PREFACE

In the last decade of the nineteenth century and the first decade of the twentieth a conflict of ideas arose within the Roman Catholic church which history now knows as the modernist crisis. In this struggle the party supported by the Roman church's full moral authority and coercive power inevitably prevailed. At no point was the crisis really a conflict between truth and error, nor even, for the most part, between genuine Christian orthodoxy and genuine heterodoxy. The group that eventually dominated did so not because what they said was true, but because what they said was enforceable. In the sixty years following that conflict much has been written about modernism, though mostly from partisan standpoints. Modernists have been concerned to defend themselves and their aims, and anti-modernists have been equally concerned to justify the conduct of the Roman authorities and the positions of Roman theologians. But for several decades now the last major figures in that historical drama have been dead, and at last the time seems ripe for a comprehensive history of the complex modernist phenomenon, expressed with as much objectivity as historical scholarship can muster, to be written.

In preparing my study of Baron von Hügel and the modernist crisis in England I have had no illusions about the nature and limitations of my work. I have not written that awaited comprehensive history of modernism, but I have tried to contribute substantially to such a future work. Before anything like a definitive history of modernism can be produced, detailed monographs on individual men and groups of men who, in their varying circumstances, constituted the so-called movement, will have to be researched and published. Any synthesis of worth necessarily presupposes careful analysis. During the past decade the monographs of Pietro Scoppola in Italy and of Émile Poulat in France have been major contributions to this analysis, though the latter, at least, has also been something of a preliminary synthesis as well. But to the extent that Poulat has been synthetic, he has also, perhaps, been somewhat premature, since, contrary to his suggestion, I cannot accept that modernism was mainly a French thing, nor that the root problem underlying the conflict was that created by biblical criticism. Historical criticism as applied to the bible was the aspect of the problem on which some of the conflict centred, especially in France. But the primary problem at issue was the larger apologetic problem – that of justifying to oneself and for one's contemporaries structural Christianity in general, and structural Roman Catholic Christianity in particular.

When a comprehensive history of the modernist phenomenon is eventually written, we can anticipate that it will have drawn on the researches of Poulat and others, but especially of others yet to come. Not only must the French and Italian scenes be further explored, but the English, German and American situations as well. Modernism was not merely, nor even primarily, a matter of certain individuals and certain books. It was the more or less simultaneous awakening of a number of Roman Catholics, in different places and different circumstances, but mostly rather well educated, and all strikingly aware of the intellectual and other advances of their own era and milieu, to the serious inadequacies of the Roman Catholic ecclesiastical system of thought and practice then current. Such an awakening and awareness transcended specific problems of biblical criticism, church–state relations, philosophy of religion and social action. This awareness was what George Tyrrell, Alfred Loisy, Romolo Murri and others shared in common, rather than the particular areas of life in which each eventually focused his awareness in an effort to change, by a diversity of means, concrete structures. This common awareness in the men who were modernists is what will, eventually, make a synthetic and comprehensive history of modernism possible. But before it can be written we must have further detailed analyses of the thought and activity of the socio-political modernists in Italy and France, of the philosophical and theological modernists in England, France, Germany and America, and of the historico-critical modernists everywhere. It is the variety of concrete undertakings, inspired by this common awareness, and aspiring to reform the Catholic system of the late nineteenth and early twentieth centuries from within, which is the historical fact denoted by the term *modernist movement*.

The single man, more than any other, who was the rallying point for modernist thinkers and their activities in western Europe was Baron Friedrich von Hügel. He alone of the modernists was truly cosmopolitan. His interests were scholarly and religious, and his orientation was broadly European. His own studies were chiefly concerned with the historical criticism of the bible and with the philosophy of religion, though he followed with informed interest the church–state developments in France and Italy, and was acquainted with some of the social action reformers in those countries as well. The free pursuit of biblical criticism and religious philosophy within the Catholic church in the late nineteenth century brought him into conflict with entrenched theological positions, and, eventually, with Roman authorities. However, they also brought him into contact with the best of those men who seemed to promise most as instruments of reform within the Roman Catholic ecclesiastical system nearly three-quarters of a century ago.

Both the limits and the theme of this book are expressed in its title. I have not undertaken to write a comprehensive history of the modernist crisis. I have studied von Hügel's involvement in the movement in its specifically English setting and circumstances. Because of his temperament, interests and values, von Hügel would probably have come into conflict with prevailing Roman theology and discipline wherever he had lived. But it was largely in the English environment that he thought and wrote and spoke, and it was usually in England and from England that his ideas and personality and writings had their first repercussions. The English side of the development of his mind, and the English aspects of the modernist conflict with Roman authority have never been adequately studied in themselves. By restricting my focus to von Hügel's activities in relation to the English scene I have tried not to misrepresent his relationship to other individual modernists and to the modernist movement as a whole. I believe that I have said enough about von Hügel's international activities to keep the pictures from ever becoming distorted, but at the same time it is evident that I have not exhaustively detailed the non-English dimensions of his work.

Hopefully, the present volume is a genuine contribution to a future comprehensive history of modernism. I have tried to clarify once and for all von Hügel's place in the movement – a place that has been misrepresented both by some of the modernists themselves and by the ecclesiastically approved Roman Catholic historiographical tradition which has grown up around von Hügel's memory and that of modernism. I believe that I have also added some fresh information and a new focus on the English dimension of the movement as a whole. The modernist crisis in England, as mostly elsewhere too, did not grow out of earlier nineteenth century liberal Catholicism. A general introduction to liberal English Catholic thought in the nineteenth century might have been interesting, but not especially relevant to the purposes of this book. The same thing might be said of the liberal schools of thought on the continent. Von Hügel was not a continuator of a school of thought, nor did he in turn influence a school. The individuals who did in fact influence him represented among themselves a variety of backgrounds, and his own relationships to them were always highly individualistic and personal. The liberal Catholic movement in England, as elsewhere, prior to 1870, was almost totally checked by the decrees of the First Vatican Council and by the practical interpretation given to them by the papacy and the majority of Catholic bishops and theologians. Significantly, it was not to English Catholic thinkers, but to the more liberal Anglican scholars, that von Hügel looked for support in the 1890s.

This book owes much to many people whose kind generosity contributed so largely to whatever of merit these pages contain. To those who have made a special effort to make available to me either their own family papers or the resources of the archives and libraries of which they are the custodians I owe a word of public gratitude and acknowledgement. These include Mrs Frank Sheed (Maisie Ward); the members of the late Canon A. L. Lilley's family – especially the Canon's daughter, the late Miss Barbara Lilley, and his grandson, Mr John L. Creed; the daughter of the late Professor Norman Kemp Smith, Mrs Janet Ludlum, and the Professor's literary executors; the Earl of Halifax and his Archivist, Major Thomas Ingram; His Eminence, John Cardinal Heenan, and the Archivist of the Archdiocese of Westminster, Miss Elizabeth Poyser; the Abbot of Downside Abbey and the Downside Librarian, Dom Mark Pontifex; Doctor Alec R. Vidler; the Librarian at St Andrews University, Mr D. MacArthur, and the St Andrews Library staff; the Fathers of the Birmingham Oratory and especially the Reverend C. Stephen Dessain; Miss Juliet Mansel; the Provincial of the English Province of the Society of Jesus and the Province Archivist, the Reverend Francis Edwards, S.J.; Mr E. V. Quinn, the Librarian at Balliol College, Oxford; the staff of the University Library, Cambridge; the staff of the Department of Western Manuscripts at the Bodleian Library, Oxford; and the Trustees of the British Museum. But my special gratitude, and that which it is a particular privilege to acknowledge, is due to Professor W. Owen Chadwick, whose suggestions, criticisms and encouragement, throughout the period of my research in England, were such important factors in my perseverance. The opinions, judgments and shortcomings of the book are, of course, the sole responsibility of the author.

LAWRENCE F. BARMANN

9 June 1970

ABBREVIATIONS

AAW – Archives of the Archdiocese of Westminster.

AEPSJ – Archives of the English Province of the Society of Jesus.

AS des B – Archives de la Société des Bollandistes.

Autobiography and Life – M. D. Petre, *Autobiography and Life of George Tyrrell*, 2 vols., London: Edward Arnold, 1912.

BCL – Balliol College Library, Oxford.

BL – Bodleian Library, Oxford.

BM, Add. Mss. – British Museum. Additional Manuscripts.

BOA – Birmingham Oratory Archives.

DAA – Downside Abbey Archives.

Diaries – The forty-three volumes of manuscript diaries of Baron Friedrich von Hügel.

HP – The Hickleton Papers, the Archives of the Wood family of Hickleton and Garrowby, Yorkshire.

LFP – The A. L. Lilley Family Papers.

Mém – Alfred Loisy, *Mémoires pour servir a l'histoire religieuse de notre temps*, 3 vols., Paris: Émile Nourry, 1930–1.

Minutes of the LSSR – Manuscript Minutes of the London Society for the Study of Religion, vol. I, 1904–25.

SAUL – Saint Andrews University Library.

WFP – The Wilfrid Ward Family Papers.

CHAPTER I

GROWTH OF AN INQUIRING SPIRIT

To KNOW the persons and ideas that dominated a man's childhood is to know, to some extent at least, the man himself. For Friedrich von Hügel's earliest years, years which psychologists increasingly emphasize as the crucial years of a person's development, little detailed evidence remains. He never had the advantages – nor the disadvantages – of an institutional education at any period of his life. As the son of an Austrian diplomat, born in Florence while his father was Minister at the Grand Ducal Court of Tuscany, and later residing as an adolescent at the Austrian Embassy in Brussels, his education was entirely in the hands of his family and of a select, and seemingly rather eccentric, group of nurses and tutors. His father's personal influence upon him was apparently very slight, for in later life von Hügel confided to a friend that 'neither my brother nor I ever directly knew him well except as a worn man of 70–75'.[1]

Friedrich's early religious instruction and training was quite as haphazard and disorganized as his general intellectual formation in those first years. His father, until the last years of his life, while 'never denying the Church, stood very much aloof from religion generally'.[2] His mother, although a Scotch Presbyterian at the time of her marriage,

[1] Von Hügel to Norman Kemp Smith, 31 Dec. 1921–3 Jan. 1922, SAUL, MSS. 30420. The letters in this collection were obtained by the author from Professor Kemp Smith's literary executors, and had not yet been deposited at St Andrews when he consulted them. Consequently, they will be referred to only by the *general* manuscript classification which the University has subsequently given them, without the individual designations from 1 to 37 for each separate letter. Baron Carl von Hügel, Friedrich's father, was 56 years old when he married, on 28 June 1851, Elizabeth Farquharson, the nineteen-year-old daughter of General Francis Farquharson and niece of Sir James Outram. Friedrich was born on 5 May 1852. See, Anatole von Hügel (ed.), *Charles von Hügel, April 25, 1795–June 2, 1870*, Cambridge (privately printed), 1903, pp. xv, xvii, 6, 10, 33, and 73.

[2] Von Hügel to Edmund Bishop, 23 May 1906, *Dublin Review*, vol. 227, no. 461, July 1953, p. 289. All of the von Hügel letters to Edmund Bishop were with the Bishop Collection of manuscripts at Downside Abbey at the time when Mr Nigel Abercrombie was preparing his *The Life and Work of Edmund Bishop*, London, 1959. In 1953 Mr Abercrombie published the entire collection of Baron von Hügel's letters in the *Dublin Review*, vol. 227, nos. 459–62, Jan.–Oct. 1953, and sometime before the author's own researches in the Downside archives in July 1967 the original letters seem to have been misplaced or lost. Mr Abercrombie has assured the author, however, that *all* of von Hügel's letters to Bishop have been published by him in the *D.R.*, and that they have not been altered nor edited.

later joined the Roman Catholic church when Friedrich, her eldest son, was three or four years old. In writing to the Baron in 1906 Edmund Bishop had presumed that von Hügel himself was a convert to Roman Catholicism. The latter responded:

I am a convert only in the sense of having, owing to a variety of circumstances, had to regain and to conquer for myself, morally, spiritually, and intellectually, a positive faith in the Catholic religion: from 13 to 18, I would have hesitated as to affirming a positive adherence to the Church; and I had considerable interior work to go through even after those early years.[1]

This statement of fact by von Hügel about his own growth as an actively believing Christian, and one who adhered to the institutional structure of Catholicism, is important. The Baron was not a man to whom religion was merely one among many factors of personality and life. It became *the* integrating factor of his own personality, and was also the dimension in which his life was most deeply lived.[2] On the other hand, he never confused nor identified religion itself with the structures within which it became institutionalized. To be true to the most important currents of his life, the religious currents, without repudiating the ecclesial structure within which he felt this life should be channelled, was the chief struggle of his adult years. As he matured the struggle intensified until it became critical; eventually it was resolved, and without compromise of principle on the Baron's part. That there should have been such a struggle at all is largely due to the radical difference between the dominant intellectual climate in the Roman church during von Hügel's lifetime, and the climate of ideas and attitudes which became his own consistent habit of mind. To understand the struggle one must have some understanding of von Hügel's mental growth and of the ideas which became his own conscious life.

On the more particularly moral and spiritual side of von Hügel's religious development, his chief mentors were, as he himself often noted, a Dutch Dominican priest, Raymond Hocking, and a French secular priest, Henri Huvelin.[3] Hocking's influence came when von Hügel was

---

[1] *Ibid.*

[2] Herbert Vaughan first met von Hügel when the latter was but twenty-one. He wrote to Lady Herbert of Lea: 'I have met von Hügel twice or three times and formed a very high estimate of his worth. He is quite unlike the ordinary run of young men, and I should think that there is in him a loftiness of view and aspiration which will very well suit Lady Mary's temperament of character. That he is not an Englishman is probably a defect which neither regeneration nor salvation will ever be able to cure or atone for...' Herbert Vaughan to Lady Herbert of Lea, 28 Oct. 1873, *Dublin Review*, vol. 219, no. 441, Oct. 1947, p. 114.

[3] References to Hocking are less frequent than to Huvelin, thus indicating, to some extent

eighteen years old and undergoing a moral crisis which in later life he referred to only in vague terms. Although this influence was, apparently, of great importance at the time in which it was felt, the relationship with Hocking was, nevertheless, only temporary. Huvelin's influence was of greater duration. Von Hügel first met him on 16 June 1884 in Paris,[1] and the relationship grew and developed, both through letters and personal visits, until the French abbé's death in the summer of 1910. Huvelin's influence was decisive; it began when von Hügel was thirty-two years old; and it lasted until his own death in 1925.[2] This influence was not that of ideas so much as it was the personal influence of a concrete life. Less than three years before his own death von Hügel publicly acknow- ledged that it was largely Huvelin's example by which he was 'helped to keep my faith and my reason through those terrible years of 1906– 1914'.[3] It was not so much what Huvelin said which helped the Baron maintain his balance, as what he was. ' *There* sanctity stood before me in the flesh,' he wrote, 'and this as the genuine deepest effect and reason of the Catholic Church; I could now utilize the sufferings of these hurri- cane years towards growing a little less unlike this mediator of Church and Christ and God.' How little the historian, even the historian of ideas, is able to chronicle a relationship and influence of this sort is demonstrated in a recent biography of Huvelin.[4]

On the more strictly intellectual side of von Hügel's interior growth, notable early influence was exerted by two of the most colourful figures of the Oxford Movement of a previous generation. In 1873, the year of his

---

at least, the relative influence of the two men. One of the most splendid expressions of what Hocking had meant to the Baron's early religious development is found in *Letters from Baron Friedrich von Hügel To a Niece*, edited by Gwendolen Greene, London, 1965, p. xxiv. Huvelin is mentioned in the same passage, and also more impressively in the Baron's *Essays and Addresses on the Philosophy of Religion*, 2nd series, London, 1963, pp. 96 and 242; *Eternal Life*, Edinburgh, 1948, pp. 374–7; and in the Baron's Preface to the Second Edition of his *Mystical Element of Religion As Studied in Saint Catherine of Genoa and Her Friends*, vol. i, London, 1961, p. vii.

[1] *Diaries*, 16 June 1884. The Baron's manuscript *Diaries*, forty-three volumes, covering the years 1877–9, 1884–1900, 1902–24, are in the author's possession. They will be referred to in the notes merely as *Diaries*, followed by the entrance date under which the material referred to can be found. In his *Life of Baron von Hügel*, London, 1951, p. 46, Michael de la Bedoyère mistakenly gives the date for this meeting as 16 May 1884, and Huvelin's biographer has merely copied de la Bedoyère's mistake (M. T. Louis-Lefebvre, *Abbé Huvelin, Apostle of Paris*, translated by the Earl of Wicklow, Dublin, 1967, p. 147).

[2] Even in his old age von Hügel felt that the advice he himself had heard from Huvelin years before would be of value for his intellectual friends of whatever religion. See, von Hügel to Kemp Smith, 1 July and 13–18 Nov. 1919, SAUL, MSS. 30420.

[3] Friedrich von Hügel, 'Louis Duchesne', *The Times Literary Supplement*, no. 1,062, 25 May 1922, p. 342.

[4] M. T. Louis-Lefebvre, *Abbé Huvelin*, pp. 145–58.

marriage to Lady Mary Catherine Herbert, at the age of twenty-one, von Hügel first came into contact with William George Ward – the 'Ideal' Ward of Oxford days. During the remaining nine years of Ward's life, he and von Hügel were now and again engaged in philosophical and theological discussion, and especially so after they became neighbours in Hampstead and took to walking on the Heath together. The influence of the older man upon the younger was, as far as positive ideas were concerned, largely negative; but his influence as an intellectual catalyst was notable.[1] Von Hügel himself speaks of Ward having drawn him out and trained him 'as to Theism and its proofs, grace and freewill, the nature and extent of Church authority, and this with a zest and a vigour, with an informality and personal unpretentiousness, with a genial, breezy defiance of all hesitation and uncertainty on any subject which was allowed a lodgement in his mind, such as I have never met with either before or since'.[2] He learned from Ward's openness in matters purely philosophical where no dogmatic question was involved; he learned from his standard of moral aims and ideals 'to find, in spite of many obstacles and prejudices, in the highest realizations of the Catholic spirit the deepest responses to all the noblest cravings of the human heart'; and he learned 'much indirectly' in matters of history

---

[1] Von Hügel himself has written an evaluation of this influence in Wilfrid Ward's *William George Ward and the Catholic Revival*, London, 1893, pp. 365–75. Writing to Wilfrid Ward from Paris in 1899, and telling Ward that he was sending him 'a copy of Armstrong's "God and the Soul"', von Hügel continued: '...I really send it because of its frequent most grateful mention of your Father, and its large indebtedness to him. Nothing can give one greater pleasure and encouragement than thus to see how persistent and fruitful is the action of rare devotedness, such as that of your Father, to whom I too owe so much.' Von Hügel, to Ward, 30 Jan. 1899, WFP, vH MSS. Wilfrid Ward's daughter, Mrs Maisie Ward Sheed, loaned the author her father's entire collection of more than 200 manuscript letters and cards from Baron von Hügel, covering the years from December 1882 till April 1916 (i.e. from the year of W. G. Ward's death till the year of Wilfrid's own death). Wilfrid Ward (1856–1916) became the most prominent of William George Ward's sons, and at the age of twenty-eight first came to public notice as a controversialist in the area of religious philosophy with his book on *The Wish To Believe*. Although to the end of his life Wilfrid Ward was concerned with and wrote about philosophico-theological problems, his greatest literary achievements were in the field of biography. His lives of W. G. Ward, of Cardinal Wiseman, and especially of Cardinal Newman, remain classical models of biographical art. With Arthur James Balfour and others Ward was a founder of the Synthetic Society in 1896, and from 1906 until shortly before his death he was editor of the *Dublin Review*. His relationship with von Hügel was at its warmest in the 1890s. As a moderate liberal, concerned to help achieve a synthesis between faith and contemporary learning and culture, he felt that some of von Hügel's special friends, men like Loisy and Tyrrell, were so excessive in their intellectual conclusions and demands as to compromise such a synthesis. Because of their different evaluations of and commitments to these men, Ward and von Hügel drifted apart, though they never fully ceased to be friends nor to respect one another.

[2] W. Ward, *W. G. Ward and the Catholic Revival*, p. 366.

and church authority.[1] While unable to accept Ward's own conclusions and attitudes and spirit on these latter topics, von Hügel was helped by the older man's conversations to see more clearly where some of the real problems in these areas lay.

But the man who first helped on von Hügel's intellectual growth in a directly positive way was John Henry Newman. And if in later years the Baron was to criticize some of the Cardinal's positions and to go beyond these,[2] he was largely able to do so because he had so thoroughly grasped and grown through contact with Newman's ideas and cast of mind. Newman's influence on the Baron began through his books while von Hügel was still a very young man. At the age of seventeen and a half he first read one of Newman's books. It was *Loss and Gain*, and of that work he has remarked that it was the first book which made him 'realize the intellectual might and grandeur of the Catholic position'.[3] In the years immediately following his discovery of *Loss and Gain*, von Hügel's intellectual debt to Newman continued to increase very rapidly. In December 1874 he wrote what seemed to be his first letter to Newman. The main business of the letter had to do with a proposed English translation of Bishop Fessler's moderate explanation of the Vatican Decrees on papal infallibility. After treating of this matter, von Hügel wrote: 'I ought perhaps to stop here by rights, but I can't keep myself from at last coming out with one of the many things I hoped some day to be able to tell you.' And he continued:

It is how deeply, profoundly indebted I am to you, for all you have been to me by means of your books. The reading of 'Loss and Gain', 'The Apologia', 'Anglican Difficulties' and 'The Grammar of Assent' has, at different times and in different ways formed distinct epochs in my young intellectual and

---

[1] *Ibid.* p. 369.

[2] One of the most significant criticisms which von Hügel ever made of a position taken by Newman had to do with public criticism of Vatican policy. In September 1911 Wilfrid Ward sent von Hügel for the purpose of criticism the manuscript Introduction to his forthcoming biography of Newman. Besides criticizing Ward's attitude expressed in the Introduction towards the late George Tyrrell [Ward removed the offending reference in the published Introduction, (see, von Hügel to Ward, 23 Nov. 1911, WFP, vH MSS.)], the Baron also made the following remark: 'I cannot but feel, more strongly than formerly and doubtless quite finally, one, to my mind now grave, peculiarity and defect of the Cardinal's temper of mind and position. His, apparently absolute, determination never to allow – at least *to allow others* – *any* public protestation, *any* act or declaration contrary to current central Roman policy, cannot, simply, be pressed, or imposed as normative upon us all. For, taken thus, it would stamp *Our Lord* Himself, as a deplorable rebel; would condemn *St. Paul* at Antioch as intolerable; and censure many a great saint of God since then. And certainly this way of taking things can hardly be said to have done much good or to have averted much harm.' Von Hügel to Ward, 2 Oct. 1911, WFP, vH MSS.

[3] Von Hügel to H. I. D. Ryder, 18 Aug. 1890, BOA, VC 20.

religious life. Such intellectual discipline as I have had, I owe it to your books. They have I hope, made up to me, at least somewhat, for the absence in my youthful years of any systematic training, any sympathetic and reliable teacher. I have no doubt I might have profited by them even more, nor have I any doubt that mine is but one out of hundreds of similar cases, and yet I hope to have won from you a permanent possession, and gratitude will out at last, anyhow.[1]

The Baron concluded his letter by telling Newman 'how eagerly, even feverishly', he looked forward to the latter's response to Mr Gladstone's pamphlet on 'The Vatican Decrees in Their Bearing on Civil Allegiance'. Von Hügel was certain, he told Newman, that this new publication from the aging Oratorian's pen 'like your other books, will be to me a fresh starting point, intellectually, and an additional link in the chain of the many helps and enlightenments that binds me to you'. In June of 1876 von Hügel and his wife spent a week in Birmingham, during which time the Baron interviewed Newman on several occasions.[2] The notes which the Baron took on these occasions indicate that Newman was quizzed, primarily, for his ideas on the problem of human certainty about God, the vicarious nature of Christ's suffering, scholastic philosophy, papal infallibility and temporal power. This list of topics about which the twenty-four-year-old von Hügel consulted the seventy-five-year-old Newman is significant, because it includes aspects of problems which would be perennial for the Baron until his death fifty years later. When Newman died in August 1890, von Hügel again commented on his great intellectual debt to the dead Cardinal, mentioning as having been especially helpful and influential in his own formation, *Loss and Gain*, the five lectures of part II of *Anglican Difficulties*, the *Parochial and Plain Sermons*, the *Letters* to Dr Pusey and the Duke of Norfolk, and 'above all' the *Grammar of Assent*. He concluded with the remark that he talked Newman even oftener than he knew.[3]

By the time that Newman came to write his essay 'On the Inspiration of Scripture' in *The Nineteenth Century* for February 1884, with its 'Postscript', printed privately and widely distributed shortly after the appearance of the initial article, von Hügel had begun to take a serious interest in critical biblical studies. In his articles Newman attempted to

---

[1] Von Hügel to J. H. Newman, 13 Dec. 1874, BOA, MS. 100a.
[2] For an account of these interviews, based on some of von Hügel's own MSS. memoranda now at St Andrews University Library, together with various letters and diaries at the Birmingham Oratory Archives, see R. K. Browne, 'Newman and von Hügel: A Record of an Early Meeting', *The Month*, n.s., vol. 26, no. 1, July 1961, pp. 24–33.
[3] Von Hügel to Ryder, 18 Aug. 1890, BOA, VC 20.

open a door for the educated Catholic of his day who seemed to be faced with an impossible dilemma – the dilemma created by the conclusions of contemporary critico-historical biblical studies contradicting (or at least seeming to contradict) the current but inadequate Catholic theology of the bible which more or less identified revelation, inspiration and inerrancy. Newman's articles were full of the subtleties which so annoyed many of his non-Catholic contemporaries; but his hair-line distinctions were gratefully received by numbers of his co-religionists faced with the spectre of another Galileo debacle. Among these latter was Friedrich von Hügel. From Valéry-sur-Somme,[1] on the first day of July, he wrote to Newman:

It is the repeated reading and study of your article with 'Postscript' on the Inspiration of Scripture which, following upon a five year's study and consideration of the Greek New Testament text and modern commentaries of various German schools upon it, leads me to wish to thank you – small as I know the value of such thanks to be – for the profound interest and subtle help your papers have been to me personally.[2]

But it was something larger than the mere conclusions of biblical criticism which primarily interested von Hügel, even here. His ultimate concern was Newman's general philosophical principles which, when treating issues touching on religious faith and certitude, gave him a sufficiently broad foundation for avoiding the traps and dead-ends which seemed to turn so many of his Catholic contemporaries into frightened reactionaries when faced with genuine biblical problems. Von Hügel concluded this letter, too, with an acknowledgment of the debt he personally owed to the general philosophical principles of Newman's *Grammar of Assent*.

In this same letter to Newman the Baron remarked that although he knew the New Testament well in its original language, the Old Testament he never expected 'to know otherwise than at second-hand'. Within a decade of writing that letter, however, he had mastered Hebrew to the extent of having read the whole of Genesis three times over in that language, besides Exodus twice and part of Leviticus. Subsequent years would include the Hebrew reading of the rest of the

---

[1] On 28 April 1884 von Hügel had gone to France with his wife and daughters for a holiday. They remained on the continent until after the first week in July. *Diaries*, 28 April– 10 July 1884.

[2] Von Hügel to Newman, 1 July 1884, BOA, VC 22. Newman's original article and the 'Postscript' have been brought out in a critical edition with introductions by J. Derek Holmes and Robert Murray, S.J., *On the Inspiration of Scripture*, London, 1967.

Pentateuch, Job, Psalms, and various of the Prophets. If in 1884 von Hügel could resign himself, however reluctantly, to never being able to approach the Old Testament as a critic at first hand, by 1890 the realization of the importance of biblical criticism for the progress of religion, as well as his own scholarly instincts, had overcome this reluctance. He was beginning to appreciate, as did few theologians or men in positions of authority in the Roman church at that time, the disaster ahead if Catholic theologians and authorities continued to refuse to acknowledge, in a thoroughly honest manner, the work of contemporary critical scholars and the general biblical problems of which even secular savants were becoming increasingly aware. In the late eighties and early nineties of the nineteenth century von Hügel made contact with the ideas of many of Europe's leading biblical scholars who were then actually labouring on the frontiers of their field of research. Through this reading and these personal contacts, and through much genuine hard work, he prepared himself as a responsible and knowledgeable biblical critic, and as a scholar prepared to defend his field of competence from the encroachments of authoritarian theologians.

Although the latter half of 1884 he spent mainly in the study of Greek sculpture and ancient coins,[1] with many visits to the British Museum, in February 1885 von Hügel paid a visit to Oxford which was to introduce him to the leading biblical critics there. He went to Oxford on Monday the 23rd and remained until Wednesday, the guest of John Wordsworth, who was at that time Oriel Professor of the Interpretation of Scripture and who would be consecrated bishop of Salisbury within the year.[2] Although the occasion for von Hügel's visit was a paper given by Charles Gore of Pusey House on the fourth century African theologian Victorinus Afer, most of the three-day visit was actually taken up in conversations with Oxford's biblical scholars. Wordsworth invited the Baron to examine his critical text of the Vulgate New Testament which at that time had reached only the first fifteen chapters of Matthew's Gospel.[3]

[1] Professor Percy Gardner once wrote to von Hügel: 'I suppose we are the only two people in Europe who combine a love of ancient coins with an eager interest in all aspects of religion.' Gardner to von Hügel, 24 Nov. 1913, SAUL, MS. 2600.

[2] *Diaries*, 23–5 Feb. 1885.

[3] While in France in 1884 von Hügel had agreed with Louis Duchesne to write occasionally for publication in the latter's *Bulletin critique* brief 'chronicles' about scholarly British publications and research. After his 1885 Oxford visit with Wordsworth, von Hügel published the following remarks in the French journal: 'Le professeur Wordsworth, d'Oxford, est arrivé enfin, après avoir employé sept ans à collationner des manuscrits par toute l'Europe, à constituer le texte de son édition critique de la Vulgate du Nouveau Testament. Pour saint Mathieu, il a sous la main les collations complètes de vingt-deux manuscrits, plus que n'en a

On Tuesday evening von Hügel dined with Samuel Rolles Driver at Christ Church in Dr Pusey's old rooms, and there he was shown the first two parts of the *Corpus Inscriptionum Semiticarum* and books on the Phoenician language. At Gore's address he had met William Sanday, and on Wednesday he had lunch with Sanday at Exeter College. But even in the midst of these discussions he found time for two visits to the Ashmolean Museum and for conversations with Arthur Evans and Robinson Ellis.[1]

While in Paris the previous year, von Hügel had made the acquaintance of Louis Duchesne, the church historian, whose scholarly and critical approach to church history, and whose personality so 'full of life and fire', had commended themselves to the Baron.[2] Although the two men remained friends, often in close communication, until Duchesne's death in 1922, it was not so much Duchesne himself, as one of Duchesne's own mentors, who most consciously and directly influenced von Hügel in the use of exacting critical historical method. Through the review section of Duchesne's *Bulletin critique*, von Hügel discovered and then read in the spring of 1885 a little French volume which considerably influenced his understanding and future use of this methodology. The book was the *Principes de la Critique Historique* by Père Charles de Smedt, the Flemish president of the Société des Bollandistes of Brussels. Thirty-five years later von Hügel reflected: 'I was coming at that time...more and more to love, to attempt to practise, and to settle down for life to the very dispositions, trainings and labours, that I saw before me, in an uplifting degree, within' de Smedt's *Principes*. 'There are chapters in the *Principes*,' he continued, 'such as the masterly analysis of the traditions and the facts concerning the baptism of the Roman Emperor Constantine, which did an abiding work for my mind and soul.'[3] De Smedt was a

---

eu Etienne pour toute la Bible. La constitution préliminaire des quinze premiers chapitres est complète; elle présente trente variantes (non orthographiques) par rapport au texte manuel de Tischendorf de 1864. Les évangiles seront publiés séparément, à mesure qu'ils seront complétés.' *Bulletin critique*, tome VI, no. 9, 1 May 1885, p. 177.

[1] *Diaries*, 23–5 Feb. 1885.
[2] According to von Hügel's own Diary, he first met abbé Duchesne on the morning of Monday, 12 May 1884. The Baron's spring holiday in France in 1884 is confirmed as the time of the two men's meeting by a letter of von Hügel to Newman, written on 1 July 1884 (BOA, VC 22). Consequently, von Hügel is himself in error when, thirty-eight years later he wrote in *The Times Literary Supplement*: 'It was in the early spring of 1885 that, myself thirty-three, I first saw Duchesne, already in his middle forties, a professor of Church history at the Institut Catholique of Paris.' *T.L.S.*, no. 1062, 25 May 1922, p. 342.
[3] Von Hügel to Père H. Delehaye, 15 Sept. 1920, AS des B, vH MSS.

9

hagiographer and historian of the early church; von Hügel was a student of and 'labourer' in the field of biblical criticism. As the Baron was aware,

these specialties are distinct and largely different, say, between a story in the earlier layers of the Pentateuch, a prophecy of Amos, or a largely apocalyptic vision of Ezechiel, on the one hand; and, on the other hand, the Acts of the Christian Martyrs, genuine or legendary, the conversations as variously reported of Saint Francis of Assisi, or the letters, autograph or otherwise, of Saint Charles Borommeo [sic!].[1]

Nevertheless, both hagiography and biblical criticism, despite their individual specializations and techniques, depend on historical method.

Biblical Criticism is an essentially historical discipline, busy with given documents and with the various kinds of literary forms, and the various degrees of historical guidance, suggested by those documents. And, so far, Biblical Criticism can learn much from so sober and circumspect, so sincere and serene a temper, method and outlook as richly characterised the labours of Père Charles de Smedt in the history of the Church and of the Saints.[2]

Not only did von Hügel learn from de Smedt's books, he also learned from the man himself. The Baron and the Bollandist first met in London in the autumn of 1897,[3] and in later years they met occasionally in Rome or London when the latter's researches brought him to England to work in the British Museum. Their meetings were not frequent, however, and they almost never corresponded. 'Yet the man,' von Hügel could say, 'what he was and what he wanted, and, again, what that personality and those ideas did for me – are still doing for me – are so clear that no documentation could make them clearer to me.'[4] De Smedt seemed to von Hügel the ideal type of one wholly and disinterestedly dedicated to the pursuit of truth within an area of research in which he was complete master of the tools necessary for such research. With de Smedt the Baron always felt that he 'stood before a man whose sheer presence drove away all suspicion of dexterously sophistic manipulation of documents, if and where they might be awkward to a less farsighted orthodoxy; all fear that the real truth might be argued down – the facts truncated or stretched upon the dread Procrustes bed of, not what *is*, but what ought to have been'.[5] Nearly eighteen years after the event, von Hügel recalled a late autumn afternoon when he had met de

[1] *Ibid.*   [2] *Ibid.*
[3] *Diaries*, 5 Oct. 1897.
[4] Von Hügel to Delehaye, 15 Sept. 1920, AS des B, vH MSS.
[5] *Ibid.*

Smedt at the British Museum. Both had finished their work for the day, and together they sat under the great front portico of the Museum, oblivious of the cold November wind blowing dust and bits of leaves and paper about their feet, and deep in conversation. The Bollandist dwelt upon and developed, with a penetration and balance which von Hügel admired, the urgent and essential need within the Roman church for 'a right and wise autonomy and encouragement for the several genuine Sciences and Researches'.[1] Regretfully he observed that only in Protestantism did there now seem to exist that liberty of investigation which was so essential to these researches, reflecting that until the sixteenth century such liberty had been part of the Catholic heritage too. When von Hügel was led to recall this conversation in 1920, he himself reflected, with all the pain and growth of the experience of the intervening years upon him, that each science and area of research

possesses its own interior structure and method, duty, autonomy and authority. It is as impossible for the student to ignore or to deny the method and ideal, specific to his special study, as it is unworthy of his high call to insist upon the sheer finality of any detail that has not been long tested and assured by the mutually independent and concurrent conclusions of many other workers.[2]

For this scholarly balance and ideal von Hügel was in part at least indebted to the Bollandist de Smedt and to his *Principes*. It is not without significance, then, that over a period of years the Baron distributed more than two dozen copies of that book to his own closest scholar friends.

With his growing involvement in critical biblical studies, von Hügel became increasingly aware of the handicap under which he laboured in lacking Hebrew as a linguistic tool of his trade. In the summer of 1890 the well-known orientalist, Dr Gustav Bickell of Innsbruck, was visiting London. Von Hügel sent him a note on 22 August, inviting this fellow Austrian to call on him, and on the 24th the two men met for the first time at the Baron's home in Hampstead.[3] During the six weeks between that Sunday afternoon and the following 4 October, Bickell visited von

---

[1] *Ibid.*   [2] *Ibid.*

[3] *Diaries*, 22–4 Aug. 1890. That von Hügel was already well aware of Bickell's scholarly work is indicated by this postscript to a letter from the Baron to Wilfrid Ward: 'Oh! the names of *Xtian* Biblical scholars. By this, I understand you to mean *living Old* and *New* T. scholars. You could add to your list: Old Testament: Dr. Gustav Bickell (Professor ["Privat Docent"] in the Innsbruck University). A Catholic priest. An admirable scholar, thoroughly critical. Dr. Driver had a review in the "Academy" on his friend Cheyne's "Book of Psalms Translated", in which you could find a wonderful eulogy of B.' Von Hügel to Ward, 17 Nov. 1888, WFP, vH MSS.

Hügel seventeen times, usually staying from tea-time through the evening meal. Twice the Baron took Bickell to the Devonshire Club for breakfast and a prolonged conversation with R. H. Hutton; and several times he invited guests to Hampstead to meet him.[1] More often, however, von Hügel and Bickell were *tête-à-tête*; and the former sometimes made notes of their conversations after the visits. Biblical studies were always at the centre of von Hügel's talks with Bickell, and, on the occasion of the latter's sixth visit, on 7 September, after the Baron had spent the afternoon looking over Bickell's own translation of Koheleth, he seems to have asked the scholar to help him with the study of the Hebrew language. At any rate, when Bickell called again on the 9th, he began to teach von Hügel Hebrew, and continued to do so for the remainder of his London stay, completing ten lessons in all.[2]

Von Hügel's introduction to Hebrew did not end with the ten lessons from Bickell. On 8 October, probably at Bickell's recommendation, the Baron sent a note to the Jewish scholar, Herr Julius Spira, asking the latter about further tutorial work in the Hebrew language.[3] On 4 November Spira went to Hampstead for his first lesson with von Hügel. Over the next five years he paid nearly 200 visits to the Baron's home on Holford Road to read with him in Hebrew various books of the Old Testament and to help him with the intricacies of grammar and oddities of vocabulary which they contained. Spira's influence was larger than merely philological, and it was with Herr Spira and his wife that von Hügel was first present at Jewish synagogue worship.[4] Very likely it was Spira's suggestion which first led von Hügel to contact Claude G. Montefiore and Israel Abrahams in 1893, and both contacts, though most especially that with Montefiore, led to life-long and fruitful friendships.[5] Even during the winters which von Hügel spent in Rome with his family, his Hebrew study continued. After his ample introduction from Bickell and Spira, most of his work was on his own. However, in the winter of 1896–7, while in Rome, he had thirty-nine sessions for Hebrew reading with a David Panziere.[6] While in Rome in the spring of 1895 he even

[1] *Diaries*, 11, 14, 18, 23 and 25 Sept. 1890. These guests included Bishop John Cuthbert Hedley of Newport and Menevia, the Rev. Walter Howard Frere, and Dom Francis Aidan Gasquet of Downside.

[2] *Diaries*, 24 Aug.–4 Oct. 1890.

[3] *Diaries*, 8 Oct. 1890.

[4] *Diaries*, 22 May 1893.

[5] *Diaries*, 23 Jan. and 2 May 1893. At this time Montefiore and Abrahams were joint editors of the five-year-old *Jewish Quarterly Review*.

[6] *Diaries*, 4 Dec. 1896 and 26 March 1897.

engaged Professor Ignazio Guidi of the Collegio Urbano for lessons in Aramaic, and these were resumed when the Baron returned to Rome again in December of that year.[1]

During the autumn of 1890 von Hügel began the study of Robertson Smith's *Religion of the Semites* and Julius Wellhausen's *Prolegomena zur Geschichte Israels*, apparently at Bickell's suggestion.[2] During the last days of October, while visiting his brother in Cambridge, von Hügel had protracted conversations with Robertson Smith on at least two occasions.[3] Their only meeting seems to have been, again in Cambridge, a brief encounter in Deighton and Bell's bookshop in the following spring.[4] And then in March, 1894, while he himself was in Switzerland, the Baron recorded in his diary the death of 'W. Robertson Smith, 49, (at Cambridge)'.[5] What von Hügel specially owed to this scholar he never so clearly stated in print as he did his debt to Wellhausen. He recalled, however, a conversation he once had with Robertson Smith in which,

when I spoke to him of his own evidently deep penetration of Arabian antiquity in 'The Religion of the Semites' (1889), he turned my look away to Wellhausen: – 'Oh, but you should know Wellhausen's gifts; I sent him some materials he has seen things in them beyond what I myself could ever have come to; his 'Reste Arabischen Heidentums' is the result.[6]

The Baron never met Wellhausen. Yet from 1890 until Wellhausen's

[1] *Diaries*, 3, 4, 10, 17, 24 April; 1 May; and 10 Dec. 1895.

[2] Both Bickell and Robertson Smith were friends and admirers of Wellhausen, and it was during Bickell's visit to von Hügel that the latter began reading both books. In his Diary for 26 August 1890, after his second talk with Bickell and after having dined with him, von Hügel noted: 'Resolved to read Kuenen and Wellhausen.' By the following March von Hügel was well enough acquainted with Robertson Smith's *Religion of the Semites* to write the following notice for Duchesne's *Bulletin critique*: 'M. W. Robertson Smith, professeur d'arabe à l'Université de Cambridge, vient de nous donner, dans le premier de trois volumes à paraître sur l'ancienne religion païenne des peuples sémitiques, un travail des plus sérieux. Toute de première main, toute pleine de faits curieux et de combinaisons toujours fines et d'une grande portée, cette première série de conférences (*Lectures on the Religion of the Semites*, Edinburgh, Black) s'occupe des institutions Fondamentales. Surtout les six dernières des onze conférences, sur les origines du sacrifice, touchent à des problèmes des plus difficiles et, en partie, des plus délicats: elles méritent, à un haut degré, plus encore par leur fond que par leur forme, l'attention de tous ceux qui s'occupent des prolégomènes historiques à l'Ancien Testament. Les deux volumes à suivre s'occuperont le premier des Institutions dérivatives, le second de la nature des dieux sémitiques et du rapport entre le paganisme sémitique et les religions juive et chrétienne.' *Bulletin critique*, tome XII, no. 6, 15 March 1891, p. 119.

[3] *Diaries*, 26–7 Oct. 1890.

[4] *Diaries*, 26 May 1891.

[5] *Diaries*, 31 March 1894. Von Hügel is mistaken about Smith's age; the latter was born in 1846.

[6] Friedrich von Hügel, 'Julius Wellhausen', *T.L.S.*, no. 842, 7 March 1918, p. 117.

death in 1918 he was a very careful and critical student of nearly everything Wellhausen wrote. Moreover, von Hügel was personally acquainted with Bickell, Robertson Smith and H. J. Holtzmann – all of whom
were, in varying degrees, personal friends of Wellhausen. Consequently,
when Wellhausen died, von Hügel felt that he had 'some right to speak
concerning Wellhausen's critical work on the Pentateuch and on the
Gospels'.[1] Von Hügel was no wide-eyed and uncritical admirer of work so
controversial and sometimes daring as were some of Wellhausen's published ideas. Much of Wellhausen's Old Testament work he thought
brilliant and of lasting significance. About his New Testament work he
was less sanguine.

Probably the deepest root of the dissatisfaction which I have never ceased to
feel with Wellhausen's outlook consists in the inadequacy and self-contradic-
tion of his positions concerning not so much God, nor even Christ, but the
Church – 'Church' taken in the most elementary, embryonic sense.[2]

But von Hügel was not one to condemn, even in disagreement. He wanted
always to learn first from another, and only where that other's conclusions were not warranted by the evidence brought forward did he find
it necessary to withhold agreement. About this time he expressed in a
letter to Wilfrid Ward his idea of how scholarly sciences are genuinely
advanced through the efforts of men like Wellhausen. He wrote:

Richard Bentley was, I suppose, the greatest Latin scholar England has yet
produced: yet he wrote nothing but was full of brilliant, daring guesses, all
unproved and almost all disproved since. Jacob Grimm was the founder of
Teutonic philology, a genius of the most stimulating kind: yet hardly a position of his but wanted modification almost as soon as it was taken up. And
as to Wellhausen, – he is a perfect God-send, in the form of a supposed *corpus
vile*, for all the conservatives, big and little, who will not learn from him first,
and experiment upon him, and prune him of his manifold excesses afterwards. Here are three out of several scholars who have dared to risk many
mistakes and have pushed on their science to a degree which restates its
problems for even the most cautious and fastidious of us, but leaving much to
such as these to correct and to improve.[3]

Von Hügel was convinced that one attained truth, in the study of the
bible as in any other field of research, only by daring to risk many
mistakes. But guardians of orthodoxy within the various Christian
churches were not always very willing to tolerate such an attitude where
the bible was concerned, and those within the Roman Catholic church
least of all. As von Hügel began to experience this intolerance, his own

[1] *Ibid.*   [2] *Ibid.*   [3] Von Hügel to Ward, 22 Feb. 1893, WFP, vH MSS.

work in biblical studies gradually became as much a plea for tolerance as it was research into and synthesis of critical biblical problems.[1]

At the same time that von Hügel began reading Robertson Smith and Wellhausen, he also read Gore's 'Holy Spirit and Inspiration' from *Lux Mundi* which he found, for the most part, 'simply admirable', and about which he consulted Walter Frere for a further elaboration of Gore's ideas.[2] At the same time he was finding a number of Canon T. K. Cheyne's shorter pieces especially relevant, including the Appendix to the latter's *The Hallowing of Criticism* which attempted to answer the question: 'To what extent should results of historical and scientific criticism, especially of the Old Testament, be recognized in sermons and teaching?'[3] This question had a practical application for the Baron since he personally undertook the methodical and detailed religious instruction of his three daughters, often preparing their lessons on the bible from critical studies by Cheyne, Holtzmann, Driver and others.[4] An article by Cheyne on 'Reform in the Teaching of the Old Testament' likewise struck von Hügel as especially worthwhile, and, again, perhaps the greatest significance of the article for him was its outline and suggestions for making relevant the core of the best from Old Testament criticism in both preaching and teaching. Most congenial to von Hügel's own way of thinking was Cheyne's plea to the clergy not to assert from the pulpit the very opposite of the sounder findings of critical biblical studies. Cheyne urged them not to treat Genesis as 'a collection of immensely ancient family records', when it was no such thing; nor to assert that various passages from Isaiah were predictions of this or that Christian doctrine, when they were not. 'Do not, my friends,' he wrote, 'give occasion to the Matthew Arnolds of the future to mock at your indifference alike to the truth of history, the charm of poetry, and the exquisite simplicity of early religion.'[5]

[1] As early as 1888 von Hügel was quite clear on what anyone who was interested in critical biblical studies and who also happened to be a Roman Catholic could expect. In answer to Wilfrid Ward's request for a bibliography of good critical and Christian biblical scholars the Baron remarked: 'May I suggest great caution both to right and left on this difficult and *special* subject? The chief help a Catholic can give and get on these points for some time to come, is, in my opinion, adding to the luminousness of other arguments in other departments; preventing any width gained from being lost; and in first-hand, *sub divo* study of the documents themselves.' Von Hügel to Ward, 17 Nov. 1888, WFP, vH MSS.

[2] *Diaries*, 18 and 21 Sept. 1890; von Hügel to Ward, 27 May 1894, WFP, vH MSS.

[3] T. K. Cheyne, *The Hallowing of Criticism: Nine Sermons on Elijah Preached in Rochester Cathedral*, London, 1888, p. 183.

[4] *Diaries*, 17, 23 and 26 March 1891.

[5] T. K. Cheyne, 'Reform in the Teaching of the Old Testament', *The Contemporary Review*, vol. LVI, Aug. 1889, p. 230.

About this same time von Hügel read Sanday's *Oracles of God* and found himself in full agreement with most of the material in the first seven chapters of the book.[1] Within these early chapters the Baron disagreed only with Sanday's approach to distinguishing true revelation from false, and with the latter's belief that the canon of scripture might yet undergo a revision.[2] Most of what he found in the last two chapters of the book, however, on 'Christ and the Scriptures' and on 'The Special Value of the Old Testament at the Present Time', he considered completely unacceptable when he first encountered them in the spring of 1891. In the chapter on 'Christ and the Scriptures' Sanday had tackled the problem of whether or not Christ's authority (and divinity) was undermined when one admitted that the Lord seemed 'to sanction the traditional views as to the origin and authorship of the Books of the Old Testament',[3] now that these views are known to be either inaccurate or false. Sanday's conclusion was that even though Jesus was God, with all that this implied, he was also really man with genuine *human* knowledge. This aspect of the divine Word's *kenosis* would seem to indicate that 'He divested Himself at least of such parts of that knowledge as enabled Him to take a real humanity on the same footing with that of His fellowmen'.[4] Thirteen years later von Hügel read a paper before a small group of Anglican clerics and scholars in which he adopted the same views as Sanday regarding the genuinely human, and therefore imperfect and developmental, knowledge of Jesus Christ, though he does not put it into the framework of kenotic theory. The reason which the Baron gave in that paper for his position on Christ's human knowledge was the compelling evidence of historical criticism.[5]

In March of 1891 von Hügel recommended to a friend an article by Driver which had appeared in the *Expositor* in 1886 on 'The Cosmogony of Genesis', but which he had himself only recently read.[6] Driver's conclusions about the first chapter of Genesis interested von Hügel less than

---

[1] *Diaries*, 11 March 1891.

[2] Von Hügel to Ryder, 19 March 1891, BOA, PC 205. 'Prof. Sanday, too, has just published a little book: "The Oracles of God": Longmans: 4/– of which the first 7 chapters contain, I think, very much that is good and but little that I could not accept (pp. 94, 95, 96, and most of chapters 8 and 9 would, of course, belong to the unacceptable).'

[3] W. Sanday, *The Oracles of God: Nine Lectures on the Nature and Extent of Biblical Inspiration and on the Special Significance of the Old Testament Scriptures at the Present Time*, London, 1891, p. 103.

[4] *Ibid.* p. 111.

[5] This paper is published in the second series of the Baron's *Essays and Addresses*, pp. 3–23, under the title 'Official Authority and Living Religion'.

[6] Von Hügel to Ryder, 19 March 1891, BOA, PC 205.

the honest attitude and general methodology with which he approached the problem. The question that Driver was concerned to face was whether or not we are 'any nearer than we were to a reconciliation of Genesis and science? and, if not, what position is the theologian to assume, and in what light is he to view the familiar and impressive narrative with which the Bible opens?'[1] Driver showed that there were three points especially at which well-established scientific evidence conflicts with the Genesis narrative. He examined the various methods used by the 'harmonizers' to get around these difficulties, and dismissed them all as inadequate. Then he indicated how the Hebrew writer borrowed stories and imagery from his polytheistic neighbours, and, with the guidance of divine inspiration, made these the vehicle for 'embodying theological teaching of permanent value'. Briefly he demonstrated the nature of this teaching, and concluded with the insistence that Christians have an obligation to help eradicate the popular misconception that the cosmogony of Genesis is an integral element of the Christian faith. He insisted that believing Christians should

distinguish between what can, and what cannot, be claimed for the Biblical narrative; we should maintain upon positive grounds, rather than as a concession extorted from us, its true position and value. We should show that it is its office neither to anticipate scientific discovery, nor to define the lines of scientific research. It neither comes into collision with science, nor needs reconciliation with it; its office lies in a different plane altogether; it is to present, under a form impressive to the imagination, adapted to the needs of all time, and containing no feature unworthy of the dignity of its subject, a truthful *representative picture* of the relation of the world to God.[2]

With nearly everything about the article von Hügel was in full accord, and wrote to a friend that 'it represents, upon the whole, the sort of attitude which, with all my heart, I believe to be the only truly loyal and prudent one for us to take up with finally'.[3] How von Hügel himself would express this same honesty of attitude in facing contemporary biblical problems he would soon have occasion to demonstrate – and even in a printed form.

[1] S. R. Driver, 'The Cosmogony of Genesis', *The Expositor*, 3rd series, vol. III, 1886, p. 23.
[2] *Ibid.* p. 45.
[3] Von Hügel to Ryder, 19 March 1891, BOA, PC 205.

CHAPTER 2

CRITICAL STUDIES AND THE BIBLICAL QUESTION

ON THE AFTERNOON of 12 December 1890, Henry Ignatius Dudley Ryder, superior of the Birmingham Oratory since Newman's death, called on von Hügel.[1] The two men had communicated earlier on theological topics, and their conversation on this particular afternoon centred on the problems connected with the idea of biblical inspiration. As a result of the discussion Ryder asked von Hügel to read through a manuscript, which he had prepared for possible publication, on scriptural inspiration and modern biblical criticism.[2] Ryder was not a scripture scholar, but he was a theologian with some reputation among the Catholic community in England, and was generally remembered for his defence of a more liberal interpretation of the First Vatican Council's decrees on papal infallibility than W. G. Ward had allowed. Ryder's paper, then, was the work of a fairly broad-minded scholastic theologian; and he approached the problem of scriptural inspiration with the traditional methodology of late scholasticism.[3]

[1] *Diaries*, 12 Dec. 1890. For a brief account of Ryder's life and family connections, see *The Tablet*, vol. 110, no. 3518, 12 Oct. 1907, p. 584.

[2] Although no copy of the original manuscript is now to be found at the Birmingham Oratory among Ryder's papers, nor with von Hügel's papers at St Andrews, the Oratory does possess a typescript of the paper as Ryder finally approved it, and this was the copy of Ryder's work used in these pages. Most of the differences between this final form of the paper and the original can be deduced through the twelve manuscript letters from von Hügel to Ryder which are in the Birmingham Oratory Archives. The article (as contained in the typescript) was eventually printed in three instalments as: 'Scripture Inspiration and Modern Biblical Criticism', *The Catholic World*, vol. LVI, no. 336, March 1893, pp. 742–54; 'Rival Theories on Scripture Inspiration', *The Catholic World*, vol. LVII, no. 338, May 1893, pp. 206–18; and 'The Proper Attitude of Catholics Towards Modern Biblical Criticism', *The Catholic World*, vol. LVII, no. 339, June 1893, pp. 396–406.

[3] The term *scholasticism* refers both to a systematic movement of thought originating in the middle ages and continuing into the present, and to a philosophico-theological method which was the instrument of developing that system of thought and which, like the system, has undergone modifications with the passing of time. Granting what values there are in late scholastic methodology, with its emphasis on logical progression through definitions, the modernists generally criticised it for its intrinsic *a priori* approach to problems. Based as it was on a framework of statements by church councils and ecclesiastical authorities, and of scripture texts wrenched from their context, and resolutely opposed to either methodological or systematic pluralism in philosophical and theological matters, scholasticism made any real advance in thought, beyond limits and a framework already implicitly determined, nearly impossible.

18

The manuscript was chiefly concerned with a consideration of the possibilities latent in Roman Catholic theology of recent centuries for explaining contemporary scriptural difficulties. Ryder distinguished between the matter and manner of scripture, the former being the revelation and the latter the vehicle of the revelation. The former he found always unchangeably true, and the latter dependent upon the time and circumstances from which it issued.

There is much, no doubt, in Holy Scripture which could never have been related in the manner it is if the writers had not been ignorant of many things of which we are aware, and so may indirectly and *obiter* convey a false impression, whilst directly they only say what is true, regard being had to their scope and circumstances.[1]

Since biblical inspiration for Ryder, as indeed for nearly all scholastic theologians of the time, meant that God was the author, very literally and rather anthropomorphically conceived, of the whole of the bible, he found it impossible to admit straightforwardly that the bible did in fact contain errors, regardless of the available scientific and historical evidence to prove it. Ryder concluded with some ideas on what he considered to be the proper attitude for Catholics towards modern biblical criticism. He referred to the type of criticism represented by Wellhausen and his school, with their concern for the rational and human explanations of all biblical phenomena, as anti-scriptural criticism. He insisted, that 'believers in the Divinity both of the Scriptures and of the Church may admit without difficulty a human element working in subordination to the Divine dispensation, whilst they reasonably refuse to find in it the one adequate explanation of the phenomenon'.[2] He denied that a Catholic man of science lacked freedom for his investigations, and claimed that the Catholic scientist had a distinct advantage over his non-Catholic counterparts, since he had as his Catholic birthright 'an intellectual system in which all things of earth and heaven find their place – and it is better to have some system, even if in certain respects imperfect, than no system at all'.[3] His penultimate paragraph insisted that Catholic theology was co-extensive with all sciences. The Catholic scientist 'will be too loyal on the one hand to faith, on the other hand to science, to believe that their last words can be otherwise than in accord'. The implied reason for the accord was science's ultimate subordination to and direction by official Catholic theology.

[1] Ryder, *Typescript*, p. 17.
[2] *Ibid.* p. 21.   [3] *Ibid.* p. 28.

Ryder's essay represented about the most moderate position one could reasonably expect from a Roman Catholic scholastic theologian in 1891. Nevertheless, it did represent, even though at its best, a tradition and a framework which had not, and, perhaps, could not, come to grips with the principles and methodology of critical biblical studies as these had developed outside the Roman church by the end of the nineteenth century. Even though Ryder was far more moderately liberal than most Catholic theologians of that day, he still placed too much emphasis on the unknowable divine element in both scripture and church, at the expense of the genuinely analysable human element. And the ideas of an autonomous biblical science, using historical rather than theological method, was more than Ryder could have been expected to accept.[1]

On 14 April von Hügel began a careful reading and analysis of Ryder's paper, and finished it a few days later. From 5 to 18 May he worked on a report for Ryder on the positions of his essay, and sent it off to Edgbaston. In July, after making a few revisions in the initial report, he had his reflections on Ryder's paper privately printed for circulation and criticism among a small circle of friends. The printed report bore the title: 'Notes Addressed To the Very Reverend H.I.D.R. upon the Subject of Biblical Inspiration and Inerrancy.'[2]

Von Hügel's report was both detailed and frank, but typically respectful and positive in tone throughout. He saw Ryder's paper primarily as an essay on the problem created for biblical study by two positions at that time commonly assumed in Roman Catholic theology. These positions had to do with the absolute and literal inerrancy of scripture, and with the total inspiration of the whole bible by God. Official Roman theology had generally, up to this time and for some time to come, refused to acknowledge that there were any real errors of any sort in the bible. The problems created by this intransigence were those chiefly preoccupying von Hügel at this particular point of his own biblical study and research.

---

[1] Loisy was not necessarily being vindictive, but merely stating the truth of the situation with which he found himself confronted at the end of the nineteenth century, when he wrote: 'Dans la conception scolastique, l'exégèse biblique n'est qu'une science auxiliaire ou, pour mieux dire, une province de la théologie. On ne lui voit pas d'autre raison d'être que celle d'appuyer les thèses dogmatiques et fournir des arguments contre l'hérésie et l'incrédulité. Que la science de la Bible puisse avoir une existence relativement indépendante, comme toutes les autres sciences humaines, avec son objet et sa méthode propres, qui seraient l'une et l'autre purement historiques, c'est pour la théologie catholique une idée absolument nouvelle et presque révolutionnaire.' *Mém.* I, p. 553.

[2] One of these printed copies, that from the Birmingham Oratory Archives, has been used here by the author. Henceforth the document will be referred to merely as *Notes*.

In his paper Ryder had mentioned certain ideas of approved Catholic authors on the concept of inspiration itself, and the Baron found several of these personally congenial. Two especially he commended: that inspiration, as a divine incitement of the will of the human writer, is not generally consciously recognized by the man who is inspired; and that of the essential distinction between divine inspiration, which merely moves the human author to write, and revelation, which is the truth communicated. This latter, von Hügel insisted, must have preceded its registration both temporally and logically, so that the unity of the sacred writer's 'spiritual life suffered no disturbance through his supernatural endowment to write'.[1] Everyone has always held that the primary and direct object of the divine influence of inspiration was the effecting of revelation, he observed, and there is no valid reason opposing an admission that 'on scientific subjects the sacred writers wrote according to the ideas and knowledge of their times and places'.[2] What, then, can it possibly mean to admit this and yet contend that 'the Holy Spirit was throughout acting upon them in such a way as to ensure their reproducing these ideas only to such an extent as to be, though not objectively quite true, never objectively quite false, – allowing them to remain inaccurate, but never, oh never, erroneous'?[3]

Von Hügel's own positive approach to the problem began with the principle that God never did, nor could He, *reveal* anything to anyone which was not true, 'at least in its degree'.[4]

But God can *inspire* a writer's mind throughout his writing, and throughout can affect the resulting writings without changing the writer's genuine even though mistaken beliefs as to matters of fact, insomuch as such matters of fact do not interfere with the object of the inspiration,[5]

i.e. the revelation. He insisted that inspiration was not intermittent and that there were no *obiter dicta* because

the moral and religious ideas and the history of the growth of such truths go absolutely throughout every story and every detail – not, no doubt, when severed from the context, but as a part of the story.[6]

He found that three things were necessarily excluded by inspiration. The first was subjective error throughout and in every respect. The second was objective error throughout as far as faith and morals and the history

---

[1] *Notes*, p. 10. [2] *Ibid.* p. 11. [3] *Ibid.*
[4] *Ibid.* [5] *Ibid.* [6] *Ibid.* p. 12.

of their revelation is concerned. The third was 'the Divine non-intendedness of such growths and changes in this History, as could fairly be argued to be compatible with subjective truthfulness and yet to be not of the substance of the History'.[1] The Baron indicated how this view of inspiration forced him to part company on some points with certain radical critics, as, for instance, Cheyne who in his *Jeremiah* held that Deuteronomy was forged in the ordinary sense of the word. And he also indicated the problems that his position had in distinguishing what does in fact belong to faith and morals and to the substance of the history of revelation. As an example of how such a critical attitude as his would work in practice, he referred, among other things, to Driver's article on the cosmogony of Genesis from the *Expositor* of January 1886.

In conclusion von Hügel pointed to some promising developments among Roman Catholic theologians and biblical critics. He singled out Loisy's *Histoire du Canon de l'Ancien Testament*, which he himself had just read at the time of writing his critique of Ryder, as an outstanding example of the change of front in some Catholic quarters 'with regard to the Unity of Authorship of Isaiah, date of Daniel, homogeneity of the Pentateuch and admission of the Hexateuch'.[2] His final recommendation to Ryder was that the latter *not* publish his manuscript. Taken alone the paper was a pleasant and inoffensive statement of Ryder's own position; but because Ryder was superior of Newman's Oratory, von Hügel believed that Rigorists would naturally enough take its publication

as an admission on the part of the most distinguished of Newman's specially theological disciples that his Scripture distinctions and theory will not work. Believing as I do that on this point it is of vital importance that the critics should be allowed more air and action, and that the great old man, with the intuition and prescience of genius, has seen where the shoe pinches and what will be the commonly accepted solution of the future, – I should be sorry to see you taking an active part on what I believe to be the mistaken side.[3]

On 30 July, just before catching a train for Malvern Wells in Worcestershire, for a holiday with his family, von Hügel sent three copies of his freshly printed *Notes* to Ryder with a few covering lines suggesting that the two additional copies be given 'to anyone who is likely to consider first and *then* condemn'.[4] He was under no illusion as to the lack of sympathetic understanding his ideas would find in English Catholic circles. Ryder's worries that his own moderate position would be criti-

[1] *Ibid.*   [2] *Ibid.* p. 14.   [3] *Ibid.* p. 15.
[4] Von Hügel to Ryder, 30 July 1891, BOA, PC 205.

cised were countered by the Baron's remark that 'you must be well aware that the general drift of Catholic opinion – in England perhaps especially, as compared with France at least – is so much against me, – that it is not *you* who need fear hasty or inconsiderate judgments, and indeed there is nothing I wish you less'.[1] At first Ryder was a bit annoyed that von Hügel should be distributing his *Notes* in printed form to others, because he felt that they exaggerated the differences between Newman's and his own positions.[2] To ease the Oratorian's mind on the question of differing with Newman von Hügel promised Ryder that he would send a copy of the latter's letter on this point to each recipient of the *Notes*. Ryder also chided von Hügel for underrating his theological liberalism. But it was not so much concessions on this or that separate point that mattered, von Hügel insisted, rather it was the whole question of critical method applied to all subject matters that the traditional inerrancy view had yet honestly to confront. 'So far,' the Baron wrote, 'the number of Theologians who do more than compare their traditional *principles* with isolated *results* of criticism is so small – that I must be content to wait and watch how they – the majority – get on without and against the critics: and myself meanwhile try hard to know much better and much more.'[3] Von Hügel also warmly recommended that Ryder read 'from cover to cover' Driver's newly published *Introduction to the Literature of the Old Testament*. The Baron had not yet had time to read the entire volume himself, but he was delighted with what he had read, especially with Driver's treatment of Wellhausen and Dillmann, and thought that Ryder would profit from it too.[4]

More than a year after this correspondence Ryder wrote to von Hügel to tell him of the developments and restatements which the Baron's comments and his own reflections had induced him to make in his essay.[5] Ryder told von Hügel that he had now made it clear that he fully agreed with Newman 'in holding that it is permissible to admit actual errors on minor points in Scripture'.[6] Moreover, he had so reformulated his own theory 'as to avoid that intermittence in Inspiration which follows if the "obiter dicta" position be pressed'.[7] With these admissions on Ryder's part, von Hügel conceded that their differences had been reduced 'to

[1] *Ibid.*
[2] Von Hügel to Ryder, 1 Aug. 1891, BOA, PC 205.
[3] Von Hügel to Ryder, 27 Sept. 1891, BOA, PC 205.
[4] *Ibid.*
[5] *Diaries*, 7 Nov. 1892; von Hügel to Ryder, 10 Nov. 1892, BOA, PC 206.
[6] Von Hügel to Ryder, 10 Nov. 1892, BOA, PC 206.
[7] *Ibid.*

differences rather of degree than of kind, – caused, I suppose, chiefly by your approaching the subject from its theological and dogmatic, and my doing so from its historical and critical side'.[1] He went on to tell Ryder that he hoped he would indicate that his concession of errors on minor points in scripture actually included even errors in the history of revelation. 'The formal (or even implied) exclusion of all the history or even of all the direct history of Revelation from the scope of your assertion, would, I am convinced, keep up the pinch exactly where the shoe pinches most.'[2] Von Hügel also mentioned to Ryder that he had been 'much interested and gratified to find that Abbé Loisy, a year after my remarks on your article, (and without any knowledge of my position), in a review of Dausch, has taken very much my line, – I rather think L.'s less formally, yet also with fewer (or at least less explicit) safeguards'.[3] Ryder's paper was eventually published in 1893, in three issues of the American monthly, *The Catholic World*. The fact that it at least allowed for many of the sounder conclusions of contemporary biblical criticism was due almost entirely to von Hügel.

About this time another Roman Catholic cleric, a man of broad views and considerable talent in the area of critical biblical studies, came into von Hügel's circle of friends. This was the Reverend Christian van den Biesen, a young professor of scripture at St Joseph's College, Mill Hill. On 11 February 1892 van den Biesen first called on von Hügel, presumably introduced by Bishop Herbert Vaughan (within two months to be Archbishop of Westminster, and shortly afterwards Cardinal of the Roman church).[4] Vaughan was both the founder of St Joseph's College and the Mill Hill clerical community, and a long time friend of von Hügel's wife and of his mother-in-law, Lady Herbert of Lea.[5] For ten years and more following their first meeting, von Hügel and van den Biesen saw one another with great frequency, even as often as twice a week during some periods.

Toward the end of July van den Biesen called on the Baron in order to read through with him an article which the former was preparing for the *Dublin Review*.[6] The paper was on 'The Authorship and Composition of

[1] *Ibid.*   [2] *Ibid.*   [3] *Ibid.*
[4] *Diaries*, 28–30 Jan. 1892. Nearly eight years after his first meeting with van den Biesen, von Hügel remarked: 'Van den Biesen came yesterday ... I do like that man, so very much'. Von Hügel to Tyrrell, 17 Nov. 1899, BM, Add. MSS. 44927.89.
[5] For an account of this latter relationship see *Letters of Herbert Cardinal Vaughan to Lady Herbert of Lea, 1867 to 1903*, edited by Shane Leslie, with an Introduction by James Brodrick, S.J., London, 1942.
[6] *Diaries*, 28 July 1892.

the Hexateuch', and was meant merely as a brief and orderly presentation of the most important conclusions on the subject already reached with some unanimity by critical scholars. Von Hügel doubted whether the publication of the article was at all wise or prudent.[1] He felt that van den Biesen's ability to use the English language was not proficient enough to assure the guarded and moderate tone necessary for making the article acceptable to Catholic authorities. Neither was 'the little Dutchman' adept enough at indicating the difficulties of the positions he attempted to explain.[2] After reading van den Biesen's second and concluding article on the same subject, von Hügel returned the manuscript to the priest with a long covering letter containing suggestions which the Baron believed would improve the papers. Van den Biesen worked on the manuscript and returned it to von Hügel for his inspection on 7 October.[3] Since the Archbishop of Westminster had effective control over the *Dublin Review*, and since, at that time at least, von Hügel seemed to have some persuasive influence with Vaughan on questions of biblical scholarship, there was an exchange of letters between the Baron and the Archbishop on the matter of van den Biesen's articles. The first of the two articles appeared in the *Dublin Review* for October; the second would appear in January. By the end of October von Hügel had prepared a rough draft of two qualifying paragraphs which he suggested that van den Biesen incorporate into the second article.[4] The suggestion was taken and van den Biesen began his second article with a statement to the effect that he was not putting forward the conclusions of the critics as established theses, but only as hypotheses which seem to explain all the critical and historical facts; that these hypotheses are not clearly condemned by the church nor contrary to the unanimous teaching of Catholic theologians; and, finally, that

even if a solemn decision of the Church or the unanimous teaching of theologians had or were to put it out of court for a Catholic's acceptance, it would still demand the Catholic's special and careful study with a view to finding the flaw in the argument, and to substituting another hypothesis, which, while fully orthodox, should be equally compatible with the facts to be explained.[5]

Since this qualifying and very balanced statement had von Hügel as its

[1] Von Hügel to Ryder, 23 Nov. 1892, BOA, PC 206. [2] *Ibid.*
[3] *Diaries*, 16–17 Aug.; 7 Oct. 1892.
[4] *Diaries*, 13, 18, 26 and 27 Oct. 1892.
[5] C. van den Biesen, 'The Authorship and Composition of the Hexateuch', *Dublin Review*, vol. cxii, Jan. 1893, p. 40.

source,[1] it is difficult to sympathize with Wilfrid Ward's estimate of the Baron at this time that his confidence in critical theories was excessive and that he over estimated the value of critical methods and their results.[2]

In 1906 von Hügel remarked that 'M. Loisy is, even since 1890, one of my closest friends'.[3] To speak of this friendship as dating from 1890 is somewhat misleading, since the two men had no direct communication at all until the spring of 1893. However, when Bickell introduced von Hügel to the study of Hebrew in the late summer of 1890, he also told him of the abbé Loisy and of his critical biblical studies.[4] Only in the previous March had Loisy published his first book, his *Histoire du Canon de l'Ancien Testament*, which had been his doctoral thesis for the Institut Catholique of Paris, consisting mainly of his lectures given during the immediately preceding years at the same Institut. In April of 1891 von Hügel began a serious study of Loisy's *Histoire*.[5] With this reading began the intellectual relationship between the two men which would survive until von Hügel's death and which would cost him more, perhaps, than any other relationship of his life.

Alfred Firmin Loisy was nearly five years von Hügel's junior, having been born on 28 February 1857.[6] In the summer of 1881 he went to Paris and the Institut Catholique, and from that time was fully engaged in biblical scholarship. While teaching a course in elementary Hebrew at the Institut in the autumn of 1882, he began following a course of lectures in Assyriology under M. Arthur Amiaud at the École Pratique des Hautes-Études. And in December of that year he began following the course of M. Ernest Renan at the College de France. This latter course of lectures he followed regularly for the next three years. Loisy himself attributed his initiation into the critical study of the text of the Old Testament to Renan, and said that he gained from these lectures a

[1] This can be shown from the *Diaries*, 26–27 Oct. 1892, taken together with von Hügel's letter to Ryder, 23 Nov. 1892, BOA, PC 206.

[2] Wilfrid Ward's own reflections on this point are found in Maisie Ward's *The Wilfrid Wards and the Transition*, London, 1934, pp. 316–21.

[3] Von Hügel to Bishop, 23 May 1906, *Dublin Review*, vol. 227, no. 461, July 1953, p. 293.

[4] This fact was mentioned in von Hügel's first letter to Loisy. See, *Mém.* I, p. 287. Although the letters from von Hügel to Loisy have now been made available to scholars by the Bibliothèque Nationale of Paris, the parts of this correspondence relevant to the present study are mostly given in Loisy's *Mémoires* and will be quoted from the published source. A comparison of Loisy's transcriptions with the original letters indicates that Loisy has been scrupulously true to the originals with the exception of touching up some of von Hügel's lapses in French grammar.

[5] *Diaries*, 18 April 1891.

[6] *Mém.* I, p. 13.

model of methodology which served him well for his future work.[1] He had no personal relations with Renan at this time, nor, indeed, at any other, and he felt both that Renan had made a mistake in leaving the church and that he was too cynical in his approach to religion in general. Renan's lectures led Loisy to prepare a doctoral thesis on the inspiration of scripture. The thesis attempted to harmonize Loisy's ideas on the bible, inspiration and true exegetical principles, with the result that the traditional idea of inspiration seemed to be jettisoned. Loisy was persuaded not to present the thesis at the Institut Catholique. Because of incipient tuberculosis he was forced to rest during the autumn of 1886 and through the following winter. During this period of enforced leisure Loisy formally decided on a life of biblical research and scholarship in the service of the church.[2]

When the first International Scientific Congress for Catholics met in Paris during April 1888, Loisy read a scholarly paper to the assembly on *Un texte liturgique Babylonien*. Among his auditors was the young vicaire général of the diocese of Soissons, Eudoxe-Irénée Mignot, the future bishop of Fréjus and eventually archbishop of Albi.[3] Through the mounting crisis of the next twenty years Mignot would be one of his few clerical friends to stand by Loisy, not only with sympathy for the man, but also with understanding of the goals and values for which he worked. This first acquaintance and the friendship which eventually grew from it was to be important for von Hügel as well as for Loisy.

In March 1890 Loisy became a doctor of theology of the Institut Catholique. His thesis on the history of the Old Testament canon was published that same month, and was followed a year later by his *Histoire du Canon du Nouveau Testament*. At the second International Scientific Congress, held in 1891, and again in Paris, Loisy read a paper on the great national gods of the Assyrians and Babylonians, Ashur and Marduk. He drew a qualified parallel between Ashur and Jahweh as the Jewish national god, and his remarks created a momentary teapot tempest which left some of the attendants at the Congress with the uneasy and lasting suspicion that the young abbé's opinions were dangerous.[4] Shortly before the summer holidays of that same year, M. Fulcran Vigouroux, professor of scripture at the Institut Catholique, had visited

---

[1] *Ibid.* p. 117.   [2] *Ibid.* p. 150.
[3] *Ibid.* pp. 162–3. Michele Ranchetti, *The Catholic Modernists: A Study of the Religious Reform Movement, 1864–1907*, London, 1969, p. 20, is mistaken when he states that Loisy did not attend any of these Congresses.
[4] *Ibid.* pp. 195–6.

Rome. On his return to Paris he told Loisy that the latter's recently published study of *Les Proverbes de Salomon*, with its novel sounding opinions on the origin of the book, had caused annoyance in high places in Rome. Vigouroux indicated clearly that if Loisy continued in this type of research and publication he would not escape the Roman Index of Forbidden Books.[1]

The second half of the nineteenth century saw the gradual emergence of the critico-historical study of the bible as a recognized science. At first these studies seemed to orthodox Christians to lead necessarily beyond the pale of orthodoxy.[2] An accepted biblical science did not yet exist, and all biblical studies were considered to belong exclusively to the realm of systematic theology. There were as yet, even on the theological side, no sufficiently full elaborations of the ideas of inspiration, revelation and inerrancy, as these were used when speaking of the bible. The serious need for a reasoned elaboration of such concepts became apparent as critical biblical scholars began to insist on the fact of historical and scientific error in the bible, and on the developmental and composite character of some of the Old Testament books. Biblical inerrancy, for example, had been taken to mean that every statement in the bible was literally true, with the historical and scientific accuracy that a nineteenth century European would require of contemporary historical and scientific studies. When the science of geology showed that the world was very much older than biblical literalism could account for, and when historical studies showed factual inaccuracies in the book of Daniel, and a multiple authorship, covering centuries, for the Pentateuch, then conflict was bound to arise. But new theologies are not born in a moment, no matter how pressing the need. And the defenders of the old orthodoxy, based as it was in part on a biblical fundamentalism, were not without their heresy trials. Two examples of such persecution, which von Hügel used to like to recall for non-Catholic audiences as evidence that the obscurantism was not entirely on the Roman Catholic

---

[1] *Ibid.* p. 199.

[2] For a good general account of this development in England see L. E. Elliott-Binns, *English Thought, 1860–1900: The Theological Aspect*, London, 1956. For a more specific account of an aspect of this development in the Church of England see *Essays and Reviews*, 12th edition, London, 1856. In this particular edition the original essays are published together with an indication of 'those portions of the Volume against which certain Charges were brought in the Ecclesiastical Court, as being contrary to, or inconsistent with, the doctrines of the Church of England'. For an account of this development in Roman Catholic thought see, James Tunstead Burtchaell, *Catholic Theories of Biblical Inspiration Since 1810: A Review and Critique*, Cambridge, 1969, pp. 164–229.

side, were William Robertson Smith's rejection by the Free Church of Scotland and Charles Augustus Briggs's rejection by the Presbyterian Church of America.[1] By the closing years of the nineteenth century, however, most Christian churches had begun to work toward a genuine synthesis of the problems raised by serious and sober critical students of the bible. The data of the new science of biblical criticism was beginning to be accepted or rejected on its own merits, and the traditional theologies were being re-thought to allow for the evidence brought forward by historical criticism. This process, like all human processes, was a relatively slow one, however, and traditionalists still expressed considerable alarm when the Lambeth Conference of 1897 suggested that it was the right and duty of Christian theologians and teachers to apply critical methods to every part of the bible.[2]

These new developments were making themselves felt among a few scholars in the Roman Catholic church too, but in disproportionate numbers because of the type of authority structure which governed that church and because of the control which this centralized authority held over intellectual developments within it. The conflict between Roman Catholic biblical scholars and their church authorities began slowly, but moved to a rapid and violent climax. In the late summer of 1887 St George Mivart wrote an article on 'The Catholic Church and Biblical Criticism' which caught von Hügel's attention.[3] In the article Mivart prophetically observed that, although the conflict between Catholic theology and biological science was at last a thing of the past, a new conflict with critical historical studies was on the ecclesiastical horizon. Mivart wrote,

There are men of mark, whose opinions cannot be lightly regarded, who think the coming conflict between authority and criticism will be the most momentous controversy in the whole history of Christianity. Some of them are convinced that the great Catholic Church – the ship of Peter – after successfully riding the swelling billows of physical science, will at last be engulfed in the whirlpool of Biblical criticism.[4]

[1] Friedrich von Hügel, *Essays and Addresses*, I, p. 259; but especially in the address delivered at Edinburgh in 1914 and published in *Essays and Addresses*, II, p. 104.

[2] *Conference of Bishops of the Anglican Communion, Holden at Lambeth Palace, in July 1897, Encyclical Letter from the Bishops, with the Resolutions and Reports*, London, 1897, p. 64. Henceforth referred to as *Lambeth Conference, 1897*. See also, Elliott-Binns, *English Thought*, p. 177.

[3] This article was published in *The Nineteenth Century* for July 1887. Von Hügel read through the article for the first time on 27 July 1887 (*Diaries*), and then went back to it for a second reading on 6 October 1890 (*Diaries*).

[4] St George Mivart, 'The Catholic Church and Biblical Criticism', *The Nineteenth Century*, vol. XXII, July 1887, p. 32.

Mivart himself would not live to see how accurate had been his judgment of the temper of the times; but von Hügel would weather the full blast of the storm. From the very beginning of the conflict von Hügel was quite clear in his own mind about what he, at least, was trying to achieve. He was convinced that the indispensable milieu within which a genuinely religious life could alone flourish was that of truth.[1] And truth about the bible was of unique importance for the Christian's religious life. Von Hügel did not deny nor minimize the need for structure, for a visible institutional church, as a requirement for the full development of religious life in the individual person. Indeed, he clearly and forcefully spoke of this latter need.[2] But he also realized that institutions inevitably spawn politics at some level or of some type, and politics within an ecclesial structure usually lead to a diminishment of authentic religious life in proportion to their strength. 'But I feel and know it well,' he wrote to Wilfrid Ward in 1892, 'I am no politician: even Church politics I quickly have too much of.'[3] To pretend that von Hügel always and solely and with utter disinterested motives pursued the truth, while the church authorities with whom he and his scholar-friends came into conflict were mere scheming ecclesiastical politicians, would be to caricature the historical reality. Nevertheless, the evidence does indicate that the conflict was not brought about merely by the disinterested pursuit of truth in historical and biblical matters by two different parties, nor does it indicate a total lack of ecclesiastical politics and authoritarian prejudice in the statements and acts of church officials. Moreover, von Hügel was primarily pursuing truth, and the church authorities were primarily pursuing a policy, and the two are not necessarily the same thing. From the early years of his involvement in critical studies, von Hügel was con-

---

[1] In a letter to Ward at the turn of the century he expressed this conviction well: 'I have not yet found time even to look at your last "XIXth Cent." paper, but expect to find that I will cordially agree with much of its matter. I put my anticipation in this way, because I have to admit that I am generally a little fearful of finding that you have treated the questions *under the aspect of their orthodoxy, and the limits of the latter.* Now whilst quite prepared to think or declare such and such a view or such and such a man, inadequate, impoverishing, or even downright untrue, I find I wd. be acting *quite* against my whole interior movement and spontaneous conscience, if I allowed myself to shift it on to the ground of orthodoxy, and drawing the line as to who or what is within, who or what is without its pale. I shd. wish to work all those questions well into a very devoted spiritual life, and, as to the results, leave the question of their orthodoxy to God and the Church authorities.' Von Hügel to Ward, 18 June 1900, in *The Wilfrid Wards and the Transition*, pp. 327–8.

[2] See especially 'Official Authority and Living Religion', and 'On the Place and Function within Religion, of the Body, of History, and of Institutions', *Essays and Addresses*, II, pp. 3–23, and 59–88.

[3] Von Hügel to Ward, 28 Dec 1892, WFP, vH MSS.

cerned to help create an atmosphere of tolerance for the work of serious scholars, an environment in which they would be truly free to make their investigations and to follow up their hypotheses, without the continual fear of censorship and condemnation, or worse, from the sensitive guardians of orthodoxy.[1]

With von Hügel's pursuit of critical studies came increased awareness of just how far the Roman Catholic church lagged behind contemporary advances in this important area of research. The appeal of men like Sanday and Driver for the Baron was not only their thoroughly scholarly approach to genuine biblical problems, but also the fact that they combined this approach with a genuine reverence for scripture as a sacred object, and with definite and solid ecclesiastical attachments.[2] The officials of the Catholic church in the nineteenth century were only too ready to equate critical biblical scholarship with anti-clerical rationalism, and to condemn both together as undermining religious faith and ecclesiastical authority.[3] Consequently, examples of the combination of reverent ecclesiastical attachment and sound critical scholarship were of great importance in von Hügel's estimation. Such examples were possibly the only available means, for the time being at least, for persuading the authorities to tolerate men who made such researches, not in a spirit of destructive rationalism, but of constructive faith. And tolerance for such studies, not positive encouragement, was all the Baron knew he dared hope for.[4] When Bickell helped give von Hügel's biblical studies

[1] Von Hügel himself has publicly stated that this plea for tolerance was even one of the themes of his interviews with the papal Secretary of State, Cardinal Rampolla, in the 1890s. See, 'On Certain Central Needs of Religion, and the Difficulties of Liberal Movements in Face of the Needs: As Experienced Within the Roman Catholic Church During the Last Forty Years', *Essays and Addresses*, II, p. 104.

[2] 'Besides, you will I hope allow me to say so, I so happily and gratefully feel uniformly sure that you always do and will look at all these matters as a true Christian and a scholar first, and, if at all as a controversialist, as a controversialist only in the 2nd place.' Von Hügel to William Sanday, 1 Aug. 1896, BL, MS. Eng. misc. d. 123(2), fol. 610.

[3] Leo XIII himself did this in his encyclical on biblical studies. See, *Acta Sanctae Sedis*, vol. XXVI, 1893-4, pp. 283-4.

[4] In the early years of von Hügel's acquaintance with Duchesne, the latter had warned him not to expect more than mere toleration for the ideas and work to which he had dedicated his life (von Hügel to Tyrrell, 19 Aug. 1900, in *Baron Friedrich von Hügel: Selected Letters, 1896-1924*, edited by Bernard Holland, London, 1928, p. 88). In 1914, when von Hügel received the honorary doctor's degree from St Andrews University, he noted in his diary: 'I went to the new hon. graduate luncheon in St Mary's Hall; sat at right of Sir James Donaldson. At end, he made a little opening speech – very warm and kind. Then I made the first of the little speeches of thanks – 7½m. long, – thanking for those who came late thus to get their 1st Univ. honour; for the natural aristocracy of Scotland (myself being ¼ Scotch); for those who would apply seriously scientific, i.e. intrinsically appropriate, method, also to the epistemology and psychology of religion; and for those who believe in the need of institutions and traditions for

definite form and direction in the autumn of 1890, he introduced him at the same time to Loisy's first book. In Loisy von Hügel found, or thought he found, and within the Roman church itself, the precise combination of definite church attachment with wide and deep critical scholarship which the Catholic church so needed. Almost as soon as he had become aware of Loisy's *Histoire du Canon de l'Ancien Testament*, he was writing to Wilfrid Ward with delight about the book:

In these 250 pp. you have an extraordinary production, the very thing we want. A series of lectures, as delivered at the Institut Catholique in Paris (directly and exclusively managed by a Committee of French Bishops), and dedicated, as such, to his pupils: and containing every date and composite authorship demanded by Wellhausen and Kuenen: you don't get that every day! I shall look out with interest as to the book's reception: it is a phenomenon, even if its history turns out to be that Loisy and d'Hulst have quietly stolen a march on the Bishops![1]

Nearly three years passed from the writing of that letter to the time of von Hügel's first personal contacts with Loisy. They were years, however, in which the Baron carefully studied nearly every printed page which Loisy produced. During the academic year 1891–2 Loisy had decided to publish in periodic instalments his course of lectures on scripture, with a bibliography of new works relative to biblical science appended to each instalment. These were the *Enseignement biblique*, and they were intended to appear in six fascicules each year. The first fascicule was published in January 1892, and the last in November 1893. The final instalment of the *Enseignement* contained his controversial article on 'La Question biblique et l'inspiration des Écritures' which furnished the pretext for his expulsion from the Institut Catholique. Through the subscription list for the *Enseignement* Loisy first learned the name of Baron Friedrich von Hügel, and through the *Enseignement* itself von Hügel grew to appreciate Loisy as a scholar whom he could not afford not to know personally.[2] Within a few weeks of publication of the first issue of the *Enseignement biblique* von Hügel was not only reading it searchingly from beginning to end, but, of course, also sharing it with interested friends like Ryder, van den Biesen, Hutton and even

---

the full vitality of religion (I a convinced practising R.C., grateful for tolerance within that greatest of all the communions). 5 other little speeches of thanks' (*Diaries*, 9 July 1914).

[1] Von Hügel to Ward, 21 Oct. 1890, WFP, vH MSS. This passage is also quoted in de la Bedoyère's *Life*, p. 69.

[2] *Mém.* I, pp. 200, 287.

Gasquet.[1] By November he was enthusiastically telling Ryder that he would like to translate into English not only the *Enseignement biblique*, but even Loisy's two studies on the canon of the Old and New Testaments, 'if my little health holds out, and our public would stand it'.[2] In one very pathetic sense, these two evils, poor health and an unsympathetic climate of opinion among his fellow English Catholics, were to be always among the chief obstacles to progress in von Hügel's work.

On 25 January 1893 Mgr d'Hulst, Rector of the Institut Catholique, published in the *Correspondant* an article on 'La Question biblique'.[3] Nine months previous to this M. Icard, the superior at Saint Sulpice in Paris, had forbidden his seminarians to attend any more of Loisy's lectures, because he considered these full of excessive novelties harmful to the faith of his subjects. By publishing his article d'Hulst hoped to counteract the public embarrassment which Icard had brought on Loisy, and at the same time to safeguard the reputations both of Loisy and of the Institut from the charge of heresy. The main problem with which the article concerned itself was that of the compatibility of error in the bible with the fact of inspiration. In his own way d'Hulst realized as well as Loisy that the traditional theology then current in Catholic institutions was strangling the legitimate development of human knowledge, in the area of history and critical studies especially, by throwing up a barrier of prejudice which masked behind the name of orthodox religion. D'Hulst's article discussed the error–inspiration problem by suggesting that there were three theological schools by which it might be approached – a broad school, a moderate one, and a traditional. This latter was equated with the narrow theology of the day, and, according to Loisy, the first two had no real existence outside of d'Hulst's imagination. The broad school was supposed to maintain that biblical truth was completely identifiable with the object of revelation, which has to do only with doctrines of faith and morals, so that everything else in the bible, whether natural science or human history, does not fall under divine inspiration and can, consequently, be erroneous. Although d'Hulst himself never mentioned Loisy by name in the article, the broad school was

---

[1] *Diaries*, 23 Feb.; 15 March; 9 June; 3 and 6 Dec. 1892. 'Here's a new Loisy just come, which I want you to read. Let me have it back with the other papers in due course – any time will do.' Von Hügel to Ryder, 6 Dec. 1892, BOA PC 206. See also, Gasquet to von Hügel, 1 Nov. 1892, SAUL, MS. 2602.

[2] Von Hügel to Ryder, 23 Nov. 1892, BOA, PC 206. In this same letter von Hügel says: 'I find they are anxious at Louvain to see Loisy translated.' Probably this information, for what it is worth, came from van den Biesen, since he was in touch with the Louvain scene.

[3] *Mém.* 1, pp. 235ff.

evidently intended to represent his ideas. The Rector identified himself with the moderate school which was supposed to combine the advantages of the two extreme positions without being encumbered with their disadvantages. Apparently d'Hulst completely accepted the principles of classical apologetics still current in the late nineteenth century, for he genuinely believed that the Gospels furnished a solid basis for a demonstration of the truth of contemporary Christianity, and, specifically, of Roman Catholic Christianity. To Loisy, on the other hand,

the bible was a book written by men and for men, and it was subject to the conditions of every human book. It could not, even in matters of faith and morals, be in complete harmony with the truth of any era except that in which it was written. The ideas of the Old Testament, and even of the New, on God and human destiny, and on the idea and the economy of salvation, are not in absolute conformity with those which the church, because of the development which biblical faith has undergone in the course of the Christian centuries, professes today in her ordinary teaching.[1]

This position neither denied inspiration nor limited it in the way of d'Hulst's broad school. Rather, it stressed the human origins, conditions and elements of the bible in a way that was calculated to, and in fact did, shock Loisy's co-religionists of the late nineteenth century. However, d'Hulst's article was not so much an essay in theological analysis as in political diplomacy, though his calculations completely misfired.

Loisy had no knowledge of the article until five days before its publication, when the Rector gave him the corrected proofs to look over. He made no remarks to d'Hulst at the time, but he later reflected that, had he been asked, he would not have approved its publication. Loisy felt that the Rector of the Institut Catholique needed to be above suspicion, so that he could intervene effectively either with the local bishops or with Rome whenever any of his professors got into trouble through the delation of the ever present heresy-hunters.[2] By publishing an article in which he equated the current theology of the Catholic schools with narrowness, and implicitly approved the basis of biblical research at that

[1] 'Selon moi, la Bible, étant un livre écrit par des hommes et pour des hommes, n'échappait pas à la condition de tout livre humain, et elle ne pouvait, même en matière de foi et de morale, être en complet rapport qu'avec la vérité d'une seule époque, celle de sa rédaction. Les idées de l'Ancien Testament et même celles du Nouveau, sur Dieu et sur la destinée humaine, sur la notion et l'économie du salut, ne sont pas de tout point conformes à celles que l'Église, en vertu de l'élaboration qu'ont subie au cours des siècles chrétiens les croyances bibliques, professe aujourd'hui dans son enseignement ordinaire.' *Mém.* I, p. 237.

[2] *Ibid.* p. 235.

time considered by orthodox circles to be excessively advanced, he had compromised his position, and someone would have to suffer.

Three weeks following the article's publication von Hügel was reading it with care and interest.[1] In early March he sent out copies to van den Biesen and Ryder, telling the latter that he thought this 'very interesting and courageous Essay'[2] might not only interest him but might also help him with an article he himself was writing. In Paris and Rome the article was also read with interest, but generally with very little sympathetic appreciation. D'Hulst was attacked in the French press and journals and, without naming him, so was Loisy. In fact, Loisy remarked that he suffered more from d'Hulst's 'La Question biblique' than he had for his own publications to that date.[3] During the Easter holidays the Rector went to Rome to explain himself. His reception was extremely cool, and it was made clear to him that his 'broad school' was totally unacceptable in Rome.[4] On 19 April, while d'Hulst was yet in Rome von Hügel wrote to him in Paris, expressing his appreciation for the Rector's article and asking his permission to translate it for publication in the *Dublin Review*.[5] Ten days passed without any answer from d'Hulst, and the worried Baron decided to address himself to Loisy. This first letter from the Baron to the abbé was dated 30 April, and explained that he had obtained Cardinal Vaughan's permission to publish 'La Question biblique' in the *Dublin*, but was still anxiously awaiting the author's consent. Moreover, he had heard rumors of d'Hulst's being summoned to Rome, and he feared condemnations which would put Catholic critical scholarship even further behind than the two hundred years of arrears under which it already laboured. Von Hügel also took the occasion of this first letter to Loisy to tell the latter of his enthusiasm for his work. The Baron mentioned the continual propaganda on Loisy's behalf which he kept up in Oxford and Cambridge, and urged the little Frenchman to come to England as soon as conceivably possible so that he could be introduced to Robertson Smith, Claude Montefiore, Driver and others of the Baron friends. Von Hügel also asked Loisy for permission to translate some of the *Enseignement biblique* for the *Dublin Review* 'when

---

[1] *Diaries*, 19 and 28 Feb. 1893. 'I have recently been reading a pamphlet by Mgr d'Hulst: "la Question Biblique"; Paris: Ponssielque: 1893, 53 pp. It is *really* a defence of Loisy, tho' his name nowhere appears. If you like, you can mention this pamphlet as an able account of what is for Catholics free and what closed in these matters.' Von Hügel to Ward, 25 March 1893, WFP, vH MSS.

[2] Von Hügel to Ryder, 12 March 1893, BOA, PC 206.

[3] *Mém.* I, p. 240.   [4] *Ibid.* pp. 243–4.

[5] *Diaries*, 19 April 1893; *Mém.* I, p. 288.

the time seemed right', and asked for two off-prints of the abbé's recent article on *Mythes chaldéens de la création et du déluge*.[1]

On 3 May von Hügel had his first letters from both d'Hulst and Loisy.[2] Although the full text of d'Hulst's letter is no longer available, Loisy told the Baron of the Rector's recent visit to Rome and of its results as these had been explained to him by d'Hulst himself.[3] At this point Loisy did not know that his lectureship in exegesis at the Institut Catholique was the price Rome had demanded for not censuring d'Hulst's article.[4] What the Rector had said to Loisy, and what the latter passed on to the Baron, was simply that Loisy's history of the biblical canon would not be put on the *Index*, and that a forthcoming papal encyclical on biblical studies would settle the so-called *question biblique*. Two days after receiving these letters, on his forty-first birthday, von Hügel spent an hour making notes on their contents which he used that same afternoon as he walked over Hampstead Heath with Cardinal Vaughan discussing the whole problem of biblical studies in the church and pleading for an openness to the sort of ideas and scholarship represented by d'Hulst and Loisy. Apparently von Hügel considered his conversation a success, for with considerable optimism he wrote to Wilfrid Ward that he had

seen Cardinal Vaughan. He kindly came up on Friday, and was really *great* in his utter non-inflation and perfect approachableness. I hope and believe he will continue to keep an open eye and ear for us and our work and principles: I think he has got them so far to a degree I should never have thought possible for him.[5]

The result of the Baron's conversation with Vaughan was an agreement that the former should write about d'Hulst and Loisy and what they stood for, apparently for publication in the *Dublin Review*.[6] The proposed

---

[1] *Mém.* I, p. 288.

[2] *Diaries*, 3 May 1893.

[3] In a letter to Wilfrid Ward the Baron quoted what he considered one of the essential points of d'Hulst's letter: 'Vous avez raison de traiter de *canard* tout ce que les journaux ont raconté d'une prétendue sommation qui me serait venue de Rome, d'avoir à m'expliquer. J'y suis allé spontanément, et j'ai beaucoup à me louer de l'accueil du Saint-Père.' Von Hügel to Ward, 8 May 1893, WFP, vH MSS.

[4] D'Hulst had written this to von Hügel, and Loisy learned it from the latter (*Mém.* I, p. 289). The recent study of Loisy by John Ratté, *Three Modernists*, London, 1968, errs in saying that in Rome Loisy's 'essay on the Old Testament canon was to be censured, and a new statement would be issued on biblical criticism' (p. 60). Mgr d'Hulst explicitly told Loisy that his *Histoire du Canon de l'Ancien Testament* was *not* to be censured (*Mém.* I, p. 246).

[5] Von Hügel to Ward, 8 May 1893, WFP, vH MSS.

[6] *Diaries*, 5 May 1893.

article never appeared. But with the beginning of active communication between von Hügel and Loisy, a new and personal influence entered the Baron's life. At no time, however, did he accept Loisy's ideas simply uncritically and blindly, and as the relationship grew so did his ability to distinguish the sounder lines of Loisy's biblical criticism from those of the less sound religious philosophy with which it was increasingly combined. But von Hügel's principle of learning from a man first, and condemning only secondly (if condemnation or non-acceptance there must be), was always operative. It was the sound general direction of Loisy's genuine biblical research that von Hügel found the Catholic church almost totally without, and which he felt must be encouraged and increased in that institution even at the risk of much that might be excessive or require alterations later on. With the opening of communications between von Hügel and Loisy the Baron's long and careful apprenticeship in critical biblical studies seems to draw to a close. For the following ten years he would speak and act more as an independent scholar in his own right. Then would follow five painful years taken up largely with his defence of the one man in the Roman Catholic church whom he felt was really a master scholar in biblical studies, Alfred Loisy.

CHAPTER 3

FIRST CONFLICTS WITH ROMAN DECISIONS

Von Hügel planned to spend the winter of 1893–4, together with his wife and three daughters, in the south of France, at Saint-Raphaël. On 8 October he wrote to Loisy to tell him that he would spend the last two weeks of October in Paris on his way south, and that he hoped to meet the abbé at that time. He arrived in Paris on the evening of 17 October, and on the following afternoon met Loisy for the first time, at the latter's residence in the rue d'Assas. This visit was followed by two others on the 20th and 24th. While in Paris von Hügel was reading with great satisfaction Loisy's 'Les Évangiles Synoptiques' which was appearing at that time in instalments in the *Enseignement biblique*.[1] Loisy's own exegetical work and the critical problems which interested both men were undoubtedly the subjects of their afternoon conversations, and when the Baron reached Saint-Raphaël, he wrote to Loisy that the visits had only 'deepened and expanded the sympathy' he felt with him. In the same letter he remarked enthusiastically on Loisy's 'La Question biblique et l'inspiration des Écritures' which he had just read, and which he thought admirably combined a clear and pointed presentation of the problem and the elements of its solution, together with a moderation and correctness of expression which should not have offended anyone.[2] This very article, nevertheless, furnished the occasion for demanding suspension of publication of the *Enseignement biblique* by Cardinal Richard, Archbishop of Paris.

Loisy urged von Hügel to call on Mgr Mignot whose episcopal residence was only a few miles from Saint-Raphaël. This the Baron did on 22 November. Loisy remarked in his *Mémoires* that 'this day is memorable in the history of Catholic modernism; I would be strongly inclined to see it as one of the dates which might be given as its beginning'.[3] On the following day von Hügel wrote to Loisy of his first visit with Mignot. Several days before going to Fréjus the Baron had learned from Loisy

[1] *Diaries*, 17–31 Oct. 1893.
[2] *Mém.* I, pp. 290–1.
[3] *Ibid.* p. 293. Von Hügel has written a moving paragraph describing this first meeting between the bishop and himself. See, Friedrich von Hügel, 'Eudoxe-Irénée Mignot', *The Contemporary Review*, vol. CXIII, May 1918, p. 519.

of his expulsion from the Institut Catholique and of Cardinal Richard's desire for the suppression of the *Enseignement biblique*. Von Hügel showed the bishop Loisy's letter telling of these latest moves in Paris, and the bishop was deeply moved. In fact, he expressed to von Hügel his great concern about the appalling state of biblical studies in the Catholic church and his anxiety over the forthcoming papal encyclical on biblical studies which the Pope was known to be preparing. Mignot had even gone so far as to write to the Pope, begging him to allow the greatest possible liberty to biblical critics, and asking that he not impede these scholars in any way nor do anything precipitously. As Loisy remarked, considering the circumstances, and the dispositions of the Roman Curia at this time, Mignot's letter was an act of genuine courage.[1]

The Bishop and the Baron met for discussions several more times during those last weeks of 1893. Both men were preoccupied about the encyclical, and von Hügel, who was convinced that Loisy either had been or soon would be denounced at Rome, asked Mignot to intervene on Loisy's behalf with the Pope. To von Hügel it seemed very important that Loisy's writings not be singled out and condemned by name, so that the scholar would be free to continue his publications. Mignot felt, however, that such specific intervention was not yet required.[2]

Leo XIII's encyclical *De studiis scripturae sacrae*, more commonly known as *Providentissimus Deus* from the initial words of the Latin document, was dated 18 November, and was formally published in the last days of the month.[3] In a letter of 6 December Loisy told von Hügel that the text of the encyclical was then known in Paris, and that by a letter dated 1 December, Cardinal Richard, standing behind the encyclical and the Instruction from the Holy Office which had accompanied it, had ordered Loisy to suspend publication of the *Enseignement biblique*. On 7 December Loisy sent the Pope his formal submission to the teaching of the encyclical and included with his letter of submission a memorandum on the biblical question as he understood it in the light of the recent papal document. On 18 December Loisy wrote to Cardinal Richard informing him that the *Enseignement biblique* had ceased publication.[4]

---

[1] *Mém.* I, p. 295.

[2] *Ibid.* p. 296.

[3] The official publication of this document is in *Acta Sanctae Sedis*, vol. xxvi, 1893–4, pp. 269–92. It is this Latin version to which these notes will refer, giving merely *Prov. Deus*, and the page numbers from the *ASS*.

[4] *Mém.* I, pp. 296–311.

Loisy's first impression of the encyclical was that it would strangle critical biblical studies in Roman Catholic circles, and reflecting on this first impression nearly forty years later he was certain that it had been correct.[1] The encyclical approached the subject of biblical studies with quotations of patristic piety and principles of scholastic theology, giving no indication that there was or could be an autonomous science of historical criticism. The conclusions of serious critical scholars and of anti-religious rationalists were lumped together in a series of generalizations, and both equally condemned. Piety and prudence were to be the chief qualifications of seminary professors of scripture, and the teaching of the ancient Fathers and the tradition of approved scholastic theologians were to set the norm for scriptural interpretation. If one found something in the bible which seemed contrary to truth, then the encyclical urged the following of St Augustine's dictum that this must be due either to a defective manuscript, or to a mistake of the translator, or to lack of intelligence on the part of the reader.[2] Seminarians were urged to prepare for scripture study by a thorough grounding in the thought of St Thomas Aquinas, since he was not only the examplar in philosophy and theology, but also in biblical matters.[3] The 'broad school' of d'Hulst's 'La Question biblique' was roundly condemned,[4] and those who might think that the bible could contain anything at all false were accused either of perverting the Catholic notion of divine inspiration or of making God the author of error.[5] None of the really critical problems of biblical study were approached with any understanding or openness, and yet the encyclical concluded with the confident hope that biblical studies might 'honestly and fruitfully' flourish under the church's moderating influence.[6]

In the memorandum which Loisy sent to the Pope with his letter of

[1] *Ibid.* p. 297. 'Ainsi ma première impression avait été que l'encyclique de Léon XIII jugulait la critique biblique. Rien n'est aujourd'hui plus certain.'

[2] *Prov. Deus*, p. 289.

[3] *Ibid.* pp. 283-4: 'Providendum igitur, ut ad studia biblica convenienter instructi munitique aggrediantur juvenes; ne justam frustrentur spem, neu, quod deterius est, erroris discrimen incaute subeant, Rationalistarum capti fallaciis apparataeque specie eruditionis. Erunt autem optime comparati, si, qua Nosmetipsi monstravimus et praescripsimus via, philosophiae et theologiae institutionem, eodem S. Thoma duce, religiose coluerint penitusque perceperint. Ita recte incedent, quum in re biblica, tum in ea theologiae parte quam *positivam* nominant, in utraque laetissime progressuri.'

[4] *Ibid.* p. 288.

[5] *Ibid.* p. 289: 'Consequitur, ut qui in locis authenticis Librorum sacrorum quidpiam falsi contineri posse existiment, ii profecto aut catholicam divinae inspirationis notionem pervertant, aut Deum ipsum erroris faciant auctorem.'

[6] *Ibid.* p. 292.

submission he had insinuated, 'discreetly but genuinely', that the encyclical was quite satisfactory for directing theologians and preachers, but that historians and critics had to be governed by other principles.[1] To orthodox scholasticism modern critical methodology in approaching the bible was simply anathema. Until church authority could recognize and accept the difference between theological exegesis and historical exegesis there could be no hope for the progress of the latter within Catholicism. On the last day of the year Cardinal Rampolla, Leo XIII's Secretary of State, wrote to Loisy to inform him that the Pope had received his letter of submission and the memorandum. He was told that the latter would receive particular attention, and that the submission had fully satisfied the Pope. Then, considering the commendable dispositions which Loisy's letter had shown, the Pope believed it 'more opportune and more advantageous' for the abbé if he employed his talent in the future, 'for the glory of God and the good of his neighbour', in some other branch of science than biblical criticism.[2] Loisy received this letter on 4 January, and, in writing to von Hügel on the 12th, he told him of Rampolla's letter, but omitted to mention the Pope's advice for his future.[3]

On the same day that Rampolla was writing to Loisy to tell him of the Pope's desire that he re-direct his entire life, von Hügel was reading *Providentissimus Deus* for the first time, and in the original Latin.[4] During January von Hügel's health broke down, with the result that almost any serious work was delayed as he tried various remedies.[5] In February, however, he was able to finish the letter to Loisy which he had begun a month earlier, and later on in the month he had a long and frank talk with Mignot on the whole question of biblical studies. The Baron told Loisy that he had gone through the encyclical twice already and that he had found several things for which to be grateful. At least the document had not explicitly insisted on defending the Mosaic authorship and the historicity of the Pentateuch, as it had for the authenticity and historicity of the New Testament. And he thought that the context in which the encyclical used the formula about there being no error in the bible was such as to make the formula analogous in meaning to the ordinary Catholic usage of the formula about there being no salvation outside the

---

[1] *Mém.* 1, p. 314.
[2] *Ibid.* p. 317.
[3] *Ibid.* p. 320.
[4] *Diaries,* 31 Dec. 1893.
[5] *Diaries,* 13 Jan. 1894; *Mém.* 1, p. 322.

church. Just as this latter formula is qualified by a corollary to the effect that any non-believer of good will who lives an upright life in accord with his conscience can, of course, be saved, so the formula about error in the bible could be qualified – even according to the mind of the encyclical, apparently. At least von Hügel thought he had found such loopholes, though Loisy was considerably more skeptical.[1] Von Hügel accepted the encyclical as an ecclesiastical fact with which a Roman Catholic had to live. But he also considered it the sort of fact which could be interpreted and used in such a way as to make ecclesial existence at least tolerable for the Roman Catholic who also happened to be a biblical scholar. Moreover, he never acquiesced in a passive acceptance of the *status quo* established by the encyclical as either desirable or as something which loyal Catholics should not work to overcome. To him *loyalty* meant working constantly to achieve within the church an ever-increasing openness and positiveness in attitude and spirit in the effort to live an ever fuller life of faith in truth; the negativism and condemnatory attitude of official Rome to most modern developments, good as well as questionable, was increasingly something he could not simply accept and acquiesce in as final. Nevertheless, he had to admit that for some months immediately following the encyclical's publication he had to pass through 'a period of fog and suspense of judgment, not one bit on questions of principle or of doubt as to fundamentals or as to the ultimate triumph of our views, but all on questions of immediate policy and practical bearing'.[2]

On 21 April von Hügel was again in Paris, and on the 23rd he had a long interview with Loisy. Before returning to London on 2 May he had three more discussions with the abbé, and borrowed a copy of the latter's memorandum to the Pope in order to copy it for his own purposes.[3] During these days in Paris both Loisy and Duchesne had drawn von Hügel's attention to an anonymous article in the April issue of the *Contemporary Review* on 'The Papal Encyclical and the Bible'. Dr Emile Joseph Dillon, at that time Russian correspondent for the *Daily Telegraph*, was the author of the article, although only three men knew this fact – Bickell, Loisy and the journal's editor.[4] The tone of that article, with its

---

[1] *Mém.* I, pp. 322–3.
[2] Von Hügel to Ward, 21 May 1894, WFP, vH MSS.
[3] *Diaries*, 24–5 April and 1 May 1894; *Mém.* I, p. 323.
[4] *Mém.* I, pp. 336–9. For an account of Dillon's fascinating career (1854–1933) as a scholar, journalist, and adventurer, see the *Dictionary of National Biography (1931–1940)*, London, 1949, pp. 277–8.

blunt indication of the Pope's failure either to understand or to face up to the real problems of biblical science, was indicative of a type of reaction in England to the papal encyclical, and it set the stage for von Hügel's activities for the following few months.

Several weeks after leaving the continent for Hampstead, von Hügel described to Wilfrid Ward the frame of mind in which he returned to the English scene:

I came home, after seeing so much of my best friends abroad & getting to know much more, I think, than any one in England knows, about what is going on under the surface and is brewing for the future, – determined upon two things: not to say one word, at least publicly, inasmuch as the Encyclical remained unattacked; but also to speak at once, off my own bat and without consultation, if it was so attacked, and that, not primarily with a view to outsiders or even generally to the immediate effect, but for the purpose of utilizing the only opportunity we insiders have, perhaps for many a long day, for respectfully widening out our bases and getting breathing-space.[1]

But the encyclical had been attacked. Writing in *The Guardian* for 11 April, Charles Gore had given an incisive analysis, commentary and prognostication of the encyclical. He believed that the papal document clearly taught the theory of verbal inspiration; that, whether or not actual infallibility were claimed for the encyclical, it certainly expressed 'with absolute decision and complete authoritativeness of tone' what Catholics must accept in practice; that it was disastrous 'from the point of view of one who desires to see a reconciliation of Christian theology with scientific criticism'; and that this ludicrous failure on the part of the very church which claimed the right of universal guidance through her supreme pastor only helped to point up the mission of the Anglican church to lead the way for the reconciliation of faith and free science among the English-speaking races.[2] A leader in *The Spectator* for 28 April, written by R. H. Hutton,[3] commented on Gore's paper. Hutton disagreed with Gore on the point about the encyclical teaching the theory of verbal inspiration, but he thoroughly endorsed his idea that, even if the encyclical is not claimed as infallible, it is bound to mislead Catholics in this direction. He lamented the obstacles which the Pope had placed in the way of Loisy and men like him, and especially regretted, as Gore had also, the enforced withdrawal from publication of the *Enseignement*

---

[1] Von Hügel to Ward, 21 May 1894, WFP, vH MSS.
[2] *The Guardian*, no. 2523, 11 April 1894, p. 530.
[3] Although the leader was not signed, the fact of Hutton's authorship was confirmed by a letter to the author from C. A. Seaton, Archivist for *The Spectator*, dated 8 Sept. 1967.

biblique. Hutton wrote,

We are told that the injunction to study Scripture diligently is in effect an invitation to free inquiry, and so it is; but when you are invited to enquire into evidence, and told at the same time that if the evidence leads you to this or that result, you are by no means to divulge nor even willingly to entertain it, the freedom disappears at once, and the inquiry becomes a farce.[1]

In the following issue of *The Spectator* Cardinal Vaughan's theologian-in-residence, Canon James Moyes, attempted to meet Hutton's charges. Moyes agreed with Hutton against Gore that the Pope had not taught verbal inspiration. He also claimed that the teaching of the encyclical was not considered by Catholics as infallible, though he quietly ignored the whole question of obedience to its teaching which Gore and Hutton had raised. Moyes told Hutton that the encyclical had not only not hindered the freedom of Catholics in biblical research, it had actually enhanced it! A man who would only be free to follow the evidence of his researches would not really be free, according to Moyes. He would ultimately be free only when he followed another light, i.e. revelation.[2]

More important than Moyes's rejoinder, however, was a series of articles in *The Tablet* by the Reverend Robert F. Clarke.[3] Cardinal Vaughan had asked Clarke to prepare some articles for *The Tablet* in response to Gore's attack.[4] Although Clarke began his first article by disclaiming any infallibility in the teaching of *Providentissimus Deus*, he concluded his final article by stating that the reason Mr Gore did not understand the encyclical was because he was unable to understand or accept papal infallibility. With the direct biblical subject-matter of Clarke's articles von Hügel was largely in agreement. But he regretted that Clarke found it necessary to put his positive material in a framework of analysing and repelling Gore's position. Writing to Wilfrid Ward the Baron explained why he too had decided to enter the discussion in print:

I was and am delighted with his [Clarke's] breadth and the fact of the 'Tab-

---

[1] 'Mr. Gore on the Pope's Encyclical', *The Spectator*, no. 3435, 28 April 1894, p. 579.

[2] *The Spectator*, no. 3436, 5 May 1894, pp. 613–14.

[3] Clarke's articles appeared in the following issues of *The Tablet*: vol. 83, nos. 2816–19, 28 April; 5, 12, and 19 May 1894, pp. 641–3, 681–3, 721–3, and 761–3.

[4] Apparently Wilfrid Ward wrote to Cardinal Vaughan about an answer to Gore's attack on the encyclical, because an undated letter [though necessarily written between 11 and 28 April 1894, and probably closer to the former date than the latter] from Vaughan to Ward reads: 'I have anticipated you. Last week I engaged Clarke for the Scripture reply to Gore. He will not be ready for a few days more. It is a most important matter, I entirely agree with your view.' Vaughan to Ward, WFP, misc. MSS.

let' taking him as our official spokesman. Such differences of taking the thing as may exist between him and me are too slight, compared with our complete agreement as to our object, for it to have been wise, or even loyal, for me to take an independent line of my own, but for one all-important fact. You know, no doubt, that the opposite party are working for an Instruction of the H. Office to be sent out to all the Bishops prohibiting the teaching of a given set of propositions. They are no doubt but waiting to see what line we fellows take, before settling upon the list. Now I thought and think it of the greatest importance that more than one form of the freer view should be before the world: if they smash *this* bluebottle, perhaps *that* bumble-bee may survive. And if, as I pray heaven, they, even they (I am of course thinking of Cornély and Co) wake up at the 11th hour to the fact that they have already gone perilously far and that discretion is the better part of valour and they let well (or ill?) alone for the present, – why, the evident good-will and evident difficulty of more than one apologist may help and confirm them in this course.[1]

The Baron's entry into the discussion took the form of a letter to the editor of *The Spectator*. Under the guise of defending the encyclical he was attempting to interpret it in as wide a sense as possible in order to make it feasible for a sincere Catholic scholar both to accept obediently the Pope's teaching and at the same time to continue genuinely scientific research. 'You will have noticed at once that I have gone as far as possible to the right as to the document's doctrinal importance', he wrote to Ward two days after its appearance, 'as far as possible to the left as to its liberal interpretation. This too I think the wiser course *with an eye to Rome*. They will either be frightened at the quasi-finality with which the pronouncement gets treated, or pleased and willing to pass a good deal of widening out.'[2] He began the *Spectator* letter by defending Loisy's action in ceasing to publish, and by stating his own credentials and position.[3] In the letter the Baron was at pains to express a theological conception of biblical inerrancy which he could square both with the encyclical and with his integrity as a scholar. He again used the analogy of the formula about no salvation outside the church which had to be immediately qualified in such a way as to negate the literal meaning of the formula, and he buttressed this with several similar analogies, i.e. that of *sacrifice*, when used of the sacrifice of the Mass, having almost

[1] Von Hügel to Ward, 21 May 1894, WFP, vH MSS. In another letter of von Hügel to Ward (27 May 1894, WFP, vH MSS.) the Baron explicitly states his regret that Clarke found it necessary to attack Gore and his position at all. A recent study of von Hügel which claims that 'von Hügel was piqued by an article on the encyclical by Charles Gore', and which pursues this approach to von Hügel's *Spectator* performance, has simply misunderstood the situation. See John J. Heaney, *The Modernist Crisis: von Hügel*, Washington, 1968, p. 40.

[2] Von Hügel to Ward, 21 May 1894, WFP, vH MSS.

[3] *The Spectator*, no. 3438, 19 May 1894, pp. 684-5.

none of the ordinary connotations of the word *sacrifice*; and that of *sin*, when used of original sin, having almost none of the ordinary connotations of the word *sin*. The body of the letter then attempted to show how the relative truth inherent in the use of language and ideas springing from a given time and place did not contradict the theological truth of the revelation communicated by this language and these ideas.[1] He also noted the Pope's silence about recent controversy over the authenticity and historicity of the Penteteuch, and concluded that if 'we would defend the Encyclical as a serious and self-consistent document, we are driven to see here a far-reaching limitation to the apparent drift of other passages'.[2]

Hutton took exception to von Hügel's views in a leader in the same issue of *The Spectator*. It was von Hügel's basic *acceptance* of the encyclical which surprised Hutton.[3] Yet the Baron had no choice if he were to remain an unharrassed Catholic, within the visible structure of that church. At the end of the nineteenth century, and especially in England, there was simply no body of public opinion within the Roman Catholic community to which appeal could be made by a sincere Catholic whose intellect and conscience were offended by one or another of the many official documents proliferating from the Roman Curia and the papal office. And to appeal to public opinion outside the Catholic community

[1] *Ibid*. p. 685: 'But we scholars should help bring into full relief those characteristics of the relative side of Scripture which rightly absolve the traditional Church from any offence against true criticism when she refuses to break with Tradition and allow in the Bible of theology any of this relative side to be simply erroneous. We could show how if Scripture employs in matters of science, as the Pope tells us, the current language of the times, yet that this nowhere expresses formal convictions on the part of the inspired writers; how if in matters of history, as even M. Vigouroux would insist, their methods and standards are astonishingly different from our own, yet that they nowhere violate the literary ethics of their time and people; how if in matters of faith and morals, the law of a very large objective development runs through the preparatory Old Testament, and of a lesser and subjective one through the final New, yet that at every stage the message as divinely fits as it divinely transcends the intelligence of its special messenger and audience; finally how, if everywhere this divine and inerrant self-adaptation can be traced and studied by the critic, it is there but as the means of an all-pervading divine self-revelation to be infallibly taught and even re-applied by the Catholic Church alone.'

[2] *Ibid*.

[3] *Ibid*. p. 679: 'The Baron Friedrich von Hügel, one of the most learned and subtle of the critics of Biblical literature in the Roman Catholic Church either in this or any other country, and to most of us, at least, not the less impressive because he is a layman who has been brought to the study of the Scriptures not by professional duty, but by the natural attraction of the subject itself, addresses us a letter in another column, in which, somewhat to our surprise, he accepts the late encyclical on this subject put forth by the Pope as a document which, if not certainly infallible, is very likely to indicate what will sooner or later assume the importance of an infallible definition, and be regarded as opening a new epoch in the doctrinal development of the Church.'

was inevitably to invite excommunication by an officialdom which condemned and stood aloof from all the world outside the Roman pale. Von Hügel's letter had been an effort to find a way of living with the encyclical without compromising his principles as a critical biblical scholar. Hutton seems to have missed this, and understandably, since he came from an ecclesiastical tradition so different from the Roman one of defining oneself into a dilemma from which one then spends a lifetime escaping. Naturally he attacked von Hügel's chief means of escape, his insistence that when the church used words she did so in a number of rather esoteric senses which took the words beyond or away from their ordinary meaning and connotation for ordinary men. And he hit at once on the crucial problem involved in so contrived a means of escape. If the highest ecclesiastical authorities could attach such esoteric meanings to the words they used, thus making them either unintelligible or misleading to the majority of men, of what value, then, was this so-called infallible guide? 'Infallibility that takes a good deal of humouring to understand rightly', observed Hutton, 'is hardly infallibility for ordinary human purposes.'[1]

Perhaps the most serious misunderstanding between Hutton and von Hügel had to do with the idea of inspiration. In his letter von Hügel had expressed his satisfaction that the encyclical had insisted on the whole of the bible being inspired, thus once for all doing away with the unsatisfactory *obiter dicta* and intermittent inspiration theories. The Baron was formulating an idea of inspiration which was completely separable from the idea of inerrancy and which, at the same time, was not limited to the revealed truths of faith and morals. Hutton, on the other hand, indicated in his editorial that his idea of inspiration was more or less co-terminus with those of both revelation and inerrancy.

On reading Hutton's editorial von Hügel wrote to Wilfrid Ward that

Hutton's triumphant war-dance over my prostrate remains, – that no. of his paper really is like a St Michael with his foot on the Dragon, in this case a blind-worm!, – I care very little about. Indeed, it is well I should be attacked from outside: I have some chance that way of being accepted, or at least being passed *sub silentio*, by our people of whose future alone I am primarily thinking.[2]

He asked Hutton to allow him a response, and von Hügel's second letter appeared in *The Spectator* for 2 June. In this letter he came closest to explaining his ideas on the compatibility of inspiration and biblical

[1] *Ibid.*
[2] Von Hügel to Ward, 21 May 1894, WFP, vH MSS.

errors in a way that clearly marked them off from theories which identified revelation, inerrancy and inspiration, and, at the same time, took
seriously the evident human error with which the bible is liberally
sprinkled. In attempting to explain how the church can refuse to admit
'in the Bible any of its relative side to be simply erroneous', he explained
this:

I mean, to be in any way an error, theologically speaking; or to be the full
connotation of error, popularly speaking. Indeed, whatever at later stages
necessarily appears erroneous, was at each stage but part of that divine
economy, that inerrant adaptation of the divine message by means of particular individuals to particular audiences, which, by some means or other, was
absolutely necessary, short of upsetting the essential conditions of all human
apprehension.[1]

This same position von Hügel had expressed in his *Notes* to Ryder two
years earlier, though in different words. The Baron's letter also repudiated Hutton's approach to inspiration as being too literally, and therefore necessarily intermittently, conceived, since Hutton believed the
bible to be the direct teacher of all men for all time. Von Hügel, on the
other hand, saw the bible only as a 'witness in the hands of the teaching
Church', and he insisted that inspiration, as he conceived it, 'need not
raise the literary ethics of the writer – need do no more than somewhat
and somehow confirm or raise the religion or morality of the people then
and there'.[2]

On the same day that von Hügel's second letter appeared in *The
Spectator*, he had a long talk with Cardinal Vaughan at the latter's official
residence in Westminster. The Baron had carefully prepared for the
interview, having written out on the previous day a paper on the present
situation of biblical studies as he understood it. Loisy had been urging
von Hügel to solicit Vaughan's patronage in Rome to obtain freedom
for the abbé to resume his publications and especially for permission to
bring out his newly prepared *Les Études biblique*. The argument which
Loisy had urged the Baron to use with the prelate was that the enemies
of the church and of the encyclical were turning Loisy's silence into
ammunition for attacking the papal document. If Loisy were to continue
his scholarly publications with the church's approval, this would silence
those who were claiming that *Providentissimus Deus* was an obscurantist
document. Vaughan, however, refused to get involved in Loisy's defence,

[1] *The Spectator*, no. 3440, 2 June 1894, p. 750.
[2] *Ibid.*

maintaining that this was an affair concerning the Archbishop of Paris and Roman authorities, and not the Archbishop of Westminster. He told von Hügel that he had recently written to Rome, sending along Clarke's articles from *The Tablet* which had interpreted the encyclical's teaching on inerrancy in matters of history and science in a broad way, asking if it were not in fact acceptable to interpret statements about science and profane history which are found in the bible as expressing the common human opinion of the writer's era. Vaughan was in no sense a scholar, nor even very understanding of the intellectual problems of his day, but he did recognize that this most recent encyclical from Rome had embarrassed Catholic apologetes before the world of educated English opinion.[1]

Nine days after his interview with Vaughan von Hügel wrote to the Cardinal offering to write an article for the *Dublin Review* on the biblical question. On 13 June, Canon Moyes, whom the Baron had met at the Archbishop's House on the 2nd, acknowledged von Hügel's letter and, as acting editor of the review, accepted the offer for the article.[2] The day after he heard from Moyes, von Hügel wrote to Wilfrid Ward that he intended to make the article 'neither a defence of the Encyclical nor an answer to Gore. It will, in form at least, only incidentally touch on either point.'[3] Ward seems to have thought that the real problem posed by the encyclical was whether or not Roman authorities should or should not encourage scholars like Loisy. Von Hügel saw the problem differently.

The real question to my mind is whether there is or is not such a thing as a science of the Bible (as distinguished from its dogmatic and devotional use); and whether it is to be allowed to pursue its own methods (as distinct from proclaiming any and every conclusion), and whether suppression of labour, or even of publication (again as distinct from broadcast dissemination), is not a danger as great as any that is attempted to be met.[4]

He also told Ward that he thought the encyclical could be interpreted in such a way as not to interfere with critical methodology. To Ward's objection that the conclusions of critical biblical scholars were upsetting people's minds, von Hügel pointed out that Loisy, and those like him, were writing in specialist reviews for scholars and clerics. 'Are we going to have no manuals of obstetrics or of gynaecology till these can be

[1] *Diaries*, 2 June 1894; *Mém.* i, p. 342.
[2] *Diaries*, 11 and 13 June 1894.
[3] Von Hügel to Ward, 14 June 1894, in *The Wilfrid Wards and the Transition*, p. 311.
[4] *Ibid.*

safely put into the hands of the average young man or woman?' he argued. And, recalling Bossuet's suppression of Richard Simon with its aftermath of the Encyclopaedists, he concluded: 'I am not going, by any well-meant apologia, to even indirectly help on the repetition and perpetration of so disastrous an experiment.'[1] Until this time Ward had generally looked to von Hügel's lead in questions of biblical criticism and church policy. But the former's interpretation of *Providentissimus Deus* as a wise policy of 'cautious tolerance' opened a little rift between the two men which gradually grew through the next ten years into a cordial estrangement. Ward himself dated the beginnings of his divergence from von Hügel from this summer of 1894.[2]

On 25 June von Hügel began collecting materials and making notes for his article on biblical studies.[3] At some point early in the composition he realized that he could never manage to express himself within the limits of the single article of twenty pages, to which Moyes and he had originally agreed, and so he arranged with Moyes for a trilogy. The first of the three articles was finished, except for a few last minute revisions, on 20 August, and appeared in the *Dublin Review* for October 1894 under the heading of 'The Church and the Bible: Two Stages of Their Interrelation'. Before leaving England for another winter abroad, von Hügel received the offprints of his article and posted them to interested friends and fellow scholars.[4] Among these latter was William Sanday, who read the paper 'with great interest & much admiration for its beautiful spirit & often felicitous expression', and wrote at once to the Baron to acknow-

[1] *Ibid.* p. 312.

[2] When Ward pressed the point of the right of church authorities to check and restrict the scholarly work of men within the church, von Hügel responded: 'There are, I take it, many things which we all admit to be true but which never really touch our mainsprings, never really help us at a pinch and the insistence on which, when at a pinch, irritate in proportion as they *are* undeniable – in their degree and their place – as to your previous letter, the body of it seemed to say excellent and undeniable things but which fall short of the concrete difficulty, and only the P.S., I thought, came to the facts of the case – that the Church can and ought when necessary, check for awhile even eventually necessary work, that the Pope acts in such cases more as a ruler than a specialist, – this and the like seems to me most true but hardly helpful when not such action in general or at its best, but a particular form of it and much specialists' prescribing is the trial in question.' Von Hügel to Ward, 19 June 1894, WFP, vH MSS.

[3] For the next two months he was busy about the first of his three articles, reading up various authors (including the seventeenth century Spanish Jesuit, Ripalda) and consulting such scholars as van den Biesen, Loisy and Bishop John Wordsworth. Although he frequently used the London and Hampstead Libraries for journal articles like Dillon's defence of Loisy in the August *Contemporary Review*, most of the major critical works which he needed for his articles, as well as a good selection of scholarly reviews, were already in his own carefully chosen and constantly growing library. See *Diaries*, 25 June–18 Aug. 1894.

[4] *Diaries*, 20, 25 and 30 Aug.; 1 and 18 Sept.; and 21 Oct. 1894.

ledge it.[1] Sanday found himself largely in agreement with von Hügel's view of critical questions, but he felt that he could not quite go along with him in the main outline of the paper's total argument, though even here he was 'by no means sure that the difference has not more to do with words & names than with realities'.[2] Von Hügel had made a distinction which Sanday was not fully prepared to accept. 'We cannot then well think of Revelation without Inspiration', the former had written, 'or some kind of assistance to speak – without the Church; but we can perfectly think of it as continuing to the end without Inspiration to write – without the Bible.'[3] Sanday commented on the distinction by noting that

it is natural to me to associate the spoken Word with the written Word. In other words my idea of the Bible rather encroaches upon your idea of the Church. But I gladly admit that both spoken and written word may be regarded as an expression of the life and thought of the Church. I noted I think that I am increasingly inclined to take that view of them myself.[4]

The whole of von Hügel's first article was a profound and moving plea to take the bible seriously as a *human* book so that it could achieve its maximum effectiveness as a vehicle for *divine* revelation. He pointed out that all human apprehension, whether of divine realities through faith, or of finite realities through reason, must constantly grow and move forward toward full understanding but without ever reaching it. He noted that reason, which begins with assumptions, leads on into faith, at its opposite extreme, and that both reason and faith are linked irrevocably with moral dispositions and moral acts and truth.[5] He wrote,

I will go on to show that the apprehensions of Faith, ever growing by development of doctrine, and the apprehensions of Reason, ever growing by the accumulation of its materials and the perfecting of its methods, have in Biblical, as in other theological sciences, each a large domain already mapped out for the characteristic activities of each; and this, by the very necessities and obligations of the Catholic position.[6]

Consequently, the bible, in so far as it is a collection of documents from

---

[1] Sanday to von Hügel, 6 Nov. 1894, SAUL, MS. 2959.
[2] *Ibid.*
[3] 'The Church and the Bible: The Two Stages of Their Inter-relation', *Dublin Review*, vol. cxv, no. 231, Oct. 1894, p. 324.
[4] Sanday to von Hügel, 6 Nov. 1894, SAUL, MS. 2959.
[5] '... still goodness is a great force, in the long run, even for purely intellectual problems, if indeed such really exist, which I doubt more and more.' Von Hügel to Ward, 14 March 1895, WFP, vH MSS.
[6] 'The Church and the Bible' I, p. 314.

human history, has a human authority which must be established by historical means and methods. And only through the divine authority within the church do we learn of the divine authority of the bible and thus learn 'certain truths and facts above and additional to the legitimate operations and conclusions of Reason'.[1] But even at this second stage, in which theological rather than historical method is most operative, 'Reason is still busy – busy with that local and temporal adaptation of the divine Message, which Faith agrees with Reason in finding throughout the Bible, whilst Faith alone can with certainty everywhere find and define the divine Message itself.'[2] In his first two articles von Hügel considered the bible merely as a human document, prior to belief in the church; the last article treated it as a literary heritage received in faith from the church.

The second article appeared in the *Dublin Review* for April 1895, and the final one in October of the same year.[3] The third article concluded with two moving paragraphs which were as thoroughly and genuinely and deeply von Hügel as anything he ever wrote at any period of his life. Moreover, they have the added pathos of embodying not only his profession of faith in the church as a divine institution, but also as expressing his implicit hope that this same church might bring to fruition her full human potential.[4] These hopes were to be shattered during his lifetime, though not his ultimate faith in the church.

Loisy remarked of the three articles that, like everything the Baron wrote, these papers on the church and the bible were a bit involved, full of metaphysics and quotations. He also felt that the critical conclusions and the theological subtleties which von Hügel intertwined in these papers harmonized less perfectly than their author imagined.[5] And, in the last analysis, the conflict between the rights of science and the rights of ecclesiastical authority remained unsolved. In the practical order no

[1] *Ibid.*

[2] *Ibid.* pp. 314–15.

[3] 'The Church and the Bible: The Two Stages of Their Inter-relation', II and III, *Dublin Review*, vol. CXVI, no. 233, April 1895, pp. 306–37, and vol. CXVII, no. 235, Oct. 1895, pp. 275–304.

[4] 'The Church and the Bible' III, pp. 303–4.

[5] *Mém.* I, pp. 386–7. After receiving all three 'Church and Bible' articles from the Baron, Sanday wrote: 'It is always a delight to me to read what you write for its very beautiful spirit – at once so wide and generous towards men of other communions & so very gentle & devout in its own inner faith. There is a particular note which I find conspicuously in yourself but also in others of your communion which seems to me to be the very essence of Christianity. Every day the attraction seems stronger – not that I am at all shaken in my own allegiance or have any thought of change, but that I feel more & more the common bond which underlies our differences.' Sanday to von Hügel, 13 Feb. 1896, SAUL, MS. 2960.

doubt they did leave the conflict unsolved. No evidence seems to exist indicating that they caused any Roman authority to alter his thinking or change his conduct. But on the theoretical level they were neither so ambiguous nor so metaphysically subtle as the impatient Loisy would have one believe. Their importance lies in the carefully worked out statement of a position which would allow both the requisite freedom for scholars to pursue serious critical historical studies of the bible, and at the same time preserve all that was legitimate in the claims of church authorities over the bible and those who would study it. The validity of von Hügel's statement is nullified neither by the unwillingness of Catholic scholars like Loisy to make such ideas their own, nor the intransigence of Roman authorities in the face of anything which looked like a challenge to or an amelioration of their claims to absolute and unqualified power. The value of the Baron's papers lies primarily in the statement of such a position at such a time in the life of Roman Catholicism. They are more a statement of the philosophy which should undergird the Christian's pursuit of critical biblical studies, than an original contribution to this pursuit itself. And yet they are this latter also. When Wilfrid Ward wrote to von Hügel to congratulate him on the appearance of the first article, the Baron answered that

tho' I have not advanced a single thing simply *de mon chef*, but have merely given, in the very words of others, a *status quaestionis*, or rather a summing up of the discriminations actually made on both sides: yet I have brought into one article what can, so far, only be found here and there, and up and down the place: the thing *looks* much more, somehow, when all added up like that.[1]

If there was a way to avoid complete suppression of critical studies by Roman authorities, von Hügel's approach was possibly the way. However, as events developed, it became clear that there was in fact no such way.

[1] Von Hügel to Ward, 14 March 1895, WFP, vH MSS.

CHAPTER 4

ANGLICAN ORDERS AND OTHER ISSUES

ROME, rather than the south of France, was the scene of von Hügel's activities during the winter of 1894–5, as it would be in successive winters. In late October he and his family began the move from Hampstead, with more than a week's pause in Paris. On the afternoon of 25 October he visited Loisy at Neuilly, where the abbé, following his expulsion from the Institut Catholique, had just been installed as chaplain to a girls' convent school.[1] Before leaving Paris on 3 November the Baron had two more interviews with Loisy; he also saw Duchesne a number of times. With Duchesne he discussed the problems raised by the reopening of the question of the validity, from the Roman Catholic point of view, of Anglican Orders. As a result of these discussions he sent a letter to *The Tablet* which appeared under the heading of 'L'abbé Duchesne and Anglican Orders', and which Duchesne himself read and approved before it was sent off.[2] In the letter Duchesne was said to have 'pronounced himself in favour of the validity'. However, because of the theological controversy on the issue and because of the historical ambiguity, Duchesne felt that if church authorities ever made a pronouncement on the matter, it would have to

be guided as ever by the ancient traditional principle of always preferring, in matters pertaining to the Sacraments, the safer opinion; and hence that the most that could reasonably be expected, short of a considerable change in the sources of information or of their appreciation, would be that Anglican ordinations should be repeated *sub conditione*.[3]

By sending this communication to *The Tablet* for publication von Hügel seemed to be aligning himself with Duchesne, though in the first part of his letter he seemed to sympathize with those who held that 'the Orders in question are, though not certainly invalid, yet not certainly valid'.[4]

When von Hügel arrived in Rome on 9 November, he found that the

[1] *Diaries*, 25 Oct. 1894; *Mém.* I, p. 357.
[2] *Diaries*, 27 and 31 Oct. 1894.
[3] *The Tablet*, vol. 84, no. 2845, 17 Nov. 1894, p. 776.
[4] *Ibid.*

question of Anglican Orders, and not the Biblical Question, was most prominent in the interest and gossip of Roman ecclesiastical circles. That the Baron should have become involved in the Orders controversy was more or less inevitable by reason of his position, his interests and his friends. The same battle that he and Loisy had been waging for an openness in the treatment of the bible as an historical document, without predetermined conclusions and limitations dictated by theology, was about to be carried on over the terrain of the historical validity of Anglican Orders. Whether or not Anglican Orders were valid by Roman criteria of validity von Hügel did not know. What he did know was that the question was primarily posed as an historical one rather than a theological one, and that consequently it must be determined by historical methods, without *a priori* determinations from scholastic theology. Soon after reaching Rome the Baron decided to seek an interview with Cardinal Rampolla in order to put before him his own views on both the Orders question and the Biblical Question. Mgr Denis O'Connell, Rector of the North American College in Rome, advised von Hügel to consult Cardinal Camillus Mazzella and Padre Salvatore Brandi first, in order to get a clear idea of the prevailing atmosphere at the Vatican. Mazzella seemed to have the greatest ascendency over Leo XIII at that time, and Brandi was not only Mazzella's disciple but also the spokesman for the powerful Jesuit hyper-orthodox group which edited *Civiltà Cattolica*. However, Padre Giovanni Semeria, a Barnabite scripture scholar whom von Hügel had met for the first time only on 14 November, counselled against seeing Mazzella and Brandi. He felt that the Baron's position, so different from that of the two powerful Jesuits, would make them suspicious of him and might cause them to take means to bar his further access to the Vatican. Von Hügel accepted Semeria's advice, and sought a letter of introduction to Rampolla from Cardinal Ledochowski. But Ledochowski was annoyed at the Baron's openly siding with Duchesne on the Anglican Orders question, and he refused to give the letter of introduction.[1] At this point von Hügel decided to ignore the

---

[1] *Mém.* 1, p. 369; *Diaries*, 14, 15, 19–22, 25 and 28 Nov. 1894. For information on Mazzella and Brandi, see Edgar Hocedez, S.J., *Histoire de la Théologie au XIXᵉ Siècle*, vol. III, Brussels, 1947. – When Semeria visited London in the autumn of 1905, von Hügel invited him to address the London Society for the Study of Religion on the topic of the state of religion in Italy. Von Hügel's notes for introducing Semeria to the Society are still available in manuscript, and they reflect von Hügel's estimate of Semeria's work after ten years acquaintance. He noted about Semeria: 'Born *1867*, near San Remo, within borders of ancient Republic of Genoa. Posthumous; his father's only child. Joined Barnabites at 15 ... It was with Paolo Savi that towards 1890, Semeria started courses of lectures on the N.T. and Primitive Church

coy intricacies of Roman politics and simply presented himself in Rampolla's ante-chamber on 29 November. Somewhat to his surprise, the Cardinal Secretary of State received him. The Baron told Rampolla who he was and why he was in a position to know the state of things in England, and especially among the educated classes. He also mentioned that his field of work was religious philosophy and biblical criticism. He then commented on Rampolla's recent letter to the abbé Portal about reunion between Anglicans and Roman Catholics, saying a few words about the actual state of English opinion for and against reunion.[1] At this point Rampolla's interest in the interview noticeably sharpened, and von Hügel was able to insinuate a number of points without committing himself more than he desired at this first meeting. Then the Baron boldly told the Cardinal that *Providentissimus Deus* had done much harm in England among the scholars and educated people, though he purposely left Loisy out of his remarks. Rampolla impressed von Hügel as being sincerely interested in all he had to say, and especially so when the Cardinal asked him to prepare a memorandum for the Pope on all that they had discussed. Rampolla concluded the interview

History. These went well, – too well. *Cardinal Graniello*, Barnabite, under *Cardinal Mazella*, the Jesuit's [*sic*!], pressure, got the courses broken up, and Semeria moved from Rome to Genoa, as head of a Commercial Academy, where he has been, ever since. He is the co-founder, with *Dre. Minocchi* of Florence and *P. Genocchi* of Rome, of the useful "Associazione promotrice della Cultura Religiosa in Italia"; and the founder of the "Scuola Superiore di Religione", for the university students of Genoa. It is the courses of lectures addressed to this audience, which have made up his four chief books: *Venti cinque anni del Xtianesimo nascente*, 1900 – in which he deliberately explains the Pentecostal gift of tongues, as an unusually striking instance of the ecstatic speaking described in St Paul's Epistles; *Il Primo Sangue Xtiano*, 1901, in which he denies any detailed prophetic value to the Apocalypse – a book of consolation addressed, in the then usual apocalyptic form, to the persecuted Xtians of the time; *Dogma, Gerarchia e Culto nella Chiesa Primitiva*, 1902 – no doubt the richest and deepest of his books, in which amongst other things, he directly attacks the Scholastic definition of Truth as an 'adaequatio intellectus et rei", and substitutes "approximatio" for the first word of this definition, making thus possible an endless growth in Truth; and *Scienza e Fede, e il loro preteso conflitto*, 1903, – really the first of two volumes, which are to present respectively a criticism of Science, in so far as materialist, pantheist, or agnostic philosophies are deduced from it; and a criticism of Theology, in so far as it occasions such excesses by excesses of its own.' SAUL, MS. 2647.

[1] On 5 October 1894 the Archbishop of Canterbury wrote to Lord Halifax: 'M. Portal gave me a copy of a letter from Cardinal Rampolla to himself, based on the representations which M. Portal had made to his Eminence of the state of religion in England. The letter breathes a spirit of charity and strong desire for unity, but is written in very general terms, which do not commit its author to any definite statement; but he apparently regards with satisfaction the arguments with which M. Dalbus (and M. Duchesne) combat the unfounded difficulties raised by ordinary Roman Catholics as to the validity of English Orders. M. Portal added that he knew from the very highest authority that M. Duchesne (whose views are known) is to be entrusted with the production of full researches upon the question. He (M. Portal) had himself had personal experience of the amicable views of this authority.' Viscount Halifax, *Leo XIII and Anglican Orders*, London, 1912, p. 137.

by telling him that he would always be happy to see the Baron if he cared to call any time after five in the afternoon.[1]

Von Hügel had another brief interview with Rampolla on 4 December, and nearly every other day for the following month found him either at the Vatican Library or the Biblioteca Vittorio Emmanuele where he used the Library's copies of *The Tablet, The Contemporary Review* and other English journals needed for his paper. On 9 January the memorandum, consisting of twenty-three pages with twelve additional pages of appendices, was finished and taken off to be bound. The following day von Hügel presented Rampolla with the bound memorandum for the Pope.[2] Both the Pope and Rampolla were completely engrossed in the Anglican Orders question, and he knew that his memorandum would not receive any attention from them unless it coincided with their current preoccupation. His whole paper, consequently, was couched in terms of the English religious scene and its problems, and under this rubric he quite effectively made his points also about the more general problems with which he was concerned. The memorandum began with observations on the question of Anglican Orders, and argued for giving the benefit of the doubt to validity, with conditional re-ordination at the time of individual or group reunion. It then took up the problems which Catholics in England faced in the social and political spheres because of their religion and the current ecclesiastical ban on attending the Universities of Oxford and Cambridge; and official approval for attendance at the universities was urged. Finally, the memorandum pointed out that, in the interest of English Catholics struggling to participate in the intellectual and scholarly life of their own time and country, the encyclical *Providentissimus Deus* must be given a broad and elastic interpretation, after the manner of Father Robert Clarke in *The Tablet* and Père Lagrange in *Revue biblique*, rather than that of Padre Brandi in the *Civiltà*.[3] It says a great deal for Rampolla that he could receive with sympathetic interest such a document, when the dominant atmosphere of Vatican politics was so opposed to every point that von Hügel had made, and when the intransigents were supported in their opinions almost unanimously by every English Catholic cleric who made his way to Rome during those years.[4]

[1] *Diaries*, 9–29 Nov. 1894; *Mém.* I, pp. 368–71.
[2] *Diaries*, 9–10, Jan. 1895.
[3] *Mém.* I, pp. 371–5.
[4] For an account of an incident which indicates the general prejudice of even the ordinary Roman Catholic priest in England towards Anglicans and towards the possibility of a declara-

Nearly every Tuesday afternoon during the late winter and early spring of 1895, from mid-January till early April, von Hügel either drove or walked with Cardinal Vaughan, who was also in Rome, and the conversation nearly always centred upon Anglican Orders, Catholics at Oxford and Cambridge, or the Biblical Question. Vaughan's outspoken opposition to Leo XIII's initial policy of reconciliation with Anglican leaders had made the Cardinal something of a *persona non grata* at the Vatican. Because of von Hügel's outspoken attitude in opposition to Vaughan, the latter continued to put the Baron off in his efforts to obtain a papal audience through Vaughan's intermediacy.[1]

In March von Hügel had his first long and serious talk with Lord Halifax on the Anglican Orders question.[2] A week after this first meeting he wrote to Halifax about arrangements he was making to introduce the latter to Padre Semeria, and took the occasion to put in writing his 'exact position as to your affairs, as I particularly fear even seeming to hunt with the hare and the hounds: I cannot bear sailing under false colours'.[3] His first statement of position was that he believed Anglican Orders to be *possibly* but not *certainly* valid. His second point was that he felt 'the attempted Catholic interpretation of *some* of the articles and of the Rubric as to the Real Presence' was precisely the sort of subtlety and special pleading which ignored the natural meaning of words and which he was 'working hard to get rid of in our treatment of scripture'. Finally, he felt that for the Pope to write a letter to the English people 'would do no earthly good, and might be even ridiculous'. A letter to the Archbishops of Canterbury and York might have a good effect, he thought; but he also worried that it might have what he would consider an evil effect, the stopping of individual conversions to Rome without aiding a corporate reunion with a portion of the Anglican body. Though von Hügel favoured treating the historical question of validity historically, he still approached the matter of individual conversions to Rome with the principles of ecclesial theology left over from the era of polemics rather than anticipating an era of ecumenism. On this point, his mind in 1895 was not totally dissimilar from that of Cardinal Vaughan and even Leo XIII himself. Von Hügel concluded his letter to Halifax with

---

tion for the validity of their Orders, see, Albert Houtin, *The Life of a Priest: My Own Experience, 1867–1912,* translated by Winifred Stephens Whale, London, 1927, p. 91.

[1] *Diaries,* 22 and 29 Jan.; 5, 12 and 26 Feb.; 5, 12, 19 and 26 March; and 2 April 1895. *Mém.* I, pp. 376–7. See also, von Hügel to Ward, 14 March 1895, WFP, vH MSS.

[2] *Diaries,* 19 March 1895.

[3] Von Hügel to Halifax, 26 March 1895, HP, MS. A4. 253.57.

typical candour: 'I hope that this may make quite clear what I think. It would be disloyal all round, I think, not to try and remind you of the limits of my agreement on this subject.' At an early Mass in St Peter's crypt on 29 March the Baron was introduced by Halifax to the abbé Portal, and later that same morning von Hügel took Halifax to meet Semeria. The following day Portal came alone for his first long interview with von Hügel. Writing to Wilfrid Ward earlier in the month, von Hügel had told him that ever since his letter to *The Tablet* in November he had

been engrossed, – for 4 weeks I read nothing else – in the Orders question: I read most carefully, weighing and sifting and analysing the evidence, all the crucial chapters in Estcourt and Hutton, and all such documents and arguments as either side press as weighty. I have come away from the study with a clear conviction that God allowed affairs so to happen in the XVIth Century, and the evidence concerning them so to come down to us, that neither we nor the Anglicans can, unless we *force the note*, make out a certainty either for or against the validity. Indeed, if we restrict ourselves to the simple question of the sufficiency of the matter, form and intention, of the ordinations according to the first and 2nd Ordinals, we can quite well maintain the moral certainty of the validity. It is, I think, only when we get out of the four corners of the strictly orders question, and get to the Baptisms, and the strong doubts felt about their validity by Fredk. G. Lee and other 'Order of Corporate Reunion' people, – that we see, clearly that there is a real doubt against these orders, and that it would be going beyond the requirements, indeed the permissions of history, to accept their validity *pure and simple*.[1]

At the time of writing his letter to *The Tablet* von Hügel acknowledged that he had never occupied himself 'in detail over this complicated question'. Circumstances, however, had since made such occupation imperative.

On his way to Rome again in the autumn of 1895 von Hügel met Charles Gore in Paris. As they had but twenty-four hours together there, von Hügel conducted Gore on a whirlwind visit to the abbés Pautonnier, Duchesne, Loisy and Portal.[2] Gore was delighted to find that 'they are vehement – especially Duchesne, Pautonnier & Loisy – in their denunciations of scholastic theology!! & uncritical history', but his own 'conservative mind' was a bit shocked at the 'very free' biblical criticism of the same French ecclesiastics. And he concluded that 'certainly

[1] Von Hügel to Ward, 14 March 1895, WFP, vH MSS. The first half of this passage is quoted in Maisie Ward's *The Wilfrid Wards and the Transition*, pp. 287–8.
[2] Gore to Halifax, 14 Oct. 1895, HP, MS. A4. 218.; *Diaries*, 8–12 Oct. 1895.

Duchesne is the most brilliant talker I almost ever listened to'.[1] By 18 November von Hügel had again reached Rome, and within the week had interviewed Rampolla, discussing once more the English religious scene. Within six weeks the Baron was writing to Wilfrid Ward with cautious optimism about the Orders question, and encouraging Ward to join him in writing for Portal's newly launched *Revue Anglo-Romaine*. He saw

many good reasons in favour of such a course: we would help inform not only *French* opinion, but also *Roman* opinion: *nothing but what is written in Latin, Italian or French really reaches the governing minds: and the 'Revue' is read regularly by our heads, I know for certain: they wd. also, I am clear, like to see Engl. Caths. working with and in it.*[2]

As the winter wore on von Hügel continued to solicit what help he could for Halifax and the Anglican cause in Rome, and in the process managed to antagonize many of the English Catholic intransigents on the Orders question.[3] Merry del Val wrote to Vaughan that 'B[n] von Hügel is leaving next week and I am not sorry, for he seems to have the art of helping to throw confusion, without possessing any of the theological or historical knowledge of the question at issue'.[4] Even after his return to

---

[1] Gore to Halifax, 14 Oct. 1895, HP, MS. A4. 218.

[2] Von Hügel to Ward, 26 Dec. 1895, WFP, vH MSS. For Ward's comments on the letter see, Ward to Halifax, 1 Jan. 1896, HP, A4. 224.1. Since the *Revue Anglo-Romaine* was so shortly to be forced to suspend publication, von Hügel never really had an opportunity to write for it. However, between 4 and 7 April 1896 (*Diaries*) von Hügel helped Portal translate for publication in the *Revue Anglo-Romaine* a paper left by Cardinal Manning at his death entitled 'Hindrances to the Spread of the Catholic Church in England' and published by Edmund Sheridan Purcell in his *Life of Cardinal Manning, Archbishop of Westminister*, 2 vols. London, 1895, as chapter XXVII of the second volume. The translation became 'Obstacles à l'expansion de l'Église Catholique en Angleterre', *Revue Anglo-Romaine*, no. 23, 9 May 1896, pp. 241–51.

[3] 'One thing, tho', is always worth repeating: as to how transparently controversial before everything else our Engl. Cath. majority is on that point of the Orders. For I too found in Rome among representatives of that party, an apparent inability to keep on believing that one in one's heart of hearts did not believe in the certain validity of those orders, seeing that one worked hard to prevent their absolute condemnation. Now, what *a priori* reason, of a philosophical or scientific kind I mean, can there be for this inability to keep on recognizing what is surely patent in so many other cases in life, – that questions are not clear to the degree to suit eager controversialists, but that they have, on the contrary, an annoying trick of, often, only testing the perfect truthfulness and balance of those who *will* try and see things as they are? ... I am still as certain about my uncertainty as to their validity as ever.' Von Hügel to Ward, 31 May 1896, WFP, vH MSS.

[4] Merry del Val to Vaughan, 2 April 1896, AAW, Vaughan MSS. VI/17. Rafael Merry del Val was 'born in London 1865, ... being third son of Don Rafael, Marquis Merry del Val, then Sec. to the Spanish Embassy, London, and subsequently Spanish Ambassador to Austria and to the Holy See ... The future Cardinal's own upbringing was more or less English, for from Baylis House, Slough, he passed to the Jesuit Coll. of St. Michel, Brussels, and thence to Ushaw. After his Ushaw course, he was selected by the Court of Madrid as private tutor to King Alfonso XII. When his father was appointed Spanish Ambassador to the Holy See, his

Hampstead in May 1896 von Hügel could write to Loisy with hopes for a middle solution to the controversy which would attribute at least a doubtful validity to Anglican Orders, though he noted that Father David Fleming, Dom Gasquet and Edmund Bishop – all either members of or consultants to the papal commission for examining the question – were all against a decision favourable to the Anglicans.[1] Yet, on the last day of May von Hügel wrote to Ward:

The opposite party believe themselves to feel quite certain of an absolute condemnation. I still doubt we shall have that. I have good news and from one who knows much in Rome, only these last 3 days, who bids me disbelieve alarmist rumours and even gives me some tangible reasons for doing so. You know I dare say, that I saw the Pope, a few days before the Commission began. *What* interesting times![2]

Nevertheless, in the same letter he wondered if it were too late for English Catholics of social prominence, men like the Duke of Norfolk and Lord Herries, to let it be known in Rome how much they would regret anything like an absolute condemnation. 'For one thing,' von Hügel thought, 'the Pope himself would at once cling to it, or lean on it, as you like.'[3]

On 19 September the Baron noted in his diary: '*Telegram in "Standard" of Bull absolutely condemning Angl. Orders having appeared in Rome previous evening.*' He had an exchange of letters with Duchesne, and then on the 27th he wrote a long letter to Cardinal Vaughan, formally accepting the Roman decision and proposing toleration for Portal's *Revue Anglo-Romaine*.[4] In response to his carefully thought out eight-page letter, von Hügel received an evasive and brief answer from the Cardinal. 'I am much obliged for your very interesting note', Vaughan wrote, and pro-

son accompanied him to Rome and entered the Gregorian Univ. to prepare for the priesthood. He was ordained at the age of twenty-four for the Diocese of Westminster, but was retained on special service of the Holy See ...' Sir F. C. Burnand (Ed.), *The Catholic Who's Who and Year Book*, London, 1909, pp. 336–7. Mgr Merry del Val was Secretary to the Papal Commission appointed to examine the question of Anglican Orders, and evidence exists that he used his position to prejudice the non-English members of the Commission against the Anglican cause. See, Moyes to Vaughan, 10 May 1896, AAW, Vaughan MSS. 1/17.10.

[1] *Mém.* I, p. 402.
[2] Von Hügel to Ward, 31 May 1896, WFP, vH MSS. The papal audience had been on 7 March. The Baron had prepared a little paper with his remarks for Leo XIII. He went with abbé Duchesne to the Vatican, and the two were with the Pope for twenty-two minutes. *Diaries*, 7 March 1896.
[3] Von Hügel to Ward, 31 May 1896, WFP, vH MSS.
[4] Von Hügel to Vaughan, 27 Sept. 1896, AAW, Vaughan MSS. VI/15; *Diaries*, 21, 24 and 27 Sept. 1896.

ceeded to tell von Hügel that he himself was 'most grateful to be out of the diplomatic mists of confusion such as poor Halifax delights in, and with a plain declaration of the truth'.[1] And to 'poor Halifax' himself Vaughan wrote several days later:

> I hope that you will come to see that the actual Pope, as Head of the Church, has the same right and duty that his predecessors had in the 16 century & in the centuries preceeding that. If after a new investigation, he has felt bound to repeat the judgment on Anglican Orders passed by his predecessors, it must be really a gain that he should have done so – unless the supposition be made (which we Catholics cannot admit) that the Supreme Judge has been wrong from the beginning.[2]

For a mind like Vaughan's, complicated problems of theology and history would always have such simple and largely juridical solutions; for von Hügel they could not. Halifax himself reflected on the decision that

> there are victories which are more disastrous than defeats, and I shall be surprised if ultimately Roman theologians do not find themselves compelled to explain away the present utterance of Leo XIII, as they now do those parts of the bull of Eugenius IV, addressed to the Armenians, which deal with the same subject.[3]

When von Hügel returned to Rome for the winter of 1896–7, he noticed a change in the atmosphere of ecclesiastical circles from that which he had left the previous April. Partly it was due to the triumph of the party in favour of an absolute condemnation of Anglican Orders, and partly it was due to a whole series of minor shifts in power among the various groups and individuals prominent in Vatican politics. To Loisy von Hügel described the difference he noticed in terms of greater narrowness and increased darkness all about.[4] And for the Baron himself a curious incident was indicative of the change. During von Hügel's previous two winters in Rome he had taken great pleasure in the company of Rome's more liberal-minded ecclesiastics, and especially in a small group of young men of whom Don Francesco Faberj and Don Brizio Casciola seem to have been the most devoted to the Baron.[5] In

---

[1] Vaughan to von Hügel, 1 Oct. 1896, WFP, misc. MSS.
[2] Vaughan to Halifax, 5 Oct. 1896, HP, MS. A4. 240.
[3] *The Guardian*, no. 2652, 30 Sept. 1896, p. 1495.
[4] *Mém.* I, p. 421.
[5] Von Hügel once described Don Brizio Casciola as 'a saint; utterly and purposely out of all touch with the official world; and as open as the day, as Loisy or Duchesne or Blondel, an admirer of the best of Wellhausen and Holtzmann, in the midst of his utter poverty and poor'. Don Francesco Faberj he described as 'very like Don C., but of another social (lower middle)

January of 1896 Don Faberj had brought Don Eugenio Pacelli, the future Pope Pius XII, to visit von Hügel, and for the next few months the Baron and Pacelli were on the most friendly and open terms.[1] Together they visited the churches and historic sites of Rome, but most significantly they discussed the great biblical problems of the day.

Some of these young and open-minded clerics had formed a *Società degli Studi Biblici* for the purpose of serious discussion of biblical questions, and in February the Baron attended one of their meetings with Pacelli and Faberj.[2] The Jesuit Gismondi read a short scholarly paper on a psalm verse, and Cardinal Lucido Parocchi, who presided at the meeting, addressed a brief exhortation to the group in terms rarely heard in those days in the eternal city.

There is a danger which Catholics must avoid: it is the danger of believing that, possessing revealed truth, and accepting the church's infallible magisterium, it is practically a waste of time to engage in scientific researches on the sources of Revelation. On the contrary, without even mentioning the needs of apologetics, a real knowledge of dogma is impossible without a critical study of the history of revelation. That which has been done thus far is insufficient, for new needs demand new studies which, while preserving in their purity the treasures of eternal truth, express it more for the grasp of the modern mind.[3]

Encouraged by these developments, von Hügel agreed to read a paper for the group when they next met in March. His remarks were described in Lagrange's *Revue biblique* as 'an important communication', and they concerned 'Certain Transpositions of Facts Which Are Noticeable in the Gospel of Luke'. In introducing his Gospel Luke remarks that he intends to relate certain facts in the life of Jesus Christ 'in order'. Von Hügel's paper showed, by a comparison of six such incidents with their counterparts in Matthew and Mark, that Luke's 'in order' could not refer to chronology, but rather must refer to theological purpose and significance. The paper, in fact, was a little cameo of *Redaktionsgeschichte* which would have done its author credit even today.[4] At any rate, it was in that atmosphere and from among those friends that von Hügel

---

class, and has (precariously) a little Professorship at the Roman Seminary. His is the same combination as Don C.; he is almost as devoted and critical as the other.' Von Hügel to Ward, 18 Nov. 1898, WFP, vH MSS.

[1] *Diaries*, 26, 28 and 31 Jan.; 2, 6, 16 and 23 Feb.; 1, 15 and 28 March 1896.
[2] *Diaries*, 6 Feb. 1896.
[3] *Revue biblique internationale*, tome v, Paris, 1896, p 470.
[4] *Ibid.* pp. 470–2.

left Rome in April 1896. When he returned in November, he found that the severe Cardinal Andrew Steinhuber had replaced the gentle Serafino Vannutelli as Prefect of the Congregation of the Index, that Duchesne was out of favour at the Vatican, and that Leo XIII found Cardinal Parocchi's ideas far too liberal. Most disappointing of all, perhaps, and most significant in the Baron's estimation, was the fact that the open, enthusiastic and enquiring mind of young Eugenio Pacelli, with which he had so often communicated in the spring, he now found quite firmly closed.[1] Several more times that winter, and in the following two winters as well, the Baron and Pacelli met, though generally in company, and after that the relationship evaporated and was never again resumed.

In January of 1897 the Holy Office published a papally approved decision on a technical point of scripture scholarship which pointed up the real source of conflict between Roman Catholic authority and Roman Catholic scholars. The Holy Office's decree stated with seeming finality that a Catholic could neither deny nor even question the authenticity of the Johannine text: 'Thus we have a threefold warrant in heaven, the Father, the Word, and the Holy Ghost, three who are yet one' (I John 5:7).[2] This particular text had long been considered by the nearly unanimous consensus of scripture scholars as a late interpolation. The Holy Office now announced that, after a careful examination of the problem, the cardinals who had voted on the question, had decided that this consensus was wrong.[3] And Leo XIII had approved, and backed with his authority, their decision. Not one of the cardinals who had decided the question was a scripture scholar, nor was there any indication that any of them understood how conclusions were reached in specialized questions of biblical research like the authenticity or non-authenticity of a particular text. What they did understand was that the particular New Testament text in question was a very important 'proof'

[1] *Diaries*, 29 Nov. 1896; *Mém.* I, p. 422.

[2] This translation, from the Knox version of the New Testament, follows the Latin Vulgate text. The RSV version, following the Greek text, does not contain this verse. The Holy Office decree can be found in *Acta Sanctae Sedis*, vol. 29, 1896–7, p. 637.

[3] This Roman propensity for pronouncing solutions to problems which had yet to be adequately formulated as questions was one of the main grievances of those men who were later branded and condemned as modernists. In December 1896 Mignot wrote Loisy of an interview he had recently held with Leo XIII. The Bishop, after having talked to von Hügel and Semeria about the problems of biblical studies in the Catholic church, decided to discuss the whole 'biblical question' with the Pope in person. But, at the time of his papal audience, before Mignot could get out more than a sentence or two, Leo had interrupted him with: 'But I dealt with all those questions in my encyclical *Providentissimus*.' Loisy aptly reflected: 'Notons que le pape se considére comme ayant, en vertu de sa fonction pontificale, à pondre des solutions, alors que l'évêque voulait l'induire à laisser étudier les questions.' *Mém.* I, p. 419.

of the New Testament doctrine of the Trinity, especially as this came to be formulated by scholastic theologians. And since the doctrine of the Trinity was one of the fundamental dogmas of Christianity, and since the church was the embodiment of Christianity, to use church authority to defend the Trinitarian dogma and its supposed scriptural justification was, of course, the correct Roman method of proceeding. The question of truth, of historical and literary truth, which the problem of textual authenticity naturally raises for the scholarly mind, had apparently never even occurred to the voting members of the Holy Office. Or, if it had, then their cavalier treatment of the whole matter, and the scandal to Christian consciences which their decree occasioned, is an interesting commentary on the state of religion in Rome at the end of the nineteenth century.[1]

Von Hügel was very much aware of the decision and of its implications, and he discussed it at great length with the young men of the scripture-study group, with Duchesne and Mgr O'Connell, with Padre Semeria and Dom Germaine Morin of Maredsous in Belgium, with the Bollandists van Ortroy and Delehaye, with Mr Norman McLean (a Syriac scholar from Cambridge), with Giulio Vitali and Baron Kanzler (friends of Roman winters), with abbate Minocchi and Padre Giovanozzi in Florence and with Batiffol, Hackspill, Hébert, Huvelin, Laberthonnière and Loisy in Paris.[2] Nevertheless, at first he remained quite

---

[1] Even two years after the decision of 1897 von Hügel was writing with chagrin of its significance. 'Still the fact remains that *in practice* the decision *has, where applied by Authority or attended to by specialists discouraged and hampered our work.* At *Propaganda* the very same Professor who, up to the decision, had been giving that formidable consensus of reasons against the authenticity, has turned right round, and demonstrates or declares the authenticity. (This he was certainly doing up to April of last year, when direct students of his attested the fact). Abbate Minocchi in Florence has had to abandon his new translation of the N.T., in which he was going to indicate the exact position of the documentary evidence in each case; and this he was required to do after, and no doubt at least in part in connection with, that decision. The Prior of Monte Cassino has a ms. which he wants to publish amongst a number of others, which involves one more conclusive proof that the "comma" is but a gloss. He came to Rome to see Cardinal Vaughan to get him to help him bring it out. I hope he has succeeded, but I see no sign in this, that the genuine and spontaneous wish or anxiety of the Roman authorities was and is not to hamper us. . . . Our position is, and indeed must be if we would be honest, *not that we ask for liberty to continue our researches on this point, but that the question has passed beyond the region of research and dispute, as far as all historico-critical evidence and principles go.* And to say and maintain this might well be conceit if it were maintained by a solitary scholar, or one here and there; or even if scholars had only just become unanimous. But, as a matter of fact, there is not one who has any reputation to lose, who would stake it upon defending this text; and for quite a quarter of a century Catholic exegetes have, with full episcopal approbation, fully and formally not simply doubted, but rejected it, – in Germany, in France, – in Italy even I think.' Von Hügel to Ward, 6 June 1899, WFP, vH MSS.

[2] *Diaries,* 4 and 20 Feb.; 2, 6, 9, 11, 16, 23, 27 and 30 March; 20, 25 and 30 April; 2, 3, 6, 7, 10, 12 and 14 May 1897. See also, *The Tablet,* vol. 89, no. 2978, 5 June 1897, pp. 896–7.

taciturn on the matter with his English friends – so much so in fact that when he returned to Hampstead in May Wilfrid Ward wrote to ask him if he were aware of the decision and its repercussions. The Baron replied:

I of course know all about that truly *phenomenal* decision of the H. Office. As there is no doubt that Cardinal Mazella [*sic*!] is somehow at the bottom of it, and as he enjoys an ever-increasing ascendancy over the Pope's mind, – said Cardinal has just been consecrated one of the suburbican Cardinal Bishops, a thing absolutely unique in the annals of the Jesuit Order and which keeps him in Rome as much as ever and with increased authority, – and as there is not the slightest chance of that neo-scholastic acquiring either special knowledge, or the instinct of the complexity of critical questions and of the wisdom of either studying them carefully or letting them alone, – we must, I think, be prepared, if His Holiness lives on, for, if that be possible, even bigger things in this kind of line.[1]

The decree occasioned a certain amount of predictable reaction in England. Cardinal Vaughan was annoyed with it, because the same Holy Office which had handed down his much-prized decision on Anglican Orders, now seemed to discredit itself by handing down a decision which the educated world could only consider a farce. He even went so far as to obtain 'from an excellent source' in Rome the assurance that the decree did not pertain to the critical evaluation of the text in John's Epistle, but only to its theological value.[2] Perhaps such a distinction made sense in Rome and to the Archbishop of Westminster, but von Hügel realized that in the practical order it was valueless. 'If our people from our Head down to our house maids would but kindly wake up to the huge arrears of self-reformation and self-education that hem them in on all sides,' he wrote to Ward, 'how little time they would find for this rankerous and unreally haughty controversy! I wonder, will that day never dawn?'[3] Charles Gore attacked the decree in *The Guardian*, and the Baron felt 'sure that Gore is doing us a timely service by pitching into this kind of thing, if only one could make sure of its being known and thoroughly digested by those whom it primarily concerns'.[4] Von Hügel himself had returned to England determined that he 'would not attempt one word in defence of this condemnation'.[5] The only three

[1] Von Hügel to Ward, 25 May 1897, WFP, vH MSS.
[2] On 4 June 1897 Wilfrid Ward addressed a letter to the editor of *The Guardian* to explain Vaughan's Roman distinction to the English public. *The Guardian*, no. 2688, 9 June 1897, p. 923. See also, *The Guardian*, no. 2689, 16 June 1897, p. 958.
[3] Von Hügel to Ward, 25 May 1897, WFP, vH MSS.
[4] *Ibid.* Gore's original letter is found in *The Guardian*, no. 2685, 19 May 1897, p. 805.
[5] Von Hügel to Ward, 25 May 1897, WFP, vH MSS.

public courses which he felt lay open to Catholics were 'silence, or frank and unqualified admission of a blunder, or brisk tho', of course, carefully limited attack'.[1] When he finally got around to reading *The Tablet*'s article which had provoked Gore's *Guardian* article, von Hügel was likewise provoked to join the attack. Though it later denied the intent, *The Tablet* had treated the Holy Office's decision as though it were final and definitive, and Gore had taken the statement at face value. The Baron's letter, which was printed in *The Tablet* on 5 June, made clear that he had no intention of discussing the Holy Office's decree itself, nor of criticizing Gore, but solely of commenting on the finality with which *The Tablet* had so happily accepted the decision. He pointed out that he had discussed the Holy Office's decree with over twenty specialists in Rome, Florence and Paris, 'men representing the most diverse degrees of age and of official position, and every kind of nationality, temperament, point of view, and theological school'. He found that not one of these men,

even from amongst the most traditional, timid, optimistic, or official-minded, but treated this decree, from the first and long before any outside attack or indeed intention, as an *ad interim* decision. There was not one who would not have found himself in serious perplexity as to the interpretation to give to this decree, were it not for the undisputed fact that the decisions of the Holy Office are not of themselves supreme or necessarily final.

He concluded the letter by challenging *The Tablet* to print a 'clear record of the actual state of Catholic theological opinion on this significant matter' of the authority of such decrees.[2]

The Tablet's editor appended a note to von Hügel's printed letter, in which he indignantly asserted that he was 'not likely to confuse a Decree of the Holy Office with the irreformable and infallible decisions which proceed from the Sovereign Pontiff himself', and accepted the Baron's challenge. In the succeeding issue of the paper appeared a lengthy article on 'The Decree of the Holy Office on the Authenticity of 1 John, V.7'. The mentality expressed in the article was such as to make any understanding of von Hügel's point of view impossible. It was stridently polemical, authoritarian and anti-intellectual, and concluded by suggesting that even among the Anglicans

there must be many pious and sincere men, free from the slightest sympathy with obscurantism or reaction, who feel that there are pastoral interests of immortal souls which after all are hardly less sacred than those of theological

[1] *Ibid.*   [2] *The Tablet*, vol. 89, no. 2978, 5 June 1897, pp. 896–7.

research, and who in turning over the leaves of certain volumes of a certain school, have come to realize the truth that the one thing which is very much worse than the supervision of a Holy Office is the lack of it.[1]

Exactly one month later the Anglican bishops, meeting at Lambeth, and concerned with the same 'pastoral interests' which preoccupied *The Tablet*'s editor, took a decidedly different approach to meeting those interests. 'The critical study of the Bible by competent scholars is essential to the maintenance in the Church of a healthy faith', they said. 'That faith is already in serious danger which refuses to face questions that may be raised either on the authority or the genuineness of any part of the Scriptures that have come down to us.'[2]

For the fourth International Scientific Congress for Catholics, which was to be held in August 1897 at Fribourg in Switzerland, von Hügel had been invited to read a paper. His contribution was to be for the scripture section of the Congress, and the paper, written in French, was entitled 'The Historical Method and Its Application to the Study of the Documents of the Hexateuch'.[3] He himself seems never to have planned to attend the Congress, probably because of his deafness, and some time during his previous winter in Italy he arranged with the Barnabite Semeria to read the paper for him. The Congress met from 16–20 August, and only on the 5th did the Baron finish his paper, covering twenty-nine foolscap pages, and send it off to Semeria.[4] On the 10th he sent four cards of introduction for Wilfrid Ward's use, since the latter was attending the Congress and was a stranger to most of the continental

[1] *The Tablet*, vol. 89, no. 2979, 12 June 1897, pp. 921–2. Von Hügel commented to Ward: 'But how irritatingly ungracious, indeed unstraight, the "Tablet" is! How easy it wd. have been for it to say, in its note on my letter: "We are much obliged to our correspondent for pointing out to us, in common with Mr. Gore, the defective and misleading wording of our 'Note'. We in no sense mean to defend this decree as necessarily final" – or something of that sort, and no one would have cared to try and show that it must have originally thought differently ... Such utter absence of gracious give and take, and of manly readiness to admit mistakes can only do harm surely ... All this bitter controversy, what harm it is doing to our people, let alone to outsiders. The whole thing is pitched in a key not made for man, at least here below, and up above, will there be a proto-typical infallible "Tablet"?' Von Hügel to Ward, 20 June 1897, WFP, vH MSS.

[2] *Lambeth Conference, 1897*, p. 20.

[3] Von Hügel's own English translation of his French paper was entitled 'The Historical Method and the Documents of the Hexateuch'. Through the influence of Mgr Denis O'Connell the paper was published in *The Catholic University Bulletin*, vol. IV, 1898, pp. 198–226, with seven further pages of appendices. This journal was an official publication of the Catholic University of America, Washington, D.C. In a previous issue of the same *Bulletin* von Hügel had published his own English précis of Lagrange's paper also delivered at Fribourg. *Diaries*, 18 and 26 Nov. 1897; 29 Jan. and 13 Feb. 1898.

[4] *Diaries*, 24–7 July and 1–5 Aug. 1897. Ranchetti, *The Catholic Modernists* p. 77, is again mistaken in thinking von Hügel himself attended the Fribourg Congress.

figures whom von Hügel now knew so well. The Baron recommended to Ward four of those attending the Congress as

most interesting men. Maurice Blondel is, I am confident, simply a genius of the first rank, little as he looks it; Pere Laberthonnière is his very thoughtful and admirably sympathetic-minded fellow-worker; P. Giovanozzi is a Scientist (Meteorology) and keenly interested besides in general Religious Apologetics; Padre Semeria you know much about, with all his rare gifts of heart and mind: he too, doesn't look what he is, a bit.[1]

Von Hügel encouraged Ward to join in the debates on Blondel's and his own subjects, though he admitted that he regarded the Congress as a not very serious affair, and judged its main value to lie in 'making acquaintances, and the Report later on'.[2] While von Hügel sent Ward on his way to Switzerland, he himself left for 'a sorely needed holiday' at Malvern Wells on the very day the Congress opened.[3] While enjoying the Worcestershire hills and reading with enthusiasm Barrie's *Sentimental Tommy*, he received a postcard from Semeria on the 23rd announcing the success of his paper. A friend of Loisy who had attended the Congress reported that von Hügel's paper had been much abridged in the actual reading and that Semeria's Italianized French made it nearly impossible to follow.[4] Nevertheless, the gist of the Baron's quiet scholarship got through to the vigilant guardians of orthodoxy because both his paper and that of Lagrange were considered excessively daring – so much so that the scripture section of the next Congress, at Munich in 1900, was cancelled. And this, of course, spelled the rapid demise of the Congresses. The greater part of von Hügel's paper was a carefully worked out demonstration of how critical scholars had reached their conclusions about the first six Old Testament books. 'For now well-nigh a century and a half', he wrote,

critical investigation has not ceased; and if system has succeeded to system,

[1] Von Hügel to Ward, 10 Aug. 1897, WFP, vH MSS.
[2] *Ibid.*
[3] *Diaries*, 16 Aug. 1897.
[4] *Diaries*, 17–23 Aug. 1897; *Mém.* 1, p. 479.
[5] *Mém.* 1, p. 481. From the first of these Congresses in 1888, because of the limitations placed on critical scriptural studies in the Catholic church, the Scripture Sections of the meetings seem to have been the weakest. 'I believe the Intern. Congress will be very good: at least some of the Presidents of Sections – e.g. the Abbé de Broglie, Paul Allard, and, above all, Père Charles de Smedt, – inspire me with much confidence. But, as usual, the Scriptural Section promises, I think, to be perhaps the most important and certainly the weakest.' Von Hügel to Ward, 12 March 1888, WFP, vH MSS. Although Loisy read a paper at this Congress in 1888, von Hügel had not yet heard of him at that time.

in at first sight barren confusion; if as a matter of fact, much has successively seemed for a while to be achieved which later on has again been called in question and been replaced by something else: yet, often hidden by much crudeness and impatience, sometimes by frivolity or rationalism, true method was being gradually learned and certain large results were being attained, a method and results which no futile ingenuity can escape.[1]

This statement of the attitude with which von Hügel approached his Old Testament investigations says much about the Baron as a scholar, and probably says as much about those who pretended to find occasion for scandal in his work. The scholars to whom he acknowledged his debt in the production of his paper were mostly German – Dillmann, Kittell, Wellhausen, von Hummelauer, and Holzinger whose *Einleitung in den Hexateuch* he found 'the most complete and critical collection of all the formidable mass of facts and analyses accumulated since Astruc's book (1753) and, indeed, before'. But alongside this formidable array of German scholarship, he cited S. R. Driver as one of the three men to whom he owed the most, and especially to Driver's *Introduction to the Literature of the Old Testament*, 'and his fine commentary on Deuteronomy, 1895'. Von Hügel's paper was, however, no mere accumulation of other men's conclusions. Although he apologized to his audience for speaking with so little that was substantially new to say, yet he also insisted that he was 'not simply compiling or copying from others'. He told them that he spoke 'with that kind of authority which the close study of all the original texts alone can give a man: and such speech may have its uses in a subject-matter as yet but little again studied historically amongst Catholics'.[2] A reader of the paper, with its tedious comparisons and analyses of texts, can sympathize with the Fribourg audience which found it hard to follow in Semeria's broken French, but he can hardly fail to admire the Baron's patient scholarship.

The last three winters of the nineteenth century von Hügel spent with his family either in Rome or southern France. His wife's nervous condition dictated in part when and where they went, and this with other family worries only added to the general sense of depression with which he watched the century draw to a close. The English Catholic party which had worked to obtain the condemnation of Anglican Orders instead of resting satisfied with their victory, continued to express a bitter tone and attitude toward those like the Baron who had been sympathetic with the investigation of the validity question.[1] He feared, too, that this same contentious spirit would carry over in the attitude of this group toward biblical criticism, and to Ward he wrote:

I feel it all too, in connection with my poor lifework. For I ask myself with some anxiety, if the feelings of what are the most influential of the personnel of Archbishop's House, and who, at the same time, have been those who have been the most open and helpful about the Scripture, – *set* hard and final against us, – well, then, by what door or window can such work as mine get into that centre. And yet such work is but little good, if disavowed, or even if only tolerated, for we are so behindhand with it, that for a long time to come, honest work on our part in this department will necessarily have to be a spreading amongst ours of the sound results of outside scholarship: the only originality of such work would just exactly consist in its finding a home in the Church.[2]

When von Hügel heard from Padre Semeria in the summer of 1898 that the Holy Office was preparing a decree on the theory of evolution which would also affect biblical criticism, he went at once to see Cardinal Vaughan to ask him to use his influence at Rome to try to prevent the promulgation of such a document. He was more than slightly disconcerted when Vaughan told him: 'We have need of truth, and we ought to be well content if the Holy Office is on the verge of giving us light on this point.'[3] And he wrote to Ward that 'everything points to Cardinal Mazella [*sic*!] and his friends gaining ever more ground; the fact no doubt is, that the Pope is getting very old, and that he leans more and more upon those who have a clear-cut programme: but this is hardly cheering news'.[4] Von Hügel also discussed with Vaughan the critical work of van den Biesen, and seems to have urged the Cardinal to encourage the Mill Hill professor in his work. At any rate Vaughan offered van den Biesen a commission to prepare a critical text and com-

---

[1] 'I had fondly imagined that, if there were people among us who, on this point, might be in danger of being sore and, for the moment at least, unable to shake hands and begin anew, it would have been us who have, roughly speaking, lost, and not they, who after all have gained their point, as to the technical matter and the having it their own way, so far, about the tone as well. But I find I was mistaken, and that the feeling is still very strong and sore. I cannot quite make out whether it is so, because of the past and settled controversy, or because they feel that, tho' we have accepted the Bull, yet that the general (and really permanent) question as to the proper attitude towards the Anglicans, remains for us substantially where it was: but I now think that even the first point has not by any means been got over by them yet, and, as to the second point, it must help to keep up the sore and angry feeling.' Von Hügel to Ward, 14 Feb. 1897, WFP, vH MSS.

[2] *Ibid.*

[3] *Diaries*, 25 July 1898; *Mém.* 1, p. 500.

[4] Von Hügel to Ward, 3 Aug. 1898, WFP, vH MSS.

mentary on the Psalms, and the latter accepted the undertaking.[1] The project, however, seems never to have gotten started before the period of repressive measures which ultimately exiled van den Biesen from biblical studies altogether.

In the late summer of 1898 Padre Giovanni Genocchi, a Roman professor of scripture and friend of von Hügel, sent the Baron the rumour that almost all of Leo XIII's entourage believed the ailing pope could not live beyond the spring.[2] But Leo was to live well beyond four more springs, and the clouds of 'regression', as von Hügel called them, were to get much thicker and much darker. The Baron felt that it was undeniably true that 'there is an attempt being made to subject the intellectual life within the Church to Thomism pure and simple'. And he believed that 'it is this rigorously unhistorically understood scholasticism which is at the root more than anything else ... of our exegetical troubles and anxieties'.[3] He too took comfort in the realization that Leo's reign must be near its end, and that in a new pontificate he could 'reasonably hope for a change, most desirable on this point'. Consequently, he postponed writing an article on 'Old Testament Criticism in the Roman Catholic Church', which D. C. Lathbury had asked him to prepare for the *Guardian*.[4] He thought he was postponing the writing only until the end of Leo's pontificate, but the article was never written.

Meanwhile the Baron used his continental winters to strengthen his friendships with the men in France and Italy especially, but also in Germany, whose own work seemed to him of the greatest importance in contemporary developments of thought. On his way home from Rome in May 1898 he made a detour to Würzburg to visit Professor Hermann Schell.[5] Already in 1895 von Hügel had 'discovered Schell's Dogmatik (really Apologetics) in 3 vols Paderborn, 1889–1893. A really fine Catholic book; powerfully original thinking and re-thinking throughout.'[6] However, in March of 1899 Rome put Schell's work on the Index of Forbidden Books, and the Baron noted in his diary that this was for himself one of the years six great trials – along with his wife's severe nerve illness; confirmation that his only sister was dying, apparently of cancer; and the British defeats in the Boer War which he believed

[1] *Diaries*, 5 Aug. 1898.
[2] *Mém.* I, pp. 500–1.
[3] Von Hügel to Ward, 30 May 1899, WFP, vH MSS.
[4] *Diaries*, 29 Aug. 1898; *Mém.* I, pp. 500–1.
[5] *Diaries*, 8–9 May 1898.
[6] Von Hügel to Ward, 14 March 1895, WFP, vH MSS.

were clear indications of 'the beginning of the break up of the Empire'.[1] From Würzburg, von Hügel went on to Jena where he spent a week with Professor Rudolf Eucken, getting to know the latter's family, sitting in on a meeting of the Professor's *Philosophische Gesellschaft* and address-ing a few words to the young philosophers there present, and, of course, holding long private philosophical discussions with Eucken himself.[2] There was much that the Baron appreciated in the development of Eucken's religious philosophy, and one point especially he shared with the Professor was the position given to suffering in any human life that realized its deepest and fullest potential. That same summer, in com-menting on the worries connected with his wife's illness and various financial problems, von Hügel reflected:

But there is no life worth living, because none developing and purifying with-out stress and strain and suffering. My beloved Eucken feels this so strongly that he and I had bracing talks as to what can be reasonably taken to be the substitute for suffering even in heaven itself. It cannot and will not be an eternal glut, although the popular presentment is often *that*, or nearly that.[3]

Loisy the Baron always visited in the spring and autumn as he passed through Paris. And when the abbé nearly died of stomach hemorrhage in September 1899, von Hügel immediately undertook to give him a pension of two hundred francs a quarter for a period of three years. Loisy refused the offer. In February 1899, while passing through Lyons, von Hügel met Henri Bremond for the first time, and was rather sur-prised to find that he was so young. Later that same month he spent a week in Aix with Blondel, and read and discussed the philosopher's

[1] *Diaries*, 1899. This entry – 'Trials of 1899' – is found on the first page marked for *Memoranda* at the front of the diary.

[2] *Diaries*, 10–17 May 1898. Several years before this visit to Jena, von Hügel was writing sympathetically of Eucken's work. See his 'Professor Eucken on the Struggle for Spiritual Life', *The Spectator*, no. 3568 14 Nov. 1896, pp. 678–81. A commentary by von Hügel on some of Eucken's key concepts is found in a lengthy letter of 26 September 1900, which the former wrote to Maude Petre shortly after introducing her to Eucken's work. The original letter is in the British Museum (BM, Add. MSS 45361.3), but it is published almost entire in Bernard Holland's edition of the Baron's *Selected Letters*, pp. 88–95. The fullest published study on Eucken by von Hügel is his 'The Religious Philosophy of Rudolf Eucken', *The Hibbert Journal*, vol. x, no. 3, April 1912, pp. 660–77. Von Hügel had originally intended to include his *Hibbert* article on Eucken in his first volume of *Essays and Addresses*. While he was working on the manuscript of the volume, Norman Kemp Smith paid him a visit in Kensington. The two men had a number of long philosophical discussions during this visit, and following one of these the Baron wrote in his diary: '*3rd talk w. Kemp Smith 10.30–12.* He made me drop out of my coming vol. the Paper on Eucken – bec. E. is 2nd rate & bec. I treat him as 1st rate; to shorten complete title to: "Essays and Addresses in the Philosophy of Religion" ...' (*Diaries*, 30 Sept. 1920).

[3] Von Hügel to Ward, 12 July 1898, WFP, vH MSS.

Letter on Apologetics while there. In March he also found time to take his daughters to watch the gambling at Monte Carlo, and to visit Aubrey Beardsley's grave on the *Côte d'Azure*. And between excursions during that March he read through John Caird's *University Sermons* with much appreciation.[1]

In *The Times* for 17 October 1899, St George Mivart addressed a letter to the editor on the subject of the Dreyfus case in France. The court-martialled Jewish captain had been the topic of journalistic headlines and editorial comment in England for weeks, and a leader in the same issue of *The Times* observed that 'Mr. St. George Mivart, with the masculine courage and scientific love of truth which have always characterized his writings, does not hesitate to look the facts in the face'.[2] The facts which Mivart was looking in the face were two: the fanaticism with which the Catholic hierarchy, clergy and press in France attacked Dreyfus as the symbol of that Republicanism which they almost universally hated; and, secondly, the silence of the Pope on this whole travesty of justice. The Pope's silence seemed to Mivart as a failure 'almost without precedent'. And observing that the scandal had been prodigious, he noted that 'no trial of any other Jew has had such world-wide consequences since that of Christ'.[3] In trying to account for the Pope's silence Mivart concluded that the daily injustices perpetrated by various Roman Congregations, and especially the Holy Office, right under the Pope's eyes and in his own name, made it impossible for the Pope to speak out on injustices committed elsewhere. 'Sad, indeed, is it', he wrote,

that so excellent and venerable a Pope as Leo XIII. should thus find himself hampered and ensnared by the neglect of his predecessors to reform their judicial procedure, as those of all other courts have been reformed, instead of continuing in a condition profoundly abhorrent, not only to Englishmen, Americans, and all English speaking people, but to the whole civilized world.[4]

Anticipating the Roman Catholic criticism of his letter, that these remarks should have been made in private and to the proper authority,

---

[1] *Diaries*, 8 and 10–17 Feb.; 19–29 March; 12 Oct. 1899; and *Mém.* I, p. 529.

[2] *The Times*, no. 35,962. 17 Oct. 1899, p. 9.

[3] *Ibid.* p. 14. 'I am feeling very sad about Dreyfus, sad I mean at the thought that there should be real doubt as to how the verdict will go, and none at all as to what large masses of leading Churchmen want – in France at all events. That being so, it is hopeless to argue that they deserve to lead on such matters: *esprit de corps* and *raison d'état* cannot and must not be our determining motive and last word on any point.' Von Hügel to Ward, 9 Sept. 1899, WFP. vH MSS.

[4] *The Times*, no. 35,962, 17 Oct. 1899, p. 14.

Mivart made a simple observation on the futility of such an approach. 'Gladly would I so act, and only so, were I not convinced that such an effort would be about as useful as would be an attempt to destroy a strong fortification by whistling.'[1] Von Hügel was in the midst of arranging numerous family problems, including various isolation cures for his wife's nerve troubles, when Mivart's letter appeared. In a hurried letter to Ward a month later, telling him that he and his family were off to Paris, Genoa and Florence on the following day, he added:

You will easily imagine that I have not the time, and am in hardly the frame of mind, quiet and reflection, to say anything worth saying about the Mivart letter. But one thing always strikes me in connection with such occurrences: nothing but a sadly large measure of truth in such criticisms can fully explain the painful, but psychologically suggestive, mixture of anger and fear shown by the official mind at such performances. They are quite transparently far from being such pieces of pure preposterousness as the comments one hears might lead one who did not know either the facts or human nature to suppose. I do not think Farm Street would show anger, if accused of attempting to poison the Queen; and I am quite sure you will not find me hot or bitter, if you spread the report of my having 3 wives, or even – only – two! And if these occurrences and recurrences, and the very reception they meet, all show plainly that they hit upon a bad, weak place, – then questions of taste and of measure (tho' of course important as *duties* for the individual speaking, and before the event), become secondary matters. To acknowledge, to investigate, to work to cure the mischief, – that is what is wanted I take it; the rest is but a palliative, that may even add, if not to the shock of the moment, at least to the unavoidable arrears and burthens of the future.[2]

From the continent von Hügel followed the final sad scene of Mivart's career. Mivart followed up *The Times* letter with other outspoken articles and a controversy developed with Cardinal Vaughan which eventually came to focus on the meaning of scriptural inspiration. Mivart's faith was called into question and he was required to sign a declaration of faith.[3] Finding himself unable to sign because he did not

---

[1] *Ibid.*

[2] Von Hügel to Ward, 20 Nov. 1899, WFP, vH MSS.

[3] Among other things, this profession of faith states: 'In accordance with the Holy Councils of Trent and of the Vatican, I receive all the books of the Old and New Testaments with all their parts ... as Sacred and Canonical, and I firmly believe and profess that the said Scriptures are Sacred and Canonical not because, having been carefully composed by mere human industry, they are afterwards approved by the Church's authority, not merely because they contain revelation with no mixture of error, but because, having been written by the inspiration of the Holy Ghost, they have God for their author, and have been delivered as such to the Church herself.' AAW, Vaughan MSS. 1/2. Confused, Mivart wrote to Vaughan for a clarification of the statement about God being the author of scripture. 'If, however', Mivart

understand the meaning of the document to which he was asked to subscribe and Vaughan referring him to Roman textbooks and Leo XIII's *Providentissimus Deus* instead of giving him straightforward answers to his straightforward questions, Mivart was excommunicated.[1] When he died very shortly afterwards, he was refused burial by the Roman church. Two things in the whole affair struck von Hügel most forcefully: the close resemblance of 'the intellectual tone and method' between Mivart and his antagonists Father Richard Clarke and Canon Moyes, and 'the sadly uncouth and unkempt, unrenovated state of our official exegetics and Historico-philosophical attitude in these Biblical regions'.[2] He felt there was something gravely defective in Mivart's 'painfully unspiritual, indeed not apparently fully serious attitude', however. And even if Vaughan had been able to offer Mivart something better than Franzelin's *Treatise on Inspiration* and Leo XIII's encyclical, von Hügel was not at all certain that they would have satisfied Mivart, because 'the soul must first be hungering for something beyond all that the science of phenomena can give, before even elementary Theism can find a deep lodgement'.[3] The Baron did not doubt that Mivart was 'a sincere believer in his own manner and degree', but he was also deeply impressed by the latter's

apparently complete absence of all response to even the most general and mystical Incarnation doctrine: and yet the Immanence of the Divine in the Human, – in Human struggle and endeavour against self and after the true enrichment of self-sacrifice: these things are the very soul of the modern spirit

---

continued, 'Your Eminence can authoritatively tell me that Divine Inspiration or Authorship, does not (clerical errors, faults of translation etc. apart) guarantee the truth & inerrancy of the statements so inspired, it will, in one sense, be a very great relief to my mind & greatly facilitate the signing of the Document sent me ... I therefore most earnestly adjure & entreat Your Eminence to allow me all the spiritual help & enlightenment you can; for the question I now ask, is my own great trouble and difficulty. I cannot & will not be false to science any more than to religion.' Mivart to Vaughan, 19 Jan. 1900, AAW, Vaughan MSS. 1/2.

[1] After referring Mivart to Franzelin's *Treatises* and Leo XIII's *Providentissimus Deus*, Vaughan added: 'But perhaps more useful to you than this would be a conversation with Rev. Dr. Clarke, or with Father Tyrrell, S.J., both of whom would be able to understand your state of mind and to give you counsel and assistance. I refer you to them.' Vaughan to Mivart, 21 Jan. 1900, AAW, Vaughan MSS. I/2.12a. Within less than two years Vaughan himself would be so mistrustful of Tyrrell's ideas that he would override the already strict censorship of books and articles which the Society of Jesus imposed on her members, and would insist on having Tyrrell's work censored in Rome. See, the correspondence between Tyrrell and Vaughan, AAW, Vaughan MSS. VI/12.

[2] Von Hügel to Ward, 18 Feb. 1900, WFP, vH MSS. This letter is quoted more fully in Maisie Ward's *The Wilfrid Wards and the Transition*, pp. 323–5.

[3] *Ibid.* The Baron expressed the same idea in a letter to Tyrrell, 4 March 1900, BM, Add. MSS. 44927.103.

at its best, and to lapse from which, would be so far to fall back into barbarism.[1]

As always, the Baron was worried that the reaction from this affair would last long and go far, – especially in the direction of checking progressive biblical scholars.

As the nineteenth century drew to its close von Hügel began to realize that Leo XIII's reign, at least, had not yet spent itself. On 6 January 1900 he wrote to Loisy about a current Roman rumour which said that the next papal election would not be bad; it would be terrible. The choice of a new pope, according to this rumour, would be a pure reactionary, and 'we shall pine for the golden days of the end of Leo XIII's reign and the ascendancy of Mazzella'.[2] In the summer of 1900, too, he wrote to Wilfrid Ward: 'Leo XIII is alive, and indeed apparently, in remarkably good physical and even mental health and vigour, at least for one so old: but his *will*, his persevering will has gone. I can give you the most final proof of that.'[3] Ward had been discussing with von Hügel the wisdom of drawing up a memorandum for presentation to the Holy See. It would be signed by prominent English Catholics, and would stress, among other things, the harm being done by Rome's restrictive measures against scholars. In October von Hügel had a 'two hours têtc-à-tête' with Archbishop John Ireland of St Paul, Minnesota, as the latter passed through London on his return from Rome to America.[4] The Baron discussed the proposed memorandum with Ireland, and wrote to Ward that as a result of this conversation he had cleared up his own mind on the question. 'I asked him directly', von Hügel wrote to Ward,

and after he had quite finished with the description and defence of his (relative) optimism, what he thought of the usefulness or at least harmlessness of such a document, supposing it carefully restricted itself to simply pointing out the danger of repressive acts, perhaps even entirely dwelling on simply possible, future ones. But even this minimum action he doubted would be wise, just now or indeed before the end of this rule. That, at the beginning of a new reign, such action, and stronger than suggested, might very well be most helpful, – but not now. I cannot help feeling that he is right; and that his opinion is, under the circumstances especially, worth attending to.[5]

Looking back to the year in which the nineteenth century became the

[1] Von Hügel to Ward, 18 Feb. 1900, WFP, vH MSS.
[2] *Mém.* I, p. 539.
[3] Von Hügel to Ward, 14 Sept. 1900, WFP, vH MSS.
[4] *Diaries*, 4 Oct. 1900.
[5] Von Hügel to Ward, 10 Oct. 1900, WFP, vH MSS.

twentieth, Loisy reflected sadly that at the time neither he nor his friends had realized that they were on the eve of a seven years war; that in the eighth year Loisy himself would be excommunicated; in the ninth Tyrrell would be dead; and that only von Hügel would remain, unbroken, on the deserted battle-field, determined to serve the church in spite of herself and by means of genuinely scientific work; while, from a distance, Archbishop Mignot, sad and pensive, watched the collapse of all their hopes.[1] On the last day of 1900 von Hügel wrote to Ward: 'May this New Year and New Century, bring us all much good, – much work, and some achievement, visible or invisible, in the direction of a synthesis of Sanctity and Science, in the Church and for the Church.'[2]

[1] *Mém.* 1, p. 578.
[2] Von Hügel to Ward, 31 Dec. 1900, WFP, vH MSS. For more on von Hügel's idea of 'a synthesis of Sanctity and Science', see, von Hügel to Tyrrell, 28 May 1901, BM, Add. MSS. 44927.162–3.

CHAPTER 5

LOISY'S TROUBLES AND THE PONTIFICAL BIBLICAL COMMISSION

FOR NEARLY EIGHTEEN YEARS, from 1890 until 1908, but especially from the turn of the century onward, von Hügel worked to prevent the total rejection of Loisy by ecclesiastical authorities in Rome. He did so not because he felt that all of Loisy's critical conclusions were necessarily correct, but because he recognized the need for an official tolerance within the Roman Catholic church of intellectual horizons broader than scholasticism, and capable both of integrating the critical and historical dimensions of contemporary thought into the church's life, and of preparing a Christian people who could respond to their own era in a positive rather than in a defensive and condemnatory manner. For official Catholicism to condemn Loisy would be to cut off one of the chief instruments for bringing about such breadth and development within the church, since at that time Loisy was almost the only Roman Catholic scholar to be completely a master of critical historical methodology in biblical matters, and was, unquestionably, something of a genius in his field. The story of von Hügel's defence of Loisy is the story of a large part of the Baron's life during the first years of the twentieth century.

As early as January 1892 von Hügel had picked up rumours of Loisy's denunciation. Duchesne wrote the Baron that the French Dominicans had denounced to the Holy Office Loisy's two studies on the canons of the Old and New Testaments. Somewhat laconically von Hügel reflected that 'it remains, of course, to be seen whether they will be censured or not; and, even if they are, it is but one of the many ups and downs the great controversy will have to pass thro', before it is satisfactorily settled'.[1] Nevertheless, the rumour was sufficiently disturbing to the Baron to cause him to ask Herbert Vaughan, who was soon to be Archbishop of Westminster, to write to Rome in Loisy's defence. This the obliging Vaughan did. Shortly afterwards von Hügel was told that Loisy had not actually been denounced at all. With chagrin the Baron observed that 'we have but put the idea of his denounceableness into the

[1] Von Hügel to Ward, 19 Jan. 1892, WFP, vH MSS.

79

heads of the Roman authorities!'[1] Several months later, however, he received confirmation that his first information about the denunciation had been correct after all. 'Also, the French (Paris) Dominicans *did* denounce my beloved Loisy sure enough,' he wrote to a friend, 'but the Roman authorities have refused to censure him. I am very pleased, but feel pretty sure, they will wait, and renew the charge later on. Still, he has already plainly shown his hand, and it seems unlikely that they will succeed, when he has still further established his influence.'[2] Whether or not the French Dominicans had really denounced Loisy at that time seems to be an open historical question yet.[3] But whether they had or not, von Hügel clearly recognized, from the time of his first acquaintance with Loisy's work, that the French scholar would have to expect considerable opposition from his fellow Roman Catholics.

Until almost the end of Loisy's struggle with the Archbishop of Paris and with the Holy Office, von Hügel seems to have been convinced that Loisy's qualities of scholarship, and the recognition of these by the scholarly world, would prevent his complete or final condemnation by Roman authorities. Most of the Baron's efforts on Loisy's behalf, therefore, were efforts to make the French scholar's work known in England and elsewhere, and to elicit a response to and marked recognition for Loisy from scholarly circles outside of France. When Loisy wrote an appreciative review of Driver's *Deuteronomy* for the *Bulletin critique*, Cardinal Richard informed the editors of the *Bulletin*, in July 1896, that he was dissatisfied with Loisy's recent contributions to that journal, and especially with his review of Driver's *Deuteronomy*. Loisy wryly observed that, since Richard did not read the *Bulletin*, it was obviously a case of denunciation again. But by whom! One immediate result of this new threat was that it caused Loisy to urge von Hügel to increase the latter's efforts at making Loisy's work known and appreciated in England.[4]

Shortly after receiving Loisy's appeal the Baron wrote to William Sanday, asking his help. The chief problem, as the Baron saw it, was to obtain tolerance for new critical work like Loisy's among churchmen unprepared for his conclusions and understanding neither his methods nor

[1] Von Hügel to Ward, 14 April, 1892, WFP, vH MSS.; *Diaries*, 29–30 Jan., and 2 March 1892.

[2] Von Hügel to Ward, 10 July 1892, WFP, vH MSS.

[3] The suspicion that Loisy had been denounced to Rome by the Paris Dominicans seems to have been fairly common even as late as 1912. Père M. J. Lagrange, himself a French Dominican, went to considerable trouble to try to show that the rumour had no foundation in fact in his *Au Service de la Bible: Souvenirs Personnels*, Paris, 1967, pp. 65–9.

[4] *Mém.* I, pp. 404–5.

motives. 'Now I need tell you', von Hügel wrote to Sanday, 'that his [Loisy's] particular tone and temper, measure and method, are as new and startling to our majority as the analogous change among your own people was to them not long ago, indeed *is* still to many, and that often precisely to many a faithful and believing soul, as among yours, so among ours.'[1] Von Hügel told Sanday that he was certain the latter was quite as anxious as he himself was 'to help on all possible common agreement and friendly interchange of happy help'. What form Sanday's help should take the Baron made perfectly clear.

Will you, at your earliest convenience say, in the 'Guardian' or 'Academy' or 'Expositor' or how or where you can and will (the 'Guardian' wd. be the best I think for the purpose I have in view), as emphatically and distinctly as would be self-respectful and wd. not even seemed forced and dragged in artificially such good as you may think of these renewed N.T. doings of Abbé Loisy? If it could take the form of a cordial welcome, expressed by yourself but as, you were sure, shared by numerous Anglican scholars and savants, and of gladness at seeing the Roman Church resuming its best traditions in this matter, and of certainty as to the importance of the work being able to be continued and finished – or some such thoroughly friendly inter-confessional form, – you wd. do much good, I am very sure. Perhaps in the case that you could do something you wd. most kindly let me have a card with place and date of appearance.

Von Hügel apologized to Sanday for his 'apparent fussiness', but he told him, too, that he was very certain that he was dreaming neither imaginary dangers for Loisy nor unreal evaluations of Sanday's help. 'I am indeed dead ashamed of myself', he concluded, 'troubling you like this, and in such hot weather too! But we are happy fellow-fighters along such a fine long bit of front: I cannot help turning to you thus.'

Sanday's response was immediate. Within three weeks of posting his letter to Sanday, von Hügel was reading and revising the proofs for the article Sanday had prepared.[2] It was entitled 'The Work of Abbé Loisy' and filled nearly two and one-half columns of *The Guardian* for 26 August 1896. Had von Hügel written the article himself it could hardly have expressed better the points he especially wanted to stress. The article began with a welcome to the revival of real critical studies among the French clergy, and especially to abbé Loisy's clear leadership in the field of French biblical criticism. Sanday expressed sympathy with those who felt uneasy at Loisy's frank acceptance of critical principles, but he

[1] Von Hügel to Sanday, 1 Aug. 1896, BL, MS. Eng. misc. d. 123(2), fol. 610.
[2] *Diaries*, 21 Aug. 1896.

also expressed his conviction that the uneasiness would give way to understanding and assurance.

The fact is that the Church of Rome in France is now going through a modified form of the crisis which began in this country some thirty or forty years ago. With us it may be said that the worst of the storm is over, and that things are settling down, if not to a state of absolute peace, yet at least to a state of mitigated antagonisms, which hold out a prospect of eventual peace. In France there is every reason to hope that the tension may be less severe. When the writers of *Essays and Reviews* put forth their volume in 1860, there was certainly much in it that was crude and aggressive. It has only been by degrees that these elements have been sifted out, and that the truths which undoubtedly were mingled with them have shown themselves capable of being assimilated with loyal and Catholic teaching. The stage at which the same truths have made their way into France is altogether more mature. In the hands of Abbé Loisy there is nothing either crude or aggressive about them. The Abbé is a dutiful son of the Church, and all that he has done has been to state modestly and reverently, but firmly, those convictions which a candid mind in touch with the more advanced methods of secular learning cannot avoid. He makes no attempt to disguise the tentative nature of many of the views which he advocates. But without discussion it is impossible to determine what is valid and what is not; and if these discussion do not take place within the Church they will assuredly go on outside it, and the pent up waters will break over the banks with all the greater fury.[1]

Nearly a whole column of praise for Loisy's use of critical methodology followed, with examples calculated to inspire confidence in Sanday's judgment of Loisy. Only once did Sanday register any dissent from Loisy's conclusions, and this was on the question of the relative importance of oral tradition in the formation of the Synoptic Gospels. Sanday would allow it a rather more important place than Loisy would seem to accept. Sanday concluded his article by observing that work like Loisy's ought to have a special appeal to those in the Church of England. 'They can sympathise with difficulties which they have felt themselves, and they enter warmly into a spirit and temper which they would be glad to make their own.' Sanday's essay was an impressive performance, and copies of it were soon in the post to Loisy from von Hügel.[2]

The final few years of the nineteenth century were full of more rumours of trouble for Loisy and for the biblical studies which he and von Hügel both had so much at heart. Several weeks after receiving Sanday's article from *The Guardian*, Loisy learned that he had again been de-

[1] *The Guardian*, no. 2647, 26 Aug. 1896, p. 1317.
[2] *Diaries*, 6 Sept. 1896.

nounced in Rome.[1] The information came initially from Padre Enrico Gismondi who was professor of oriental languages and scripture at Rome's Gregorian University, and in 1904 would lose his chair because of his sympathy for Loisy. Even in his *Mémoires* Loisy paid tribute to the honesty and courage of Gismondi 'who supported us and discreetly protected us to the extent of his ability to do so, with a consistency equalled by no other Roman theologian'.[2] The denunciation at Rome, however, seemed to receive no encouragement nor was it acted upon. But with the death of Leo XIII this pattern of procedure would change radically.

In the issue of the *Revue du clergé française* for 15 October 1900 Loisy published an article on the origins of Israel's religion, most of which had already appeared earlier in the *Revue Anglo-Romaine*. The article was signed with the pseudonym Firmin, but, since this was Loisy's middle name, the actual authorship was an open secret. Two further articles on the religion of Israel were to follow in continuing issues of the *Revue*. However, by a letter to the journal's editor, dated 23 October, Cardinal Richard condemned the article as being contrary to the teaching of the decree *Dei Filius* of the First Vatican Council, and to Leo XIII's *Providentissimus Deus*. Moreover, he forbade the publication of the two remaining articles, and commanded the *Revue* to print a notice to this effect in its next issue, which it did on the 1st of November. Loisy learned of his condemnation, not from the Archbishop of Paris, but from the editor of the *Revue*. Almost at once Loisy wrote to both Mignot and von Hügel of his latest conflict with authority. Mignot answered by return of post, sympathizing with Loisy, and remarking that Richard certainly had gone too far in condemning the two articles which had not even appeared in print.[3] On 30 October von Hügel recorded in his diary: 'Letter from *Loisy: fresh trouble for him*: Card. Richard prints in "Revue du clergé française" a prohibition of further Origins du Peuple d'Israël arts. there, by Firmin.' Two weeks passed, however, before he wrote to Loisy, and when he did write, he seemed to Loisy to be overly philosophical in his acceptance of these developments.[4]

If in November 1900 von Hügel could receive the news of his friend's condemnation with relative calm, the developments of less than a year's

---

[1] *Mém.* I, p. 408.
[2] *Ibid.* p. 422. Von Hügel himself once remarked of Gismondi: '... in his inner mind, and with friends he can trust, he is as wide as Loisy.' Von Hügel to Ward, 11 Jan. 1902, WFP, vH, MSS.
[3] *Mém.* I, pp. 563–77. [4] *Ibid.* p. 576.

time would make him come to consider any check at all to Loisy's freedom as seriously detrimental to the cause of free scientific inquiry within the church. Loisy himself, however, saw the condemnation of 1900 as a major turning point in his own career. In his *Mémoires* he wrote that

until the 1st of November 1900 my person and my opinions had not been formally denounced as suspect, my expulsion from the Institut Catholique in 1893 having been rightly regarded as a political manoeuvre, and the pontifical decrees in which I figured at all being of a character so majestically vague as to render them ineffectual. Now I was nearly made into a heretic, and it was not difficult to forsee that I would soon be an heresiarch. Thus the moment seemed to have come, not only to preserve, but also to guarantee, my independence.[1]

His first move was to secure a post at the École des Hautes Études. Although no chair was available there, he did receive an appointment as a free lecturer with a temporary grant, and as an assistant in the preparation of the *Corpus Inscriptionum Semiticarum*. His course, entitled *Mythes babyloniens et les premiers chapitres de la Genèse*, began almost at once. Loisy realized that by taking this position in a department of the state university he had unmistakably joined battle with the Archbishop of Paris, but he seemed to have no other course left open to him if he wished to continue his pursuit of critical biblical studies freely.[2]

Although Loisy wrote to von Hügel in early December of his new course at the École des Hautes Études, he had no response from the Baron for three months. The silence was not due to indifference, but largely caused by an excessive weight of family problems and worries. His wife's nervous condition was requiring constant attention and arrangements for travel, and at Boscombe his only sister, Pauline, was slowly dying. In January 1901 Lady Mary went off to Cannes with Hildegard, and the Baron, with his youngest daughter Thekla, went back and forth between London and Boscombe until Pauline's death on 29 March.[3] Early in March von Hügel finally acknowledged Loisy's

[1] *Mém.* II, p. 5.
[2] 'Si une difficulté survenait, je ferais observer au cardinal que l'objet de mon cours est purement scientifique et ne tombe pas sous sa compétence. Mais c'est justement ce que les autorités ecclésiastiques ne veulent pas comprendre. Il leur répugne d'admettre que la Bible puisse être l'objet d'un examen scientifique et historique, qui se constitue par sa nature même en dehors de la théologie et échappe à son contrôle direct aussi bien que toute autre science.' Loisy to Paul Desjardins, 9 Dec. 1900, quoted in *ibid.* p. 13. This was a major aspect of the real controversy between Loisy and the ecclesiastical authorities, and the aspect which von Hügel tried with most effort to help clarify and solve.
[3] Von Hügel to Ward, 31 Dec. 1900, WFP, vH MSS.

letters, and then, after his sister's death, wrote again in April to say that he would soon be in Paris. Writing to Wilfrid Ward from Boscombe just two weeks before Pauline's death, the Baron told him that he presumed the latter had heard of Loisy's 'fresh trouble these last six months'. Briefly he told Ward what he himself thought of these developments.

But at the end of Dec. he had an interview with the Archbishop of Paris: and I think the latter, *then* at all counts, saw (and I hope still sees) that enough and more than enough has been done to please L.'s antagonists. But if so, this would not, in this case at all events, proceed from any special or indeed sufficient knowledge of the subject-matter in dispute. Perhaps the better safeguard is the possible or probable fear of those who have pushed the good Archbishop, as to the difficulties they may bring on themselves by too drastic a repression. – Well, well – these obscure tracasseries are really not impressive to know about and watch at close quarters and from day to day. Let us hope that many among the juniors are growing up determined to know before speaking, and to learn before repressing.[1]

At the end of April and for the first few days of May von Hügel was in Paris, visiting Loisy twice, and seeing his other friends there. After the Baron had gone on to Genoa and then Milan, Loisy learned from Archbishop Mignot that a new denunciation of himself had been made to the Holy Office. When von Hügel learned that Loisy was in really serious danger of receiving a formal condemnation, he reflected that 'if it happens, we can prophesy the appearance of a book someday, which will carefully explain, how that no such condemnation ever took place; it is a base invention of the Free-Masons!'[2] Mignot wrote at once on Loisy's behalf to Cardinal Mathieu in Rome, asking his help. Mathieu urged Mignot to write directly to the Pope, and suggested that Loisy himself write to Padre Lepidi, the Master of the Sacred Palace and the man with special influence, apparently, in such affairs. Both Mignot and Loisy sent off their letters, and neither had even an acknowledgement in return.[3]

Von Hügel pondered this state of affairs for a few days and then decided himself to write to Cardinal Rampolla. Rampolla had been open and sincere in listening to von Hügel in the past, and the Baron felt that in this situation a letter to him could not possibly do any harm and might even do some good. Unlike Mignot in writing to the Pope, the Baron did not write from a theoretical point of view, but from a practical

[1] Von Hügel to Ward, 14 March 1901, WFP, vH MSS.
[2] Von Hügel to Maude Petre, 18 May 1901, BM, Add. MSS. 54361.5.
[3] *Mém.* II, pp. 34 and 40.

one. He told Rampolla that a condemnation of Loisy would utterly discredit the Roman Catholic church in English educated circles and especially at the universities. He pointed out that over the past ten years, an acquaintance with Loisy's critical work, combining as it did a true religious sense and the best of contemporary critical thought, and the fact of the apparent non-condemnableness of Loisy's work, had largely helped any number of educated Englishmen come into the Roman church. Moreover, a condemnation of Loisy would jeopardize Leo XIII's reputation at the English universities as 'the patron of science and letters'. All of this good will and influence, he told Rampolla, should be carefully considered before the Holy See set out to lose it through acts of condemnation and repression.[1] This was the same practical approach that von Hügel had used before with Rampolla, and, as before, this time, too, he made some impression. Writing to Loisy in late June from Airolo in Switzerland, where the Baron and his family spent the summer of 1901, he told him that he had received an answer from Rampolla, telling him of his interest in all that von Hügel had written, and assuring him that Leo XIII too was pondering his letter.[2] Where Mignot and Loisy had apparently failed, von Hügel had succeeded to a degree and for a time, at least. Loisy attributed the success to von Hügel's practical approach.

In October von Hügel and his family moved on from Switzerland to Rome, where they would spend the winter. The Baron was discouraged to find Duchesne so sceptical and indifferent to the whole development of events concerning Loisy and the future of critical biblical studies in the church. 'He could do so much,' von Hügel wrote to Loisy, 'but he does nothing, on the pretext that there is nothing to be done.'[3] Within a few days of his arrival in Rome von Hügel had an interview with Rampolla, and again he stressed the points he had made in his letter of the previous May, giving the Cardinal detailed examples in proof of his assertions. Through his friend Padre Genocchi the Baron also gained a lengthy interview with Padre Lepidi who put him through a rigorous examination of his ideas on 'Inspiration, Inerrancy, Development, Relativity, Scandal, Pious Ears, German Rationalism, French *fougue*' and cognate subjects. 'I like him as a man sincerely', von Hügel wrote to Tyrrell, 'and I felt that he somehow liked me too; and such a thing

[1] Von Hügel to Tyrrell, 28 May 1901, in *Von Hügel and Tyrrell*, pp. 78–9. See also, *Mém.* II, pp. 41–2.
[2] *Mém.* II, p. 44.
[3] *Ibid.* p. 66. See also, *Von Hügel and Tyrrell*, p. 99.

helps. And then I felt sure that much was said and put because it was his business to do so; and I got the impression (and I have since had occasion to think I was right) that he is really against any censure.'[1] For Wilfrid Ward the Baron also described the same interview and pointed out how utterly without any historic sense he found Lepidi to be, and how little reassuring this was. But the two interviews seem to have clarified for the Baron the general pattern of his future action.

But two points these interviews have taught me, with unforgettable vividness: (1) we must be careful *not* to cease quoting or praising, when the natural occasions come, our true scholars, Loisy especially; and (2) we must not, even by our acts and adhesions, imply our acceptance of the present situation, still less of the possible immediate future as satisfactory. Nothing, I now see and know, would, within the limits of the little we can do or hinder, help on more conclusively, the consummation of all we wish to see avoided. I could give practical proofs and illustrations of the truth and meaning of what I am saying. But I must stop.[2]

The Baron admitted that he found all this 'labour and battle' in Rome taxing in the extreme, but he likewise admitted to Tyrrell that he found it exhilarating and would be unwilling to exchange it for a quiet existence elsewhere. 'And I am having the strange, very sobering impression that God is deigning somehow to use me, – me, in my measure, along with others who can and do do more, much more – towards making, not simply registering, history. And, dear me, what a costing process *that* is!'[3]

Both Archbishop Mignot and Monsignor Batiffol were likewise in Rome that December of 1901. The Baron and the Archbishop had five long meetings to discuss Loisy and his problems and, at the end of the month von Hügel wrote Loisy a fifteen page letter to tell him about it. Once von Hügel remarked to Loisy that the latter's crises had made intimate friends of Mignot and himself.[4] Batiffol, too, called on von Hügel, three times in fact, and talked constantly in a nervous effort to justify his attitude toward Loisy. Batiffol was himself a critical historian and was, ecclesiastically, in something of a delicate position as Rector of the Institut Catholique of Toulouse. In order to stress his own orthodoxy he had, both in print and by word of mouth, shown himself hostile to Loisy's work. When he came to see the Baron, von Hügel stressed two

[1] Von Hügel to Tyrrell, 18–20 Dec. 1901, in *Von Hügel and Tyrrell*, pp. 91 and 94–5.
[2] Von Hügel to Ward, 22 Nov. 1901, WFP, vH MSS.
[3] Von Hügel to Tyrrell, 18–20 Dec. 1901, in *Selected Letters*, pp. 102–3.
[4] *Mém.* II, pp. 75 and 82.

points with him. He told Batiffol that Loisy had many friends and admirers in England, especially at Oxford and Cambridge, and these friends of Loisy could easily be turned against Batiffol if he wrote or did anything unfriendly to Loisy. Von Hügel then stressed that he was neither asking Batiffol to say anything positive in Loisy's favour nor asking him to refrain from genuine and sincere scholarly criticism of Loisy's writing. What he was asking was that he simply cease trying to give the impression that Loisy was an author unacceptable for orthodox Catholics.[1] How little effect the Baron expected his words to have is reflected in a comment to Tyrrell: 'I want to put in a word, disagreeable but necessary to say, as to Mgr Batiffol. Alas, *he is a man not to be trusted*: pray take my word for it, and look out.'[2] The Baron was afraid that Batiffol would try to undermine Tyrrell's position with the authorities as he had tried to do to Loisy.

During the interview which von Hügel had with Lepidi in November, the latter asked the Baron to become a founding member of a Roman Society for Biblical Studies.[3] The Biblical Society to which Lepidi referred, and which was still in the planning stage, was apparently what later became known as the Pontifical Biblical Commission. Von Hügel refused Lepidi's overtures on the grounds that he could not possibly lend the little influence of his own name and presence to such an authority-sponsored organization until he saw clearly that this same authority meant to give sufficient breathing space to men like Loisy who were engaged in serious biblical work. Lepidi pressed von Hügel to accept his offer, however, and the Baron agreed to think it over and to give a final decision later. On 7 December he wrote to Lepidi a firm but respectful refusal to have anything to do with the proposed Biblical Society. His reasons were the same as those he had earlier given orally.[4] Plans for the organization had been developing in Vatican secrecy since August, apparently, and in January 1902 the London *Tablet* was the first paper to announce the creation of the new Biblical Com-

---

[1] *Ibid.* pp. 75–6.

[2] Von Hügel to Tyrrell, 18–20 Dec. 1901, in *Von Hügel and Tyrrell*, p. 83.

[3] *Ibid.* p. 98; *Mém.* II, p. 79.

[4] 'Que pas même l'Église et notre respect à tout jamais pour ses droits et devoirs imprescriptibles ne pouvaient nous dicter les conditions nécessaires de notre activité: sans une suffisance d'air, nous ne pourrions respirer, même si l'on nous le commandait. Que je devrais à tout prix respecter l'Église, et partant garder une grande loyauté dans mon attitude envers elle. Je ne pourrais donc l'aider par mon action à croire que nous étions contents et sûrs de notre présent et de l'avenir immédiat. Je devrais donc attendre et voir ce qui se ferait, moi avec mes amis, avant de pouvoir nous-mêmes agir avec l'autorité.' Von Hügel to Loisy, 30 Dec. 1901–1 Jan. 1902, in *Mém.* II, p. 79.

mission. The London-based Vicar-General of the Franciscan Order, Father David Fleming, was the Secretary for the Commission, and he had brought the news to Vaughan and to *The Tablet*.[1] With a bit of a flourish *The Tablet* made the most of the information:

We are privileged to make an announcement which must necessarily be of the profoundest interest to the whole of the Christian world. Leo XIII has appointed a special Pontifical Commission for the consideration of all questions connected with Biblical studies. Catholic scholars all the world over will have the fullest opportunity of stating their views and difficulties, and bringing them to the direct notice of the Holy See.[2]

Leo XIII's original idea for the new Commission seems to have been that theological problems raised by the critical work of men like Loisy should be placed before it, not so that the Commission should then produce instant answers to difficulties, but so that the real problems should have prolonged and competent study. The creation of the Commission, in brief, was a delaying tactic, to prevent the Index and Holy Office from issuing condemnations of men and ideas which were new, before the truth of the ideas and the motivation of the men could be weighed and ascertained. Von Hügel felt certain '*that the appointment of this Commission, at all events if taken in connection with the list of names constituting it, and with what the zealots wanted, – is a gain*, certainly a relative, and possibly even a positive gain'.[3] The President of the Commission was Cardinal Parocchi who had already shown himself sympathetic to critical biblical study and aware of the church's need for such studies. 'As to the President', observed von Hügel, 'Cardinal Parocchi is not, I think, in these matters, more than a *dilettante* of considerable reading and some real culture. But he is certainly the best resident Cardinal they could have chosen.' And on the Commission, as the Baron noted, 'have been put 12 consultors, not one of whom, with the exception of Vigouroux, belong to the strictly narrow set; and even V. never denounced us here, and has moments (tho' not more) of wide outlook'. Although Fleming, the Commission's Secretary, had been one of those who had worked in Rome for the condemnation of Anglican Orders, von Hügel could yet say in January 1902 that 'Fleming is still, I feel sure, at heart, with us'.

Three facts about the Commission especially encouraged von Hügel

[1] *Mém.* II, pp. 88–9.
[2] *The Tablet*, vol. 99, no. 3217, 4 Jan. 1902, p. 10.
[3] Von Hügel to Ward, 11 Jan. 1902, WFP, vH MSS. All quotations from von Hügel in this and the following paragraph are taken from this same letter to Wilfrid Ward.

at its inception. 'For one thing, this Commission is a *permanent* one, like that for the Reunion of the Churches. This, I think, makes just all the difference. It can thus take its time, – any length of time it likes, – the longer the better.' And the quality of the original twelve men on the Commission made its permanency especially desirable. Von Hügel's second fact was

that *this Commission*, in the idea of those that started the plan, and according to the willingness of the authorities here (so long as they are not exposed to too great a pressure from the zealots, or as long as such pressure can be counteracted by something like an equal pressure by our side), *is intended* and may, I trust will work, *as a substitute for condemnation and restrictions*. Nothing is more certain, I think, than that, (without any kind of enthusiasm for, or even understanding of us, on the part of the authorities here), there is (and indeed in large part just because of that absence of all real knowledge, or continuous activity or spontaneous interest of and in our question) a real weariness of the subject, not only a willingness but a wish to delegate the shocks and circumstances of war, the meeting the onset of the zealots, to others, provided only such delegation leaves to the authorities the appearance of active management, and the power of really resuming this management at any time. I could give you many instances and indications of this spirit: the Temporal Power, the Congregations in France, *these* are questions on which they feel spontaneously: on the Bible question, except as far as they feel it to involve their own authority, they have no such instincts.

The Baron's third point was that the authorities in Rome felt they could not stop the serious critical investigations of Catholics into biblical problems, and that 'as long as we ask for no kind of approbation or authorization, and as long again as the others do not press them too much on the point, or as counterworked by us, so long shall we be able, *if we can continue to find in God and ourselves the vigour and devotedness necessary*, to continue to work'. In fact, the critical work of biblical scholars was necessary if the Commission as it was originally conceived was to have any subject matter for its deliberations, or even if it was to have a *raison d'être*. Consequently, von Hügel felt that there was even an obligation to work to get Catholics to see the values of the Commission and to be reasonably optimistic about its future prospects.[1]

---

[1] An article which contributed to this end and which almost certainly had von Hügel for its chief source of information and for its main inspiration was Austin West's 'The Abbé Loisy and the Roman Biblical Commission' *The Contemporary Review*, vol. LXXXI, no. 436, April, 1902, pp. 497–507. West was at this time the Roman correspondent of *The Daily Chronicle*; he was a convert to Roman Catholicism, the son of a Nonconformist minister of Norfolk, and had tried his vocation as a Dominican. He saw a great deal of von Hügel during January and February of 1902, and was given information and writings by the Baron which went into the

From the very beginning of the Commission's unofficial existence, however, a tug-of-war went on in Rome as to what its purpose and powers and personnel should be. As the winter wore on von Hügel's optimism about the ability of the new Commission to withstand the opposition of the intransigents began to wane. Fleming kept *The Tablet* informed of developments, and the tone of that journals' first full-scale account of the Commission was disquieting.[1] The article also spoke of the possibility of more cardinals and more consultors being added to the Commission, which suggested that the demand of the intransigents for a voice in its sessions was at least under consideration. As the months of 1902 began to pass no official Roman publication of the names of the members of the Commission yet appeared, and von Hügel took this to mean that the intransigent party, which would have liked to have Loisy condemned and the Biblical Commission turned into a biblical branch of the Holy Office or of the Index, was strongly exerting pressure in high places. In early April the Baron even presented Cardinal Rampolla with yet another memorandum in an effort to try to provoke official publication of the appointment of the Commission and to obtain some moderation of the attacks on Loisy which were becoming increasingly vehement.[2] On the afternoon of 22 April, the day before von Hügel was to leave Rome – for the last time until he returned there in 1915 to be with his dying daughter Gertrude – he received distressing news of fresh opposition to Loisy.[3] The Baron had been to tea with Padre Genocchi, and was just coming away with Arthur Headlam who had also been at Genocchi's,[4] when they encountered Padre Gismondi in the street. The latter excitedly told them that he had news that new pressure on

---

article. See *Diaries*, 3, 6, 12, 15, 19, 23 and 26 Jan.; and 4, 13 and 25 Feb. 1902. E. J. Dillon, who also wrote for English journals on Loisy's plight, but with considerably more acid in his pen than West manifested, thought West's article was too moderate (*Mém.* II, p. 16). This moderation was very much a Hügelian characteristic.

[1] *The Tablet*, vol. 99, no. 3218, 11 Jan. 1902, p. 58.
[2] *Diaries*, 1–5 April, 1902.
[3] *Diaries*, 22 April 1902.
[4] Arthur Cayley Headlam (1862–1947) was rector of Welwyn in Hertfordshire at the time that von Hügel first met him on 15 April 1902 (*Diaries*) in Rome. In 1903 Headlam became principal of King's College, London, and from 1901 to 1921 he edited *The Church Quarterly Review*. In 1910 von Hügel mentioned to A. L. Lilley, concerning an address Headlam was to give to the London Society for the Study of Religion, that, whereas they could be certain that Headlam's talk would be well informed, von Hügel himself nevertheless always felt 'too much the coming Dean or Bishop in the worthy H[eadlam]'. Headlam was appointed Regius Professor of Divinity at Oxford in 1918, and bishop of Gloucester in 1923. See *Concise Dict. of Nat. Biog.* II, p. 203.

Rome had just come from Paris to procure Loisy's condemnation.[1] With little time to spare, the Baron decided that the only practicable thing he could do would be to remind the Pope of his promise, made in December to Archbishop Mignot, not to condemn any individual biblical scholars, but to examine the whole biblical question through the Commission he was establishing for this purpose.[2] Before leaving Rome alone[3] on the following morning at 8.15, the Baron sent a letter to Mgr LeCamus, the Bishop of La Rochelle who happened to be in Rome, asking him to undertake this delicate mission to the Pope. Within two weeks LeCamus wrote to Mignot: 'We have gained the victory all along the line!'[4]

Not until the end of October, however, did the Pope sign the papal letter, *Vigilantiae studiique memores*, which officially and publicly estab-

[1] On 17 March Picard of Paris had published Albert Houtin's *La Question biblique chez les catholiques de France au XIXᵉ siècle*. The book was immediately attacked by members of the French hierarchy, and Loisy thought that it was the publication of this book which had brought new pressure from Paris to Rome for his own condemnation (*Mém.* II, p. 116).

[2] The French correspondent for *The Pilot* had informed the English public of this promise some months earlier: 'Mgr Mignot was in Rome only a few days ago. The Pope has received him with the greatest kindness. Their conversation was mostly about the Biblical question. The old Pontiff, with incredible insight in a man of his years and so foreign to the details of these questions, declared that he would allow no personal condemnation, and would see that the new Commission took its time to do its work. Two of the members of that Commission, both heads of powerful Orders, are favourable to M. Loisy. This is all we know of the immediate future; it is on the whole more cheering than alarming.' *The Pilot*, no. 99, vol. v, 18 Jan. 1902, p. 68.

[3] On 23 April the Baron went to Genoa, to visit Semeria and research some material for his study of St Catherine of Genoa. On the 28th he went on to Milan meeting Lady Mary there and spending a few days with his friends Marchese Tomassino Gallarati Scotti, Padre Gazzola, Professor Morando, and a young man named Gallavresi to whom Semeria had introduced him at the same time he first met Scotti (i.e. 27 Nov. 1899). On 2 May he and Lady Mary went on to Heidelberg. Ernst Troeltsch came to the Baron's hotel on the following day for a long visit, this being the first time the two men had actually met. The 4th of May von Hügel spent almost entirely with Troeltsch and his family, and on the 5th he and Lady Mary left for Jena. There the Baron's wife met Rudolf Eucken and his family for the first time, and the two men spent most of the following few days in lengthy philosophical dialogue in which von Dobschütz and Scheler also sometimes participated. Leaving Lady Mary to visit friends near Neuss, the Baron returned to London on the 15th (*Diaries*, 23 April–15 May 1902).

[4] *Mém.* II, p. 117. The third chapter of Loisy's *Autour d'un petit livre*, 2nd edition (Paris, 1903), pp. 61–108, entitled 'Lettre à un Évêque, sur la critique des Évangiles et spécialement sur l'Évangile de saint Jean' was addressed to LeCamus. Von Hügel's observations on the bishop, made several years later, are relevant: 'I know him personally, a little, and have had a good many bits of his writings before me at various times, and I must say that I do not think Loisy's criticism of him in his "Lettre à un Evêque" (the Evêque = LeCamus), is at all excessive. He is a man who just sprinkles his books with (entirely intermittent) *velléités* of criticism, and who loves to talk as though he had, even 30 and 40 years ago, settled for good all but such touches, which can and do get modified by him in successive editions. He has travelled a good deal in Palestine: his topography is generally fair. But it would not do to take him as a true critic, although he is not a fanatic or pure scholastic as a good many are.' Von Hügel to Ward, 13 Feb. 1906, WFP, vH MSS.

lished the Biblical Commission.[1] And even then, as von Hügel observed, 'there has been, as far as I know, no official publication of any particular names, – so that even now a tustle *may* again take place over this important matter of the personnel'.[2] On 8 February 1903 von Hügel was dining at Arundel Castle with the Duke of Norfolk and his family, where he happened to glance at a copy of *The Tablet* for the previous day which was lying about there. In it he read the lengthy communication from Fleming in which the complete list of the Commission's consultors was at last made public. The list included the original twelve, as the Baron noted in his diary, but the strength of these twelve had been thoroughly diluted with the names of twenty-eight other men, all of whom were either scholastic-trained non-critical biblical scholars or else men of no scholarly repute at all.[3] The news considerably upset the Baron, and the following day he sent a note to Loisy saying that he considered the forty names a clear 'victory for the other side'.[4] He suggested that perhaps among this 'mob' there would be so little unity and ability to work together that they would do nothing, or, if they did do something, it would be so worthless as to fail to convince even Catholics. And if the new Commission was unwilling to offer tolerance to genuine critical scholars, the Baron hoped that it would at least make a condemnation so patently absurd as to create a counter-reaction.[5] In a very short time there would be a number of such absurd condemnations, but there would be no counter-reactions – with the exception of von Hügel's nearly solitary voice of protest.

[1] This document was published in *Acta Sanctae Sedis*, vol. xxxv, 1902–3, pp. 234–8. Loisy remarked of the document: 'C'est la première fois depuis dix ans que le pape parle de la Bible sans me dire des choses désagréables.' *Mém.* II, p. 155.

[2] Von Hügel to Ward, 24 Nov. 1902, WFP, vH MSS.

[3] *Diaries*, 8 Feb. 1903. *The Tablet*, vol. 101, no. 3274, 7 Feb. 1903, pp. 213–14.

[4] *Mém.* II, p. 217.

[5] *Ibid.* pp. 217–18. Loisy remarked: 'Spéculations de contemplatif.' And when von Hügel returned to the same subject in another letter later that same month, Loisy similarly reflected: 'Rêves d'un saint qui faisait beaucoup de crédit à la Providence, et aussi à l'intelligence humaine.'

CHAPTER 6

'L'ÉVANGILE ET L'ÉGLISE'

A FEW DAYS after von Hügel returned from the continent to his home in Hampstead in May 1902, Loisy wrote to him about an idea which he had for a new book.[1] In working out his commentary on the Synoptic Gospels, Loisy had reached the passage in Matthew upon which Adolf Harnack had largely based his interpretation of Christianity in his widely discussed *Das Wesen des Christentums*. For Harnack this passage (Matt. 11:25-30) was the one sure touchstone with the Jesus of history, and most of the rest of the New Testament he considered to be the theological adumbration of early tradition. But Loisy had come to the conclusion that Harnack's crucial passage in Matthew was almost impossible to explain *historically*, and that it was very likely 'the work of a Christian prophet coming somewhere between the Christ of history and that of John's Gospel'.[2] Consequently, the text on which Harnack rested his whole system of Christianity was no more a contact point with the Jesus of history than was the whole of John's Gospel. Loisy felt that with the French translation of Harnack's book just coming on the market he had an ideal occasion for challenging the Berlin scholar in print. By August he had nearly finished the manuscript. Mignot and von Hügel were the only two friends that he told of his project, and von Hügel seems not really to have taken the scheme seriously until the book was nearly published.[3] Mignot, on the other hand, felt that the time was not quite right for the proposed anti-Harnack essay, but agreed to read the manuscript for Loisy. When the Archbishop returned the manuscript on 17 September, he told Loisy that he felt this to be the most comprehensive and objective thing that the latter had yet written. 'I think that no one can condemn you', Mignot wrote, 'and, on the contrary, this publication will place you in the first class of Christian critics.'[4] The book, of course, was *L'Évangile et l'Église*.

[1] *Mém.* II, p. 121.   [2] *Ibid.*

[3] Meriol Trevor, *Prophets and Guardians: Renewal and Tradition in the Church*, London, 1969, p. 65, has ignored the evidence (*Mém.* II, pp. 124-5), when she states that von Hügel 'urged Loisy to publish' *L'Évangile et l'Église*. Loisy himself remarked that von Hügel never mentioned the book to him until *after* it was published, although Loisy had several times written about it to the Baron.

[4] *Mém.* II, pp. 126 and 133.

On 10 November, the same day that they went on sale in the Paris bookshops, von Hügel received from Loisy copies of his *Études Évangeliques* and *L'Évangile et l'Église*.[1] Although the Baron began reading the latter book on the day after receiving it, he did not finish it for nearly a month.[2] He was working hard on writing his own *Mystical Element of Religion* at this time, and was rather sparing of the amount of time he gave to reading other than that which was necessary for his own book. However, within a few days of receiving *L'Évangile et l'Église* he began sending copies of the book to his friends, and he began soliciting reviews for it by men whom he thought could best represent it in the various types of English journals.

He sent a copy of *L'Évangile et l'Église* to Percy Gardner, hoping for a notice in *The Hibbert Journal*.[3] Gardner read the book 'with the greatest interest and much appreciation'. He told von Hügel that 'in many ways it runs parallel to my Exploratio; and I often agree with Loisy's criticisms of Harnack'.[4] In his review, however, Gardner approached Loisy's book as though it were primarily a piece of polemic which had been unfair to Harnack's real position. Loisy's theme and principle of development seem to have caused Gardner the most annoyance, and the latter remarked caustically of Loisy's assurance that the Roman Catholic church could adapt in the twentieth century as she had in the past: 'It is strange to say of a church which degrades or ejects all who dare to think differently from the Roman curia that it can adapt itself to modern conditions.'[5] The Baron thanked him for the review, but he told Gardner that both he himself and Loisy were disappointed with it and felt that Gardner had 'not fully grasped the precise object and drift of the book'.[6]

[1] *Diaries*, 10 Nov. 1902. The best analysis in English of *L'Évangile et l'Église* is still Alec. R. Vidler's *The Modernist Movement in the Roman Church, Its Origin and Outcome*, Cambridge, 1934, pp. 113–22.
[2] *Diaries*, 7 Dec. 1902.
[3] Von Hügel to Gardner, 13 Nov. 1902, in *Selected Letters*, p. 112.
[4] Gardner to von Hügel, 30 Nov. 1902, SAUL, MS. 2589.
[5] *The Hibbert Journal*, vol. I, no. 3, April 1903, p. 604.
[6] Von Hügel to Gardner, 25 April 1903, in *Selected Letters*, p. 118. – Eighteen months later Gardner again criticized Loisy in print ('M. Alfred Loisy's Type of Catholicism', *The Hibbert Journal*, vol. III, no. 1, pp. 126–38). His article was polemically anti-Roman and based on the assumption that Loisy was really anti-Protestant. He strongly criticized Loisy's radical separation of history and Christian doctrine. Alfred Fawkes, under the signature of 'Romanus', attacked ('Discussions', *The Hibbert Journal*, vol. III, no. 2, Jan. 1905, pp. 376–80) Gardner's assumption that Loisy's *L'Évangile et l'Église* was really anti-Protestant, and even claimed that 'Liberal Catholicism is in no sense the antagonist or rival of Liberal Protestantism. The two are varieties of one and the same standpoint, as it is found in this or that environment, that of Latin or of Reformed Christianity' (p. 277). When von Hügel read Fawkes' rejoinder, he wrote to Loisy that 'Fawkes is a good and intelligent man; but I often ask myself just where

Much of the structural development of Roman Christianity Gardner had challenged in his review, and he had asked the question of Catholics: Why cling to the Roman form of Christianity? Von Hügel gave Gardner his own answer by telling him that, although religious toleration and intellectual freedom had been more characteristic of Protestantism than of Catholicism in recent centuries, nevertheless, 'Catholicism, *at its best*, still somehow produces saints of a depth of other-worldliness, of a delecate appealing heroism, and of a massiveness of spiritual wisdom, greater than I can find elsewhere. And indeed I note that men so much outside our system as William James are generally ready enough to admit this.'[1] And this holiness, the Baron stressed, was not in spite of the Roman church's developments of dogma, cult and structure, but in part because of and in relation to these.

If Gardner's review of *L'Évangile et l'Église* was, in part at least, a disappointment to von Hügel, other of the Baron's efforts to gain favourable recognition for Loisy's book were more successful. One of the first people to receive a copy of the book from von Hügel was Eucken. Writing to Wilfrid Ward the Baron told him:

Eucken writes to me delighted with it, and declares that he considers it unquestionably superior to Harnack, and as, in its general view of the nature of religion in general and of Primitive Xtianity in particular, simply impregnable. Only, with regard to the Roman Church does he think it lacking, – in a sufficiently full and historic appreciation and admission of the grave checks and oppressions generated by that system in the course of its development. It is, I think, deeply instructive to note how it is the very (soundly scientific) Radicalism of the premises which makes the Catholic conclusion irresistible to at least the speculative reason of any one determined to still hold to Xtianity as *normative* even for our times. My own close studies in N.T. matters make it quite clear to me that L.'s view is the solid and eventual one; and that H.'s will

---

his Catholicism lies. I find bloody little of it here' (*Mém.* II, p. 425). Moreover, the Baron answered both Gardner and Fawkes in print ('Discussions', *The Hibbert Journal*, vol. III, no. 3, April 1905, pp. 599–600). The *Hibbert*'s editor had limited him to one and a half pages, and so he answered each of Gardner's and Fawkes' points with a very few penetrating sentences. In the light of the overall controversy which *L'Évangile et l'Église* had raised by this time, von Hügel's answer to Gardner's objection, that Loisy had too much separated history and doctrine, was important. The Baron answered that Gardner 'assumes history, philosophy, faith, to be all on the same level. Yet we distinguish between and combine neurology, and belief in a spiritual soul; evolution, and faith in a creative Intelligence; indeed, this discipline brings a virile depth to our convictions' (p. 600). As von Hügel insisted against Blondel in 1904, Loisy's position was not that of either history or dogma, but of both history and dogma, though at different levels and with different methodologies to explicate them.

[1] Von Hügel to Gardner, 25 April 1903, in *Selected Letters*, p. 120.

go and is going. May we on our part, wake up to the true and necessary lines of our growth and defence! The 'Month' is having a very appreciative 3½ pp. review.[1]

The review in *The Month* was non-committal about the conclusions found in *L'Évangile et l'Église*, and the reviewer, Herbert Lucas, S.J.,[2] confined himself to emphasizing the great debt which Catholic biblical scholars owed to Loisy whether they agreed with his conclusions or not. According to Lucas this debt was based on the fact that Loisy had 'done more than anyone else to wake up Catholic students to the need of a more thorough investigation of the grounds on which the conclusions of modern biblical criticism are based, and to the possibility (to say the least) that there is a larger element of truth in these conclusions than an older school of exegesis had been willing to admit'.[3] The tone of the whole review was positive and open, and this, more than anything else, was what von Hügel hoped for and worked toward for Loisy among his fellow Catholics in England.

William Barry, Roman Catholic priest and theologian, one time professor of divinity at Oscott, and the author of novels and light history, was asked by von Hügel to review Loisy's book in *The Pilot*.[4] This Barry did, at great length, approaching his subject with sincere objectivity and little criticism based on norms external to the book's plan or aim. 'Every page of M. Loisy bears on it the token of severe and subtle thought,' Barry wrote.[5] And although he felt obliged to point out that some would not be able to accept 'the daring view and almost unlimited scope which he [Loisy] assigns to the evolution of dogma', Barry also noted that Loisy 'restores the true historical lines upon which we go back from the Church of our own day to St. Augustine, St. Paul, and so on to

[1] Von Hügel to Ward, 24 Nov. 1902, WFP, vH MSS.
[2] Although *The Month* review was unsigned, the reviewer was in fact Herbert Lucas, S.J., (von Hügel to Tyrrell, 28 Nov. 1902, BM, Add. MSS. 44928.44; and Tyrell to von Hügel, 4 Dec. 1902. BM, Add. MSS. 44928.48). Lucas was born in 1852 and entered the Society of Jesus in 1869. He was educated at Beaumont and London University, and became professor of scripture at St Beuno's College, St Asaph, Flintshire. In the spring of 1902 he lost his chair because his moderate espousal of critical biblical methods and conclusions scandalized his fellow Jesuits of the theological faculty there (Tyrrell to von Hügel, 12 April 1902, BM, Add. MSS. 44928.12). His review of *L'Évangile et l'Église* also had repercussions: 'Lucas too is in one of his states of re-actionary penitence. I despair of him. By-the-way his critique of L. in the *Month* brought a thunderbolt from Rome & an editorial "climb-down" in the next number. The Editor has closed his columns to scripture subjects & even refused my *Chapter of Ethics* as "strange sounding". What a terrorism it is to turn free men into cowards all round! Surely it cannot go on forever' (Tyrrell to von Hügel, 8 April 1903, BM, Add. MSS. 44928.87).
[3] *The Month*, vol. c, Dec. 1902, p. 643.   [4] *Diaries*, 22 Nov. 1902.
[5] *The Pilot*, no. 144, vol. vi, 20 Dec. 1902, p. 532.

Christ'. But Barry was not entirely at ease with the radical criticism of the Gospels which Loisy's little book represented, and a short time after his review appeared he told von Hügel that there were Catholics 'not in any sense personally hostile, who feel that when he [Loisy] has completed the task of dissection, nothing definite, nothing sufficiently solid, will be left on which to build dogmatic religion'. And he added that these same Catholics 'obey their deepest intimations of conscience in holding to the Christ whom the Gospels reveal, and as they reveal Him. The tradition which interprets the record is, at last, the very same in the light of which it was written.'[1] A few days after receiving Barry's letter von Hügel sent it to Mignot with the remark that Barry's mentality was that of a good number of those but semi-initiated into critical studies among English Catholic clerics.[2]

Edward Caird, Scottish philosopher and Master of Balliol College, Oxford, was another recipient of Loisy's *L'Évangile et l'Église* from von Hügel.[3] The Baron hoped to enlist Caird's interest, and help, if possible, for Loisy's book. Caird was one of the very few authors to be quoted by name in *L'Évangile et l'Église*. The quotation from Caird did not mean, as some of his Roman Catholic detractors would claim, that Loisy knew and agreed with all of Caird's philosophy nor, much less, that he was a neo-Hegelian. Loisy's quotation came from a single article which Caird had written, 'Christianity and the Historic Christ', which had appeared in the American journal *New World*, and which von Hügel had sent to Loisy.[4] But because Loisy had found this article useful, and had, in fact, used it, the Baron felt that there was sufficient warrant to attempt to interest Caird in Loisy's book. After reading through the book, Caird wrote on Christmas Day to thank von Hügel for sending it to him.

In the main thesis of it, as to the impossibility of separating Christianity from its developments both in and out of the Churches, I agree thoroughly, & also in his criticism of the unhistorical method of Harnack in his attempt to extract an essence of Christianity which is independent of all particular forms of thought and life.[5]

[1] Barry to von Hügel, 31 Dec. 1902, SAUL, MS. 30306/17.

[2] Von Hügel to Mignot, 5 Jan. 1903, SAUL, MS. 30306/17. The original letters of von Hügel to Mignot are in the files of the Archdiocese of Albi, though photocopies of all these letters are available at the Library of St Andrews University. The letter from Barry to von Hügel above was sent to Mignot by the Baron, and is also photocopied under the same manuscript number as the von Hügel letter which enclosed it.

[3] *Diaries*, 18 Nov. 1902; von Hügel to Caird, 21 Nov. 1902, BLC, vH MS.

[4] *Mém.* II, pp. 179 and 199.

[5] Caird to von Hügel, 25 Dec. 1902, BCL, Caird MSS. (copy).

He had but one criticism of Loisy's book, and this was that Loisy seemed 'to exaggerate somewhat the negative aspects of the Fourth Gospel, & to forget that it was the Gospel of those who looked for a Kingdom of God, State or Will or Church, to be established on earth in a few years'.

Neither Loisy nor von Hügel was under any illusion as to the risks that were taken in publishing *L'Évangile et l'Église*.[1] The Baron knew that Catholics would be alarmed at Loisy's thorough-going criticism of the Gospels as historical narrative, and this was why he so eagerly sought sound and sympathetic propagandizers for the book. *L'Évangile et l'Église* was a sincere defence of Catholicism, but a defence on the only grounds on which Loisy felt it could be sincerely defended. He saw Catholicism as the legitimate growth of the very same tradition which had produced the Gospels in the first place. Rather than being direct historical accounts of Jesus and his teaching, Loisy considered the Gospels to be the beginning of the tradition which Jesus's life and teaching had produced in the first generation of his followers. By refusing to divide the Gospels up into patchworks of, on the one hand, eternally true teachings of Jesus which can be historically certified, and, on the other, relative truths which were merely the developments of Jesus's teaching by his followers, Loisy seemed to undercut the foundations of current theological orthodoxy. He insisted on taking seriously the relativity of the human side of Christianity, and this included the Gospels in so far as they are documents from the hand of man in a given historical time and milieu. Less than six weeks after the book's publication, Mignot wrote to Loisy to tell him that in Rome *L'Évangile et l'Église* had been denounced as a purely natural history of the Gospels and of Christianity, after the manner of Auguste Sabatier.[2] Whether or not Rome would act on this denunciation remained to be seen.

At first a considerable amount of enthusiasm was generated by the book among Catholics. The branch of the Pustet publishing firm at Rome asked for the rights of an Italian translation. George Tyrrell pressed Loisy to agree to an English translation. A woman whom von Hügel did not know wrote to ask him about the possibility of her making an English translation. He put the woman off until he had some proof

---

[1] On the occasion of the publication Loisy wrote in his journal: 'J'ai rarement été aussi inquiet sur l'effet moral de mes publications que je le suis pour les deux volumes qui vont paraître. Tous les deux représentent un effort pour adapter le catholicisme théorique aux faits de l'histoire, et le catholicisme pratique aux réalités de la vie contemporaine.' (*Mém.* II, p. 149).

[2] *Mém.* II, p. 177.

of her ability with the French language and her knowledge of theology, but he wrote to Longmans nevertheless, to ask them to undertake publication of the English version.[1] Then suddenly, but not unexpectedly, the balloon burst, and Cardinal Richard condemned *L'Évangile et l'Église* and forbade the reading of the book by those subject to his diocesan jurisdiction. The reasons given for the condemnation were that the book was published without the authorization of the ecclesiastical censors, and that it was of such a nature as seriously to trouble the faith of Catholics on matters of fundamental dogmas and Catholic doctrine, notably on the authority of the scriptures and of tradition, on the divinity of Jesus Christ, on his infallible knowledge, on the redemption brought about by his death, on his resurrection, on the eucharist, and on the divine institution of the papacy and episcopate.[2] Loisy wrote to the Baron with the news almost at once. Apparently Longmans had already agreed to an English translation of the book because von Hügel noted in his diary that he wrote to the firm 'getting Loisy off the English translation of *L'Évangile et l'Église*'.[3] Before the year was out, however, there would be an English edition of the book, published by Isbister and Company, Limited, of London, but without von Hügel's influence or encouragement, and, in fact, against his wishes.[4]

On the same day that von Hügel learned of Richard's condemnation, he wrote to Loisy and indicated that he considered the one really important point, and that which must be achieved at any cost, was the non-condemnation of Loisy *by Rome*.[5] He took the attitude that Richard, as Archbishop of Paris, was acting solely on his own initiative in condemning *L'Évangile et l'Église*, and that Rome's slowness to make any move was a hopeful sign. He also encouraged Loisy to forget about any translations or new editions of the book. This advice annoyed Loisy, who already had the second French edition of the book ready for the press, and he avoided answering the Baron for a time.[6] But it was Loisy's

---

[1] *Ibid.* p. 170; *Diaries*, 2, 8 and 15 Jan. 1903.

[2] *Mém.* II, p. 194.

[3] *Diaries*, 5 Feb. 1903.

[4] *Diaries*, 21 Jan. 1903. *Mém.* II, p. 248. E. J. Dillon was Loisy's agent for arranging the publication of the English translation (*Mém.* II, p. 204). Since Isbister had published Dillon's *The Original Poem of Job*, it was not unusual that he would make arrangements with that firm for Loisy.

[5] 'Avec vous je vois et crois qu'il est de la toute dernière importance d'empêcher à tout prix que cette persistante non-condamnation par Rome soit interrompue. Si vous n'aboutissiez pendant votre vie qu'à cela, ce sera déjà, vu la grandeur du point en débat, un gain immense.' Von Hügel to Loisy, 21 Jan. 1903, in *Mém.* II, p. 201.

[6] *Mém.* II, p. 201.

non-condemnation by Rome that von Hügel worked for throughout
1903; and until he was presented with the actual irreversible evidence
to the contrary, he was willing to believe that anything was possible in
this increasingly tightening situation.[1] Because of the Baron's attitude,
however, Loisy consulted Mignot rather than von Hügel for advice on
how to respond to the condemnation. Loisy preferred simply to remain
silent. Mignot felt that his silence could be exploited by the wrong people,
and suggested that either Loisy write to the Cardinal with the offer
to withdraw the book from sale and to cancel the second edition, or he
should write with the offer to prepare a second edition with explanatory
notes on the ideas which were misleadingly expressed in the first, and
thus do away with any doubts that might exist as to Loisy's full adherence to Catholic doctrine.[2] In the end Loisy did not really follow
either of Mignot's suggestions fully. On 3 February he wrote a respectful letter to Richard, telling him that out of deference for his decision he
would withdraw the second edition from publication, and that he himself likewise condemned all the errors deducible from his book which did
not coincide with his intention in writing it.[3] Loisy also decided to publish a new book in which he would draw out clearly the implications
of *L'Évangile et l'Église*, leaving no doubt as to his meaning. This he did
in October with the publication of *Autour d'un petit livre*.

In England von Hügel was eagerly looking out for any positive signs
of understanding and support for Loisy. Two such signs appeared in *The
Guardian* for 25 February and in *The Commonwealth* for March, both from
the pen of the Reverend A. L. Lilley, Anglican Vicar of St Mary's,
Paddington Green.[4] Lilley's articles were not only totally sympathetic
in tone but showed also a real familiarity with the personnel and

---

[1] 'L. wrote me 3 letters, all increasingly convinced that the little book wd. certainly be
put on the Index; but now (day bef. yesterday) he writes: "Le Cardinal Satolli dit qu'on ne
condamnerait pas mon livre, mais qu'on voulait m'empêcher d'écrire." Both points, interesting. I had anyhow already noted the emphasis on the non-approvedness of the book laid by
Cardd. Richard and Perraud in their prohibitions of it. Yet, even the simple non-condemnation (Roman) of the book, after all this attention drawn there to it, wd. be, in its way, a
veritable triumph, to be used cautiously & without exultation: we are not nearly out of the
woods yet: but still, I think, with a feeling that Rome is somehow waking up to the formidable-
ness of trying to directly break the movement.' Von Hügel to Tyrrell, 3 April 1903, BM, Add.
MSS. 44928.83.

[2] *Mém.* II, p. 202.

[3] *Ibid.* p. 207.

[4] 'Biblical Criticism in France, II', *The Guardian*, no. 2986, 25 Feb. 1903, pp. 267–8;
'L'Affaire Loisy', *The Commonwealth*, vol. VIII, no. 3, March 1903, pp. 73–6. Both of these
articles were later reprinted in A. L. Lilley's *Modernism: A Record and Review*, London, 1908,
pp. 55–64 and 185–94.

problems of the French crisis. They also showed genuine appreciation for Loisy as a person and for the quality of his work, and they analysed the ultimate significance of his writings with unusual insight and clarity. For this reason von Hügel felt impelled to thank Lilley for what he had done. The Baron's letter was sent off on 6 April 1903, and with that initiative began a lifelong friendship between the two men. After explaining to Lilley how close was his own friendship with Loisy, von Hügel told him:

You can, then, easily imagine with what pleasure I read your papers. I think what especially struck, and indeed delighted me in them, was the way in which you appeared conscious throughout of the first-class quality of his mind and of all that he has got to teach anyone and everybody; and then the manner in which, throughout again, the problems and solutions discussed and propounded by him, were felt by you as, practically, quite inter-confessional, as concerning all Christians of any and every kind, who find that they must and do *think*.[1]

In the same letter the Baron proposed a meeting with Lilley. The meeting took place on 20 April, with the Baron walking from his Hampstead residence to Lilley's Vicarage, and back again after a two hour conversation and tea.[2]

Several of von Hügel's Roman Catholic friends in England also came out in print in defence of Loisy and his book, even after Richard's condemnation. *The Tablet* had refused to review *L'Évangile et l'Église* in its pages, and communications from its 'Roman Correspondent' were not friendly to Loisy's cause. One such communication reported on a pamphlet released in Rome by the Jesuit Palmieri which pretended to show that Loisy had 'not merely prescinded from revealed doctrine, but has in many instances denied it'.[3] To prove his point Palmieri gave a long list of errors compiled from Loisy's book, and *The Tablet* printed the list. In the subsequent issue of *The Tablet* appeared letters from both

---

[1] Von Hügel to A. L. Lilley, 6 April 1903, LFP, I, vH MSS. – Most of the letters from von Hügel to Lilley were on loan from the Lilley family to Dr Alec Vidler at the time the author consulted them, and have since been depositied at Saint Andrews University Library. These letters are referred to in the notes, as here, as LFP, I, vH MSS. A smaller collection of letters from von Hügel to Lilley remained in the possession of Miss Barbara Lilley, daughter of A. L. Lilley. These were loaned directly to the author by Miss Lilley, and will be referred to in the notes as LFP, II, vH MSS. The present location of this smaller collection of letters, since Miss Lilley's death in June 1970, is unknown to the author.

[2] *Diaries*, 20 April 1903. Even by the end of 1903 von Hügel could say to Lilley: 'It is indeed a great consolation and one to thank God for, – the finding in you, one more of the few minds and souls that understand the situation!' Von Hügel to Lilley, 14 Dec. 1903, LFP, I, vH MSS.

[3] *The Tablet*, vol. 101, no. 3282, 4 April 1903, p. 534.

Dom Cuthbert Butler, at that time resident in Cambridge though later to be abbot of Downside, and Father W. H. Kent, of Manning's clerical foundation at Bayswater, protesting the injustice done to Loisy. Dom Butler's letter insisted that Loisy should be judged only on what he intended and what he achieved, and that he had achieved his intention in an admirable way. Butler pointed out:

A statement of Catholicism may be true from the critic's historical standpoint and yet be theologically inadequate: but it is important in face of current modes of thought to have an expression of Catholicism in the bare language of severely critical history. An algebraic equation is a true expression of a curve, and may be of great value in mechanics and engineering; but from the point of art, which I imagine is a higher plane, the formula is not a satisfying representation of the line.[1]

Kent's letter attacked Palmieri's list of errors, and commented that not only was it ungenerous to compose such a list after the book had been withdrawn from circulation, but that most of the sample errors printed by *The Tablet* were 'grotesque perversions of the French author's meaning'.[2] The following week Wilfrid Ward published a letter in *The Tablet* supporting Kent and Butler, and drawing attention to Newman's principle that it is better for great minds to write, with no matter how inadequate an expression of their thoughts, than not to have written at all. This principle Ward felt was especially important for the present time, when so many problems raised by criticism had to be faced. He stressed that the incidental errors of men like Loisy

and the misconceptions of their critics may take time to correct; but their work is surely, in spite of its defects, a far more important intellectual aid to faith than the simply correct treatise which advances neither any statement whose sound is new to the theological ear, nor any statement betraying an appreciation of those considerations whereby the faith of Christians is in our own day tried.[3]

To all three men von Hügel expressed his gratitude for their public support, and he sent their letters to Loisy.[4]

The summer months of 1903 were days of change, of transition and of death. On 19 June Cardinal Vaughan died, at his own clerical establishment at Mill Hill, and in the arms of von Hügel's cleric–scholar

---

[1] *The Tablet*, vol. 101, no. 3283, 11 April 1903, p. 578.
[2] *Ibid.*
[3] *The Tablet*, vol. 101, no. 3284, 18 April 1903, p. 617.
[4] *Diaries*, 13, 19, 21 and 22 April 1903.

friend, Christian van den Biesen.[1] Although the Baron wrote a letter of condolence to Lady Herbert of Lea, and took his youngest daughter Thekla to pray beside the dead Cardinal's coffin in Westminster cathedral, he himself did not attend the funeral.[2] In July occurred another death which would affect the course of events for the Baron and his friends in their relation to ecclesiastical authority; it was the death of Pope Leo XIII on the 20th. Writing in *The Fortnightly Review* Wilfrid Ward spoke of the dead Pope's life and achievements, but denied that he had been a liberal pope or even that he understood or much valued true liberty. He even went so far as to suggest that 'Pius IX. had more of genuine Liberalism in his composition than his successor', and gave interesting reasons for this judgment.[3] Von Hügel thought Ward's paper was 'truly admirable. Especially the bit about the supposed "liberality" or "liberalism" of the Pope, was to my mind, exactly right and most suggestive.'[4] He told Ward that he read most of it twice over 'with the most complete appreciation and sympathy'. But Leo, too, would probably look like a liberal pope to those who survived the reign of his successor, though few surmised this at the time. *The Pilot's* reflection on the outcome of the papal election well summarized the hesitancy and expectancy with which the majority of those who concerned themselves with such things watched Pius X ascend the papal throne. 'Meanwhile', Lathbury wrote, 'all Europe will be interested in watching the new career of the simple country curate of the Veneto, who has emerged as Pope from the first Conclave of the twentieth century and has assumed the heavy burden so long borne by the scholarly diplomatist of Carpineto.'[5] At Westminster Vaughan's successor was to be the former Bishop of Southwark, Francis Bourne. Although von Hügel knew Bourne hardly at all, he wrote to congratulate him on his new appointment, and within a short time visited him to discuss the burning issues of criticism and authority.[6] After his visit to Bourne, von Hügel wrote to Archbishop Mignot to suggest that the French prelate invite Bourne to visit him at Albi when the latter returned from his first Roman visit as Archbishop.[7]

[1] Among the unsorted papers of Canon James Moyes in the Archives of the Archdiocese of Westminster is a manuscript letter from van den Biesen, addressed simply: 'Right Reverend & Dear Monseigneur' and dated 29 June 1903. It is an account of Cardinal Vaughan's last moments from the pen of the only cleric who was actually with him. See, AAW, 168, Misc. Moyes MSS.

[2] *Diaries*, 20, 22, and 25 June 1903.

[3] 'Leo XIII', *The Fortnightly Review*, no. ccccxl, new series, 1 Aug. 1903, p. 263.

[4] Von Hügel to Ward, 21 Sept. 1903, WFP, vH MSS.

[5] 'Pope Pius X', *The Pilot*, no. 177, vol. viii, 8 Aug. 1903, p. 121.

[6] *Diaries*, 2 Sept. and 23 Oct. 1903.   [7] *Diaries*, 24 Oct. 1903.

The Baron felt that Mignot's broad views and openness might encourage Bourne in the direction which von Hügel hoped he would take as Archbishop of Westminster.

With the change of personnel in high places only just complete, Loisy published his *Autour d'un petit livre*, and almost immediately the tensions of the spring came fully to the fore again.[1] In Rome the changes consequent on the end of one papal reign and the beginning of another were most significantly marked, perhaps, in the appointment of the new papal Secretary of State. Cardinal Rampolla, who had been Leo XIII's Secretary of State, was made President of the Pontifical Biblical Commission to replace Cardinal Parocchi who had died. And Cardinal Merry del Val became Pius X's Secretary of State. Merry del Val, son of a Spanish diplomat to England, educated at Ushaw near Durham and at Rome's clerical establishments, was the narrow product of a totally scholastic training and was one of the single most powerful influences at Rome to oppose ruthlessly the aims of von Hügel and his friends.[2] But von Hügel's family had known Merry del Val's family in England, and during the Baron's winters in Rome the Cardinal had been kind, in a social way, to his daughters. Consequently, von Hügel felt obliged to write a letter of congratulations when Merry del Val received his appointment, though it cost the Baron 'much pains'.[3] He took the occasion of the letter to tell the new Secretary of State how necessary was Roman toleration for Loisy if the church was not to lose many whose faith had been strengthened by Loisy's work. Within a week of writing his own letter the Baron had an answer from the Cardinal, a curt snub which merely thanked von Hügel for his letter and for remembering the small bit he had tried to do for the von Hügel children. Whether or not Merry del Val's answer was to be taken as an indication that action was already being taken in Rome regarding Loisy, thus making any comment

[1] On 7 October, von Hügel received Loisy's four latest books (*Autour d'un petit livre*, *Le Quatrième Évangile*, *Discours sur la Montagne*, and the 2nd edition of *L'Évangile et l'Église*), – the one to cause the greatest immediate sensation, of course, being *Autour d'un petit livre*. The tone of this book seemed to some rather heavily sarcastic, and this, probably more than any other factor, was the real reason behind the eventual rejection of the book by the Roman authorities. While reading the book, von Hügel wrote to Loisy (*Diaries*, 10 Oct. 1903): 'Vous savez bien que je suis tout avec vous; et que ce (les péripétites éventuelles) sont *nos* affaires, *nos* espérances, *nos* sueurs et *nos* couronnes; ou non, ces dernières, elles sont pour vous presque exclusivement, tout comme les sueurs ont été tellement plus abondantes chez vous' (*Mém.* II, p. 264).

[2] See, Pio Cenci, *Il Cardinale Raffaele Merry del Val*, Rome, 1933. This volume of more than 800 pages, written by the archivist of the Secret Vatican Archives, mentions merely in passing that Loisy and the modernists were 'unmasked' and 'defeated' (p. 192) by Pius X and Merry del Val.

[3] Von Hügel to Ward, 18 Nov. 1903, WFP, vH MSS.

impossible, or whether it merely meant that the Cardinal considered such questions to be beyond the competence of a layman, von Hügel did not know. But he did know that he had never been treated in this manner by Cardinal Rampolla, and if Merry del Val's note was indicative of the Roman atmosphere of the years immediately ahead, it was a very discouraging indication.[1]

The last six weeks of 1903 were increasingly full of new efforts on von Hügel's part to help Loisy. In mid-November one of his continental friends sent him a letter with the request that he translate it for publication in *The Pilot*. The letter was printed under the heading of 'History and Dogma' on 28 November.[2] It was a defence of Loisy's position on the relationship of history and dogma – that history cannot 'prove' the dogmas of Christianity, since history deals solely with phenomenal reality and Christian dogmas deal with divine realities beyond the phenomenal categories of time and space. Roman Catholic orthodox theology, however, still tended to imply that Jesus's divinity and resurrection were facts capable of historical proof, so that Loisy's insistence on the limits and aims of critical history sounded alarming to the ears of conservative Roman theologians. Von Hügel appreciated the value of repeating as often and as publicly as possible the legitimacy of Loisy's methodology and aims, even by published letters in *The Pilot*. When Archbishop Mignot went to Rome in late November, the Baron wrote to tell him that he himself would be happy to come to Rome to help Loisy's cause, if the archbishop thought that he could really help there.[3] Members of the French hierarchy and other anti-Loisy ecclesiastics were concentrating their efforts to bring about a Roman condemnation of the French scholar. Whether or not there would be a specific condemnation remained uncertain until about the middle of December.

As the opposition began to close ranks in Rome, von Hügel worked on as best he could in England. On 11 December he received, through the intermediacy of Padre Giovanni Semeria of Genoa, the first of a series of letters which praised and defended Loisy's *L'Évangile et l'Église* and

---

[1] *Ibid.*; *Diaries*, 18 Nov. 1903.

[2] *Diaries*, 16 Nov. 1903; *The Pilot*, no. 193, vol. VIII, 28 Nov. 1903, p. 529. 'You will have noticed the 1st letter in the "Pilot" Dec. 5th "History and Dogma". I have no idea who wrote it, – except that the writer is an admirer of L's in a high eccles. position; and I translated the ms. as sent to me by a friend.' Von Hügel to Tyrrell, 15 Dec. 1903, BM, Add. MSS. 44928.132. – The Baron has erred in giving Tyrrell the date of the *Pilot* letter's appearance. It was 28 November rather than 5 December.

[3] *Diaries*, 27 Nov. 1903.

the whole of Loisy's critical historical enterprise.[1] The letters were in French when the Baron received them; and he was asked to polish their literary quality, to find a journal in which to publish them and, in fact, to supervise the details of their publication.[2] These letters were the mysterious *Lettres Romaines*, and von Hügel arranged for their publication in the *Annales de philosophie chrétienne*. He himself revised the French before sending each of the six letters to the journal's editor, and he corrected the proofs before the final printing. Who the original author was von Hügel seems never to have known.[3] The letters were printed in the *Annales* between January and March 1904, and were later published in Italian too. Another of the Baron's efforts was his attempt to get D.C. Lathbury to take a clear stand for Loisy in *The Pilot*'s policies, but he had to settle for something less definite – an offer to himself for a review of Loisy's new study of the fourth gospel.[4] However, when Lathbury published a lengthy article by a 'Roman Catholic Correspondent' on 'A Question of Attitude', von Hügel felt that the old editor had been unfair and sent him a 'hot' letter of protest.[5] The offending article, written on the presumption that Loisy would soon be condemned in Rome, asked the

---

[1] *Diaries*, 11 Dec. 1903. Although von Hügel's diaries do not explicitly state that Semeria was the intermediary between the author of the *Lettres Romaines* and von Hügel, they do have this entry: 'Letters from ... Abbé Denis, urging continuation of "Lettres Romaines". Sent this on to Semeria' (*Diaries*, 1 Jan. 1904).

[2] On the day following his reception of the first *Lettre*, von Hügel wrote to the abbé Charles Denis, editor of the *Annales de philosophie chrétienne*, to try to have them inserted in that journal. They were accepted. Shortly afterwards Semeria wrote to von Hügel that Denis's Lenten Sermons had just been placed on the Index, and the Baron had a pang of regret that he had placed these Loisy-defending *Lettres* with an editor who had just been condemned (*Mém.* II, p. 298). See, 'Lettres Romaines', *Annales de philosophie chrétienne*, 3rd series, tome III, nos. 4–6, Jan.–March 1904, pp. 349–59, 473–88, and 601–20.

[3] The authorship of the 'Lettres' is still not known with any certainty. Loisy surmised that probably Giovanni Genocchi had written them (*Mém.* II, p. 298). The most recent scholarly study of the modernist crisis discusses the history of the surmises about the authorship, and concludes that Genocchi is still the most likely candidate: Émile Poulat, *Histoire, dogme et critique dans la crise moderniste*, Paris, 1962, pp. 671–2. However, if in the abstract Genocchi seems a likely choice for the authorship of the 'Lettres Romaines'; there are, nevertheless, some practical problems against it. On 31 December 1903 Genocchi wrote to von Hügel (SAUL, MS. 2605) *from Sicily* where he had been for two weeks and where he would remain for another week. Moreover he was there 'for the preaching of a retreat', and he also told the Baron that he was 'busy with confessions and sermons'. These circumstances make it unlikely that he would also have had time to compose three of the carefully thought out 'Lettres', and yet during these same three weeks that Genocchi was away from Rome doing pastoral work in Sicily, von Hügel received three of the 'Lettres Romaines'. The fact that he received them at intervals of nearly a week apart suggests that they were actually being composed during that time. It is unlikely that the Baron ever knew who the author was, and if he did know, the secret seems to have gone with him to the grave.

[4] Von Hügel to Lilley, 14 Dec. 1903, LFP, I, vH MSS.; *Diaries*, 13 and 21 Dec. 1903.

[5] *Diaries*, 23 Dec. 1903.

question: Why are some men condemned and others not, when both condemned and uncondemned seem to hold similar positions? The writer's answer was that 'it is not a question of position or of opinion. It is a question of attitude.' And just what this objectionable attitude was, the writer tried to clarify.

Let him have the reverential, cautious, obedient spirit of Newman, and he may write the letter to Ullathorne, or may criticise the proofs of Christ's divinity from miracles and prophecy. Let him have the spirit of insubordination, criticism, and irresponsibleness, let him scandalise the little ones, and lecture prelates, and, were he as accredited as a Galileo in science, or a Lamennais in politics, the likelihood is that he will be struck off the roll of the Church's official apologists. In ceasing to acknowledge her indebtedness to him, the Church will take less account of the objects than of the spirit, of his denial.[1]

To insinuate that Loisy, at this particular point of his ecclesiastical career, manifested, 'the spirit of insubordination, criticism, and irresponsibleness', was unjust. And von Hügel who, was excessively sensitive to injustice toward his friend, was bound to react.

As December wore on von Hügel and Lilley worked out some plans for publications which they thought would help Loisy's cause, the first being an article by Lilley for *The Pilot* on Loisy and the Holy Office.[2] Von Hügel also wrote to Robert Dell[3] to ask him to prepare an article on the same topic, and on Christmas Day he wrote to Lord Halifax to suggest that he too write something against a condemnation of Loisy.[4] Until the very end the Baron believed that if Rome could be made to see that a condemnation of Loisy would seriously offend all intelligent and sincere Christians, she would not condemn him. From Hickleton Hall Halifax answered at once that he would be happy to do what von

[1] *The Pilot*, no. 196, vol. VIII, 19 Dec. 1903, p. 598.
[2] *Diaries*, 23–4 Dec. 1903.
[3] Robert Dell was born in 1865, the son of the Vicar of South Baddesley, Hampshire. He was educated at University College, Oxford, and joined the Roman Catholic church in 1897. His life's work was largely journalistic. From 1899–1900 he edited the Catholic *Weekly Register*, and then in 1900 *The New Era*. In 1905 Dell went to Paris where he operated an art gallery, and where he gained a close knowledge of the French church–state problems. In 1906 he translated Paul Sabatier's *A propos de la Séparation des Églises et de l'État* into English. He became political correspondent for the *Manchester Guardian* in 1912, but was expelled from France in 1917 by Clémenceau for favouring the peace projects of Prince Sixtus of Bourbon-Parma. He died in New York in 1940. See, Burnand, *The Catholic Who's Who*, 1909, p. 133; and the biographical section by Poulat in A. Houtin and F Sartiaux, *Alfred Loisy: sa vie et son oeuvre*, Paris, 1960, p. 345.
[4] *Diaries*, 25 Dec. 1903.

Hügel suggested if he could think of an appropriate way to do it. He told the Baron that he would write again in a few days when he had decided on a mode of procedure. 'Meanwhile,' Halifax continued,

I think to insist upon any *retractions* or to put out any *Decrees* condemning as it would all sorts of things would be a misfortune for everyone & that for all sorts of reasons. But I don't know that one can be surprised at the books being put on the *Index*, for surely they are not suited, nor are they good for *general* reading. I know lots of people in whose hands I should be very sorry to see *Autour d'un petit livre*.[1]

But even before von Hügel had received Halifax's first letter, the condemnations had fallen. On the 27th, while at tea with his friend of many years, Mrs Cecil Chapman, the Baron picked up her copy of the previous day's *Times* to read 'the news of Loisy's condemnation, by Holy Office and Index, published on Xmas Day by Cardinal Richard'.[2]

On 17 December 1903, a decree of the Inquisition had been signed in Rome, stating that five of Loisy's publications should be inscribed on the Index of Forbidden Books.[3] The five were *La Religion d'Israël*, *Études Évangeliques*, *L'Évangile et l'Église*, *Autour d'un petit livre*, and *Le Quatrième Évangile*. No reasons were given in the decree for this condemnation. This document, together with a general statement of condemnation by the Holy Office and a covering letter from Cardinal Merry del Val, was sent to Cardinal Richard on the 19th, publication in Rome being delayed until Richard made the documents public in Paris. Merry del Val's letter informed Richard that Loisy's 'grave errors' principally concerned 'primitive revelation, the authenticity of the facts and teaching of the Gospels, the divinity and knowledge of Christ, the resurrection, the divine institution of the church, and the sacraments'.[4] The list clearly resembled the group of generalizations which Richard had put forward as unsatisfactorily treated in *L'Évangile et l'Église* when he had

[1] Halifax to von Hügel, 27 Dec. 1903, SAUL, MS. 3227. What Halifax actually did was to write a short preface for a pamphlet by T. A. Lacey (*Harnack and Loisy*, London, 1904). Lacey's paper had originally been an address given at Oxford on 27 November 1903. Halifax's introduction was printed also as a separate article in *The Pilot*, no. 200, vol. IX, 16 Jan. 1904, pp. 56–7. Halifax's concluding words stressed a theme often to be repeated in the press in the ensuing months: 'All Christendom is concerned with the honour and dignity of the Roman Church. And more, a blunder of this kind injures religion at large, injures the general authority on which religion rests, tends to throw men back upon purely individual sanctions for the truth. The case of Galileo wounded Christianity sorely for two hundred years, and the wound is not yet healed. Is the case of Loisy to repeat the blow?' (From page 57 of *The Pilot* edition, and page 7 of Longman's pamphlet.)
[2] *Diaries*, 27 Dec. 1903.
[3] *Mém.* II, pp. 283, 299–300.
[4] *Ibid.* p. 301.

condemned that book in the previous January. Before Richard could privately inform Loisy of the condemnation of his books by Rome, the news was leaked to the Parisian press, apparently by the Papal Nuncio in Paris, and so Loisy learned of the condemnation of his life's work from the Paris newspapers and the communications of his journalist friends.[1] Just as the decree of condemnation gave no reasons for its decisions, so no opportunity was given Loisy to justify or to explain to the authorities his own understanding of whatever it was that offended them. In fact, what offended them was never made explicit. Loisy was expected to make an unqualified submission to the decree, and to repudiate absolutely the books condemned. Customarily, when such submissions and repudiations were received in Rome following upon a condemnation, the Inquisition published its victory notice in the traditional Latin formula: *Auctor laudabiliter se subjecit et opus reprobavit.* If no such complete submission was forthcoming, the author was usually given a formal warning, and then, if he still refused to make a satisfactory submission, he would most likely be excommunicated.[2] The creation of this situation for Loisy by a Roman condemnation of his books was precisely what von Hügel had dreaded and worked against. Yet the eventual condemnation had not been unforeseen, and now that it was a fact the Baron was catapulted into action.

It was a Sunday evening when von Hügel first learned of the Roman decree, and early Monday morning he sent a telegram to Lathbury of *The Pilot*, offering to write an article on the condemnation. By a return telegram within a matter of hours Lathbury had accepted the offer, and the Baron at once set to work on his first major piece of propaganda in this new campaign.[3] He himself looked on the article as an act of public support for the position he knew Loisy would have to take if he were not to compromise his conscience and scholarly integrity, and he told Loisy that he hoped it would back up the latter's position in dealing with Merry del Val.[4] Covering almost two full pages of *The Pilot* for 9 January 1904, the article was published under the heading of 'The Case of the Abbé Loisy'. It was a highly personal, disarmingly frank, and utterly sincere, piece, which, as well as giving an excellent defence of Loisy,

[1] *Ibid.* p. 288.
[2] This 'juridical lore' was explained to the English public by the French correspondent of *The Pilot* (no. 198, vol. IX, 2 Jan. 1904, p. 10), who had himself consulted a Roman Catholic priest experienced in Canon Law.
[3] *Diaries*, 28 Dec. 1903.
[4] *Mém.* II, p. 309.

contained in miniature many of the main features of von Hügel's religious philosophy.[1] Starting with the Roman condemnation as a fact to be accepted and somehow balanced with the fact of the objective legitimacy of Loisy's work, the Baron stated that he conceived the first of these two facts to be primarily a disciplinary matter. He was certain that Loisy would 'respectfully submit himself, and condemn whatever may be reprehensible in his writings, with the obvious and due reservation of his self-respect as an historian, and of adhesion to the general historical method and its legitimate applications'.[2] Using examples from history von Hügel showed how other men and ideas had been condemned by Rome because they were in advance of the general mentality of the majority of Christians in their day, and how eventually these very condemned ideas found acceptance within the church. He insisted that men of Loisy's calibre cannot cease to think, nor to pursue truth even at the risk of error, without becoming something less than human. Moreover, he advocated sincerity, rather than orthodoxy, as the road by which truth was to be sought, and showed how the Christian can share Christ's cross precisely in this approach. Finally, he felt certain that history would place Loisy with the great men of the past who had suffered for truth and sincerity. Von Hügel sent off-prints of his article to dozens of friends in England and on the continent, and through the mediation of Padre Genocchi in Rome it was printed in February in Italian in the *Rassegna Nazionale*.[3] The Baron himself made a French translation of the article which he sent to abbé Charles Denis, the editor of the *Annales de philosophie chrétienne,* for placing in a French journal, though it seems never to have been actually published in France. A typescript of the French translation, however, was sent to Padre Lepidi in Rome at the Baron's request.[4]

[1] Loisy felt that the article had not been of much help to his cause (*Mém.* II, p. 309). However, von Hügel was more optimistic, especially as he received numerous letters of congratulations for it. 'I think I have good reason to hope that it really *has* done good, – even in the very precise and immediately practical sense in which I hoped it would operate. For, already when writing it, the Censure, inasmuch as Disciplinary, was understood and accepted by us. Yet the matter was not by any means just so much past history: for the important point of what Rome would accept as a sufficient-submission was still ahead, and is still undecided. And it is quietly plain not only to me and L., but to I think all of even his partial friends or moderate antagonists, that a simply absolute submission would, in the long run, do as much harm to the cause of authority as it would *instantly* discredit L. in the eyes both of the learned world and of even the most violent of his assailants themselves.' Von Hügel to Ward, 22 Jan. 1904, WFP, vH MSS.
[2] *The Pilot*, no. 199, vol. IX, 9 Jan. 1904, p. 30.
[3] *Mém.* II, p. 309.
[4] *Diaries*, 20 and 23 Jan. 1904. Lepidi did not read English, but he did read French. As

From the first von Hügel realized that the main problem with a Roman condemnation would be to find a form of submission which would both satisfy the authorities and at the same time not compromise Loisy. Early in January Loisy told Cardinal Richard that he would soon write to Merry del Val with a statement 'of adherence to the judgment' of the Roman Congregations which had condemned him. What Loisy meant by this remark was not what Richard took it to mean, and on the 9th the *Semaine religieuse* for Richard's diocese published a statement of Loisy's unqualified submission.[1] *The Pilot*'s Paris correspondent picked up this information and repeated it,[2] thus calling forth a letter to that journal from von Hügel. The Baron denied, on the basis of his own communications from Loisy, that any such unqualified submission had been made. 'No act of submission was made by him to the Archbishop', von Hügel pointed out, 'and the act which he has now made in Rome will, no doubt, have been thoroughly respectful and sincere, and cannot therefore have been without some reasonable and necessary reservation in the matter of his historian's conscience and method.'[3] And this was exactly the sort of qualified submission that Loisy had sent to Merry del Val on 12 January. The Baron had so little confidence in Loisy's submission being accepted by the Cardinal, however, that he wrote to Loisy on the 15th suggesting that the latter send a memorial directly to the Pope, affirming his 'lively and full faith in the divinity of Jesus Christ and all the dogmas of the church', but also pointing out his obligations to his conscience and his science.[4] His suspicions of Merry del Val's frame of mind were soon confirmed. Loisy was summoned before Cardinal Richard on the 23rd and was told that the Archbishop had just received an answer from Merry del Val regarding Loisy's attempted submission. This answer demanded an immediate retractation, without any reservations whatsoever, of the five volumes which had been placed on the Index and of their entire content. If the retractation were not received straightaway, the letter continued, then the Holy Office would

---

soon as his article appeared in *The Pilot* von Hügel sent a number of copies to Genocchi in Rome for distribution there. Genocchi reported back to the Baron: 'As for your article on Loisy, I gave it, as you wished, to the appointed men and to some others; but F. Lepidi told me he does not understand English. Send him, please, a copy in French' (Genocchi to von Hügel, 17 Jan. 1904, SAUL, MS. 2606).

[1] *Mém.* II, p. 309.
[2] *The Pilot*, no. 200, vol. IX, 16 Jan. 1904, p. 58.
[3] *The Pilot*, no. 201, vol. IX, 23 Jan. 1904, p. 94.
[4] *Diaries*, 15 Jan. 1904; *Mém.* II, p. 315.

proceed with further measures. Loisy accepted this as the first formal warning of his impending excommunication.[1] Almost as soon as he came away from the Archbishop's residence Loisy wrote this information to von Hügel, and within twenty-four hours of receiving the news the Baron had himself written to Merry del Val. He wrote in English and at great length; he identified himself with Loisy and his cause and told the Cardinal Secretary of State that any submission demanded 'must allow us some room for self-respect and for our reputations as scholars and responsible men'; he stressed once again that an absolute condemnation of Loisy would hurt Rome far more in the estimation of educated Englishmen than it would hurt Loisy; and he warned the prelate 'as to not going too fast, finally or far, against Loisy'.[2] Von Hügel posted this letter to Merry del Val on the same day that Loisy posted his second attempt to satisfy the Cardinal with a limited submission.

The English press kept up interest in Loisy's vicissitudes with various types of articles, communications and letters. Some of these the Baron was responsible for either directly or indirectly; but some of them, too, were quite unsolicited and some he even found upsetting. One of the latter type appeared in the same issue of *The Pilot* in which his own letter clarifying the matter of Loisy's supposed submission had appeared. It was entitled 'An Anglican View of M. Loisy', and it was written by William Sanday. If in 1896 Sanday had publicly expressed unqualified praise of Loisy's use of critical method, eight years later he was publicly criticizing his use of that same method. And the factor which had largely changed Sanday's attitude was the publication by Loisy of his study of the fourth gospel. Loisy's radical criticism of the historicity of that Gospel had seemed to Sanday so excessive that Christian doctrine seemed to be left 'suspended in the air', unable to show historic links beyond the early second century. 'M. Loisy has given us a great deal that is of high value,' Sanday conceded, 'but I hope that, as a whole, his books will be used with discrimination, and that English scholars and the English people will not be too much carried away by the prestige of his name.'[3]

---

[1] *Mém.* II, p. 319.

[2] *Diaries*, 25–6 Jan. 1904; *Mém.* II, p. 324.

[3] *The Pilot*, no. 201, vol. IX, 23 Jan. 1904, p. 85. Significantly, Charles Gore had concluded two papers on the Fourth Gospel less than two years earlier with these remarks: 'It has been the object of these papers only to renew the old but by no means antiquated contention that we must, on the evidence, accept the Johannine authorship of the Fourth Gospel; that we must recognise that St. John both realised the importance of really reporting what Jesus had done and said, and also believed himself and his fellows to be specially qualified by the Holy Spirit to recall and record it; that the evidence of the rest of the New Testament, and such other

This was the sort of criticism which could most seriously damage von Hügel's English propaganda efforts for Loisy, and the Baron, consequently, reacted at once. On the very day that Sanday's article appeared in print von Hügel went to see Lilley, and together they laid their plans for a counter-attack. Lilley was to prepare a brief article at once, and the Baron would follow this up with two longer ones a bit later on. When they asked Lathbury to go along with their plan for publishing these articles in *The Pilot*, he refused, though he once again offered von Hügel space for a lengthy review of Loisy's *Le Quatrième Évangile*. Because Lathbury's idea would not be especially helpful as an immediate counteraction to Sanday's article, Lilley and the Baron worked out a letter-to-the-editor which they felt Lathbury would have to print. Since Lilley had actually composed the letter, it appeared under his name in the following issue of *The Pilot*.[1] Lilley's attack on Sanday was very clear and very incisive. The difference between Sanday and Loisy, according to Lilley, was not merely that of conclusions reached, but rather of methods used to reach them. Loisy stood for free and autonomous criticism, whereas Sanday insisted on introducing theological considerations into his criticism. And the result, as far as Lilley could estimate it, was that Loisy had created a Christian apologetic as relevant to the educated secular mind of the twentieth century, as Athanasius's had been for the Hellenistic mind of the fourth. Sanday, on the other hand, with 'a latent distrust of the critical method' and a fear 'of the consequences of a too rigid application of it', was forced to fall back on theological considerations and into a conservatism more rigorous than many orthodox Roman Catholic commentators.[2]

The journalistic exchange, however, which hit most clearly at the heart of the Loisy affair was that which appeared in *The Times*. On 21 January the paper printed a letter over the signature 'Vidi' which

considerations as are available, support his testimony; and that thus we may unhesitatingly accept St. John's Gospel as giving us a true picture, and as preserving for us elements in the Christ of history without which we should indeed have suffered loss ... I would only conclude these papers with a real appeal to Englishmen to use their own judgment on the subject of St. John's Gospel, and not to be carried away by a mere fashion of deference to "critics". And if we must introduce the question of contemporary intellectual authority, we should remember that there are no saner or fairer judgments to be found in the last generation of historical scholars or the present than Lightfoot's and Sanday's.' (*The Pilot*, no. 105, vol. v, 1 March 1902, pp. 230–1.) Von Hügel sent Gore's two articles on St. John's Gospel to Loisy (*Diaries*, 12 March 1902.)

[1] *Diaries*, 23, 25 and 26 Jan. 1904. *The Pilot*, no. 202, vol. IX, 30 Jan. 1904, pp. 116–17.
[2] *The Pilot*, no. 202, vol. IX, 30 Jan. 1904, p. 116.

defended Loisy as the ablest apologist the Roman church possessed, and implied that his condemnation by that church was indicative of the church's lack of sincerity and faith in her own mission. The writer concluded by saying that

the question is not one to be settled by praise or denunciation, but rather to be fought out slowly between the partisans of authority and the partisans of religious sincerity. It suffices to register the fact that the latter have never been so numerous in the Roman Church as now.[1]

A few days later the letter was answered by another, this time over the signature 'Catholicus'. In his letter 'Vidi' had listed seven conclusions held by Loisy as a result of his critical studies, most of them having to do with the composition and authorship of the books of the Old Testament, and indicated that such conclusions were at the centre of Loisy's troubles with Roman authorities. 'Catholicus' primarily attacked 'Vidi's' list of critical conclusions, stating that all these were now held and taught by Catholics without any harassment from authorities, and that the real issue between church authorities and Loisy had to do with critical conclusions about the New Testament, i.e. Jesus' self-consciousness as God, the origin of the church and sacraments, and the historicity of the Resurrection.[2] Since the writer of that letter was almost certainly David Fleming, the Secretary of the Pontifical Biblical Commission, his statement of the problem represents the view of the conflict as seen from Rome. But the statement which 'Catholicus' evoked from von Hügel was likewise the most succinct presentation of the issues at stake as seen from Loisy's side of the struggle – at least as the Baron understood that conflict.

After reading the 'Catholicus' letter in *The Times* and concluding that Fleming was its author, von Hügel decided to answer it. He wrote to Loisy and Tyrrell asking for their suggestions, but, although both responded, and the Baron used some of their ideas, the finished letter was unmistakably von Hügel's. He signed the letter 'Romanus', and took it off personally to *The Times* editorial offices where he was interviewed by the sub-editor who was rather vague about whether or not the letter would be printed. A few days later the editor told von Hügel that he doubted whether the letter would appear, since so much other news was waiting to be covered.[3] The Baron observed, nevertheless, that

---

[1] *The Times*, no. 37,296, 21 Jan. 1904, p. 4.
[2] *The Times*, no. 37,299, 25 Jan. 1904, p. 4.
[3] *Diaries*, 27 and 30 Jan.; and 1–3, 5 and 6 Feb. 1904. See also, von Hügel to Tyrrell, 5 Feb. 1904, in *Von Hügel and Tyrrell*, p. 142.

'Bailey Saunders and Dell, both experienced in the "Times" ways, are convinced that that mighty organ is going to publish it, but have warned me to wait patiently for 3 to 4 weeks from date of sending it in'.[1]

The warning was prophetic and the letter was published in *The Times* on 2 March. It was double the length of the 'Catholicus' letter and it was very direct and hard-hitting. Von Hügel pointed out that if, as 'Catholicus' claimed, 'Vidi's' list of conclusions about the Old Testament were now allowable in the Roman church, they were so allowed almost solely because Loisy's patient and careful work had made them at last acceptable. Then he turned to the five propositions pertaining to Christ and the New Testament on which 'Catholicus' had challenged Loisy's position. Here he hit on the heart of the conflict:

But all turns really upon whether, as Historian, he [Loisy] gives us these successive facts and attestations according to sound – i.e. universally applicable – historical method; and whether, as Apologist, he sufficiently retains, whilst reinterpreting under pressure of these facts, that substance of the faith which necessarily transcends and interprets, but may not contradict or ignore them.[2]

The Baron then took 'Catholicus's' five propositions, and placed beside each one the main facts adduced by historical criticism regarding that proposition. He asked 'Catholicus' whether he himself rejected these facts, and if so, on what critical grounds. And if he accepted them, von Hügel asked 'what more orthodox but equally sincere interpretations he has to offer, as compared with M. Loisy'. In two lengthy and movingly personal paragraphs von Hügel concluded the article by stating his own 'deliberate conviction as to our conscientious obligations'. These obligations included acceptance of the Index decree as a disciplinary measure, and acceptance of the Holy Office decree as a doctrinal measure since it is the church's right and duty to determine whether or not any given apologetic really is an adequate presentation of the faith. 'But we cannot make our submission to the decree of the Holy Office in so unqualified a form as to let it include historico-critical method and its direct subject matters, as such, even though these latter be the records of primitive Christianity.' The Baron's final declaration was that 'we are, with God's help, determined to remain deeply convinced Catholics, and, if required, to suffer respectfully whatever the Church authorities may determine for the Church's good'. Although

[1] Von Hügel to Tyrrell, 11 Feb. 1904, BM, Add. MSS. 44928.163.
[2] *The Times*, no. 37,331, 2 March 1904, p. 15.

von Hügel's use of a pseudonym was justified beyond question by the similar use of the writer he was answering, it was also prompted by a growing realization of the serious hopelessness of Loisy's position and the utter intransigence of the Roman authorities. 'I have not myself only to think of', he wrote to Tyrrell in explaining why he had not signed *The Times* letter with his own name, 'but a dear wife, only by affection with me in this attitude, and three good girls to marry. I really must, short of low cowardice (and, as for *that*, I have already by my signed *Pilot* article and two letters – last one on 23rd January, to Card. Merry, shown my colours beyond a shadow of a doubt), now avoid directly prodding or worrying the powers that be.'[1]

On 11 February von Hügel received a letter from Loisy telling him that the latter's second submission had been refused by Rome. Sending the letter on to Tyrrell that very day the Baron told him that 'it seems clear, that Rome is determined not to let him off, under less than his own interior self-annihilation'.[2] Immediately von Hügel set about arranging for various articles to be published in the event either of Loisy's suspension as a priest or of his complete excommunication. He also wrote to Loisy suggesting that the latter should not accept excommunication with silence.[3] On the last day of the month Loisy sent a *cri du coeur* directly to Pius X. 'Most Holy Father,' he wrote in a simple, direct and non-curial manner,

I know the universal kindness of Your Holiness, and it is to this heart of Yours to which I address myself today.

I wish to live and die in communion with the Catholic Church. I have no desire to help on the destruction of the faith in my native land.

It is not in my power to destroy in myself the result of my researches.

As far as I am able I submit to the judgment brought against my writings by the Congregation of the Holy Office.

As proof of my good will, and in order to pacify others, I am ready to give up my course of lectures at Paris, and I shall suspend publication even of the scientific works which I have in preparation.[4]

Loisy's abandonment of his lectures at the Sorbonne and of his publications was a truly great personal sacrifice, and this more than anything

---

[1] Von Hügel to Tyrrell, 5 Feb. 1904, in *Von Hügel and Tyrrell*, p. 143. Von Hügel has made a mistake in his dates here. Loisy himself only learned on the 23rd of Merry del Val's refusal of his submission. The Baron received this information from Loisy on the 25th and wrote to Merry del Val on the 26th. See, *Diaries*, 25–6 Jan. 1904, and *Mém.* II, pp. 319 and 324.

[2] *Diaries*, 11 Feb. 1904; von Hügel to Tyrrell, 11 Feb. 1904, BM, Add. MSS. 44928.162.

[3] *Diaries*, 14 Feb. 1904.

[4] *Mém.* II, p. 351.

else at the time is an objective indication of his sincere good will. Rumours of his excommunication by Rome abounded, and both Italian and French newspapers even published it as fact. On 12 March he was summoned before Cardinal Richard to hear the Pope's answer to his letter. What he heard was one of the main factors in detaching his heart forever from the Roman Catholic church.[1] The Pope began by denying Loisy's sincerity. He said that all of Loisy's other declarations were rendered meaningless by his insistence that he had not the power to destroy within himself the result of his researches. If Loisy's declarations were to be accepted in Rome, the Pope concluded, 'it is absolutely essential that he admit his own errors, and that he submit completely and without reservation, to the judgment pronounced against his writings by the Holy Office'.[2] The remainder of the interview with Richard was stormy. After returning to his residence in Bellevue, Loisy penned the following few lines to Richard: 'Monsignor, I declare to Your Eminence that, out of a spirit of obedience to the Holy See, I condemn the errors which the Congregation of the Holy Office has condemned in my writings.'[3] This was Loisy's last effort to appease Rome. It was never formally accepted, but Loisy was left in relative peace for four more years. The rumours of an impending excommunication remained for a time, and then were later replaced with other rumours of a syllabus of propositions to which Loisy and others would be forced to subscribe. The real reason for Rome's temporary abandonment of the pursuit of Loisy, however, was the growing involvement of the papacy in the French church–state crisis. Pius X was increasingly intervening in the French hierarchy's own attempted solutions to their problems with the state, and the risk of a French reaction to an outright Roman excommunication of Loisy was too great at that particular moment in history.

---

[1] *Ibid.* pp. 362–3. Pius X's letter to Richard for Loisy is printed in full in Cenci's *Il Cardinale Raffaele Merry del Val*, pp. 187–8.

[2] *Mém.* II, p. 361. 'But as in Galileo's case, they will not stand the frank holding, in science and hence as subject to further scientific correction, points or facts as long as they appear acutely to conflict with the Faith. Yet we all bear, as well as we can, the presence of "evil" in a world rightly proclaimed by us to be the handiwork of the all-powerful, all-knowing, all-good God. No antimony presented by the historico-critical workers comes near to this one, in its stupendous weight.' Von Hügel to Ward, 10 March 1904, WFP, vH MSS.

[3] *Mém.* II, p. 367.

CHAPTER 7

INTERLUDE IN L'AFFAIRE LOISY

FOR NEARLY THREE YEARS following Loisy's interview with Cardinal Richard in March of 1904 communication between the abbé and the Roman authorities ceased. No one, least of all Loisy or von Hügel, was led to believe that the Loisy affair was ended. It had only been temporarily shelved, and an eventual showdown was inevitable. At first no one seemed to realize that the war of nerves had actually reached even a temporary respite, and when the Paris correspondent for *The Times* commented on the probable results of the Vatican's 'successful stifling of the Abbé Loisy',[1] von Hügel put into print a plan prepared months earlier. In January Thomas Bailey Saunders had written to Loisy to console him on his condemnation by Rome, and to express himself on the matter of intellectual freedom and Vatican obscurantism. Loisy had answered the letter at once, saying that it was not yet possible to estimate the consequences of the condemnation, but giving his own ideas on its implications and making clear his own understanding of his personal responsibility to truth and to his science. Bailey Saunders had shown the correspondence to von Hügel, and the latter had obtained Loisy's permission to publish the two letters in *The Times* in the event of Loisy's excommunication.[2] However, when *The Times* printed their article about Loisy from their Paris correspondent, treating the matter as a closed issue, and suggesting that the Vatican had demanded and obtained an absolute and unqualified submission from him, von Hügel decided that the time was right for publishing the Bailey Saunders–Loisy letters. Without consulting Loisy, the Baron touched up Loisy's letter, and wrote a half-column introduction himself.[3] In this introduction he denied that Loisy had been forced to sacrifice his intellect, stating that the real fact was 'that the Abbé's last act of submission, despatched by Cardinal Richard to Rome as far back as March 17, which there is good reason to trust will turn out to have been acceptable to Rome, was not meant or understood by himself as a renunciation of his entire

---

[1] *The Times*, no. 37,371, 18 April 1904, p. 15.
[2] *Diaries*, 14 Jan., and 3, 6, 12, and 17 Feb. 1904.
[3] *Diaries*, 26 April 1904.

historico-critical conscience'.[1] Yet the sort of annihilation which *The Times* writer was speaking of seems almost to be admitted by von Hügel in his following paragraph when he wrote: 'It is true that the Abbé has abandoned his lectureship at the Sorbonne, and has offered not to publish any further works within the next few years; that this double sacrifice appears a very great, and, taken in itself, a very saddening, self-immolation to all his many friends; and that he has made it in the belief that it would be acceptable to the Roman authorities.' After going over both letters and the introduction with Bailey Saunders, von Hügel sent the documents to *The Times*, and they were printed on the last day of April.[2] The *Matin* of Paris reprinted Loisy's letter alone, without von Hügel's introduction or Bailey Saunders' initial letter, and with no further explanation.[3] When he saw the *Matin*, Loisy was upset at the thought of how this indiscretion might unsettle the delicate balance of his relations with ecclesiastical authorities. Other papers, however, soon began to fill out the story of the correspondence, and von Hügel hastened to explain what had prompted him to act without Loisy's knowledge.[4]

The defence of Loisy which seemed to cost the Baron most, both emotionally and intellectually, was the article he published against his friend Maurice Blondel. From his first reading of *L'Évangile et l'Église* Blondel had been unhappy with Loisy's implicit Christology.[5] Eventu-

---

[1] *The Times*, no. 37,382, 30 April 1904, p. 6.

[2] *Diaries*, 27, 28, and 30 April 1904.

[3] *Mém.* II, p. 383. *The Tablet* did almost the same thing that the *Matin* had done. A week after the correspondence had appeared in *The Times*, *The Tablet* (vol. 103, no. 3339, 7 May 1904, pp. 743–4), published Loisy's letter, without either von Hügel's introduction or Bailey Saunders's initial letter, but with this introduction: 'Replying to an Anglican who had expressed sympathy with him abbé Loisy wrote the following letter on January 8, which was published in *The Times* on Saturday.' Abbot Gasquet then wrote a letter to *The Tablet* (vol. 103, no. 3340, 14 May 1904, p. 776), in which he complained that Loisy's letter had been unjust to Merry del Val since it seemed to imply that Merry del Val's letter to Cardinal Richard at the time of Loisy's December condemnation had been an expression of his own private opinions rather than an expression of the Pope's mind and intentions. Gasquet's intrusion annoyed the Baron and he proposed to Bailey Saunders that the latter answer Gasquet's letter, and even suggested what he should say in a general way (*Diaries*, 17 May 1904). In the next issue of *The Tablet* (vol. 103, no. 3341, 21 May 1904, p. 817) Bailey Saunders's letter appeared. He denied that Loisy's letter was open to the implication which Gasquet was so eager to find in it; he pointed out the unfairness of publishing Loisy's letter without the context in which it had appeared in *The Times*; and he insisted that to publish the single letter out of context and without any explanation of why the correspondence had now, at so late a date, been put into print was a further injustice. 'But I cannot stand by', Bailey Saunders concluded, 'and see a friend exposed to possible misrepresentation through a failure to mention matters essential to a full and fair view of his attitude.'

[4] *Mém.* II, pp. 383–4.

[5] Blondel to abbé Wehrlé, 10 Dec. 1902, in René Marlé, *Au cœur de la crise moderniste*, Paris, 1960, p. 49. This entire volume is a study of the history-and-dogma conflict of the

ally he wrote a long essay on 'History and Dogma', attempting to solve the philosophical problem he felt Loisy had evaded.[1] It was published in three instalments of *La Quinzaine* during January and February 1904. What Blondel disliked about Loisy's work was the latter's insistence on taking a purely historical view of the Gospels, prescinding from all metaphysics and theology as unattainable by historical method. By this historicism, as Blondel called it, Loisy could treat Christ's knowledge, for instance, as purely human, and imply that if there was divine omniscience in the earthly Jesus, the historian found little evidence for it. Yet Blondel seemed to think that Loisy was somehow trying to justify the objects of faith on purely historical grounds.

In early March 1904 von Hügel began an answer to Blondel.[2] Later in the month he wrote what he considered an important letter to Blondel, telling him, among other things, that he felt the latter had little understanding of what Loisy was actually saying, and that to have this understanding one needed 'a sympathy more or less instinctive' for Loisy's work.[3] The Baron felt Blondel lacked this instinctive sympathy because he had no real appreciation for any study of the merely relative and contingent, i.e. the purely historical. Henri Bremond translated the Baron's article into French,[4] and it was published in *La Quinzaine* on 1 June[5] with the title 'Du Christ éternel et de nos christologies successives'. The first two, and larger parts of the article, were a profound statement of the meaning of Christ for the Christian,[6] and the third part was an

---

modernist crisis, from Blondel's point of view, and is based primarily on the correspondence in the Blondel Archives at Aix-en-Provence.

[1] The copy of Blondel's 'Histoire et Dogme' used here by the author was von Hügel's own off-print, found in the von Hügel collection at the St Andrews University Library, von Hügel unbound papers, Box no. 10. For the English translation see Maurice Blondel, *The Letter on Apologetics and History and Dogma*, translated by Alexander Dru and Illtyd Trethowan, London, 1964.

[2] *Diaries*, 19, 23, and 24 Feb., and 3 March 1904.

[3] *Diaries*, 19 March 1904. 'Je crois que vous comprenez fort peu Loisy. On ne comprend bien que ce pour quoi l'on a une sympathie plus ou moins instinctive. Vous ne l'avez pas cette sympathie. Ce n'est nullement un péché: mais enfin vous montrez bien les conséquences d'un tel manque. Je crois aussi que, tout à fait en dehors de lui, vous n'arrivez point à une idée *intérieure* et de contact sympathique quant à l'esprit, au caractère, à la fonction de l'étude du contingent et du relatif.' Von Hügel to Blondel, 19 March 1904, in *Au coeur de la crise moderniste*, p. 218.

[4] *Diaries*, 22 and 29 April, and 2, 3, 4, 6, 8, 9, and 10 May 1904. Bremond arrived in London on 3 May 1904 from Paris, and spent a week at the Baron's Kensington home. In the summer of 1903 von Hügel had moved from Hampstead to Kensington, and at 13 Vicarage Gate, Kensington, he lived until his death.

[5] Poulat, *Histoire, dogme et critique dans la crise moderniste*, p. 575, is mistaken in saying that von Hügel's article was published on 1 April. It was not even completely written by that date.

[6] Two weeks after von Hügel's article appeared in *La Quinzaine*, he had a request from the

appeal to Blondel to take the Incarnation seriously. Christian faith demands historical facts. Although historical facts neither cause faith (philosophically speaking) nor explain it, without them there can be no belief in the Jesus who was really man as well as God. Von Hügel suggested that Blondel was unwilling to make a sufficient distinction between historical phenomena and their spiritual significance.[1] One of the points on which Loisy had most insisted was the fact that historical criticism cannot establish the existence of the spiritual realities which are the objects of Christian faith.[2] Blondel seems to have misunderstood Loisy completely on this point, and thought he claimed too much for historical method. Von Hügel pointed out that Blondel was unwilling to allow for an adequate distinction between the earthly Jesus and the heavenly Christ, though the distinction is as old as St Paul's theology itself. In

Italian Christian-Democrat priest Romolo Murri to translate the first part of the article (*Diaries*, 13 June 1904). Within less than a month the Baron had received the Italian off-print from the *Cultura Sociale* for 1 July 1904 (*Diaries*, 8 July 1904).

[1] 'Du Christ éternel et de nos christologies successives', *La Quinzaine*, vol. LVIII, 1 June 1904, p. 21. The copy of this article used by the author was von Hügel's own off-print found in the von Hügel collection at St Andrews University Library, von Hügel unbound papers, Box no. 5. The pagination for the off-prints is different from that of the article as it originally appeared.

[2] Most of the writers who have treated of the Blondel–von Hügel controversy have been Frenchmen and Roman Catholic clerics with a theologico-metaphysical bias in approaching the problem here involved. Blondel and his sympathizers really did fail to understand historical method, both in its manner of proceeding and in the objects of its research. All that von Hügel was trying to express in the controversy was that what a believing Christian knows about Jesus Christ through faith, he does not know as a result of the application of historical method to the few really historical phenomena concerning Jesus of Nazareth which are now available to the historian. But when he said this, Blondel and the others, thinking in metaphysical categories, immediately presumed that the Baron was postulating two really separate and distinct Jesus Christs. When the Baron, and Loisy too for that matter, spoke of the Jesus historically reconstructed from the phenomenological evidence left to history, and of the Jesus of faith, he was not making an absolute separation in the *object* of one's knowledge. Rather he was separating the *methods* by which one knows, each method attaining different aspects of the ultimately one object of knowledge. That Blondel's defenders never really accepted the different methodologies involved, nor apparently understood them, is exemplified by Maurice Nédoncelle, *La Pensée religieuse de Friedrich von Hügel*, Paris, 1935, p. 200, when he wrote: 'Le problème de l'existence et celui de la nature sont inséparables dans l'histoire profane. A combien plus forte raison le sont-ils dans la détermination des origines chrétiennes!' But *existence* and *nature* are metaphysical categories and are never, as such, the object of historical science, and method. When Nédoncelle writes (p. 201): 'En séparant la critique et la foi, en établissant le Christ sur deux plans à peu près entièrment séparé, Loisy a suggéré au Baron une conception qui était au fond très peu hügelienne', he shows both his misunderstanding of the type of 'separation' von Hügel and Loisy were talking about and fighting for, and he also shows a lack of knowledge of the history of von Hügel's thought. This distinction, which Nédoncelle finds 'très peu hügelienne', is discernible in the Baron's Notes to Ryder of 1891 – nine months after he had first heard the name of Loisy, before he had either corresponded with or met Loisy, and before Loisy had published anything other than his history of the Old Testament canon! The distinction is profoundly 'hügelienne'.

Blondel's thought the Jesus of history seems to disappear into his Christ of faith, and this most clearly shows itself when Blondel speaks of Jesus's self-consciousness. For von Hügel's tastes Blondel showed too great a certainty about the limits, contents, and mode of Jesus's knowledge as both God and man; the Baron preferred to admit that one who approaches Jesus both historically and with Christian faith confronts an insoluble mystery in this matter of Jesus's knowledge and self-understanding.[1] Nevertheless, he would insist that one who approached the Synoptic Gospels as just an historian, as Loisy had tried to do, would find definite limits and lacks in the knowledge of the man Jesus, i.e. his own belief in the proximity of his second coming. And these lacks and limits had to be faced, regardless of what problems they might pose for theology or Christian philosophy. When von Hügel's article was attacked by Blondel's friend the abbé J. Wehrlé in a later issue of *La Quinzaine*, the Baron was especially pained because he detected the hand of Blondel in the most personal and violent sections of the article.[2] He answered Wehrlé briefly, and there the discussion ended as far as von Hügel was concerned.[3]

By the summer of 1904 the frantic activity of the winter and spring had eased off, and von Hügel was able once again to resume work on his study of St Catherine of Genoa and the mystical element of religion. A physically exhausting but psychologically rewarding event of that summer for the Baron was the ten-day visit which Archbishop Mignot paid him. Besides sights of interest to a foreign visitor, von Hügel arranged for Mignot to meet an extraordinary number of outstanding men in English academic, religious and political life.[4] This was the

[1] 'Du Christ éternel et de nos christologies successives', *La Quinzaine*, pp. 25–7.

[2] 'As to myself, I have had an article published against my "Xt. Eternal" in the "Quinzaine" of Aug. 16th, which has been in so far a pain to me, as I have inevitably recognized, in over one half, and precisely in the most strenuously rhetorical, most implacably heresy-hunting paragraphs, not only the inspiration but the actual writing of my close friend Maurice Blondel; and that I cannot avoid admitting to myself that, even tho' he is sincere in his opinions, his present distinctly feverish and over-emphatic insistence upon them, cannot be altogether dissociated from the storm-clouds visible on the ecclesiastic heavens.' Von Hügel to Bishop, 16 Sept. 1904, in *Dublin Review*, vol. 227, no. 460, April 1953, p. 182.

[3] *Diaries*, 30 and 31 Aug.; and 1–5 and 21 Sept. 1904.

[4] The Baron wanted Mignot to meet a certain number of people and to visit certain places, but because the Archbishop neither spoke nor understood spoken English, and since von Hügel was himself deaf, this involved much anxious pre-arrangement. On 16 July von Hügel met Mignot at Charing Cross Station, and from then until the morning of the 27th, when Mignot left again for France, nearly every hour had its set engagements. Drives through the more scenic parts of London were mixed with, for instance, a visit to Archbishop Bourne, lunch at the Deanery of Westminster Abbey with the Dean, Armitage Robinson, dinner at the House of Commons as guests of James Hope (Wilfrid Ward's brother-in-law) and with Sir R.

English leadership that von Hügel wanted the French prelate to glimpse at least, because this was the England for whom a Vatican condemnation of Loisy could only be understood as a repetition of the Galileo affair, and before whom the Baron had tried for so long to gain a sympathetic hearing for the Roman church.

The year which had opened with such anxiety seemed to draw calmly to a close, though the anxiety had only gone underground. In the November number of *The Fortnightly Review*, Robert Dell tried to summarize the actual state of things in his trenchant article on 'The Crisis in the Catholic Church'. To Dell the issue at stake was 'whether and how far it will be possible in the future for traditional Christianity to retain its hold on educated men'.[1] The problems creating the current crisis, he said, were from the areas of philosophy and history, and they were 'felt with particular force in the Catholic Church, since the official Church is at present committed to a system of philosophy discarded by all philosophers (including those that are Catholics) and to a view of history that cannot be supported by evidence'. This commitment to worn out theories by the Roman officials was maintained with a claim to absolute authority in every area, and resulted in condemnations or frustrations for nearly every Catholic capable of independent thought. 'In the English Catholic body few of the laity', Dell wrote, 'and fewer still of the clergy, take any interest in intellectual matters; but there are signs of grave mischief among the younger laymen even in England.' Since Rome was not likely to moderate nor to limit her claims to absolut-

---

C. Jebb, Lord Hugh Cecil and George Wyndham. Another day was spent in visiting the Tower, and then to St Paul's where Arthur Headlam gave them a conducted tour; an afternoon reception for various of the Baron's friends like William Gibson, Basil Maturin and Dr van den Biesen; and dinner with Lilley and his wife and Miss Maude Petre. Two days were spent in Oxford, with Lilley accompanying them since he was 'at home in colloquial French'. The Baron and Mignot were guests of J. A. Smith of Balliol, where they had lunch in the common-room and were entertained to dinner, and where von Hügel had his first sight of Edward Caird. The second day in Oxford included lunch at New College with Hastings Rashdall, tea with the Master of Balliol, and dinner at Magdalen as guests of Clement Webb. From Oxford they travelled to Cambridge, where they met the Baron's mother and brother, and were entertained by various of von Hügel's friends. A morning trip to Ely, where they were met at the station and then shown over the cathedral by Bishop Lord Alwyne and Lady Compton, was followed by an afternoon reception given by Dom Cuthbert Butler, and followed by dinner at Trinity College where they were entertained afterward by F. C. Burkitt and Sedley Taylor. Back in London there were more receptions and more visits to museums and places of interest. The final day was spent at Eton where Lord Kynnaird's son accompanied them over the school and 'little Sidney Herbert came to lunch', and from Eton they toured the grounds and state apartments of Windsor Castle. (*Diaries*, 16–27 July 1904.)

[1] *The Fortnightly Review*, no. CCCCLV, new series, 1 Nov. 1904, p. 846. Further quotations from this article are taken from this same page and pages 850, 855, and 860.

ism, Dell felt impelled to answer both the Ultramontane and the Agnostic who would query his remaining in the Roman church. His answer very much anticipated those which many of the men condemned as modernists within a few years would give, and was basically a statement of the fact that his faith was not ultimately dependent on the unsubstantiable claims of a clique of authoritarian extremists. 'In that faith we look, not backward', Dell wrote, 'but forward, with confidence to the Church of the future, however dark may be the immediate outlook.' And in conclusion he observed that 'the experience of the last thirty years almost justifies one in prophesying that the historian of the future will regard the definition of papal infallibility as a turning point in the history of the Catholic Church, marking the climax of the era of absolutism and scholastic dogmatism – and the beginning of their decline'. As soon as the early November issue of *The Fortnightly* was on the bookstalls, von Hügel sent a copy off to Loisy, remarking that he thought Dell's article 'excellent'.[1]

The year 1905 and the early months of 1906 were again a relatively tranquil period for von Hügel's efforts to help Loisy and to gain breathing space for critical studies in the Roman church. Loisy felt that von Hügel was too patient and sanguine in evaluating the real situation, but Loisy was far more emotionally agitated than was the Baron by the Vatican's interference in the French church–state relations which were at the peak of their crisis. 'The events of 1905–1906 concerning the separation of church and state in France', Loisy reflected years later, 'contributed as much as the directly ecclesiastical acts and my own laborious thought on the religious problem to erase the last traces of profound attachment which I had for the church.'[2] But if von Hügel preferred to be optimistic and hopeful about the direction of Loisy's thought and affection and even about his ecclesiastical future, it was at least partly Loisy's own fault. 'Loisy wrote me such a beautiful, calm, happy, humorous letter, a week ago'; the Baron told Maude Petre,

he is engrossed in field-and-farm-work; and is full of gratitude that, just when he badly required this complete rest and tonicking of nerves and brain, he is able to get it, in the best form, – that form most appropriate to himself. He

---

[1] *Mém.* II, p. 416. 'Le 1er Nov. parait aussi un art. dans la "Fortnightly Review", par M. Dell (vous l'avez vû ici), qui me semble (je l'ai soigneusement lie en épreuves) fort opportun et puissant, – Je ne vois pas comment les autres sauront ou l'ignorer ou y repondre. Il montre comment toute l'apologetique, tout la science et critique Catholiques vraiment serieuses et effectives ont été fait *en dépit de Rome*.' Von Hügel to Mignot, 28 Oct. 1904, SAUL, MS. 30306/26.

[2] *Mém.* II, p. 441. See also, von Hügel to Ward, 26 Jan. 1907, WFP, vH MSS.

believes that Rome will move again, as soon as ever Church and State are really separated.[1]

However, the Baron was himself no more indifferent to the Vatican's misplaced interference in political matters than in its interference in scientific and historical matters. When he read in *The Daily Chronicle* of 2 March 1906 that Pius X had attacked the Pastoral Letter on church–state relations which the liberal Bishop Geremia Bonomelli of Cremona had written for his diocese,[2] and that the Pope had ordered the Bishop to appear before the Holy Office on the 8th for a formal retraction, von Hügel spoke up.[3] He sent Bonomelli a telegram, written in French, which only he could have composed in the circumstances: 'Profound respect – lively sympathy – complete assurance that God will aid to combine deference to authority with resounding loyalty to principle of common law – unshakeable foundation of English Catholicism – Baron Huegel – London.'[4]

In the autumn of 1905 von Hügel met for the first time the Reverend Gerald Christopher Rawlinson, the Anglican curate of St Barnabas, Pimlico.[5] Rawlinson was not only well read in French classical spirituality and ecclesiastical literature generally, but was very well informed on current developments in France and was sympathetic to Loisy. Although Rawlinson came to the Baron's home at least once that autumn

[1] Von Hügel to Petre, 5–7 Sept. 1905, BM, Add. MSS. 45361.11.

[2] For a very strong attack on Bishop Bonomelli in the English Catholic press, and a rejection of the principle of separation of Church and State, see *The Tablet*, vol. 107, no. 3435, 10 March 1906, p. 373.

[3] Bonomelli was an old man in 1906, having been born in 1831. He was consecrated Bishop of Cremona at the age of 40, and remained in that post until his death in 1914. He was largely concerned with a Christian approach to contemporary social problems, and had already been condemned by the Index for his efforts to work out a realistic existence for the church in Italy *vis-à-vis* the new Italian state. But to Vatican intransigents of that period, a willingness to abandon the claims to temporal power by the papacy was tantamount to heresy. Consequently, when Bonomelli sided with the majority of the French bishops in desiring to cooperate with the French government at the time of the Separation Laws in France, Pius X who was interfering in the French church–state crisis was bound to be annoyed. Von Hügel knew of Bonomelli, but had no contact with him until 18 November 1902 (*Diaries*) when he both sent the bishop a copy of Loisy's *L'Évangile et l'Église* and wrote him a letter. He received an answer on 15 December (*Diaries*) which has apparently been lost, but which must have impressed von Hügel since he continued to send Bonomelli off-prints of articles and books relevant to Loisy's struggle during the following years.

[4] *Diaries*, 3 March 1906. 'You will have read about Mgr. Bonomelli's trouble, – at 75, after 50 years of Priesthood and 35 of Episcopate. He may have been a bit tactless, and his details may be wrong and his enthusiasm excessive: but as to the substance of his contention, – will any of your Reverences kindly get up and preach in any English Pulpit the contradictory of that, and let us see the reception of it! Why, even Farm Street would not dare to do so!' Von Hügel to Dom Cuthbert Butler, 7–8 March 1906, DAA, Butler MSS.

[5] *Diaries*, 6 Oct. 1905.

for tea, the curate's crippled condition probably explains the fact that von Hügel himself carried books and back issues of Loisy's *Revue d'histoire et de littérature religieuse* to the former at his residence in Warwick Street.[1] When Rawlinson was travelling in France in the autumn of 1906, von Hügel arranged for him to visit Loisy. On his return he told the Baron that

at the risk of boring you I must write to tell you of my visit to M. Loisy. I spent a night at Dreux on my way from Rouen to Chartres, & drove over to Garnay, spending about a couple of hours with M. Loisy. I tore myself away at the end of that time for fear of trespassing unduly on his kindness. He was most kind & friendly, which touched me very much, & saw me off with a most hearty *au revoir*. One thing he said struck me very much, though I am sure on thinking it over that he is right, namely that the great question of the next twenty years will be, not any critical questions, but the fundamental question of all – *la question de Dieu*. He told me that his seven years leave to say Mass in his own house expired on the 18th October, a week after I saw him, & that he had applied to Rome for a renewal, but had not then had an answer. You will hear what the result of that application is, & if you would let me know I shall be deeply interested to learn. He told me that, unlike Harnack, his opinions did not get nearer to tradition as he went on. I must thank you very sincerely for the opportunity you gave me of making his acquaintance, it was more than a pleasure to me.[2]

The permission to celebrate Mass was not granted, and Loisy offered his last Mass on 1 November 1906, twenty-seven years and four months after his first one.[3]

In late November 1905 Lady Mary von Hügel had gone to Paris and Rome for a six weeks holiday with a friend. Shortly before returning to England, she had an audience with Pius X, on 4 January 1906, in which she was very outspoken in favour of Loisy.[4] She told the Pope that if he had read the correspondence between her husband and the abbé, he would have been most edified. As the Baron told Loisy, she really did not know what Loisy's ideas were, but she simply followed the impulse of her heart. Pius X was, apparently, both impressed and amused, and he admitted to Lady Mary that Loisy was a brave man but 'a little too excited about a certain idea'.[5] As the year 1906 progressed, however,

---

[1] *Diaries*, 18 Oct., and 14 and 20 Nov. 1905.

[2] Rawlinson to von Hügel, 26 Oct. 1906, SAUL, MS. 2916. See, also, *Diaries*, 11 and 27 Oct. 1906. W. J. Sparrow Simpson in his Memoir of G. C. Rawlinson, *An Anglo-Catholic's Thoughts on Religion*, London, 1924, p. xxiv, seems to have known only of Rawlinson's visit to Loisy in 1908 and not of the visit in 1906.

[3] *Mém.* II, p. 493.

[4] *Diaries*, 4 and 8 Jan. 1906; *Mém.* II, pp. 462–3.   [5] *Mém.* II, p. 463.

there was increasingly less evidence that the Vatican was either impressed or amused with the ideas of von Hügel's friends. In March the Pope had personally attacked Bishop Bonomelli. In April Dell wrote to the Baron to tell him that the Paris newspapers had carried the story of a new decree of the Index, condemning Fogazzaro's *Il Santo*, Laberthonnière's *Essais de Philosophie religieuse* and *Le Réalisme chrétien et l'Idéalisme grec*, and Paul Viollet's *L'Infaillibilité du Pape et le Syllabus*.[1] In all of these works von Hügel had taken great delight,[2] and on the very day he heard the news of their condemnation he wrote letters of sympathy to Laberthonnière and Viollet.[3] A few days later Wilfrid Ward paid him a visit and told him that the epilogue to Ward's own *The Life and Times of Cardinal Wiseman* had been denounced to Rome by Archbishop Bagshawe,[4] the former Roman Catholic bishop of Nottingham. And a week later, while von Hügel and his wife were spending a few days at the Royal Crown Hotel in Sevenoaks, Kent, they heard a very depressing sermon preached, 'as to how the Church was coming back to the Age of Catacombs'.[5]

As the darkness seemed to increase all round, two English laymen, converts to the Roman Catholic church, approached von Hügel with the suggestion that they and some like-minded laymen should meet to discuss the situation and to try to determine whether anything could be done to help alleviate it. The originator of the idea was G. B. M. Coore, a senior examiner on the Board of Education and a fellow member with von Hügel of the London Society for the Study of Religion; his seconder was Robert Dell, the outspoken journalist. Von Hügel agreed to the meeting, and to its being held at his own house in Kensington, 'on con-

---

[1] *Diaries*, 10 April 1906.

[2] Von Hügel's own copy of Viollet's *L'Infaillibilité*, which was presented to him by the author, is at St Andrews University Library, with the von Hügel unbound papers, Box no. 4. In von Hügel's handwriting the following is inscribed on the inside of the 1st page: 'Étudie: Avril 28, 1905 – Un travail excellent. Je ne voudrais rien changé, si ce n'est, les pp. 50–57, qui, je ne sais pas trop pourquoi, me semblent faibles; et certaines touches aux pp. 107, 108, qui me semblent trop *autoritaires*. Tout le reste est admirable.'

[3] *Diaries*, 10 April 1906.

[4] *Diaries*, 14 April 1906. Interestingly, Maisie Ward, *Insurrection versus Resurrection*, London, 1937, pp. 221, 228, 235, seems to know of neither a rumour nor a fact of Bagshawe's denunciation of her father's *Life of Wiseman* before 1907. '... you will have heard, – [Wilfrid Ward] has been denounced by Archb. Bagshawe for "Heresy" in his "Functions of Prejudice" to Holy Office. I wish W. W. no evil, but honestly think this experience may be very good for him.' Von Hügel to Butler, 7–8 March 1906, DAA, B. MSS. In another letter of this same time von Hügel speaks of Bagshawe denouncing both Ward's *Wiseman* and his 'Functions of Prejudice' (von Hügel to Petre, 17 April 1906, BM, Add. MSS. 45361.33, also quoted in de la Bedoyère's *Life of Baron von Hügel*, p. 182).

[5] *Diaries*, 22 April 1906.

dition that there was no kind of commitment to anything beforehand', and on the understanding that von Hügel was himself 'averse to any action previous to a serious modification by Rome of the present *status quo*.'[1] The Baron hoped that Edmund Bishop would be able to chair the meeting, and when Bishop could not, von Hügel wrote to tell him why he had wanted his leadership.

You are now the one Catholic layman in England, – at least any one of mental training and activity, – who has been through the fiery waters of 1870, – through them as then already a formed, thoughtful man; and you are the most finished and thorough Historical Critic and Scholar of any kind that we Catholics, lay or clerical, have got in this country.[2]

Most of the invitations to attend the proposed meeting were sent out by Dell. Von Hügel, however, invited the young Lord Acton and Professor Bertram Windle, the President of Queen's College, Cork. Acton was in Spain at the time and Windle in Ireland, and, besides, von Hügel sent Acton's invitation in Windle's envelope and *vice versa*, so that the meeting had come and gone before the confusion was straightened out.[3] The meeting was held on 2 May, with ten men in attendance. The Baron chaired it and Coore assisted him.[4] Coore's main intention in desiring such a meeting was to try to determine how

to seize a right and fitting opportunity and mode for letting the Authorities know unmistakably that all this silence and deference, on the part of such men as himself, must not be taken as assent to this their present policy and action towards men and work which have helped the faith of these silent and deferential men, amidst hard trials:

'This *did* and does seem to me', von Hügel told Bishop, 'a thing to give satisfaction to, if and when we can'.[5] Coore seems to have thought that either a public Declaration on this point, or a Deputation to Archbishop Bourne, would be the most suitable form of action. Edmund Bishop had suggested by letter that perhaps an Address of appreciation for

[1] Von Hügel to Bishop, 23 May 1906, *Dublin Review*, vol. 227, no. 461, July 1953, p. 289.
[2] Von Hügel to Bishop, 3 May 1906, *Dublin Review*, vol. 227, no. 461, July 1953, pp. 285–6.
[3] *Diaries*, 25 and 28 April; and 5 May 1906.
[4] '8.30. Meeting here, 13 Vicarage Gate: 10 present: I, in Chair; Coore, my right hand man; James Hope; Corrance; Bland; Stokes; Dell; Gibson; Williams; Sir R. Blennerhasset: to consider if anything cd. usefully be done, in this crisis for Bibl. critical & Rel. philosophy.' *Diaries*, 2 May 1906. Michael de la Bedoyère, *Life of Baron von Hügel*, p. 183, has mistaken 'critical' for 'Political' in transcribing this passage.
[5] Von Hügel to Bishop, 23 May 1906, *Dublin Review*, vol. 227, no. 461, July 1953, pp. 289–90.

presentation to Loisy would be appropriate. The one positive decision reached on the evening of 2 May was to draw up such an Address for Loisy, to be presented to him in the event that Rome drew up a Syllabus of propositions which he would be required to sign and accept, and that being unable to sign he would be excommunicated.[1]

The Address, as it came to be conceived, was never intended as a challenge to ecclesiastical authority; rather, it was thought of by the men who proposed it as a discharge of a duty in conscience, at a time when to remain silent would be an act of moral cowardice. The Address was intended strictly as an affair of Roman Catholic laymen,[2] and it was to be signed by a small group of men whose positions and attainments would stress the quality, rather than the quantity, of those concerned about Loisy's condemnation. Edmund Bishop, who eventually backed out of associating himself with the document altogether, suggested that, rather than have the Address composed in English and then translated into French, it would be preferable to have it actually composed in French. Von Hügel accepted this idea and first approached M. François Thureau-Dangin, a former pupil of Loisy and a promising young Assyriologist, thinking that he might be willing to write the final text of the Address.[3] Thureau-Dangin refused absolutely to be associated with the Address in any way,[4] and the Baron then approached Edouard LeRoy who, eventually, accepted the responsibility.[5] At first von Hügel hoped for six prominent signatures from each of England, France, Italy,

[1] *Diaries*, 2 May 1906; von Hügel to Bishop, 23 May 1906, *Dublin Review*, vol. 227, no. 461, July 1953, p. 290.

[2] Von Hügel to Bishop, 23 May 1906, *Dublin Review*, vol. 227, no. 461, July 1953, p. 291.

[3] *Ibid.* p. 291. François Thureau-Dangin had built for Loisy a cottage on his own country estate near Dreux, and it was there that Loisy resided from the time of his retirement from Neuilly until the spring of 1907.

[4] 'I first of all wrote to François Thureau-Dangin ... [who] answered as enclosed, – letter no. 1 – His answer settles *him*: but I expect he is wise, for I am convinced he is determined not to cease harbouring L., even if all happens that we fear; and his keeping thus out of *everything*, even so correct an affair as ours, would probably render such action more feasible without causing too great a shock.' Von Hügel to Bishop, 13 June 1906, *Dublin Review*, vol. 227, no. 461, July 1953, p. 294.

[5] *Diaries*, 7, 13, 19, 26 and 30 June 1906. From the very first LeRoy told the Baron that he would be honoured to help with the Address, but feared that his name being attached to it might cause more harm with the authorities than von Hügel cared to risk. LeRoy, mathematician and philosophical disciple of Bergson, had published an article entitled 'Qu'est-ce qu'un dogme?' in *La Quinzaine* for 16 April 1905. The article immediately caused an ecclesiastical uproar. It was published in book form in 1906, together with some of LeRoy's answers to his critics, and this volume, entitled *Dogme et critique* was put on the Index in 1907. Von Hügel overcame LeRoy's scruples about accepting the task of composing the Loisy Address. See, LeRoy to von Hügel, 9 June 1906, SAUL, MS. 2750; LeRoy to von Hügel, 24 June 1906, SAUL, MS. 2751.

Germany, Austria, and even Russia.[1] Within a very few weeks, however, he was beginning to realize how hopeless so ambitious a project really was, as post after post brought polite, and sometimes not so polite, refusals to be associated with an Address to Loisy. Antonio Fogazzaro, who had agreed to obtain the Italian signatures, alone was successful in persuading the full number of acceptable men to sign the document; and, when even England and France could ultimately muster only four signatures apiece, he had the embarrassing task of asking two of the Italian signatories to retire.[2] Von Hügel's inability to find English Catholic laymen of social or intellectual standing who were willing to sign the Address was characteristically demonstrated in his efforts to obtain Lord Acton's support. On 17 July von Hügel entertained Acton to lunch. They had their meal alone while the Baron explained to the younger man his own views on Loisy's situation and its importance. Acton was 'kind, but very "correct" and cautious, and asking to refer everything to his wife'.[3] Nevertheless, von Hügel gave him Tyrrell's *Letter to a Professor* and *The Church and the Future* in the hope that these might reinforce his own words. Several days after the luncheon engagement Acton wrote to the Baron, hesitating about signing the Address, but not actually refusing. After a few more weeks had passed von Hügel wrote again to Acton a long letter, asking outright for his signature. Finally, on 13 August Acton agreed to sign. As the weeks and months went by, however, it became increasingly clear that there would be no representation from Germany and Austria, let alone Russia, and to find even a fourth French name of real stature seemed like an impossible task. By early December the Baron felt that in fairness he must tell Acton of the state of affairs as regards the German and French signatures, since the maturity and responsibleness of the foreign signers had apparently been one of the conditions for Acton's finally agreeing to sign himself. Four days after writing to Acton the Baron had the former's answer; he had backed out of the project entirely.[4] It was not until the spring of 1907 that even four satisfactory French signatures had been obtained,[5]

[1] *Diaries*, 17 Aug. 1906; and 2 April 1907.
[2] *Diaries*, 4, 9, and 21 June; 31 July; 3 and 20 Aug. 1906; 18 and 23 Feb. 1907.
[3] *Diaries*, 17 July 1906.
[4] *Diaries*, 20 July; 8 and 13 Aug.; 6 and 10 Dec. 1906.
[5] *Diaries*, 28 March 1907. It was only in the previous month that the Baron had finally decided to settle for four signatures, since almost no Frenchmen of any standing were willing to sign the Address (*Diaries*, 12 Feb. 1907). In late January von Hügel had written to LeRoy to tell him that if proper French signatures were not soon forthcoming, he would have to cut down the English and Italian signatures to four (*Diaries*, 28 Jan. 1906).

and that von Hügel was at last able to give the document with its twelve signatures to a printer in Fleet Street. The printed Address itself was to have been given to Loisy, and copies of it were to have been printed in leading newspapers in England, France, and Italy.[1] A few months after the Address had been printed, however, Loisy's position had become so ambiguous that the publication of the document could not possibly help him, and it could cause serious harm to the men who had signed it. Loisy himself, consequently, asked that they withdrew it, which they did.[2]

During this year of turmoil over the Loisy Address and the effort to obtain signatures, von Hügel became involved in one last major symbolic act of defence, not only of Loisy, but of the larger cause of intellectual freedom and honesty within the Roman Catholic church. In late June of 1906 the Pontifical Biblical Commission issued a decision which stated that Catholics must hold the Mosaic authorship of the entire Pentateuch, though they were free to hold that Moses had employed a number of secretaries who 'faithfully recorded his meaning, writing nothing against his will, and omitting nothing'.[3] Since the Biblical Commission had not been established to act as another tribunal for settling questions of orthodoxy, von Hügel at first insisted on accepting this decree merely on its merits 'of helfpulness, – of its workableness along the lines of scholarship'.[4] He considered it, of course, completely hopeless along these lines, and another victory for the 'neo-scholastic, utterly un-historical, un-critical minds' in Rome. In late August the Baron had a letter from Padre Semeria, calling the Commission's decision 'simply grotesque' and giving him good reasons for thinking that

an attempt is to be made, with this *ballon d'essai*, to impose these positions as *scientific* and with *scientific authority*. If the Decision is well, or at least silently, received, it is to form part of the coming 'Syllabus', – probably at New Year, and such incorporation would inevitably mean an accession of *doctrinal* authority. If so then *all that is done, between now and then, to make this as yet only would-be scientific decision appear wise and right, will but help its transformation into a far more binding, a 'dogmatic' proposition.* And if and where any criticism is

---

[1] *Diaries*, 14 Aug. 1906.

[2] *Mém.* II, p. 613. 'P. C. from Loisy, *releasing all signatories* of "Lettre" from presenting it' (*Diaries*, 21 Jan. 1908). One of the original copies of the Address (or 'Lettre' as von Hügel sometimes refers to it), written in LeRoy's hand, is among the von Hügel manuscripts at St Andrews University Library.

[3] *Acta Sanctae Sedis*, vol. 39, 1906–7, p. 377.

[4] Von Hügel to Ward, 20 Aug. 1906, WFP, vH MSS.

impossible, there a suggestive silence and embarrassment would certainly be, I think, the right and alone solidly helpful line to take.[1]

Von Hügel was writing to Wilfrid Ward, who, as editor of the diocesan owned and controlled *Dublin Review*, might be in a position 'where any criticism was impossible'. But the Baron was not in such a position, and he was determined to do what he could to prevent this Roman decision from becoming a dogmatic proposition. He felt he could best achieve this objective by bringing about a public outcry against the decision by scholarly and serious men. While he and Lady Mary were spending their late summer holiday near Haslemere, von Hügel wrote to Professor' Driver, proposing that the latter write a critique of the Pentateuch decision for publication either in *The Times* or in *The Guardian*.[2] Several days later he wrote to Professor Charles Augustus Briggs, asking him also to write a criticism for publication in some prominent place, and sending him a copy of the Roman decision as published in *The Tablet*. Von Hügel had met Briggs for the first time in November 1897 while in Rome, and since that time the two men had corresponded on biblical and allied topics, and Briggs had visited the Baron in London. Although Driver answered von Hügel with a flat refusal to do anything in the way of criticising the Pentateuch decision, Briggs, who was vacationing in Genoa, sent von Hügel a formal 'Letter' on the Biblical Commission decision which the Baron was free to place in whatever publication he should think best.[3] He wrote to Briggs suggesting that the 'Letter' be altered into a query, and von Hügel himself then proposed to express his own ideas as an answer to Briggs's query. He then wrote to Sir James Knowles, the editor of *The Nineteenth Century*, to ask if he would be willing to insert in the November number of his journal a correspondence between Dr Briggs and himself in respectful but firm criticism of the recent Roman decision.[4] Meanwhile, at Haslemere, the Baron was

[1] Von Hügel to Ward, 30 Aug. 1906, WFP, vH MSS.

[2] *Diaries*, 25 Aug. 1906.

[3] *Diaries*, 28 and 31 Aug. and 9 Sept. 1906. There seems to be no evidence for de la Bedoyère's statement (*Life of Baron von Hügel*, pp. 186–7) that von Hügel wanted to associate with himself an Anglican scholar in publicly attacking the Biblical Commission's decision, that he asked Driver to join in this project, and that, when Driver refused, he turned to Briggs. The evidence, on the contrary, quite contradicts this version. The Baron's diaries show that he first wrote to Driver, merely asking him alone to attack the decision in either *The Times* or *The Guardian*. Before the Baron had any answer from Driver, he also wrote to Briggs, asking him to place a similar criticism in some journal. Only several days after writing to Briggs did the Baron receive Driver's letter, refusing to attack the decision. Moreover, it was the form of Briggs's own open 'Letter' to the Baron which seems to have suggested the query–response approach which ultimately associated von Hügel with Briggs in the attack.

[4] *Diaries*, 14 Sept. 1906.

enjoying the company of F. C. Burkitt, Norrisian professor of divinity at Cambridge and a scripture scholar, who likewise was on holiday there with his family. The two discussed the whole Pentateuch question and the implications of the Biblical Commission's decision, as they rambled across the Devil's Punch Bowl and over the undulating Surrey country-side.[1]

On the same day that von Hügel heard from Knowles agreeing to a 'favourable consideration' of a Briggs–von Hügel correspondence for the November *Nineteenth Century*, he also had a note from Briggs together with the latter's formal 'Letter' altered according to the Baron's suggestion. At once he began making a few revisions in Briggs's query, and then began work on his own response. By 12 October the two 'Letters' were in Knowles's hands.[2] The Baron, who believed that Rome would soon be issuing a syllabus of condemned propositions, including the proposition that Moses had not composed the Pentateuch, considered it of the utmost importance that his correspondence with Briggs should appear at once in print so as to have time to make its impression. Accordingly, when more than a week had passed without any communication from Knowles, he gave the editor an ultimatum, and the manuscript was promptly rejected.[3] At this development von Hügel decided to publish the correspondence as a small book. After once more going through the whole manuscript to settle on final corrections, this time with Tyrrell's help, the Baron wrote to Longmans to ask for an interview. On the afternoon of 1 November he had an interview with Mr Charles Long-man who readily agreed to publish the correspondence as a pamphlet of sixty pages, cloth bound, at a retail cost of half a crown. One thousand copies were to be printed, the authors were to receive a royalty, and the book was guaranteed to be in circulation before the month was out.[4] Almost at once von Hügel began trying to find French and Italian publishers to issue translations of the correspondence. When he wrote to the Casa Editrice Docca, he promptly had a return telegram telling him that they were not interested. He then asked Semeria to try to find an Italian outlet, and he himself wrote to Picard in Paris to ask if they would bring out a French translation.[5] On 9 November von Hügel returned Longmans's proofs corrected, and sent a copy of these to his young French

[1] *Diaries*, 17 Sept. 1906.
[2] *Diaries*, 20, 24–9 Sept., and 5, 8, 9, and 11 Oct. 1906.
[3] *Diaries*, 23–4 Oct. 1906; von Hügel to Ward, 30 Aug. 1906, WFP, vH MSS.
[4] *Diaries*, 28–9 Oct., and 1 Nov. 1906.
[5] *Diaries*, 2, 5 and 8 Nov. 1906.

friend Augustin Leger,[1] a disciple of Blondel at that time living in
England, to ask if he would make the French translation, if Picard
accepted. On the following day the Baron received a telegram from
Picard agreeing to publish the French translation, and he in turn at once
telegraphed to Leger to tell him that the plan was on. When he had
Leger's letter of acceptance two days later, the Frenchman had already
translated half the little book. By the 17th, the French translation, carefully revised by von Hügel, was in the post to Picard, and within a few
more days the Baron had agreed to let the Italian translation appear as
part of the initial number of the journal *Il Rinnovamento* which was to be
launched in January.[2] On 3 November von Hügel had written the little
prefatory note which introduced the book, and on the 6th he determined
on the title – *The Papal Commission and the Pentateuch*. Only then did he
write to Briggs to tell him of all the arrangements and revisions that he
had undertaken in both their names.[3]

By the middle of November the book was ready for distribution, and
von Hügel sent his first and only free copies to his eldest daughter
Gertrude, then resting at Cannes, to Loisy, and to Semeria. Immediately
he set about enlisting the aid of friends to place helpful reviews of the
book in all the prominent newspapers and journals in England. Lilley,
Rawlinson, Barry, Headlam, and a number of others, all promised to do
whatever they could for the volume.[4] When he wrote to John St Loe
Strachey of *The Spectator* to solicit help for the book, he had in return a
'most warm letter, promising perhaps a leader'.[5] The editor was true to
his word, and took the occasion to notice both *The Papal Commission and
the Pentateuch* and Tyrrell's *A Much-Abused Letter* in a lengthy leader
under the heading 'Liberal Roman Catholicism'. The Baron, no doubt,
would have preferred a different tone and emphasis from that which St
Loe Strachey gave, and especially so in the writer's concluding paragraph. 'How can the Roman Church do as these men would have her?'
he wrote.

With the millstone of her own infallibility round her neck, how can she pursue
the truth and seek the strayed sheep down the new paths which science has

[1] Leger had been a student of Blondel at the École Stanislaus in the 1890s. In the first
years of the twentieth century he lectured at Lavel University in Canada, and then returned
to Europe, spending a number of years in England. He was one of the original members of the
Sillon group in France which was condemned by Pius X in 1910.
[2] *Diaries*, 5, 10, 12, 13, 14, 15, 17, 18, 25, 26, and 28 Nov. 1906; and 13 Jan. 1907.
[3] *Diaries*, 3, 6 and 7 Nov. 1906.
[4] *Diaries*, 14, 16 and 17 Nov. 1906.
[5] *Diaries*, 19–20 Nov. 1906.

made for humanity? How can she cast aside the false treasure of her sanctified ignorance and start afresh in Christian poverty ready to enter the Kingdom of Heaven as a child?[1]

A happier approach, from von Hügel's point of view, was Arthur Headlam's review in *The Times Literary Supplement* which seemed to the Baron rather 'longish' for a mere notice of such a book in such a journal, and which he thought was 'very good'.[2] When von Hügel told Briggs what he had done about publishing their correspondence on Rome's Pentateuch decision, the latter responded: 'We did not do the thing for gain or for renown, but in a spirit of love and of sacrifice; and we must be prepared for a good deal of misconception and abuse.'[3] Although the misconception and abuse would come later, the Baron could still write to a friend at the year's end that *The Papal Commission and the Pentateuch* had 'as yet received only one unfavourable review'.[4]

The late winter and early spring of 1907 was a time for concluding yet unfinished business and, as the Baron fully realized, of preparing for new and difficult contingencies ahead. He had been asked to write the article on 'The Gospel of St John' for the 11th edition of the *Encyclopaedia Britannica*, and this was to have been in the editor's hands by the end of 1906.[5] But 1906 had been a difficult year, and von Hügel had to ask for several extensions of his dead-line. And only in May 1907 was the article finally finished.[6] In April the completed Address to Loisy had at last been ready for the printers, and, most importantly, in April too the definitive manuscript of the Baron's *Mystical Element of Religion* was handed over to an International Publishing Bureau in Covent Garden

[1] *The Spectator*, no. 4092, 1 Dec. 1906, p. 878.

[2] *Diaries*, 10 Dec. 1906. Headlam began by saying: 'To any one interested in theological progress the struggle at present going on in the Church of Rome for freedom of thought in matters of Biblical criticism is of profound interest.' And he concluded the review by saying: 'We would only add two things in conclusion. Although these letters deal with the situation in the Roman Church, there is little in them which will not be applicable to any Christian Church; and all those who are interested in or disturbed by Biblical criticism will find what they say valuable. It is of enormous importance for the good of the nations whom it teaches that the Roman Church should clear itself of those unnecessary restrictions on thought which make it so difficult for an educated man of science in countries where it holds sway to be a believing Christian' (*The Times Literary Supplement*, no. 256, 7 Dec. 1906, p. 410).

[3] This passage is quoted in a letter written by von Hügel to Delehaye, 5 Dec. 1906, AS des B, vH MSS.

[4] Von Hügel to Delehaye, 29 Dec. 1906, AS des B, vH MSS. The unfavourable review was in a Unitarian Journal called *Christian Life*.

[5] *Diaries*, 14 July, and 4 Aug. 1905; 19 and 22 Feb., 18 Sept., and 5, 6, 10, 12, 13, 14 Dec. 1906. Friedrich von Hügel, 'John, Gospel of St.', *The Encyclopedia Britannica*, 11th ed., vol. xv, Cambridge, 1911, pp. 452–8.

[6] *Diaries*, 15, 18, 22, 24, and 27 Dec. 1906; 5, 24, 29, and 31 Jan., 14 and 26 Feb., 5, 9, and 11 March, and 14 May 1907.

for placing with a satisfactory publisher. On the same day that von Hügel left his *magnum opus* with the publishing bureau, his youngest daughter Thekla entered the Carmelite convent at St Charles Square, Notting Hill, to begin life as a nun.[1]

Two days later he and Lady Mary left London for a week in Paris. There they visited old friends, and the Baron met for the first time Edouard LeRoy with whom he had corresponded so frequently over the Loisy Address during the past year. He called on abbé Huvelin and 'found him very gouty, but as movingly spiritual and great as ever'. At a small gathering he saw Père Laberthonnière who had 'a worried, angry look and tone not him'.[2] He went to a meeting under the abbé Portal's auspices which was attended by about '40 young men', three-quarters of whom were clerics, and whom he addressed on 'The "New Theology" and Religion in England'.[3] On the same day he was taken by LeRoy to visit Henri Bergson, and the two had a 'long talk'.[4] But the most moving event of the week was his visit to Loisy. They spent most of a day together at Garnay near Dreux, and von Hügel left his *Encyclopaedia Britannica* article with Loisy to read. They walked back together in the late afternoon towards the place where the Baron could catch the Paris train. Because Loisy's health was bad, he would be leaving Garnay within a few days to return to Montier-en-Der where his few remaining relatives lived.[5] But as the two men walked 'along the upper High-road' toward Dreux, their thoughts and hearts were heavy. Both sensed that they were not likely to meet again, and both knew that the months and years immediately ahead were likely to destroy completely all that for which they had both longed and worked.[6]

[1] *Diaries*, 6 April 1907. Duncan Macpherson, 'Baron von Hügel on Celibacy', *The Tablet*, vol. 223, no. 6741, 2 Aug. 1969, p. 757, is mistaken when he asserts that 'his daughter Thekla decided to become a nun in 1910'. She had been in the Carmelite convent for three years by 1910.

[2] *Diaries*, 10 and 12 April 1907.

[3] *Diaries*, 14 April 1907. On the previous 4 March von Hügel had agreed to write a review of R. J. Campbell's *New Theology* for *The Christian Commonwealth* on condition that he have three weeks to prepare it, a certain word limit which he considered adequate, perfect liberty to express his 'respectful' opinions, and would receive 100 off-prints of the review (*Diaries*, 4 March 1907). The editor accepted his conditions (*Diaries*, 8 March 1907), and on the 15th von Hügel received Campbell's book. Because of the pressure of events the review was not ready for the editor until 21 June, and then it had to be turned down, perhaps because of excessive length (*Diaries*, 21 and 27 June 1907). On 4 July von Hügel sent it to the editor of *The Albany Review*, and there it was eventually published (Friedrich von Hügel, 'The Relations Between God and Man in "The New Theology" of the Rev. R. J. Campbell', *The Albany Review*, vol. 1, Sept. 1907, pp. 650–68).

[4] *Diaries*, 14 April 1907.   [5] *Mém.* II, pp. 518–19.

[6] *Diaries*, 11 April 1907; *Mém.* II, p. 516.

CHAPTER 8

FRIENDSHIP WITH TYRRELL AND MORE CONFLICTS WITH AUTHORITY

BARON VON HÜGEL had first been attracted to Loisy because of the latter's discriminating biblical scholarship both within and for a church which had fallen woefully behind in such critical work. He was first, and continually, attracted to George Tyrrell because of the latter's penetrating and discerning emphasis on the more mystical aspects of religion[1] within a church whose official emphasis had become, he thought, too much centred upon scholastic rationalism and the external, structural aspects of religion.[2] But even before the nineteenth century had completely run its course von Hügel told Tyrrell that 'it is, alas, so evident that they [the Roman authorities] really fear as much, and understand as little, even sane and sober Mysticism, as they do critical and scientific method'.[3] As the Baron shared with Loisy his critical interests and was to suffer for and with him because of them, so did he share with Tyrrell his mystical and specifically religious interests and would also suffer for and with him.[4] But von Hügel's sharing in each of the two situations was different. For Loisy he had mounted a publicity campaign in England, and had exerted as much direct influence as he could in Rome itself. For Tyrrell, on the other hand, there were no such efforts. The reason for

[1] The expression 'mystical aspects of religion' is used here in the sense in which von Hügel distinguishes the 'mystical' elements from the 'institutional' and from the 'intellectual' (i.e. analytic, philosophic or scientific) elements in his *The Mystical Element of Religion*. Of this mystical element he wrote: 'Man's emotional and volitional, his ethical and spiritual powers, are now in ever fuller motion, and they are met and fed by the third side of religion, the Experimental and Mystical. Here religion is rather felt than seen or reasoned about, is loved and lived rather than analyzed, is action and power, rather than either external fact or intellectual verification.' Baron Friedrich von Hügel, *The Mystical Element of Religion As Studied in Saint Catherine of Genoa and Her Friends*, vol. 1, London, 1908, p. 53.

[2] For Tyrrell's ideas concerning the effects of scholasticism on genuine religion see, Tyrrell to Bailey Saunders, 25 Oct. 1907, in M. D. Petre's *George Tyrrell's Letters*, London, 1920, pp. 53–4.

[3] Von Hügel to Tyrrell, 4 Dec. 1899, in *Selected Letters*, p. 81.

[4] 'Then Father Tyrrell was ever a mystic; and I myself have found full religious peace only since deeply spiritual Catholic clerics helped me to understand and to assimilate the simpler elements of the great Catholic mystics. So we have a central requirement and help in common; and it was in this interior life that I ever longed to see his sorely harassed soul continuously find its fundamental peace.' Von Hügel, 'Father Tyrrell: Some Memorials of the Last Twelve Years of His Life', *The Hibbert Journal*, vol. VIII, No. 2, Jan. 1910, p. 235.

the difference in von Hügel's activities on behalf of the two men is twofold. In the first place, Tyrrell's aims and efforts did not lend themselves as readily to objective defence as did Loisy's, because they were less easily separable from his own personality. Tyrrell's thought grew in the directions in which, as a matter of fact, it did develop, partly because of the conflicts and frustrating situations with which he was confronted. Loisy's thought was, in so far as the Baron was inclined to defend it, scientific and objective. Von Hügel was as concerned about Loisy's person as he was about Tyrrell's. But it was Loisy's scientific rights and work that the Baron's campaign was concerned with primarily. Tyrrell's writings were far less easily separable from his personal problems within the church. Then, secondly, Tyrrell's first major conflicts with authorities came later than Loisy's earliest difficulties; they reached critical proportions at a time when the barest hope of modifying the extreme Roman line and attitude against any liberal thought was, to all practical purposes, gone. Consequently, von Hügel's relationship with Tyrrell was less overtly dramatic than his relationship with Loisy, but it was no less poignant or significant. In the course of their exchanges the differences between the two men, differences not only due to temperament but also due to their varying estimates of men and of circumstances, became somewhat marked. Yet the underlying bond of their relationship seemed only to deepen. To follow some of the more important developments in this quiet exchange will demonstrate the nature and extent of their friendship, but it will also add another dimension to the understanding of von Hügel's involvement in the modernist crisis on the English scene.

George Tyrrell was nearly nine years von Hügel's junior, having been born in Dublin on 6 February 1861.[1] He was raised with his older brother and sister in genteel poverty by his mother, as his father had died several weeks before George's birth. His brother's seering scepticism about every aspect of religion seems to have helped to start the adolescent Tyrrell on a religious quest which eventually led him into the Roman Catholic church in 1879. In the following year he joined the English Province of the Society of Jesus, and embarked on the long years of ecclesiastical training demanded by that order. He was ordained a priest on 20 September 1891, and spent the two following years in further

[1] M. D. Petre, *Autobiography and Life of George Tyrrell*, vol. I, London, 1912, p. 3. All of the factual material contained in this paragraph is to be found in this two-volume work. The first volume consists of Tyrrell's own autobiography, covering the years 1861 to 1884, and arranged, with supplements, by Miss Petre. The second volume, written by Miss Petre, covers Tyrrell's life from 1884 until his death in 1909. Henceforth, *Autobiography and Life*.

ecclesiastical studies, before being sent to St Helen's in Lancashire for a year of pastoral work. In 1894 he was assigned to St Mary's Hall, Stonyhurst, as philosophy master to the young Jesuit students. His zeal for the doctrine of Thomas Aquinas, in accord with the directives of Leo XIII's *Aeterni Patris*,[1] and in opposition to the traditional Jesuit preference for their own Suarezian doctrine, led to his removal in 1896 to the Jesuit residence at Farm Street in London.[2] From this London base, in a very short time, Tyrrell's reputation as a confessor, a retreat-master, and a director of men and women with 'religious problems', grew to impressive proportions. Although he had contributed his first article to *The Month* in 1886, it was likewise from his Farm Street days that his *Month* articles, and eventually the books to which they often gave rise, began to attract attention.

On 20 September 1897 von Hügel wrote his first letter to Tyrrell, whom he had never before met nor even seen.[3] He told the thirty-six-year-old Jesuit priest that he had been impressed with his recently published *Nova et Vetera* which so abounded with 'ideas and tendencies that have now for long been part and parcel of my life, its aims and combats'.[4] The Baron also invited Tyrrell to lunch or tea at the latter's earliest convenience. On 9 October the two men met for the first time.[5] At even this first meeting they seem to have recognized in one another the shared source of hopes and aims toward which they would work together in the

---

[1] *Acta Sanctae Sedis*, vol. XII, Rome, 1879, pp. 97–115. When the Franciscans continued to follow Bonaventure and Duns Scotus in their seminary teaching, rather than the Dominican Aquinas, Leo XIII addressed a letter to the order's superior: 'De studio majorum disciplinarum satis commonstrant Litterae Nostrae Encyclicae *Aeterni Patris*, qua sit ingrediendum via. Discedere inconsulte ac temere a sapientia Doctoris angelici, res aliena est a voluntate Nostra eademque plena periculi.' *Acta Sanctae Sedis*, vol. XXXI, Rome, 1898–9, p. 264. A similar letter, but a secret one, was said to have gone out to the Jesuit General, since Suarez and the seventeenth century Spanish Jesuit scholastic theologians were still preferred in Jesuit institutions to Aquinas. When Wilfrid Ward objected to an article which had maintained that there was an attempt being made to subject the intellectual life within Roman Catholicism to 'Thomism pure and simple', von Hügel responded: 'Indeed it is supported by the fresh fact of that secret encyclical to the Jesuits. *That* and the Letter to the General of the Franciscans closes the door upon any attempt to describe such action as a simple slowness in adopting new paths: *it is not a question of slowness of movement, but of a marked movement backwards.* One need surely only stop and try and realise for a minute what it means to order the Franciscans, after 5 centuries, to drop St. Bonaventure, and the Jesuits, after 2 centuries and more, to drop Suarez and Vasquez – to see that this is so; indeed it is so to such a degree, that from the excess will, I think, spring the remedy: whether you or I will stand it, may (I think does) matter little except for our interior sincerity: but these orders themselves will not stand it, – not for ever and aye.' Von Hügel to Ward, 30 May 1899, WFP, vH MSS.
[2] *Autobiography and Life*, II, pp. 40ff.
[3] *Diaries*, 20 Sept. 1897.
[4] Von Hügel to Tyrrell, 20 Sept. 1897, in *Von Hügel and Tyrrell*, p. 10.
[5] *Diaries*, 9 Oct. 1897.

following years – the common desire to eliminate the sectarian spirit in its various manifestations within Roman Catholicism. Their eventual conflicts with authority, too, and ultimately their failure, were largely due to the triumph of this sectarian spirit.[1]

Von Hügel planned to leave England at the end of October with his family for six months in Rome. However, his eldest daughter Gertrude, then twenty years old, was undergoing a period of religious uncertainty and reaction which the doctor diagnosed as an 'over-wrought state of nerves and imagination', and which he hoped to cure by 'a six months' complete change of environment'.[2] The change of environment seems to have meant primarily being away from her family, and consequently Gertrude was not to accompany them to Rome that winter. The Baron wrote to Tyrrell to tell him of his daughter's trouble, and told him that Gertrude 'much fancies, what I too would much like, that she should come to you, if not for ordinary confession, at least occasionally for sympathy or advice'.[3] He also told Tyrrell that he would like to discuss his daughter's situation with him before he himself set out for Rome. Tyrrell, accordingly, spent the afternoon of the 27th with the Baron, and from that time undertook the spiritual direction of his eldest daughter, at least for the duration of von Hügel's Roman sojourn.

In the course of the following few months Tyrrell wrote several letters to Gertrude's anxious father, informing him of her progress, in so far as he could without any breach of confidence. He likewise pointed out to the Baron that a certain amount of the responsibility for Gertrude's religious difficulties were due to her father's over-eagerness to share his own mature religious ideas, problems and aims with her. Tyrrell warned

[1] See, von Hügel to Ward, 14 Oct. 1897, WFP, vH MSS. By 'sectarian spirit', as used here, is meant a denial in practice of the mystical element of religion, and the excessive and authoritarian insistence on all aspects of the institutional elements which, in turn, are rationalized and justified by a single, and therefore necessarily narrow, official theological system. After reading A. Houtin's *La Question biblique chez les catholiques de France au XIXe siècle*, Paris, 1902, which von Hügel had sent to him (*Diaries*, 27 March 1902), Tyrrell commented on the roots of such sectarianism: 'I was most keenly interested in Houtin's book which is surely a strange revelation. That authority should blunder now and then were natural; but to see it always & systematically on the wrong side suggests a sort of inverted infallibility that is hard to account for on natural principles until one digs down to "the roots of all evil". These formulate themselves more & more clearly in my mind, as (1) the political conception of the Church, embodied in the claim to temporal power; (2) the substitution of the mechanical pseudo-consensus of seminary text-books for the consensus ecclesiae which I might call "scholasticism"; (3) the principle of "protection" which adapts the environment to the organism, to the prejudice of true vitality; embodied in Jesuitism.' Tyrrell to von Hügel, 12 April 1902, BM, Add. MSS. 44928.11.
[2] Von Hügel to Tyrrell, 19 Oct. 1897, in *Von Hügel and Tyrrell*, p. 14.
[3] *Ibid.*

von Hügel that he had

neglected St. Paul's caution against giving to babes the solid food of adults. The result is indigestion. Things that your formed mind can easily swallow, without any prejudice to simple faith, may really cause much uneasiness in a mind less prepared ... If you want your daughter's company you must shorten your steps and walk slowly, else she will lose her breath in her desire to keep up with you.[1]

But already von Hügel had partly come to the same conclusions about Gertrude's trouble, and Tyrrell's admonitions and suggestions were humbly and heartily accepted. The Baron was less anxious over the fact that Gertrude seemed to have lost, temporarily at least, her faith in the church and in fundamental Christian dogma, as over the fact that she seemed to have lost 'true creatureliness of mind'. He told Tyrrell that he had written to his daughter telling her

how this moral, humble, creaturely attitude towards God, one's own ideals; one's own achievement compared with those ideals; one's own achievement compared with others' achievements – the consciousness of incompleteness and of failure, of one's life being unlivable without its being lived co-operatively between the soul and God – how I found this in several friends who are no Catholics, no historic Christians of any kind; and that, as long as she can keep, and by daily practice and prayer ever regain this spirit, I can wait so far happily, quite indefinitely, as I should feel that she keeps in her the germ of full life, and is still living, in her degree, the one true life, and is still moving in the one true direction.[2]

To Catholics less secure, perhaps, in their faith than her father, and certainly more narrow in their approach to Catholic life and practice, Gertrude's attitude and remarks were a source of scandal and dismay. When von Hügel's mother and sister tried more direct methods to bring her back to the practices and ways of thought which they considered essential, the Baron remonstrated that 'if they want to help, and not to do more harm, and not to deliberately go against my, her father's, deliberate wishes and unshakeable responsibility, they will leave her to God, and love her dearly all the same, only speaking as occasion serves'.[3] By the middle of February 1898 Tyrrell could already tell the Baron that he thought he detected symptoms of reaction in Gertrude against her scepticism and abandonment of Catholic practice.[4] Within a few weeks

[1] Tyrrell to von Hügel, 6 Dec. 1897, in *Von Hügel and Tyrrell*, p. 17.
[2] Von Hügel to Tyrrell, 26 Jan. 1898, in *Von Hügel and Tyrrell*, pp. 21 and 22.
[3] Von Hügel to Tyrrell, 26 Jan. 1898, BM, Add. MSS., 44927.17. This portion of the above letter was not published by Maude Petre.
[4] Tyrrell to von Hügel, 16 Feb. 1898, *Von Hügel and Tyrrell*, p. 26.

of von Hügel's return to England Gertrude had again assumed Catholic sacramental practice,[1] and what ever remained of her difficulties seems never again to have unsettled her seriously. Tyrrell's part in helping the young woman regain her spiritual balance was another reason for von Hügel's drawing closer to him in friendship.

Shortly after the Baron's return to Hampstead in the late spring of 1898 he was invited to contribute an article to *The Hampstead Annual* for that year. He chose to write about St Catherine of Genoa, probably because he had been especially interested in her life for some years and was familiar with the physical locale in which her life had been lived. On 30 May he told Wilfrid Ward that he was sending him 'a photograph of St Catherine of Genoa's portrait, – a photo I have just had taken, and which cannot be bought. Isn't it a winning countenance? I am writing a little paper on her.'[2] Apparently his paper had been promised for October, but by September he still had a third of it to write, and this was the most difficult section, i.e. that in which he tried to relate mystical theory to the concrete practice of the mystic he was writing about; and, even more difficult, that in which he tried to explain the relationships between her nervous illness, her so-called mystical phenomena, and the end result of her genuine mystical experiences. On all these points the Baron wrote long letters to Tyrrell, as much for the clarification of his own ideas as for seeking Tyrrell's advice and observations.[3] The paper was written and in the publisher's hands by 24 October, but by the end of the month von Hügel was in the hospital, and the correction and revision of the proofs was left to Tyrrell.[4] The article was printed before the year was out.[5] Sidney Mayle, the publisher, was apparently impressed with von Hügel's efforts, because he offered to publish at his own risk an expansion of the article into 'a little book on St Catherine of Genoa'.[6] From this small beginning grew the two stout volumes of von Hügel's *The Mystical Element of Religion As Studied in St Catherine of Genoa and Her Friends*. The undertaking coincided with the beginnings of the

[1] *Diaries*, 2 June 1898.

[2] Von Hügel to Ward, 30 May 1898, WFP, vH MSS.

[3] Von Hügel to Tyrrell, 26 Sept. 1898, in *Selected Letters*. pp. 71–4, and also in *Von Hügel and Tyrrell*, pp. 29–35; von Hügel to Tyrrell, 3 Oct. 1898, in *Von Hügel and Tyrrell*, pp. 41–7.

[4] *Diaries*, 31 Oct.; and 9 and 10 Nov. 1898. See also, von Hügel to Tyrrell, 27 Oct. 1898, in *Von Hügel and Tyrrell*, p. 53.

[5] Baron Friedrich von Hügel, 'Caterina Fiesca Adorna, the Saint of Genoa, 1447–1510', *The Hampstead Annual*, London, 1898, pp. 70–85. On the final page of the article, a *Postscript* makes the following declaration: 'The above article gives but the outlines of a little book which I am preparing for publication in the early part of 1899.'

[6] Von Hügel to Tyrrell, 21 Nov. 1898, in *Selected Letters*, pp. 74–5.

Baron's acquaintance with Tyrrell, and the final results were only published a few months before Tyrrell's death. The whole period of the two men's relationship coincided with the gradual growth of the Baron's book. The storms gathering around Loisy in the early years of the twentieth century, von Hügel's own ill health, and his many family problems and worries, all delayed the book's appearance year after year. At nearly each stage of the book's growth, however, von Hügel discussed aspects of it with Tyrrell. In 1901, for instance, he told Tyrrell that he was 'working at the doctrine chapter ... but the two points on which I would desiderate your special kind attention, are my English and my orthodoxy. What lies between these two poles I am more confident about. But without those two points in order the rest will hardly get a chance.'[1] Finally in the late summer of 1906 he sent the whole of the work in manuscript to Tyrrell for the latter's careful reading and critique, and from Tyrrell's pages of remarks von Hügel's final revision began.[2] The book was not published until December 1908, and Tyrrell's own lengthy estimate of it in *The Quarterly Review* coincided with his premature death in July of 1909.[3]

In November and December of 1899 Tyrrell published in *The Month* and in *The Weekly Register* respectively two articles of significance not only to his own career, but also, indirectly, to his relationship with von Hügel. The first of the two was entitled 'The Relation of Theology to Devotion', and was, apparently, considered by Tyrrell himself to be the best expression of his religious philosophy's main theme 'and as the kernel of whatever original contribution he had made to religious thought'.[4] Tyrrell was convinced that scholastic theology's excessive rationalizing both of the data of revelation, and of the spiritual realities of the Christian life, was turning Catholicism into an abstract and arid intellectual system, instead of helping it grow into the life it was meant to be. He did not deny the need for theological precision, abstraction and development, but he saw this rather as a corrective to any excessive anthropomorphism in religion which might result from the more

[1] Von Hügel to Tyrrell, 6 Aug. 1901, BM, Add. MSS. 44927.169.
[2] *Diaries*, 11, 17, 18 and 27 Aug.; 13 Sept.; and 6, 12 and 15 Oct. 1906.
[3] G. Tyrrell, 'The Mystical Element of Religion', *The Quarterly Review*, vol. 211, no. 420, July 1909, pp. 101–26.
[4] *Autobiography and Life*, II, p. 98. Von Hügel also acknowledged that 'there is nothing to which he [Tyrrell] himself (in numerous confidential conversations) attached greater importance than "Theology and Devotion",' and also that Tyrrell used to say that in this article 'he found, looking back, the root and substance of all he had striven and suffered for'. Von Hügel to G. E. Newsom, 7 Sept. 1909, in *Selected Letters*, p. 166.

spontaneous and popular reactions of faith. In his 'Relation of Theology to Devotion' article he expressed this with great strength and clarity.[1] Before the article was published Tyrrell sent it in proof sheets for von Hügel to read. After carefully reading through it twice, the Baron returned the proofs to Tyrrell, telling him that the article was his finest achievement to date, at least of the writings which he himself had yet read. 'It is of course a deep encouragement to me in my work', von Hügel continued,

– not only my book, but my poor life's work generally, – which is so entirely on these lines, which aims at them, – to find you giving such crystal-clear expression to my dearest certainties, to the line of thought and living which alone can and does bring me light and strength; and to find too, that you are let say these things in your Order, and by your Order.[2]

Tyrrell's second article, entitled 'A Perverted Devotion', and appearing in *The Weekly Register*, was not to receive so gentle a reception in and by his order. The article was an attack on the contemporary fashion among some theologians and preachers of describing with great certainty, and apparently with great self-righteous delight, the exact nature and duration of the punishment allotted to those damned to hell. Tyrrell preferred to admit the Christian doctrine of hell as simply a very great mystery, one difficult to reconcile with any just appreciation of the concept of an all-loving God. He insisted that the doctrine of hell was one of the most obscure of Christian mysteries, and he felt that those who could detail its torments and duration without seeing any apparent contradiction to other Christian doctrines had, indeed, a perverted devotion to the doctrine of hell. Von Hügel had gone abroad at the end of November, nearly three weeks before the article had been published, and it was in Rome in early January that he first read 'A Perverted Devotion'.[3] By the time he saw the article it had already been delated to the Jesuit General, and Tyrrell had been ordered to confine his writing to the Jesuit controlled *Month* until the offensive article had been examined and censured. The three priests appointed by the English

[1] George Tyrrell, S.J., 'The Relation of Theology to Devotion', *The Month*, vol. xciv, Nov. 1899, p. 473. The article was reprinted in *The Faith of the Millions*, first series, London, 1901, pp. 228–52.
[2] Von Hügel to Tyrrell, 8 Oct. 1899, in *Selected Letters*, p. 77. Von Hügel's enthusiasm for the article led him to send it to his various continental friends, and within months he was telling Tyrrell of Eucken's appreciation of it, and that Laberthonnière had arranged its translation into French for the *Annales de philosophie chrétienne*. Von Hügel to Tyrrell, 4 March 1900, BM, Add. MSS. 44927.102.
[3] *Diaries*, 7 Jan. 1900.

Vice-Provincial to examine Tyrrell's article all pronounced it 'theologically blameless and calculated to do good'[1] This judgment was unsatisfactory to the Jesuit superiors in Rome who decided to have the article re-examined there. At this juncture Tyrrell wrote to the Baron:

Bremond will have told you that my hell was not hot enough for the Spanish[2] taste, and I delayed writing in hopes of telling you the issue. The last oracle was: Quidquid sentiat Reverentia Vestra (our Vice-provincial) et consultores, hic Romae longe aliter sententiae and so on; but nothing definite, for the best of reasons that I left them nothing definite to get hold of, – tho' of course they can always say: 'Offensive to pious ears.' I wish they would define the precise length of a pious ear, and we should know where we were.[3]

When von Hügel answered, he expressed great sympathy for Tyrrell in his troubles. He told Tyrrell that 'since Newman's death, there has been no English-speaking Catholic whose work appeals to me, and pierces, I think, to the very centre of questions, to a degree at all really comparable to yours. And *your* trouble has, hence, been most really *my* trouble also.'[4] As to the condemned article itself, he felt that Tyrrell had never written anything quite so fine. 'It is so deep and tender, too, so full of the mystery of Faith and of the world unseen', he told him. But the Baron could also appreciate the annoyance of the paper's opponents, since 'they evidently feel themselves hit, without being able, really, to hit back. It is somewhat as with Loisy, as Duchesne says of him – he worries his antagonists, his whole attitude of mind and treatment of subjects being so different from theirs, that they slip about the premises, trying to find a common starting-point and measure, and failing utterly.' Tyrrell's situation became doubly complicated when, in an article having nothing directly to do with his own article, Robert Dell, writing in the April issue of *The Nineteenth Century*, complimented Tyrrell at the expense of the Society of Jesus.[5] The Jesuit authorities demanded that

[1] Tyrrell to von Hügel, 10 March 1900, in *Autobiography and Life*, p. 119.
[2] The Jesuit General at that time, Luis Martin, was a Spaniard.
[3] Tyrrell to von Hügel, 14 Feb., 1900, BM, Add. MSS. 44927.99.
[4] Von Hügel to Tyrrell, 4 March 1900, in *Von Hügel and Tyrrell*, p. 123.
[5] The offending sentence read: 'Above all, as was pointed out quite recently in a Catholic paper by an English Jesuit father, whose views seem to be as much out of harmony with the spirit of his Society as his abilities are superior to those of his *confrères*, our neo-scholastic theologians try to accommodate to reason mysteries which can only be accepted on faith.' Robert Edward Dell, 'A Liberal Catholic View of the Case of Dr. Mivart', *The Nineteenth Century*, vol. XLVII, no. 278, April 1900, p. 676. The main thrust of Dell's article was a condemnation of the principles which seemed to govern the Jesuit order as a whole at the end of the nineteenth century. When Wilfrid Ward wrote to von Hügel deprecating Dell's attack on the Jesuits, the Baron responded: 'I have been, necessarily and of course, much interested in your two letters, ... I can find but *one* criticism to make, – and it is the very one which Schell

Tyrrell publicly repudiate Dell and give a satisfactory re-statement of the doctrine of hell. The only repudiations and re-statements which Tyrrell was willing to write were rejected at Rome. Finally, one of the assistants to the Jesuit General dictated some statements which Tyrrell was ordered to accept and submit to *The Weekly Register* for publication. Tyrrell wove the statements into a letter which rendered them meaningless, and they were duly published.[1] Although this long, drawn-out affair had seemingly ended by June, this first formal check to Tyrrell's writing activities was the beginning of a series of restrictions and frustrations which would largely make the last nine years of his life a period of prolonged conflict.

During the summer of 1900 Tyrrell left the Farm Street community in London and took up residence at the Jesuit parish in Richmond, Yorkshire. He remained there until the end of 1905, and it was in the quiet and leisure of Richmond that the main ideas which dominated the final years of his life were clarified and refined. In trying to articulate the idea of Christianity more in Gospel terms than in those of scholastic theology and canon law, Tyrrell had come into conflict with ecclesiastical authority. It was this evangelical and mystical approach to religion which had initially brought about his relationship with von Hügel, and it was this approach which largely sustained and deepened the friendship.[2] As Tyrrell increasingly sought and took the necessary freedom for

---

made of me, when I urged upon him the wisdom (and indeed justice) of recognizing two drifts and tendencies amongst the S.J.'s, as really as elsewhere. He said: "I know, of course, that there are individuals amongst them, and the Bollandist body, who are wide enough; I also am aware that the Belgian and English Provinces are, even as wholes, more moderate and reasonable than others. But it would, for all that, be untrue and misleading to make it appear as though the influence of the order at headquarters, and inasmuch as official and determining, were not truly self-consistent and steadily repressive, – for *it is*." And he is no doubt right. Hence tho' I think that it *was* inconsiderate and wrong in Dell to quote Fr. T. by name, and though it may be unwise to present the Society as practically acting bodily on the repressive side, – yet the latter assertion is, in a very true sense, unfortunately correct. And for one who had made up his mind that this fact should be stated, – it was necessary, – as Schell urged upon me, – to in *some* way meet by anticipation the argument that would be sure to be brought forward by some, – of the existence of such types as T.'s in the Society. But this much does not justify, though I do think it largely excuses, D.'s action on this point.' Von Hügel to Ward, 5–7 July 1900, WFP, vH MSS.

[1] The details of this affair are given in *Autobiography and Life*, II, pp. 112–30; the letter to the Editor of *The Weekly Register* is reproduced in full on pp. 128–9. For Tyrrell's own description of the affair for von Hügel see, Tyrrell to von Hügel, 6 June 1900, BM, Add. MSS. 44927.115–16.

[2] Two years after their first meeting von Hügel told Tyrrell that he was 'the Catholic, with whom of all English-speaking ones, I feel myself the most completely at one. I have, of course, other gratefully cared for friends amongst them, but they are either not intellectually

expanding and expressing his religious philosophy and observations on the Christian life, his conflicts with authority increased proportionately. Eventually the conflict dominated and broke his life, though the mystical *attrait* ever struggled for expression to the end. While von Hügel encouraged Tyrrell in the development of his religious philosophy and spirituality, and could often appreciate the rightness of Tyrrell's strictures on the misuse of authority within the Church, he did not always agree with Tyrrell's methods of fighting that misuse. From the summer of 1900, the problem of authority within the church, not so much in the abstract as in the concrete experience of his own life and that of those he knew and worked for, came to dominate Tyrrell's thought and activities.

In June Tyrrell told von Hügel that he had been going over the history of the Vatican Council again, looking for a way out of the difficulties which the definition of papal infallibility seemed to occasion. 'I expect ecclesiastical infallibility really means that the Church is infallibly moving through tortuous paths to the right end, even when her back is turned to the goal', he told the Baron;

that we are infallibly right in holding to her winning, though many a hare may seem to out-strip the old tortoise for the present; that all heresy rises from forgetting the organic oneness of her doctrine, and tearing bits off and judging them as wholes in themselves, whereas they are essentially parts and lose their meaning and intelligibility when isolated.[1]

Tyrrell admitted that he was still groping his way on the problem. He also noted that he was 'struck by the apparently *radical* opposition of principle between Vaticanism and anti-Vaticanism; between viewing the Pope as the *mind* of the Church, and as merely the *voice* of that mind'.[2]

---

alive, or active largely on other subjects or in other directions, – at least more so than you are. The mystical attrait is a point that really speaks volumes, all round.' Von Hügel to Tyrrell, 17 Nov. 1899, BM, Add. MSS. 44927.88.

[1] Tyrrell to von Hügel, 6 June 1900, BM, Add. MSS. 44927.115–17.

[2] Tyrrell to von Hügel, 6 June 1900, BM, Add. MSS. 44927.118. A letter which Tyrrell wrote to Wilfrid Ward at about this time expands the same idea: 'The test question is: If the Scriptures and the Fathers and all written documents were destroyed (all allow that these are contingent), where lies the *depositum fidei*? In the Pope's single brain, or in the collective brain of Christendom? If in the former, then the Pope may say *L'Église c'est moi*; the Spirit works directly on his mind; and only through it on the Church. If in the latter, then the Pope is infallible in declaring the general mind in cases of sufficient magnitude to threaten unity; in such matters as formerly justified an Ecumenical Council; when he publicly and notoriously does investigate the *depositum fidei* contained in the general mind; then, as the Catechism says, he speaks as Head and Teacher of the Universal Church, in functional union with it; and not severed from it as a local bishop. It is, then, not a question of the "form" of a docu-

At the end of the year 1900 the Roman Catholic bishops of England created a situation which made the pieces of Tyrrell's puzzle on authority fall more readily into place. On 29 December Cardinal Vaughan and the fifteen bishops of the Province of Westminster issued 'A Joint Pastoral Letter on the Church and Liberal Catholicism'. The 'liberal Catholicism' which occasioned the bishops' Pastoral seems to have been that expressed in the recent articles and letters of the late St George Mivart. However, the bishops were far less interested in describing liberal Catholicism than in making explicit the nature and rights of authority within the Roman church. This latter they did in the most extreme and unqualified terms. Man has a 'Divine Teacher' with him upon earth to guide him in matters of salvation, the bishops asserted.

Now God Himself is the Divine Teacher of whom we speak. When our Lord Jesus Christ was upon earth, God spoke through the lips of His Sacred Humanity. After He had ascended into Heaven the Divine Teacher spoke through the mouth of Peter and the Apostles; and He now teaches and will continue to teach through their legitimate successors, 'until the consummation of the world'.[1]

For readers of the Pastoral to conclude that the bishops really believed that, just as once God spoke through the lips of Jesus of Nazareth, so now he speaks through the lips of the pope, was logical. The Pastoral also divided the church into two distinct and totally separate groups, the *ecclesia docens* and the *ecclesia discens*: 'the small body of chosen men, assisted by the Holy Ghost, who represent the authority of Jesus Christ; and the large body of the faithful taught, guided and guarded by the Divine Teacher, speaking through the audible voice of the smaller body'.[2] The *ecclesia docens* was limited to the pope ultimately, since the bishops were considered to be authentic teachers only to the extent that they were united to him in mind and will. The ecclesia *discens* was

---

ment, but of a fact which justifies the form. The "Immaculate Conception" was such a case obviously; the "Providentissimus" as obviously not. The *L'Église c'est moi* position is a perversion of the papal conception due to an ambiguity; where the true conception is a legitimate and necessary development of the dogma of ecclesiastical infallibility, determining more exactly what was previously more vague. Is not all we are now suffering from Rome due to the perversion aforesaid, to what is practically a belief in papal inspiration!' Tyrrell to Ward, 10 Sept. 1900, HP, A4.224. This is a copy of the original letter. In January 1910 Ward made copies of Tyrrell's letters to himself and sent them to Lord Halifax. This letter, copied, and the others, are in the Wood family archives at Hickleton Hall.

[1] The Cardinal Archbishop and the Bishops of the Province of Westminster, *A Joint Pastoral Letter on the Church and Liberal Catholicism*, London, 1900, p. 5.
[2] *Ibid.* p. 7.

defined as consisting 'not only of the laity, but also of Ecclesiastics and even Bishops in their individual and private capacity'.[1] Their duty was made clear as consisting in passive submission of their minds and wills to the church, i.e. the pope and those acting in his name. The Pastoral asserted that Catholics had a serious obligation not only to assent to truths revealed by God and taught infallibly by the church, but also to assent in religious obedience to everything taught by the church when exercising her 'ordinary authority to feed, teach and govern the flock of Christ'.[2] This ordinary authority seemed to be without limits and to be co-extensive with all knowledge. The bishops summed up the argument of their Pastoral by stating: 'There is but one fitting attitude for a Catholic toward the Church, namely, that of unswerving loyalty.'[3]

The reaction to the Pastoral was immediate and loud, and it lasted for well over six months. The Baron was almost completely occupied with family troubles at the time the Pastoral was issued and for quite some months to come. Nevertheless, in a hasty letter written to Wilfrid Ward on the last day of the year, he described exactly, though briefly, what he considered to be the great defect of the document.

The double apprehension that we all have to be ever learning; and that a simple passivity, a mere receptivity is as impossible in religion, and therefore also for a religious- and intellectual-minded layman, as it is impossible in any other subject-matter, or for any other class of men, if they are at all made of one piece, and if they are to be centres of conviction: this is, I think, so sorely wanted, so absent, e.g. from such a document as this Joint Pastoral on Liberal Catholicism. Every detailed structure of it may or might be true, and yet the absence of any consciousness of those two, I think essential concomitants of all fruitful present-day faith amongst the educated, whether priest or layman, – would strike one painfully.[4]

Tyrrell, too, in his criticism of the Pastoral, stressed this same defect lamented by von Hügel, but he also stressed the untenableness of its specific claim for papal absolutism. He took the unqualified statements of the Pastoral in their literal, and presumably, intended sense, and pointed out the absurdities to which they logically led.[5] Because the Baron was preoccupied with assisting at his sister's slow death-bed for

[1] *Ibid.* p. 9.
[2] *Ibid.* p. 13.
[3] *Ibid.* p. 26.
[4] Von Hügel to Ward, 31 Dec. 1900, WFP, vH MSS.
[5] One of Tyrrell's finest expressions on the subject was his letter signed 'A Conservative Catholic', *The Pilot*, no. 53, vol. III, 2 March 1901, p. 282. Tyrrell's authorship is proved by a letter from von Hügel to Tyrrell, 28 May 1901, BM, Add. MSS. 44927.162.

the first three months of 1901, he and Tyrrell did not at once exchange observations on the Joint Pastoral. In a letter toward the end of February Tyrrell seems to have mentioned the document for the first time in communicating with von Hügel. 'The bishops have mounted on metaphors as witches on broomsticks', he wrote, 'and have ridden to the devil. It is the "sheep & shepherd" metaphor that does the trick. The sheep are brainless, passive; their part is to be led, fed, fleeced & slain for the profit of the shepherd for whose benefit solely they exist. Apply this to the constitution of the Church & where are you to stop?'[1] The Baron did not reply to Tyrrell's comments until the end of May, when he wrote a lengthy letter from Milan. 'Certainly the clouds are very thick and black and low everywhere just now', he told Tyrrell, 'in these, the deepest matters, the requisites for the soul's breathing space in our times and latitudes.'[2] He mentioned how struck he had been by Tyrrell's remarks on the Joint Pastoral, and told him that he agreed with Tyrrell's interpretation of the unqualified absolutism of the Pastoral: 'The point that that document really puts the Pope outside of the Church is most strikingly true.' He also told Tyrrell that Dom Gasquet had likewise pointed out to him that the Pastoral 'had, whilst insisting upon the Vat. Council's positive teaching, entirely omitted the limitations which even it had introduced, so that as you say, we have in this document a really unlimited authority'.

In *The Nineteenth Century* for May of 1901 Lord Halifax published an article on 'The Recent Anglo-Roman Pastoral'. The purpose of the article was to draw attention to 'the nature and extent of the authority claimed by that pastoral for the rulers of the Church, and to the grounds on which it demands assent, exterior and interior, to the utterances of ecclesiastical authority'.[3] Wilfrid Ward published a reply to Halifax in *The Pilot* for 22 June. Ward's article appeared nearly eight weeks after

[1] Tyrrell to von Hügel, 20 Feb. 1901, BM, Add. MSS. 44927.155.

[2] Von Hügel to Tyrrell, 28 May 1901, BM, Add. MSS. 44927.162. It would seem that J. Lewis May, *Father Tyrrell and the Modernist Movement*, London, 1938, p. 196, had not heard of The Joint Pastoral, or at least had never read it, nor paged through the *Acta Sanctae Sedis* from, say, 1879 to 1909. In discussing the extreme ultramontanist absolutism against which Tyrrell fought, May remarks: 'But the important point to note is that the idea which he [Tyrrell] combated was mainly one of his own creation.'

[3] Halifax, 'The Recent Anglo-Roman Pastoral', *The Nineteenth Century*, no. 291, May 1901, p. 737. The body of this article was, apparently, actually written by Tyrrell. 'Halifax (between ourselves) once covered an article of mine to the XIX Century, by a short head-and-tailpiece. (May 1901).' Tyrrell to Lilley, 20 May 1904. This letter is part of a collection of Tyrrell's letters to Lilley, all of which were on loan to Dr Alec Vidler at the time this book was being written. Dr Vidler kindly obtained this reference for the author.

that of Halifax, and it asked why in all that time there had been so little notice taken of Halifax's criticism by Roman Catholics. Was it because Catholics had to admit the justice of Halifax's criticism and, consequently, had no response to make? Certainly not, said Ward! The limitations on authority which Halifax required were, according to Ward, simply presumed by the Joint Pastoral, and were taken for granted by every Catholic who knows anything about theology. Ward insisted that Halifax's interpretations of the Pastoral's teaching were extreme, and had

long since been universally rejected, and no theologically instructed Catholic would think of accepting them. An average Catholic would regard the Pastoral as an emphatic protest against a form of 'Liberal' Catholicism which required to be denounced; as an insistence on truths known to theologians, but which 'Liberal' Catholics have in practice forgotten.[1]

Ward's response to Halifax was considered unsatisfactory by both Tyrrell and von Hügel. 'A Pastoral is not directed to "educated theologians"', Tyrrell commented, 'but to the faithful at large; if, then, it puts before these a doctrine which is saved from absolutism only by limitations which have to be sought for in books of theology, it must be allowed that such half-truth is as dangerous and mischievous as any heresy.'[2] Halifax himself sent von Hügel a copy of his article, and from Switzerland the Baron wrote to thank him. Von Hügel told him how much he agreed with the large and open idea of Catholicism for which the article pleaded, and at the same time how pained he was 'the moment it is made (or allowed) to appear as not involving and requiring contributions of light and love from all the members of the Church, and

[1] Wilfrid Ward, 'Doctores Ecclesiae', *The Pilot*, no. 69, vol. III, 22 June 1901, p. 774.
[2] E.F.G., 'The Anglo-Roman Pastoral', *The Pilot*, no. 71, vol. IV, 6 July 1901, p. 23. The author has discovered no conclusive external evidence for Tyrrell's authorship of this letter. He is convinced of Tyrrell's authorship, however, on internal evidence. The tone, arguments, style and expressions of this letter are all similar, and even in places identical, with those found in other observations made by Tyrrell on the Joint Pastoral. Moreover, a letter known with certainty as Tyrrell's, had appeared in the same journal several months earlier, and was identically signed (E.F.G., 'M. Blondel's Dilemma', *The Pilot*, no. 35, vol. II, 27 Oct. 1900, p. 534). When the author consulted Dr Vidler for his judgment as to Tyrrell's authorship, he received the following reply, dated the 29th of May 1969: 'The letter to *The Pilot* of 6 July 1901 I have marked in my copy of *The Pilot* but I haven't noted there its attribution to Tyrrell as I should have done if I had come across an actual acknowledgment of authorship. But I agree from internal evidence it must be by T.' T. M. Loome, 'A Bibliography of the Published Writings of George Tyrrell (1861–1909)', *The Heythrop Journal*, vol. x, no. 3, July 1969, pp. 298, 305, 306, notes that Tyrrell used on several occasions the signature of E. F. G. Loome, however, seems unaware of this letter to *The Pilot*, nor does he mention it in his follow-up article of *corrigenda* and *addenda* in the *Heythrop Journal* for April 1970.

hence friction, obscurity, difficulty; but also in due subordination, variety, breathing-space and air'.[1] Von Hügel, too, felt that the Pastoral, which was supposedly a carefully thought out document, representing the thought of the entire Roman Catholic episcopate in England, 'must be strangely open to misconception and (at least so far) to legitimate attack', if all the wise things which Ward and the other defenders of the Pastoral say about it 'have to be fetched from outside the document'. The Baron also wrote to Ward about his article, but he did not hesitate to tell him that he 'felt, – a point you will yourself have felt and have discounted even before sitting down to write the paper, – that it was not *really* an answer to Halifax; but, under form of an answer to him, a communication of useful and important truths'.[2] The Baron even told Ward that he considered Halifax's paper, in its substance, unanswerable. 'And I think we all', he added, 'will be uncommonly glad when the day comes on which we shall have less frequently and copiously to draw upon the wisdom and balancing counter-considerations somehow left out, or even apparently denied by such documents as the one in question.' Throughout the whole of the discussion generated by the Joint Pastoral, von Hügel and Tyrrell were at one in their grasp of the real problem presented by the bishops' statement. When the dust of the controversy had again settled, von Hügel thanked Tyrrell for forwarding

the philosophy of the whole question by the distinction, surely new, or at all events, either unknown to or forgotten by myself, between the independence of the Pope, as far as his settling to define, and actually defining goes, and his dependence for the subject-matter of all his definitions upon the mind of the Church at large. This is truly admirable, and full as only deep thinking ever is.[3]

The problems highlighted by the Joint Pastoral continued to pre-occupy Tyrrell, since their solutions touched his life deeply both as a Catholic and as a priest. Aspects of these problems were treated in nearly everything he wrote during the next several years, whether printed anonymously or under his own name. In April of 1903 he told von Hügel that he was printing for '*very* private circulation' a study which he called 'Catholicism Re-stated'. 'Of course neither Blondel (nor even Loisy, nor perhaps even you)', he told the Baron, 'will follow me in my radicalism, though I think I make out my case so that the

[1] Von Hügel to Halifax, 21 July 1901, HP, A4.253.
[2] Von Hügel to Ward, 22 Nov. 1901, WFP, vH MSS.
[3] Von Hügel to Tyrrell, 6 Aug. 1901, BM, Add. MSS. 44927.167.

most liberal Catholicism is essentially distinct from Protestantism & has its right place in the Church.'[1] The book was eventually printed under the name of Hilaire Bourdon and had as title *The Church and the Future.*

After reading the book von Hügel sent Tyrrell his impressions and observations. 'It seems to me then', the Baron told Tyrrell,

that putting aside certain subsidiary thinkings, the book is composed of five closely connected theses; and that, – whilst all of them are, in their various ways and degrees, of most living, poignant importance and interest, – you have driven home two of them with an extraordinary force and consistency, but have been, I feel, less successful with the two [*sic*!] others.[2]

The two ideas for which von Hügel especially praised Tyrrell were that of his 'cooperatively corporate conception of the Church' and of his realization 'that the inerrancy claimed for the Church by the first thesis, will have to be conceived in a mode corresponding to the change necessitated in our conception of Biblical inerrancy'. The Baron was less satisfied with Tyrrell's efforts to indicate precisely in what the deposit of faith, about which the church was thought to be inerrant, consists. He admitted, however, that what Tyrrell was searching after here seemed to be identical with what he himself was seeking. But in Tyrrell's ardent denunciation of a scholastic intellectualism which too readily identified in practice the theology of Roman seminaries with divine revelation, he ran the risk of sinking into an equally unworkable sentimentalism. 'I know from my own case', the Baron told him,

how difficult it is, to avoid such slips, still I think our view is doomed before-hand, if it cannot manage to avoid them: for its very strength consists, not in a simple and direct reaction from, and an entirely understandable but still unworkable exaggeration against, Intellectualism, but precisely in getting higher up or deeper down than either Sentimentalism or Intellectualism: whatever we do, let us not push any part of ourselves, out of our lives and our religion and its making.

The fourth thesis which the Baron found in Tyrrell's book, and the second of those he found not wholly satisfactory, had to do with Tyrrell's expression of the Catholic position 'towards the non-Catholic Christian, and non-Christian religious levels and bodies'. With most of what Tyrrell had to say on this point von Hügel agreed; though he asked him:

But why is it necessary to declare 'one universal religion' to be a 'crude dream', as much as that of a universal language or of a universal empire?

[1] Tyrrell to von Hügel, 8 April 1903, BM, Add. MSS. 44928.85.
[2] Von Hügel to Tyrrell, 22 June 1903, BM, Add. MSS. 44928.101.

Of course, any thought of such a consummation, as other than an indefinitely remote and unpicturable terminus *ad quem*, which can and should only indirectly and very interpretatively regulate our immediate judgments and actions, is indeed to be abandoned. Yet, whilst too weary to argue it out, I must, in honesty, put upon record, that it hurt my poor instincts a bit, to find that formal repudiation of so touchingly grand a conception there.

The fifth and final thesis concerned the knowableness of God and the various human conceptions of him. Here, too, von Hügel largely agreed with what Tyrrell had written; but he felt that in some of the book's passages either modifications or additions were needed 'to prevent the impression that God may, after all, be something less than (human) spirit, reason and will'. He sympathized with Tyrrell's problems of expression, but he told him that although he saw

plainly how little we can define God: yet I am sure that any Hébertian[1] evaporation of all attribution, however analogical it may have to remain, of spirit, self-consciousness etc. to Him, – anything that would ever leave out of sight that He cannot be below or less than all these our own highest realities, – must be most vigilantly avoided by us.

The Church and the Future was Tyrrell's most synthetic and important book at the time it was first printed, and, perhaps, of all his works to the time of his death. It included the great themes and insights of his 'The Relation of Theology to Devotion', his scattered reflections on the Joint Pastoral, his soon to be published *Lex Orandi*, and most of his other works too – all worked into a careful synthesis on the meaning and constitution of the church. The importance of the book was evident to von Hügel, and he told Tyrrell that he felt as if he were 'committing a mean action by apparently discounting my acceptance of your noble, touching, deep

[1] This refers to the ideas being expressed at that time by Marcel Hébert. Hébert was born a year earlier than von Hügel, in 1851, at Bar-le-Duc, and when the Baron first met him (April 1896) was Director of the École Fénelon of Paris. In July 1901 Loisy wrote to von Hügel that Hébert's *Souvenirs d'Assise* had been denounced to Cardinal Richard, though it had been privately printed and distributed only to friends. Its theme, in Loisy's analysis (*Mém.* II, p. 48), was the familiar one of reform of the church. Richard was scandalized at Hébert's ideas on the church, Christ's resurrection, and the idea of God. Within a short time Hébert's ideas on God had evolved to the point of denial of all personality to the deity. In the winter of 1902 von Hügel had two interviews in Rome with Cardinal Vives y Tuto on Hébert's behalf (*Diaries*, 23 Feb. and 9 March 1902), and three of his letters to Hébert, one written on the day following the first interview with Vives y Tuto, are published in *Selected Letters*, pp. 100–2, 103–8. Von Hügel had great personal sympathy for Hébert, who seems from all accounts to have been a warm and likeable man. Loisy calls him *homme aimable et sympathique entre tous* (*Mém.* II, p. 49). But in a letter to Maude Petre the Baron made perfectly clear that he distinguished the man from his ideas. (See von Hügel to Petre, 29 April 1902, in *Selected Letters*, p. 109.)

and singularly courageous book' by criticizing it. 'But indeed', he added, 'I doubt whether it is, if only because I know so well how solid and fundamental is my adherence to, and profit from, all the substantial parts, all the fully deliberate and entirely self-consistent utterances of your noble confession of Faith.'[1] Tyrrell was grateful for the Baron's sympathy and approval, and told him how much he valued these. 'In my own inward history', he wrote, 'the book ends a painful process of necessary readjustment, and I feel as one who after much uncertainty has at last chosen a path that is clear, however difficult and uninviting in many ways.'[2]

The main difficulty in the path that Tyrrell had chosen was the fact that the prevailing Roman theology on the nature and constitution of the church was radically different from that expressed in his book.[3] This theology of the Roman schools had become, moreover, the practical norm by which authorities distinguished the orthodox from the

[1] Von Hügel to Tyrrell, 22 June 1903, BM, Add. MSS. 44928.103.
[2] Tyrrell to von Hügel, 27 June 1903, BM, Add. MSS. 44928.105.
[3] The exemplar *par excellence* of prevailing Roman theology on the church is to be found in Louis Billot, S.J., *Tractatus de Ecclesia Christi*, 2 vols., 4th edition, Rome, 1921–2. Billot was Professor of Theology in the Gregorian University; at one time was thought to be largely responsible for the doctrinal sections of *Pascendi dominici gregis*; and was eventually created a cardinal. His theological work had far-reaching influence in Roman Catholic schools and seminaries. Billot's two-volume work on the church is divided into three sections. The first section is entitled *Demonstratio veritatis Ecclesiae Catholicae Romanae necnon et falsitatis omnium sectarum quae ab ae separantur*. This so-called demonstration is made by a series of *a priori* theses which wrench scriptural passages, patristic texts and conciliar documents out of context as proofs of the theses, and which treat unproven didactic statements as historical facts. The second section is entitled *De intima constitutione Ecclesiae*. After a brief introductory treatment of fifty-three pages on membership of the church, there follow three hundred and seventy-one pages on the various authority structures within the church and on the powers and rights of these structures. The final section is entitled *De Habitudine Ecclesiae ad civilem societatem*, and this section is further subdivided four times. The four divisions treat 'Of the Error of Liberalism and its Various Forms', 'Of the Indirect Subordination of the State to the Church', 'Of Those Things Which Follow from This Subordination', and 'Of Ecclesiastical Immunity'. Billot's attack on liberalism was really an attack on all that has come to be accepted as the secularization of society. Billot was fighting not only secularism, which was an anti-religious ideology, but also secularization, which was a neutral historical process. *Liberalismus, secundum quod dicit errorem in materia fidei et religionis, doctrina est multiformis quae plus minusve emancipat hominem a Deo, et a lege ejus, et a revelatione ejus, et ex consequenti solvit civilem societatem ab omni dependentia a societate religiosa, hoc est ab Ecclesia quae legis divinitus revelatae custos est, et interpres, et magistra* (Billot, vol. II, p. 15). By quietly assuming that the church was the realized kingdom of God, that the pope, who called himself Christ's vicar, regularly expressed God's will and intentions, and wielded God's direct authority and power, Billot would naturally consider, – as he did, – that any and every civil, social, and intellectual development which marked a further emancipation of these areas of life from clerical and ecclesiastical control, was anti-religious and even diabolical. The old mediaeval concept of a world-embracing Christendom was very much alive in the closed world of Roman theology and ecclesiastical and clerical life. The rejection of this 'Ptolemaic world system', as Tyrrell often called it, and an acceptance of the 'Copernican revolution', was basically what the modernist crisis was all about.

heterodox. To prevent Tyrrell's book from falling into unsympathetic hands was of considerable importance, therefore, and was a problem to which von Hügel immediately addressed himself. He drew up a list of the names of men in England and on the continent for whom he felt *The Church and the Future* would be suitable 'both on account of their gained-ness or gainableness to such ideas; of their importance; and of their loyalty and discretion'.[1] Tyrrell's recognition of the risk he ran was no less than the Baron's, but his concern for his own safety was not as marked as von Hügel's concern for him. 'I wrote the book to convince myself that my position as a Catholic is an honest one', Tyrrell told the Baron,

but I could not expect to convince officials, & in the event of conflict they would be subjectively justified in imposing tests which I could not honestly accept. Still I felt that there are a few here & there, & will be more as time goes on, to whom the book might suggest a *modus vivendi*, whom it might keep in the Church for leavening the whole mass.[2]

In January of 1905 the Baron wrote anxiously to Tyrrell that a copy of *The Church and the Future* had found its way into Archbishop's House, Westminster; but he had not been able to discover whether Archbishop Bourne himself had actually seen it, nor whether Tyrrell's authorship was known there.[3] More than two years after the book's first printing von Hügel sent a copy to Edmund Bishop, telling him that he did so because Bishop was 'so utterly trustworthy and understanding a reader of Catholic writings of the *coming* type', and because he hoped that Bishop would find the book deeply stimulating.[4] The book's importance and value continued to increase in von Hügel's estimation. Even a week after making his first critique of it he told Tyrrell that it struck him 'as greater at a little distance now, than it looked when I read it: and yet, then already, it impressed me deeply'. And he added: 'That increase of impressiveness at some distance like that, is, I think, one of the surest tests and signs of the livingness and true greatness of a work: this one certainly has that quality in a rare degree.'[5]

Six months after reading *The Church and the Future* von Hügel began to

[1] Von Hügel to Tyrrell, 22 June 1903, BM, Add. MSS. 44928.103.
[2] Tyrrell to von Hügel, 27 June 1903, BM, Add. MSS. 44928.106.
[3] Von Hügel to Tyrrell, 10 Jan. 1905, BM, Add. MSS. 44929.2.
[4] Von Hügel to Bishop, 29 Sept. 1905, in *Dublin Review*, vol. 227, no. 460, April 1953, pp. 187–8. For Bishop's appreciative response to his first reading of the book see, Bishop to von Hügel, 8 Oct. 1905, SAUL, MS. 2215.
[5] Von Hügel to Tyrrell, 28 June 1903, BM, Add. MSS. 44928.109.

gather his own thoughts for presentation on the relationship between the individual's Christian life and the authority of the institutional church. The occasion was an invitation, probably at the suggestion of A. L. Lilley, to address a group of Anglican clerics known as 'The XII Silent Men'. The address was to be given at the end of January, and January of 1904 was one of the most hectic months in Friedrich von Hügel's entire life. Loisy had been condemned by Rome at the end of December, and January was filled with the Baron's efforts to defend him. In the midst of these trials von Hügel began sketching out the rough draft of his address for 'The XII Silent Men'. He finished it six days later, on the 28th.[1] On that very morning he sent a newly received letter from Loisy, together with five others received in the previous few days, to Tyrrell with a covering note: 'On the verge of breaking down, even as it is, – I have been quite unable to even forward letters or crucial news. I now send you his last 6 letters, – the ultimate one received only 2 hours ago. Return them all, sometime soon, *registered*, please ... Pray for me and my poor labours.'[2] Yet on the evening of the same day that he wrote those lines, von Hügel dined with and addressed 'The XII Silent Men'. The host for that evening was Charles Robert Shaw Stewart, Anglican Rector of Sanderstead in Surrey, and at the dinner von Hügel was seated next to Lilley, his friend of less than a year and fellow-defender of Loisy. The Baron addressed the group – which numbered fifteen instead of twelve – on the subject of 'Official Authority and Living Religion'.[3]

The Baron's address had three parts. In the first section he pointed out seven constitutive differences between the institutional officialism of the church on the one hand, and the living forces of religion in the individual on the other. These differences necessarily lead, in the concrete, to conflicts for the individual within the institution. So the second part of the paper tried to show 'how the very acuteness of the conflict and pressure suggests, not only certain irrepressible rights and functions of officialism, but also certain abiding, immanental discriminations and limitations'.[4] The final section of the paper showed how 'these discriminations and limitations are reinforced, and rendered quite inevitable,

[1] *Diaries*, 22, 23, 26, 27, and 28 Jan. 1904.
[2] Von Hügel to Tyrrell, 28 Jan. 1904, BM, Add. MSS. 44928.149.
[3] *Diaries*, 28 Jan. 1904. This address was published in von Hügel's *Essays and Addresses*, second series, pp. 3–23.
[4] *Essays and Addresses*, second series, p. 4. The other quotations in this paragraph are taken from pp. 4 and 19 of the address.

by the clear results of historico-critical research'. The whole address was concerned with some of the larger problems dealt with in *The Church and the Future*, but von Hügel's perspective and angle of approach differed considerably from Tyrrell's. This difference, however, was entirely in the sense of complementarity, and not in that of contradiction. In the paper's third section von Hügel came closest to paralleling Tyrrell's approach. Like Tyrrell, the Baron completely rejected the contemporary trend of Roman theology to find a full-blown Roman Catholic system in primitive Christianity. Any serious understanding of contemporary biblical criticism made that impossible; and, as a result of his own critical studies, von Hügel explicitly accepted the full *human* dimensions of Jesus's knowledge as well as Jesus's belief in his own proximate second coming. 'Now this conclusion', the Baron pointed out,

necessarily involves the recognition that all and every officialism beyond that humble brotherhood, so simply trained, organized and sent out by Him, can but go back germinally and not formally and materially to Him, somewhat as the visible universe itself was germinally created by God in the beginning and not in the state or form in which we now see it.

The implications of this for ecclesiastical life were important, and von Hügel did not hesitate to make them explicit. To one who merely heard his remarks without knowing him, this address might have sounded like the tranquil reflections of a philosopher far removed from most of life's real turmoil. In fact, it grew directly from the living forces of religion in von Hügel's own life and those of his friends in their conflicts with the contemporary authority structures of the Roman Catholic church.

After the meeting with 'The XII Silent Men' von Hügel touched up his paper and had it professionally typed. Then, more than six weeks after its delivery, he sent a copy to Tyrrell.[1] Although Tyrrell was impressed with its contents, he did not hesitate to tell the Baron that its presentation was excessively dense. The paper was 'most satisfactory & constructive', Tyrrell thought,

but I wonder how much the 12 masked conspirators understood of it. It requires awful concentration of attention & it was only in making a careful synopsis of it, that I really seized its full import. I should have put all that into 300 8v. pp. & sold it for 5/– net; & people would have said it was over crowded & obscure.[2]

He tried to show von Hügel that, although the latter chose and placed

[1] *Diaries*, 19 Feb., and 17 March 1904.
[2] Tyrrell to von Hügel, 20 March 1904, BM, Add. MSS. 44928.183.

each word of his address 'with full explicit consciousness & meaning', no audience could be expected to grasp it all at once in one delivery. The Baron should have more concern for 'the average man', Tyrrell told him. And he added:

Solid, liquid, gas – are the three forms in which thought can be presented; the last for an audience; the second for a book; the first for an archangel in retreat. I don't think anything has helped & satisfied me so much as this last paper of yours, & I shall be doling out bits of it for years to come according as it sinks into my mind & bears fruit there.

The Baron thanked his friend for his 'praise and most useful criticism', and promised to try to be more aware for the future of the 'fault' which Tyrrell had pointed out.[1] He seems not to have bothered further with the paper until March of 1907, when he considered offering it to *Il Rinnovamento* for publication in Italian. To this end he asked Tyrrell to go over the paper again, to help to clarify words and expressions that might be misleading or provoke unnecessary trouble. This Tyrrell did, with the comment that he thought he had made the paper 'quite clear with no more than a number of small tinkerings – parenthesis; numerations; excises of avoidable duplications; transpositions; full stops; here & there an audacious explanatory insertion; or even a substitution of terms'.[2] The immediate development of events in 1907 made the paper's publication impossible for years to come, however; and it was printed only after the Baron's death.

[1] Von Hügel to Tyrrell, 23 March 1904, BM, Add. MSS. 44928.185.
[2] Tyrrell to von Hügel, 15 March 1907, BM, Add. MSS. 44930.13.

CHAPTER 9

TYRRELL AND THE JESUIT ORDER

As TYRRELL began to wrestle seriously with the larger problem of ecclesiastical authority, he likewise continued to examine with searching thoroughness his position as a member of the Jesuit order. He had joined the order as a young man of nineteen and without knowing very much about it. However, his youthful Jesuit ideal, based primarily on what he had read in the pages of Paul Féval, was rapidly and rather rudely tempered by the rougher realities of Jesuit life in the English Province of the order at the end of the nineteenth century.[1] Although the relationship of the ideal to the reality had troubled him from the days of his novitiate onward, Tyrrell's first really serious disillusionment seems to have set in after his removal from the chair of philosophy at St Mary's Hall, and to have rapidly increased with his experiences while at the Jesuit residence in Farm Street.

In the summer of 1898 Tyrrell received a letter from Henri Bremond, a French Jesuit who was four years his junior, and who had been impressed with his contributions to *The Month*.[2] This correspondence opened a friendship between the two men which ended only with Tyrrell's death. At the time of Bremond's earliest contact with Tyrrell, the former was himself experiencing much dissatisfaction and considerable disillusionment with his own position as Jesuit. When Bremond put his difficulties to Tyrrell, the latter responded with an explanation of his own temporary solution to his analogous problem. Writing to von Hügel, who himself met Bremond for the first time in February of 1899,[3] Tyrrell told the Baron that he had heard from Bremond who

seems troubled with the consciousness of being in a false position; so I have written explaining my own *modus vivendi* which is practically that life forces us to make certain decisions more or less in the dark, which once made, a man's martyrdom lies in standing loyally to the consequences, so long as conscience is not violated.[4]

[1] *Autobiography and Life*, I, pp. 226–7.
[2] *Ibid.* II, pp. 71–5.
[3] *Diaries*, 8 Feb. 1899. Loisy, *George Tyrrell et Henri Bremond*, Paris, 1936, p. 2, is inaccurate when he states that this initial meeting was in March.
[4] Tyrrell to von Hügel, 23 July 1899, BM, Add. MSS. 44927.81–2.

161

Tyrrell left no doubt about the quality of the loyalty which he had in mind. 'My father's first wife', he told von Hügel, 'was a painted Jezebel of 45 – he being 18 and yet he seems to have been kind to the old hag who lived some 25 years. This fact has helped me much to see my own duty in a somewhat similar alliance.'

In the summer of 1899 Tyrrell considered his commitment to the Jesuit order as analogous to that of a man who had contracted an unfortunate marriage. His obligation of loyalty seemed fairly straightforward. Throughout the year 1899 he continued to be optimistic, not about the Jesuit order as a whole, but about his (and Bremond's) ability to remain within it and to work for the ends which he considered authentically Ignatian. During that year he wrote an introduction and an epilogue for a new translation of St Ignatius's autobiography. In this epilogue Tyrrell justified his own existence as a Jesuit.[1] Tyrrell saw that Ignatius's great insight had not been in the goal he set for himself and for his followers, i.e. the greater glory of God through the service of men for their own salvation. This goal was Christ's and St Paul's and that of the whole Christian tradition. According to Tyrrell, what was specifically Ignatian was the insistence that the means for achieving this goal must be flexibility and adaptability in the use of whatever raw materials of thought and achievement any given age or culture produced. To cling to old forms and customs, which had outlived their genuine usableness for a given milieu and mentality, would be to subvert the goal, substituting for it the very means which were meant to achieve it.[2] Tyrrell's implication was that this subversion had taken place in the Jesuit order

---

[1] Tyrrell explicitly stated this in a letter to his provincial superior: 'When I edited the "Testament of S. Ignatius" & wrote the Epilogue to it, it was to justify myself in having joined the S.J. & to put forth the aspect under which it appealed to me. As long as I could think that even with 99 p.c. of failure due to human frailty the Jesuits were really true to that ideal & were striving however imperfectly to realize it, I could not in conscience say I had joined in substantial ignorance. But what I suspected at the time, & suspect more strongly now, is, that the existing Society is diametrically opposed to those principles of accommodation & vitality which S. Ignatius preached & by which the Church was then saved; & that she is heart & soul with that fierce reactionary party whose policy is preparing the way for wholesale apostasies in the near future. If I joined the Society, as I did, solely to work for the cause of Catholicism; how shall I stay, if I am forced to regard her as one of the worst enemies of that cause? That is roughly how the case presents itself to me. If I had married a harlot, thinking her pure, I should feel bound, not to love or honour her, but to hold to her in justice – for the risk is inherent in the contract. But if I joined a Conservative Club & found it defending & acting on anarchic principles, – who could say any vow could bind me to it? Still I cherish a faint hope that the dry bones may by some miracle be made alive again; & should be glad to find myself wrong.' Tyrrell to Reginald Colley, S.J., 10 Aug. 1901, AEPSJ, CD/2, Tyrrell Letters, no. 24.

[2] The Testament of Ignatius Loyola, translated by E. M. Rix, with a Preface by George Tyrrell, S.J., London, 1900, pp. 197–206.

after Ignatius's death, and that only a return to his principles of adaptability and mobility would justify the continuance of the order. However, even before the epilogue was in print, Tyrrell's article on 'A Perverted Devotion' had been denounced, and a new series of events was set in motion which would eventually cause him to conclude that to stand by his Jesuit commitment any longer would be to violate his conscience.

Not until June of 1900 was the storm over the article on hell concluded, and by August Tyrrell was no longer resident in London, but in far away Richmond. Moreover, his freedom to write and to preach were somewhat restricted, and the means by which he personally had striven to attain the Ignatian goal were no longer at his free disposal. Although he was soon to resort to publication under a pseudonym or anonymously as means both of overcoming this handicap and, at the same time, of not compromising the Jesuit order, this was but a temporary measure and clearly not a solution to the problem. When the superior of the English Jesuits asked him later that year to consider writing some controversial pamphlets of a philosophical nature for *The Catholic Truth Society*, Tyrrell was honest and blunt in his refusal. He told the Provincial that controversy was neither his line nor the need of the times. 'Supposing I could throw cold water on evolution', he asked, 'would that help any man towards faith?'[1] It was the 'large class of reluctant unbelievers (again, of every grade) who are affectively & often effectively, religious-minded' that Tyrrell was concerned about and for whom he intended his religious dedication to serve. It was this class with whom he had worked in London, and it was for these that he wrote. Tyrrell told his superior that

the tide is upon us & we are unprepared; we have obstructed every attempt to build an ark of escape, & don't know where to turn for materials or skilled workmen. We have refused to bend, & now we must break. Whatever respite can be won by a policy of repression & brute-force, by brazening things out; by asserting what every educated man denies, & denying what he asserts, can only be partial and temporal; the tide will come in, & round, & over, notwithstanding.

The letter drew out in moving detail the problems of contemporary unbelief which, in Tyrrell's estimation, neither the Roman Catholic church in general nor the Jesuit order in particular were making any serious and sympathetic efforts to understand and meet. From the very beginning of this prolonged inward struggle Tyrrell left no doubt as to

[1] Tyrrell to John Gerard, S.J., 17 Nov. 1900, CD/2, Tyrrell Letters, no. 4. All further quotations in this paragraph are taken from the same lengthy letter.

where he stood, when he discussed the situation with those authorities who had some right to know his mind.

In 1901 Tyrrell was involved not only in controversy over the Joint Pastoral, but also in efforts to satisfy the requirements of ecclesiastical censorship for a new book which he had hoped to be able to publish under his own name and with diocesan approval. The book was a volume of seventy-three reflections, varying in length from less than two pages to a bit more than twelve, on subjects concerned with faith and love and the Christian life generally, and embodying the best of Tyrrell's religious philosophy and spirituality. Originally he had called the book *Vetera et Nova* 'because it is like and unlike "Nova et Vetera"', and he had told von Hügel that it was 'a sort of advanced "Nova et Vetera" for senior students'.[1] When the volume was finally printed, however, it bore the title *Oil and Wine*. Customarily, Jesuits of the English Province submitted their manuscripts of books for publication to their province superior who, in turn, gave them to two Jesuit censors in the province for criticism and comment. If the Jesuit censors passed a manuscript, Cardinal Vaughan had always before granted his *imprimatur* without further diocesan censorship. When Tyrrell presented his *Oil and Wine* to the Jesuit censors, they at first demurred, 'being timid in the light of past events'.[2] Eventually they passed the manuscript. At the time that the routine application for the *imprimatur* was requested of Cardinal Vaughan, the book was already being set up in type. Vaughan refused to give his *imprimatur* until he had himself first seen the book. When Tyrrell wrote to Vaughan, protesting this unprecedented double censorship, the latter replied that 'objections had been made about "Theology & Devotion"',[3] and that he would not approve this new book without first examining it. Exasperated, Tyrrell wrote to Vaughan on Christmas Day a letter utterly devoid of the usual exaggerated deference toward ecclesiastical authorites, but clearly expressing the state of his mind and emotions. Tyrrell told Vaughan that he felt constrained to lay down his pen so far as the defence of Catholicism was concerned. 'One thing I am resolved on', he added; 'that I shall cause all the reasons why I lay it down to be well and widely known – chief of which is this unmanly unchristian system of government by secret tattling and organized slander.'[4]

[1] Tyrrell to von Hügel, 3 Jan. 1902, BM, Add. MSS. 44928.3; Tyrrell to von Hügel, 12 April 1902, BM, Add. MSS. 44928.11.
[2] Tyrrell to von Hügel, 12 April 1902, BM, Add. MSS. 44928.11.
[3] *Ibid.*
[4] Tyrrell to Vaughan, 25 Dec. 1901, AAW, Vaughan MSS. VI/12.4a.

Tyrrell's letter seems to have frightened Vaughan, since he sent the book's proofs to Rome itself for censorship rather than trust his own diocesan censors. At this move Tyrrell threw in the sponge and told the Cardinal that if the book puzzled him, 'it will puzzle the average Catholic intelligence; so I will give it to an Anglican friend to publish in his own name for Anglicans'.[1] Vaughan thanked Tyrrell for his 'virtuous submission' and sent him the reports of the three Roman censors. Every one of the points censored by the Roman critics of *Oil and Wine*, Tyrrell told von Hügel, were to be found over and over in his other books, all of which had Vaughan's *imprimatur*, and some of which Vaughan had earlier gone out of his way to eulogize. Tyrrell reported that he then told the Cardinal 'that numbers have been drawn toward & kept in the Church by those books & that it would be only fair to such deluded individuals that I should withdraw those books & publish all my reasons for doing so', – since the church now seemed to repudiate the ideas contained in them. Alarmed, Vaughan informed Tyrrell, through the latter's own provincial superior, that such a step would cause serious scandal. 'I think they will leave me alone another time', Tyrrell told von Hügel, in summing up the whole sad business of *Oil and Wine*, 'but of course this double censorship, which H. E. will now always insist on makes it impossible to publish under my own name.'[2] A few copies of the book were run off nevertheless, and, with the Baron's help, these eventually attained a relatively wide private circulation.

The spring of 1902 was underway before Tyrrell was certain of the fate of *Oil and Wine*. The obstacles and opposition with which increasingly he met seemed both to depress him and yet to stimulate him to further literary efforts.[3] The Baron was greatly concerned about the ambiguity of Tyrrell's position, and each summer from 1902 until 1905 he spent from two to three weeks of his holiday at Richmond with his troubled friend.[4] Except for the year 1904, these visits were always pre-

---

[1] Tyrrell to von Hügel, 12 April 1902, BM, Add. MSS. 44928.11.

[2] *Ibid.*

[3] 'For my own liberty, inward & outward, I keep up my "irreconcilable" attitude with the S[ociety of] J[esus]; they are far more civil to me in consequence & will not easily provoke me by any needless interference. Were I to sink differences, it would mean taking some active part in the corporate life of an order whose whole present spirit & policy is odious to me; it would mean simulating interests & sympathies that I do not feel – for example every excitement that thrills the Farm Street community pleasantly or unpleasantly would thrill me in an opposite sense. It is therefore only as *notoriously* a dissident that I can honestly stay where I am' (Tyrrell to von Hügel, 10 July 1902, BM, Add. MSS. 44928.22).

[4] *Diaries*, 16 Aug.–6 Sept. 1902; 18 Aug.–4 Sept. 1903; 10 Aug.–5 Sept. 1904; and 7–29 Aug. 1905.

ceded by or concluded with a brief visit to Lord Halifax at Hickleton Hall. While in Richmond itself the Baron stayed in lodgings, and spent a major part of every day in conversation and long walks with Tyrrell. It was at Richmond in 1902 that Tyrrell first presented von Hügel with some of the privately printed copies of *Oil and Wine* as well as with his pseudonymous *Religion as a Factor of Life* by Dr Ernest Engels.[1] Tyrrell was deeply grateful for von Hügel's interest and help, and after the first Richmond visit he wrote to tell the Baron 'what a great help & pleasure your visit has been to me & how greatly it has stimulated my flagging interests & filled me with hope & desire to work on through thick and thin. I am afraid however, it was but little of a rest for you; & that between us all we are largely responsible for your present weariness.'[2]

Once back in London von Hügel sent copies of *Oil and Wine* and *Religion as a Factor of Life* to various scholar friends and men sensitive to religious problems and values whom he hoped to interest in Tyrrell's works and ideas.[3] When these men wrote their appraisals of the books to the Baron, he in turn usually sent them on to Tyrrell as means of encouraging and sustaining him in his efforts. After receiving a number of positive comments on *Religion as a Factor of Life* from von Hügel's friends, Tyrrell told the Baron that he had 'been much encouraged by the kind words of such men as Eucken, Holtzmann, Sauer, Semeria, etc.; although it would have been so much more encouraging had it been possible to put my name to "R." & not necessary to speak the truth under one's breath, as it were something obscene'.[4] The Baron also continued to stimulate Tyrrell's interests and flagging spirit by recommending books and authors to his attention, especially in the areas of philosophy and biblical criticism.[5] Philosophical works predominated in the lists of

[1] *Diaries*, 21 and 24 Aug. 1902.

[2] Tyrrell to von Hügel, 16 Sept. 1902, BM, Add. MSS. 44928.28.

[3] With his first letter to A. L. Lilley von Hügel sent a copy of *Oil and Wine*, telling Lilley: 'I also venture to send you a copy of a book by my close friend, the Revd George Tyrrell, a truly deep and brilliant Irishman, and a Jesuit as liberal as his close friend Père Bremond, the Frenchman. The book was approved by the Censors of his order, but met with difficulties of approbation from the *entourage* of our good Cardinal: hence its non-publication. I cannot but think you will find it *full* of deep and delicate thinking and experience about and of religion.' Von Hügel to Lilley, 6 April 1903, LFP, 1, vH MSS. See also, von Hügel to Tyrrell, 30 June 1904, in *Selected Letters*, p. 128.

[4] Tyrrell to von Hügel, 14 Oct. 1902, BM, Add. MSS. 44928.37.

[5] Von Hügel to Tyrrell, 8 Sept. 1902, BM, Add. MSS. 44928.26. – Maude Petre has accused von Hügel (*My Way of Faith*, London, 1937, pp. 290–3; *Von Hügel and Tyrrell*, pp. 103–4, 118–20) of being largely responsible for the unhappy development of Tyrrell's career with its tragic climax. She felt that by introducing Tyrrell to the best of contemporary biblical criticism, the Baron had led him away from his natural field of action which was the pursuit of 'religious truth', and into an alien sphere which was the pursuit 'of the exegetical questions

von Hügel's reading suggestions during these years, though he likewise recommended such studies as Weiss's *Die Predigt Jesu von Reiche Gottes* and Percy Gardner's *A Historic View of the New Testament*. The former seems to have had some influence on Tyrrell's *The Church and the Future*, and the latter he found 'eminently satisfactory & clear'.[1] All of Loisy's writings and ideas were also constant topics of conversation, both verbal and written, between the two men, almost from the time of their first meeting.[2] The Baron's enthusiasm for Troeltsch was bound to lead him to want to share this friend with Tyrrell too.[3] He sent Troeltsch's *Geschichte und metaphysik* to Richmond at the end of October 1902. Within a few months Tyrrell told him that 'Troeltsch's problems give me most pause; they are those *towards* which, rather than *from* which my mind seems to be working; the question of the relation of Christianity to other religions is just the *whole* question'.[4] But as the days and months wore on, after Cardinal Richard had condemned Loisy's *L'Évangile et l'Église*,

---

of the day'. Although Miss Petre knew these letters well, an examination of the Tyrrell–von Hügel correspondence in the British Museum seems to discredit her contention. Tyrrell was an apologist, and he was by temperament polemical. Some of the ideas and readings suggested to him by von Hügel were undoubtedly grist for Tyrrell's polemical and apologetic mill. But to suggest as Miss Petre does that Tyrrell would probably have lived a quiet life in the pursuit of religious truth had he never met von Hügel, is to ignore the basic realities of Tyrrell's situation. By the time the Baron came to know Tyrrell, the latter already had a reputation as a counsellor for Christians whose consciences were troubled and whose efforts to reconcile their religion with their contemporary thought-patterns and milieu seemed frustrated. The biblical problem was one of the main problems on the religious horizon of this period, and unless Tyrrell had come to grips with it in some way, he could hardly have been of help to the Christians whom it troubled. The unwillingness of Roman Catholic ecclesiastical authorities either to concern themselves about such intellectual problems of believers, or to allow other clerics to be concerned about them, antagonized Tyrrell and was largely responsible for the rather violent polemics which coloured his final years.

[1] Tyrrell to von Hügel, 11 Jan. 1903, BM, Add. MSS. 44928.63.

[2] The whole of their correspondence is full of references to Loisy and his books, ideas, and problems, e.g., Tyrrell to von Hügel, 2 April 1900, BM, Add. MSS. 44927.111, and von Hügel to Tyrrell, 27 May 1900, BM, Add. MSS. 44927.113). Loisy, *George Tyrrell et Henri Bremond*, p. 9, quotes a letter from Tyrrell to himself in which Tyrrell told Loisy that the latter's *Études bibliques* had brought him to a real cross-roads in his own thought. This letter is published entire in *Autobiography and Life*, II, pp. 394–6.

[3] When the Baron returned from the continent and his first meeting with Troeltsch in the spring of 1902, he wrote to Tyrrell: 'Then I got on to Heidelberg, where I at last met my good Prof. Ernst Troeltsch in the flesh ... He has the most sensitive consciousness of the complexity and relativity of all history and its evidences; an extraordinary speculative, metaphysical competence and revealing power; and finally a truly touching spiritual and personally devotional sense and experience, which runs through all, and hallows, steadies and deepens it. And his knowledge of the history, of the literature, of the present requirements of all these three things is *astonishing*; and his honesty, and straight cleanness and clearness of vision is, of itself a true moral tonic, which comes from a robust, truly manly faith, and leads straight on to its strengthening in others.' Von Hügel to Tyrrell, 4 June 1902, BM, Add. MSS. 44928.16–7.

[4] Tyrrell to von Hügel, 11 Jan. 1903, BM, Add. MSS. 44928.64.

and the rumours and threats from Rome grew louder and more ominous, von Hügel himself found it increasingly difficult to be optimistic and encouraging. And in a moment of depression he told Tyrrell:

Alas, alas: that any men or body of men should think they simply hold the final truth and final statement of it *hic et nunc*. You remember Browning's 'Ixion' and how a rainbow of Hope is formed by the tortured one's sweat and tears and blood. Not only the rainbow of hope but the sun of Truth is largely seen by us, through, and only through, a mist as painfully expensive to us as *that*.[1]

While Tyrrell's relationship to the Jesuit order continued to deteriorate gradually but inexorably, Bremond's similar relationship reached its terminus rather more suddenly, and certainly more satisfactorily. In April of 1903 Tyrrell told von Hügel that 'Bremond has been in very hot water; they have been collecting evidence against him at Rome for 4 years & have now exploded the bomb. He was first sentenced to banishment from Paris & incarceration in some college or big residence; now it has been rather ludicrously mitigated to residence at Farm Street.'[2] Tyrrell suggested that Bremond should ask to come to Richmond 'as a sort of Siberia; but London with all its wickedness & heterodoxy was judged less spiritually perilous than the desert with the Devil in it'. During the summer and autumn of that year Bremond went to Hampstead and to Kensington on a number of occasions to visit von Hügel. After one such visit in June the Baron reported to Tyrrell that their French friend was 'certainly very run down: nervous, restless, depressed, easily irritated'.[3] And after a July visit von Hügel noted how Bremond was 'in a sadly battered condition'.[4] The Baron saw Bremond at least twice in January 1904, and then on the morning of 11 February Bremond paid him a brief farewell visit. He was off on the 2.00 p.m. train that day from Victoria to Paris and Aix-en-Provence where his secularization was being arranged for him by his Jesuit superiors.[5] This meant

1 Von Hügel to Tyrrell, 11 Feb. 1903, BM, Add. MSS. 44928.73.
2 Tyrrell to von Hügel, 21 April 1903, BM, Add. MSS. 44928.93–4.
3 Von Hügel to Tyrrell, 28 June 1903, BM, Add. MSS. 44928.108.
4 Von Hügel to Tyrrell, 7 July 1903, BM, Add. MSS. 44928.110.
5 *Diaries*, 14 and 25 Jan., and 11 Feb. 1904. 'Poor Bremond turned up here, at 11, practically on his way to the station, as he was leaving for Paris at 2. Is to be 3 weeks away, but intends then to be back in London. But he himself will have written you word about it all: he says the last steps have been made fairly easy and pleasant for him by the Order. I do hope, he may now manage to find and utilize an environment better suited to him, to his growing. He has kindly agreed to translate my anti-Blondel papers. I may be trying his patience with my slowness: I simply cannot do such things very quickly and so far, I have not even seen an extract, from even the first of B.'s 3 articles. Bremond warns me, to be prepared to find them very hard and absolute.' Von Hügel to Tyrrell, 11 Feb. 1904, BM, Add. MSS. 44928.163.

that Bremond's vows as a Jesuit would be terminated, and that he would join the ranks of the diocesan clergy under the nominal jurisdiction of the bishop of Aix. Eleven days after Bremond's departure the Baron received a postcard from him, written from Locarno, and stating that the secularization had been successfully and amicably completed.[1] How much Bremond influenced Tyrrell in the further evolution of the latter's position as a Jesuit remains to be documented. Although the basis for Tyrrell's eventual rupture with the Jesuits, and many of the factors actually operative in that rupture, were already manifest before he ever knew Bremond, and were totally independent of Bremond; still, that there was some element of influence and interaction, no matter how indirect, seems clear.[2]

As Bremond quietly terminated his relationship with the Society of Jesus, Tyrrell began once more to review and reconsider his own situation *vis-à-vis* the order. The Society, 'by the necessity of its circumstances, and by its instinct of self-preservation', was so committed to the cause of reaction, Tyrrell concluded, as to make his own commitment to the cause of progress and adaptation an intolerable anomaly.[3] In order to make his own position an honest one, he saw only two alternatives open to him. Either he must lay down his pen and cease working for the liberal cause, or he must leave the Society. If he accepted the first alternative, he would be failing those who had come to trust and to depend on him, and he would be compromising his conscience. If he accepted the second, he would face almost inevitable ecclesiastical harassment and disgrace. Although for Tyrrell there was never really any option, since the first alternative was never a serious choice for him, dread of the consequences of the second choice caused him to hesitate yet longer.[4]

Finally, toward the end of the summer of 1905 Tyrrell formally requested of the Jesuit General in Rome a release from his religious vows.[5] Since Tyrrell was a priest, and since there was no question of his reduction to the lay state, it was necessary, according to current canonical law

---

[1] *Diaries*, 22 Feb. 1904.

[2] One might deduce this even from no more evidence than that contributed by the letter of von Hügel to Tyrrell, 30 June 1904, in *Selected Letters* (top) p. 129, and from the letter to von Hügel to Petre, 28 Oct. 1912, in *Selected Letters*, p. 199.

[3] *Autobiography and Life*, II, p. 278.

[4] 'I have tried to make out a case for myself, and all I can see is that my position is not yet so demonstrably dishonest as to force me to go. If I go, nothing could excuse me from speaking out all I think about the S.J. and explaining how I remained in it so long.' Tyrrell to von Hügel, 3 July 1904, in *Autobiography and Life*, II, p. 236.

[5] Tyrrell to Luis Martin, S.J., 6 Aug. 1905, in *Autobiography and Life*, II, p. 238.

and practice, to find a bishop willing to accept him into his diocese before the Jesuit superiors could release him from his obligations of obedience. A priest without either a bishop or the superior of an order to whom he was juridically subject would be in an extra-canonical state, and technically, suspended from the basic ministerial activities of the priesthood. When the Jesuit General approached the Sacred Congregation of Bishops and Regulars to obtain the necessary dispensation for Tyrrell, he was told that the Congregation was well disposed to grant the secularization, but that it desired a direct application from Tyrrell himself. During these negotiations Tyrrell kept von Hügel abreast of developments, even sending on to his friend the letters received from his local Provincial and from the General.[1]

When Padre Semeria visited England for a few weeks in the autumn of 1905, von Hügel consulted him, as one familiar with Roman juridical practice, on the best way for Tyrrell to proceed in meeting the Congregation's request for a personal application for dispensation from his Jesuit vows. As a result of Semeria's advice the Baron wrote to his prospective son-in-law, Count Francesco Salimei, then resident in Rome, asking him to inquire confidentially about the most satisfactory canonical form in which Tyrrell's request should be cast. Semeria had also suggested that as much external influence as possible be brought to bear on Cardinal Dominic Ferrata, the Prefect of the Sacred Congregation, to impress him with the need to make as few difficulties as possible in granting Tyrrell's request. Von Hügel decided that the best way to accomplish this would be to have the English Ambassador in Rome contact Ferrata in order to let the latter know that Tyrrell was 'a person of consideration in England; that it is of importance for the public credit of the Church & Religion in England, that [Tyrrell's] request should be granted in as amicable a way, and with the least onerous conditions possible'.[2] The Baron proposed to persuade the Ambassador to undertake this mission through Tyrrell's own cousin, William Tyrrell, who had once been a secretary at the English Embassy in Rome.[3] Toward the

[1] Von Hügel to Tyrrell, 16 Oct. 1905, BM, Add. MSS. 44929.53–4.   [2] *Ibid.*

[3] William Tyrrell (1866–1947) was George Tyrrell's cousin, the latter's father and the former's grandfather having been brothers. William was educated at Balliol College, Oxford, and entered the Foreign Office in 1889. Among other positions, he was one time principal private secretary to Viscount Grey of Fallodon, and he was head of the political intelligence department. He attended the Paris peace conference in 1919 where he strongly opposed Lloyd George; and he was principal adviser to Lord Curzon at the Lausanne conference in 1922–3. From 1928–34 he was British ambassador in Paris. In 1929 he was created baron, and among other honours he held were the K.C.V.O., G.C.M.G., G.C.B. and P.C. See, *The Concise Dict. of Nat. Biog.*, II, p. 443.

end of October von Hügel told Tyrrell that he had approached his cousin, and that this latter had decided to approach the Ambassador through Mr E. W. Howard 'who was an Engl. Emb. Secretary in Rome up to last year; is much considered by Church-Officials in Rome, where he now resides with his upper-ten wife; and who is a convert, well disposed toward your cousin, and who is sure to act promptly, tactfully, firmly, and impressively'.[1] This, at least, was what William Tyrrell told von Hügel. The Baron also mentioned that Salimei had sent exact information on how best to draw up the petition for the Sacred Congregation, and added:

Grieved as I am to think it, I cannot but fear that this matter of a Bishop may easily turn out *the* stumbling-block in the way of the whole movement. I know well how determined you were to keep yourself unattached; and see too how difficult, even apart from any such wish of yours, it would be or will be to find, under the precise combination of circumstances in question, a Bishop who would take you, under conditions that would not more or less nullify the objects of your move.[2]

The question of obtaining a bishop willing to accept Tyrrell into his diocese did, as a matter of fact, turn out to be *the* stumbling-block of these negotiations. All through October and November von Hügel warned Tyrrell against leaving Richmond until he had made certain of a bishop's acceptance.[3] However, a more immediate difficulty, and one with rather remarkably ironic overtones, resulted from the effort to approach the English Ambassador through Mr Howard. This latter was on diplomatic service in Crete when he received William Tyrrell's letter asking him to persuade the Ambassador to approach Cardinal Ferrata. When he received the letter, instead of following its suggestion, Howard simply sent it on, with a covering note, to his personal friend Cardinal Merry del Val. 'Your letter, as coming from one of the family, will do much more than anything I could say', Howard told William Tyrrell. 'M.d.V. will of course treat it as private and merely make such use of it as may be possible under the circumstances. I know of no better man to go to in any case of trouble: there is no one more large-minded or more ready

[1] Von Hügel to Tyrrell, 24 Oct. 1905, BM, Add. MSS. 44929.56.

[2] Von Hügel to Tyrrell, 24 Oct. 1905, BM, Add. MSS. 44929.56-7.

[3] Von Hügel to Tyrrell, 24 Oct. 1905, BM, Add. MSS. 44929.57; von Hügel to Tyrrell, 28 Oct. 1905, BM, Add. MSS. 44929.58; von Hügel to Tyrrell, 15 Nov. 1905, BM, Add. MSS. 44929.64. Maude Petre remarks: 'In deferring, as he did, to this advice, Father Tyrrell probably acted against his own judgment. In the first place, he had little hope of finding such a bishop; in the second place, he doubted the wisdom of seeking one.' *Autobiography and Life*, II, p. 239.

with sympathy.'[1] Von Hügel's reaction to this strange twist of irony was not uncharacteristic. 'On first reading this', he told Tyrrell,

I was absorbed in musing on the utter absence of all intellectual interests among such no doubt representative upper-ten and official men as Mr H. represents; who, a convert, will know and care precisely about those things only, on which our average officials would be quite understanding and help-ful. – But, though I would not myself have taken the step he has taken, I think now that it can do no harm and *may* do some good: for M.d.V. is pretty sure to hear of (perhaps even have a word to say to) the case, before it is over: and his having to show his hand, a hostile one, to a man so entirely a novice and so trusting to M.d.V.'s friendliness towards you, – would be for the said M.d.V. far more difficult than any amount of fighting of 'Liberalistic' per-sons – I am, therefore, sorry at this step only because it deprives us of H.'s offices with Cardinal Ferrata; and that, this being so, I am at my wits' end as to whom to find for that approach. – I am thanking your cousin and trying to allay his fears of possible harm coming from Mr H.'s action. I am quite certain that M.d.V. if he does act at all, will carefully take his cue from the General S.J., whom he visits, I know, often and lengthily.[2]

When Tyrrell heard this news, he reportedly spent the morning 'in gusts of laughter', and observed that Merry del Val and the Jesuit General were 'as identical as any two persons of the Trinity'.[3]

As the year 1905 drew to a close, Tyrrell seemed as far away from a satisfactory solution to the problem of his ecclesiastical status as he had ever been. When he appealed to Archbishop Bourne to be received into the archdiocese of Westminster, he met with a refusal, on the plea that Bourne had an inviolable rule against receiving ex-order priests. 'Arch-bishop Bourne's letter is courteous', von Hügel pointed out to Tyrrell, 'even kindly in tone, I think; and I expect that it is literally true what he says, that, if he *did* take you, it would be the first exception to a fixed rule of his.'[4] The archbishop of Dublin was likewise approached, and with the same results. Several other attempts were planned, including a request to the archbishop of San Francisco. But as Tyrrell told the Baron with frank realism: '... a bishop who takes me knows well enough that he is freely patronizing a known "liberal" and that he will be responsible to Rome for my pranks. It may really prove impossible to get out except as suspended, i.e. a pacific solution may not be viable.'[5]

[1] *Diaries*, 28 Oct., and 17 Nov. 1905; von Hügel to Tyrrell, 18 Nov. 1905, BM, Add. MSS. 44929.65.
[2] Von Hügel to Tyrrell, 18 Nov. 1905, BM, Add. Mss. 44929.65–6.
[3] *Autobiography and Life, II*, p. 243.
[4] Von Hügel to Tyrrell, 6 Nov. 1905, BM, Add. MSS. 44929.60.
[5] Tyrrell to von Hügel, 13 Nov. 1905, in *Autobiography and Life*, II, p. 242.

Early in the new year of 1906 Tyrrell's problems with ecclesiastical status took an unexpected turn. On 7 January the Jesuit General wrote to Tyrrell, asking whether or not the latter was the author of a 'Lettera Confidenziale ad un amico professore di antropologia' ascribed to an 'English Jesuit' in a recent issue of the Milanese *Corriere della Sera*.[1] The Italian article in question was a rather sensationalistic account of a little work which Tyrrell had written two years earlier for private and limited circulation, and it included a few of the more radical sounding passages from Tyrrell in a not always accurate translation. Tyrrell's original booklet had been intended as a help for those educated Catholics who confused their inability to accept much of current Roman theology and practice with loss of faith, and it attempted to suggest the direction in which such individuals might search in order to live Catholic lives without compromising either their intellects or their consciences. When Tyrrell answered the General's query on 10 January, he told the latter that 'it will be better to keep to one question at a time and to settle my relations with the Society before proceeding to further issues'.[2] Consequently, he neither denied nor affirmed that he had written the 'Lettera Confidenziale'. Three days later, however, Tyrrell wrote the General again, telling him that at the time of writing the earlier letter 'it seemed to me better to deal with the camel before discussing the gnat ... But on reflection I see that the latter discussion may help to determine the former, and so I hasten to acknowledge as much responsibility as I honestly can for the "Lettera Confidenziale".'[3] He told the General that he did not know who had translated it, nor had he himself read the translation, and that he had been told that his original 'Letter' had been freely adapted to meet local needs. 'But I have no doubt', Tyrrell added,

that the substance of it – all that you would most dislike – is founded on a letter written by me two or three years ago to meet a particular yet not uncommon case. There is no statement of that original letter that is not theologically defensible. Yet as a whole it is a medicine for extreme cases; not for common ailments.[4]

[1] *Autobiography and Life*, II, pp. 249–50.
[2] Tyrrell to Martin, 10 Jan. 1906, in *Autobiography and Life*, II, p. 250.
[3] Tyrrell to Martin, 13 Jan. 1906, in *Autobiography and Life*, II, pp. 250–1.
[4] *Ibid*. Tyrrell was not being sarcastic, but factual, when he remarked that the General would dislike the substance of his *Letter to a Professor*. In 1896 Father Martin, in his capacity as General of the Society of Jesus, had addressed a letter to the entire Society throughout the world. The letter was entitled 'On Avoiding Some Dangers of Our Times', and its whole mentality was negative, fearful and condemnatory. Whereas Tyrrell's approach, and the more authentically Ignatian approach, had been to encourage the use of all the best creations and developments of contemporary society as means for bringing that society to higher values;

On 20 January the General told Tyrrell that he must either submit a repudiation of the 'Lettera' suitable for publication in the papers, or prepare himself to face dismissal from the Society of Jesus. Tyrrell answered on the 24th, leaving the matter of the dismissal to the General, and submitting a letter of explanation for the newspapers. Tyrrell's explanation was considered unsatisfactory in Rome. The papers authorizing his dismissal from the order were sent to the English Provincial for transmission to Tyrrell. On 19 February the Provincial formally presented the letters of dismissal to Tyrrell, and with their acceptance the latter's relationship to the order was ended. Yet Tyrrell's ecclesiastical status was more confused than ever. The General had dismissed Tyrrell from the order, but the Sacred Congregation had not thereby secularized him. He was a Roman Catholic priest and thus juridically required to have an ecclesiastical superior. He had been repudiated by his legitimate superior, and not yet, nor likely to be, accepted by another. In the meantime his rights to administer the sacraments or in other ways to exercise the functions of his priesthood were denied him.[1]

Martin's approach was to condemn all that was new, in every area, and to insist on fleeing to contemplative security. One relevant example from Martin's letter was his insistence that the desire on the part of some Jesuits to supplement the study of scholastic philosophy and theology with historical and scientific studies was a machination of the devil. The letter also condemned for Jesuits the reading of newspapers, novels and magazines. See, R. P. M. Ludovici Martin, 'Epistola ad Patres et Fratres Societatis Jesu de Aliquibus Nostrorum Temporum Periculis Cavendis', *Epistolae Praepositorum Generalium ad Patres et Fratres Societatis Jesu*, tome IV, Brussels, 1908, pp. 282–3 and 294–311 especially. The thirty-first General Congregation of the Society of Jesus, held in Rome from May to July 1965, and from September to November 1966, vindicated Tyrrell's spirit rather than Martin's. See, *Documents of the Thirty-First General Congregation*, Woodstock, Maryland, 1967, p. 5.

[1] *Autobiography and Life*, II, pp. 251–5. Several days after Tyrrell's dismissal, the following note appeared in *The Tablet*: '*The Daily Chronicle*, in its Roman Correspondence published on Tuesday, under the obviously misleading heading "Jesuit Secedes", a statement that Father George Tyrrell, S.J., in consequence of an old correspondence between himself and a Professor of Science, lately published in Rome, had left the Society of Jesus. Father Tyrrell has favoured us with a copy of the following letter which he has now addressed to the Editor of *The Daily Chronicle*: "Sir, – I learn with some regret that more attention has been given in your columns to my ecclesiastical difficulties than they are really worth. I wish to remark that the conflict, such as it is, is one of opinion and tendencies, not of persons; that, on both sides, it is the result of mental and moral necessities created by the antitheses, so far irreconcilable, with which the Church is wrestling in this period of transition; that, however harsh ecclesiastical action may seem, it is the usual harshness of a general law rather than that of personal rancour. Let me add that while I am most grateful to those who come forward to speak for me at a time of misunderstanding, I would far rather be left defenceless than that anything should be said that might be hurtful to my Jesuit and pro-Jesuit friends who are very many and very dear; or that would seem to deny to the opinions and tendencies of others that broad-minded toleration which, in the name of Catholic Liberty, I claim for my own. I am, &c., George Tyrrell."' *The Tablet*, vol. 107, no. 3433, 24 Feb. 1906, p. 286.

Tyrrell himself learned on 8 February that the letters dismissing him from the order had been received in England and were awaiting him. From his cousin's house in London he wrote to von Hügel, informing him of these latest developments, and asking: 'Is it desirable that, under the circumstances I shd. call upon you; or would it not be better if you could look me up some day? I shall be here for a fortnight; then to Paris with Bremond for a sort of wanderjahre before settling down.'[1] Von Hügel answered at once, telling Tyrrell 'how wise I think your line of conduct, and admirable your balance, strength and temper'. With the frankness of friendship the Baron added: 'I *think* whilst your status is still so much in *nubibus*, it will save me possible anxieties as to my wife's and girls' taking of it all, if you do not come here.'[2] He arranged to see Tyrrell on the following day, Sunday the 18th, and spent 'a good while' with him that day at the house of William Tyrrell.[3] On the next day Tyrrell received his dismissal papers from the English Provincial, and on the 20th he and von Hügel spent the afternoon walking and discussing the situation.[4] The two men met again on the 25th, and on the 27th Tyrrell left for Paris. Several weeks later von Hügel wrote to his friend Dom Cuthbert Butler:

As to Tyrrell, I had three long interviews with him during the 12 days he was in London, before going abroad on Shrove Tuesday. His dispositions were admirable: no bitterness or excitement but also no indifference or spiritual relaxation. And, alas, I am somewhat of a specialist by now, in symptoms at crises in people's lives ... Certainly, as far as I can judge, he is in a solid, balanced frame of mind; as his old friends in the Order are sticking to him finely. He has joined Bremond in Paris, and the two have gone together for a couple of months to Freiburg in Breisgau, where the excellent Sauer will learn from and, in return, benefit them. I think that not many months will pass, before the number of those who believe in him will be materially increased.[5]

The Baron was in constant contact with Tyrrell by letter during the two months in which the latter was on the continent. On 23 April he received a copy of the newly published *Lex Credendi* from Tyrrell, and on the 27th they had lunch and a walk together, – their first meeting after Tyrrell's return to England.[6]

1 Tyrrell to von Hügel, 16 Feb. 1906, BM, Add. MSS. 44929. 85.
2 Von Hügel to Tyrrell, 17 Feb. 1906, BM, Add. MSS. 44929.87.
3 *Diaries*, 18 Feb. 1906.
4 *Diaries*, 19 and 20 Feb. 1906.
5 Von Hügel to Butler, 7–8 March 1906, DAA, Butler MSS.
6 *Diaries*, 2, 15, and 20 March; 10, 14, 20, 23, 24, 25, 26, and 27 April 1906.

In mid-June von Hügel had an unexpected telegram which informed him that Tyrrell had suddenly gone abroad again with Bremond.[1] Although he was surprised at Tyrrell's sudden decision and move, he was not alarmed since he presumed that the action was mainly caused by Tyrrell's 'evidently shattered condition of nerves, and his wanting change and solitude even from Storrington'.[2] The first two postcards which the Baron received from Tyrrell only reinforced this impression, making it clear that the latter 'was immensely strained and weary, and only slowly and intermittently his "true self" again'.[3] Then, on 2 July, Alfred Fawkes[4] lunched with von Hügel and showed him a postcard which he had just received from Tyrrell. It spoke rather ambiguously of some 'fresh Roman excessive requirements', and it requested Fawkes to publicize Tyrrell's plight in the English press. Alarmed at this development, von Hügel wrote to Maude Petre on the following day to tell her that he was now convinced that Tyrrell 'has gone abroad *at least* as much because he wants to be in a position where he can "throw bombs" without injuring or distressing *directly* those that have grouped themselves about him.'[5] The postcard to Fawkes confirmed a 'longstanding conviction' which the Baron had about Tyrrell, and which he told Maude Petre he thought she shared. Tyrrell 'ever reminds me', he told her,

of those beautifully delicate, and *in their own way*, wonderfully strong marine creatures, plants, zoophytes, jelly-fish etc., which, as a child, used in the summer Mediterranean bathings, to delight and to affect me, – for in water and sunshine, how expansive, how delightful, how happy they were; and out of water and in the bleak winds, how shrunken, limp, mere husks and weeds they were! If ever a soul required trust, sympathy, affection, expansion, to be itself and do its great, very great, work, it is his! – But note, please, what follows from this. I think, taking circumstances as they are, and as they are not going to be materially changed during his and our life-times, – that *this* follows: not only that he should get the sympathy etc. which you want to keep

---

[1] *Diaries*, 15 June 1906.
[2] Von Hügel to Petre, 3 July 1906, BM, Add. MSS. 45361.39.   [3] *Ibid.*
[4] Fawkes, who was two years von Hügel's senior, was educated at Eton, and Balliol College, Oxford, where he had been an ardent latter-day Tractarian. In 1875 he entered the Roman Catholic church, and was ordained to the priesthood by Cardinal Manning in 1881. He was a close friend of Tyrrell, and expressed the desire to be buried beside him at Storrington. In 1909 Fawkes returned to the Anglican church and spent the rest of his life in a small country parish. ('Rome represents a stage through which the Christian idea has passed, but a stage from which it has emerged and to which it will not return. And "the Sabbath was made for man, not man for the Sabbath": Rome was for religion, not religion for Rome.' Alfred Fawkes, *Studies in Modernism*, London, 1913, p. 387.) Fawkes died in 1930.
[5] Von Hügel to Petre, 3 July 1906, BM, Add. MSS. 45361.39.

and get for him, but also that there should be as little as possible of fighting and collision between himself and the authorities. I now feel as if even our sympathy would not turn him into a 'good' fighter, by which I mean, not an 'effective' fighter, but a fighter *who does not damage his own self* by the fighting. He is too utterly sensitive, in a sense feminine a nature not to get dried-up, embittered, unbalanced over such conflicts. – Yet if this is true, the situation is indeed difficult: for it would be difficult on its directly *spiritual*, his spiritual advancement side. And I do not see how he is going to keep his liberty of *printing and circulating uncensorized* theological matter, without continuous battles and an ever growing ecclesiastical isolation. – I now feel inclined not to his making any of the doubtless very absolute engagements which, on this point, Rome is asking in return for his getting back his Mass, but to his not publishing anything further just at present, – not at least anything aggressive. I quite think there may be men who could and ought to do this, and now, – because they could do so well, – both for others and for their own soul's health; but I doubt whether he is that kind of man, – at least, just now. And certainly much [as] I wish to keep him unmuzzled, I do not want nerves or bitterness or temper to speak: is not blank silence far better than that? ... I know, of course, that he hoped to be able to keep the Authorities at least at bay. And perhaps he could do so, if he kept both his nerve *and* his temper. I pray God he may do so, – not merely or chiefly for our cause's sake, but for his own continuous deepest self-identity.[1]

That estimate by von Hügel, based on observation, reflection, and affection, is important. It was made on 3 July 1906, *before* Tyrrell's serious 'bomb throwing' had begun, and *before* the distressing events of Tyrrell's final three years of life. Had Maude Petre and Henri Bremond been less emotionally entangled with Tyrrell's every changing mood, had they been able to make an objective estimate of von Hügel's relationship to him during the following three years, and had they been able to recall this carefully thought out letter of the Baron's, in the light of which his future action was both intelligible and consistent, their judgments and accusations against von Hügel after Tyrrell's death might have been different.[2]

A week after Fawkes had shown Tyrrell's card to him, von Hügel received from Fawkes another card which the latter had just received from Tyrrell.[3] This second card explained what the earlier card

[1] *Ibid.*

[2] Maude Petre's full criticism of the Baron in his relationship to Tyrrell was only expressed in print after von Hügel's own death in 1925. See, for instance, her 'George Tyrrell and Friedrich von Hügel in Their Relation to Catholic Modernism', *The Modern Churchman*, no. 3, vol. XVII, June 1927, especially pp. 150, 151, and 153; *Von Hügel and Tyrrell*, especially pp. 5–9, 70–2, 103–4, 118–20, 121–2, 145–6, 165–6, and 197–203; *My Way of Faith*, especially pp. 256–9, 267, and 291.

[3] *Diaries*, 9 July 1906.

had meant by 'fresh Roman excessive requirements'. While Tyrrell had been in Freiburg in April, he had written to Cardinal Ferrata, asking that his ecclesiastical position be regularized at once and that his *celebret* (permission to offer Mass) be immediately restored so as to avoid scandal among Catholics and others who did not understand the situation.[1] Ferrata neither answered nor acknowledged the letter. Again in early May Tyrrell wrote to him, and stated that he intended to publish the correspondence and documents of his case in order to alleviate the scandal which his position was provoking. He also asked permission to approach the sacraments as a layman.[2] In the meantime, Archbishop Mercier of Malines in Belgium had been persuaded to accept Tyrrell into his diocese.[3] Accordingly, Mercier wrote to Ferrata, asking for Tyrrell's secularization and the regularization of his status. On 18 June Ferrata wrote to Mercier to tell the latter that he could accept Tyrrell, with his right to offer Mass restored, *colla condizione però che il medesimo P. Tyrrell prenda formale impegno di non pubblicare nulla in materia religiosa e neppure di tener corrispondenze epistolari senza la precisa approvazione di persona competente designata dalla Signoria Vostra.*[4] This condition of submitting his letters, in so far as they treated of religious matters, to ecclesiastical censorship was the 'fresh Roman excessive requirement' against which Tyrrell was reacting and about which he had written to Fawkes, – but not to the Baron. Only on 11 July did von Hügel himself hear from Tyrrell about the new restriction and about the 'decisive action' which Tyrrell had taken as a result.[5]

Tyrrell's action was 'decisive' in that it almost certainly put an end to the possibility of his reaching a satisfactory solution to his irregular ecclesiastical situation during the Roman reign of Pius X and Merry del Val. He wrote and printed an open letter of nearly 3,000 words to Cardinal Ferrata, dated from London (though he was actually in France) on 4 July 1906. Tyrrell recalled for Ferrata the brief history of their relationship, i.e. the two unanswered letters. 'Courtesy, charity, justice, demanded a reply,' he told the Cardinal, 'but none came.'[6] At once he proceeded to the condition which Ferrata had attached to his reception

[1] Tyrrell to Ferrata, 7 April 1906, in *Autobiography and Life*, II, p. 503.
[2] Tyrrell to Ferrata, 4 May 1906, in *Autobiography and Life*, II, p. 504.
[3] *Autobiography and Life*, II, p. 299ff.
[4] Ferrata to Mercier, 18 June 1906, in *Autobiography and Life*, II, p. 504.
[5] *Diaries*, 11 July 1906.
[6] Tyrrell to Ferrata, 4 July 1906, privately printed. The copy of the letter used by the author was von Hügel's own, which is found in the von Hügel collection at St Andrews University Library with the Baron's unbound theological pamphlets and papers, Box no. 8.

by Mercier into the diocese of Malines. 'I write now to tell Your Eminence that if this is to be the condition of my reinstatement I decline finally and categorically to be reinstated on a condition so dishonouring both to me and to the tribunal which imposes it.' And Tyrrell added: 'My rights and duties as a man are distinct from my rights and duties as a Catholic and a priest. As prior in nature, the first neither derive from nor can they be controlled directly by the Church or her officers.' He suggested that it was not 'with the knowledge or consent of the Holy Father that this indefensible condition has been imposed upon me. But from its inherent character as an artifice of inquisitorial police-control, and from all the circumstances under which it has been laid upon me, I have little doubt as to the true inspirers of this suggestion.' These, he told Ferrata, were the Roman officials of the Jesuit order. Tyrrell pointed out that to impose such conditions for his reinstatement implied that his suspension was penal. Yet he had never been accused or convicted of any crime against the church. 'Plainly the whole of my supposed offence', he argued,

is simply and only that I have left the Society of Jesus on a question of principle, about which Catholics and their spiritual rulers, even the most eminent, are equally divided, and consequently at perfect liberty to think as they choose. Belief in Jesuitism is no article of faith.

In concluding his letter Tyrrell told Ferrata that he would 'accept this present *impasse* as permanent rather than plead any further with authorities who have already treated my pleadings with a seemingly contemptuous silence', and who had imposed such outrageous and undignified conditions to his reinstatement as a priest.[1] In order to discomfort Ferrata with the idea that a large number of people had already seen the printed letter, Tyrrell numbered the first copy, the one which Ferrata received, as 67.[2] On 20 July Tyrrell wrote to Merry del Val asking him to

---

[1] Von Hügel defended Tyrrell's decision. '... I do not think it would be fair by Tyrrell, if we took the offers of the Bishop of Aberdeen and of the Archb. of Malines, alone, and then said "it is a pity he didn't accept, there was nothing seriously to prevent his accepting; it would have been all right". No: I quite agree that if these offers had stood unhampered by any other impossible condition, I should have regretted his not accommodating himself to them, at least as an experiment and for a time. But this was not the actual situation. Cardinal Ferrata's condition was (without any wish on those Bishops' part) an unescapable constituent of the whole offer. I am very sure that I could not, in his place, have accepted such an impossible, dishonorable condition; and I could not and cannot blame him if he felt and feels the same. But I feel confident that nothing remains to be done for him, with the Congregation, during this Pontificate. With the next one, I hope this and many another analogous situation may get improved; and meanwhile his friends will stick to him, quietly but firmly.' Von Hügel to Ward, 30 Aug. 1906, WFP, vH MSS.

[2] Tyrrell to Dell, 17 Aug. 1906, in *Autobiography and Life*, II, p. 306.

arrange to have the letter to Ferrata 'translated to His Holiness by some-one whose competence and honour are above suspicion'.[1] And he told the papal Secretary of State that since his writings and ideas were un-acceptable to Roman authorities, he would soon publish this fact, so that troubled souls kept in the church by these very ideas and books would no longer be misled, and so that the full burden of giving relevant help to such troubled seekers would fall heavily on the Roman authorities themselves.

On the same day that Tyrrell was writing to Merry del Val, von Hügel was entertaining the former's cousin, William Tyrrell, to breakfast, where he had a 'capital talk with him about Fr Tyrrell'.[2] Three months later the Baron wrote to Maude Petre about this talk in a way that left no doubts about his own dispositions and attitudes in regard to his much-harassed friend. He told Maude Petre that he had managed

a good visit and talk from and with Mr William Tyrrell. I think Fr.T. is rather tried and irritated by him; and I myself know him *very* slightly, so do not know whether or not he would affect me similarly. But it was very plain how utterly sincere and solid was that good, simple man's self-identification with his cousin's lot. – I found him, I thought more than in mere words, readily with me, when I insisted that the situation was so supremely difficult, that we, Fr. T.'s relations and friends, must not make our adhesion to and sympathy with him dependent upon his doing only what we may think the prudent and wise thing; but that, short of his doing clearly indefensible things (a most unlikely contingency) we should and will stick to him quietly but quite firmly and persistently. And again that he, Mr T. and his immediate belongings had a quite unassailable position and right in the matter. He entirely agreed and wrote me a very good little letter later on about the matter.[3]

To the end of George Tyrrell's life this cousin remained a sincere and loyal friend.

In August von Hügel sent his entire manuscript of *The Mystical Element of Religion* to Tyrrell for his criticism and suggestions.[4] Tyrrell worked through the manuscript with great dedication, spending as many as six hours a day over a period of weeks on it. On 6 October the Baron received a postcard from Tyrrell, telling him that the manuscript was on its way back to Kensington and that Tyrrell himself soon expected to take up residence in Clapham. When the manuscript arrived six days later,

[1] Tyrrell to Merry del Val, 20 July 1906, in *Autobiography and Life*, ii, p. 505.
[2] *Diaries*, 20 July 1906.
[3] Von Hügel to Petre, 19 Oct. 1906, BM, Add. MSS. 45361.43-4.
[4] *Diaries*, 11, 14, 15, 17, 18, and 19 Aug. 1906.

von Hügel wrote Tyrrell of the fact and also invited him to stay at the von Hügel residence for at least a week on his return.[1] Then on the 18th the Baron received another postcard from Tyrrell, one that really worried him. Tyrrell thanked von Hügel for his proffered hospitality, but told him that he had

already arranged as paying-guest with some friends at Clapham & I shd. not like to disappoint them. Besides I am sure it would not be prudent for you to entertain me in my present dismantled state. Indeed I am going to ask you to erase my name when it occurs in 2 or 3 places of a certain little MS. I never felt less inclined to be 'good', and so we had better confine our meetings to the neutral territory of K[ensington] Gardens.[2]

The allusions to Tyrrell's name in a certain little manuscript were to von Hügel's acknowledgment of Tyrrell's help in *The Mystical Element*. But the Baron felt that Tyrrell's request to have these acknowledgments removed was '*not* solely prompted by regard for my peace or with respect to his, Fr. T.'s actual, achieved doings and position, but as tho' they looked to some future, more "revolutionary" action of his, and as tho' it fretted him to feel us on his back or holding by his coat-tails, – something like the occasional temper I see in him with regard to Storrington also.'[3]

Tyrrell returned to England in late October and lunched with the Baron on the 23rd for the first time after his return. At that meeting von Hügel loaned him the typed manuscript of the Briggs–von Hügel correspondence which would become within a few weeks *The Papal Commission and the Pentateuch*.[4] They discussed the manuscript at later meetings, as they had discussed together so many other manuscripts in other years. Tyrrell had, meanwhile, prepared for publication the *Letter to a Professor* which had been instrumental in his dismissal from the Society of Jesus. He included with the *Letter* a long introduction which explained the reasons for publication, and gave the origins and purpose of the *Letter*. He also appended a number of notes which developed several ideas less fully developed in the original *Letter*. The new work was entitled *A Much Abused Letter*. On 3 November the Baron received his copy from Tyrrell himself.[5] The following six months were full of similar examples of mutual interest and help with one another's manuscripts

---

[1] *Diaries*, 27 Aug.; 6 Sept.; and 6 and 12 Oct. 1906.
[2] Tyrrell to von Hügel, 17 Oct. 1906, BM, Add. MSS. 44929.131.
[3] Von Hügel to Petre, 19 Oct. 1906, BM, Add. MSS. 45361.45.
[4] *Diaries*, 23 Oct. 1906.
[5] *Diaries*, 3 Nov. 1906. It was published in London by Longmans, Green and Co., 1906.

and writing schemes, but all the time von Hügel was increasingly aware of his need to help sustain the attitudes and dispositions in Tyrrell which he knew to be for the latter's own deepest and most lasting interests. Von Hügel continued to loan Tyrrell books and journals, and to suggest ideas and articles of interest for his perusal. In the last weeks of 1906 and through the early months of 1907 they met every few weeks for a walk or lunch or tea.[1] When Tyrrell prepared a preface for his new edition of *Oil and Wine*, von Hügel read and commented on it. And when the Baron had nearly finished his article on the Fourth Gospel for the *Encyclopaedia Britannica*, Tyrrell read it and gave him a long written critical evaluation.[2] Together they attended meetings of the London Society for the Study of Religion, and together they continued to plan and work for the future.[3] When the Baron returned from his week in Paris in April, he and Tyrrell spent an afternoon walking in Kensington Gardens while the former recounted all that he had seen and heard and done in Paris.[4] In June Tyrrell left London again for a more or less permanent residence at Storrington. But with the arrival of the summer of 1907 came the decisive Roman acts which were finally to destroy the hopes and dreams and much of the work of these friends of now ten years.

[1] *Diaries*, 11, 22, and 27 Nov.; and 2 Dec. 1906; 27 Jan.; 12 and 21 Feb.; 3, 9, 19, and 28 March 1907.
[2] *Diaries*, 5 and 7 March 1907.
[3] *Diaries*, 19 March, and 4 June 1907.
[4] *Diaries*, 16 April 1907.

CHAPTER 10

THUNDERBOLTS FROM ROME

BY THE SPRING of 1907 no doubt at all remained about the attitude of Pius X's pontificate toward modern ideas. Contemporary historico-critical studies of the bible had been rejected as early as December 1903 by the unqualified condemnation of Loisy's books. Philosophical and religious thought which expanded the traditional scholastic system had been rejected with the condemnation of Laberthonnière's and Viollet's books, and with the relegation of Tyrrell to an ecclesiastical no-man's land. The suggestion of ecclesiastical reform had been rejected with the condemnation of Fogazzaro's *Il Santo*. And political ideas and aspirations which wholeheartedly accepted democratic principles had been rejected with the papal interference in French political life, with the papal attempt to disgrace Bishop Bonomelli, and with the suspension from his priestly office of Romolo Murri.[1] To make the rejection of contemporary thought and life complete, and to ensure the large-scale retreat of Roman Catholics back into the mediaeval mould there only remained for the Pope to universalize his condemnations, and to enforce them with all the moral pressures available in his armoury of spiritual weapons. Before the year was out this final step also had been taken.

On 4 May Cardinal Steinhuber,[2] the Prefect of the Sacred Congregation of the Index, published in the *Osservatore Romano* a letter condemning the Milanese Review *Il Rinnovamento*.[3] According to Steinhuber, the Review was 'notably opposed to Catholic spirit and teaching'. He asserted that its writers were causing disturbance to consciences, and

[1] Murri (1870–1944) was founder of the National Democratic League which he declared to be independent of the hierarchy; he was suspended on 15 April 1907. Six weeks later von Hügel remarked: '...and tho' Murri's direct thinkings and temper of mind are far too absolute and theocratic for me, his opposition to the ever-increasing direct claims of the Pope and Bishops in Italy in *even* simply political and social affairs, is, in its substance, at least, undeniably legitimate.' Von Hügel to Ward, 28 May 1907, WFP, vH MSS. In January 1909 Murri's *I problemi dell' Italia contemporanea* was placed on the Index of Forbidden Books, and in March 1909 Murri received the major excommunication, i.e. he was nominally excommunicated by the Vatican, and Roman Catholics were required to disassociate themselves from him. *Acta Apostolicae Sedis*, vol. I, no. 2, p. 157, and no. 4, p. 276.

[2] Steinhuber died on 15 October in this same year. A brief account of his ecclesiastical career can be found in *The Tablet*, vol. 110, no. 3519, 19 Oct. 1907, p. 606.

[3] The official publication of the letter in Italian is found in *Acta Sanctae Sedis*, vol. XL, Rome, 1907, pp. 272–3.

posing 'as masters and almost as doctors of the Church'. And 'among those who seem to wish to arrogate to themselves a magisterium in the Church and to teach the Pope himself, are to be found names already known for other writings dictated by the same spirit, such as Fogazzaro, Tyrrell, von Hügel, Murri, and others'. Steinhuber castigated the 'self-conceit' of these men who dared to speak 'of the most difficult theological questions, and of the most important affairs of the Church', and who 'make distinctions between official and non-official Catholicism, between the dogmas defined by the Church as truths to be believed, and the immanence of religion in individuals'. Steinhuber expressed the belief that *Il Rinnovamento* had 'been founded with a view of fostering a most dangerous spirit of independence from the authority of the Church, and the supremacy of private judgment over that of the Church herself and of erecting itself into a school to prepare an anti-Catholic renewal of minds'. The letter concluded by condemning the spirit and unspecified 'errors' of the Review, and by calling on the Archbishop of Milan 'to summon the editor of the said review to desist from this undertaking so misguided and unworthy of a true Catholic'.[1]

When von Hügel received a copy of the *Osservatore Romano* containing the condemnatory letter, he wrote a lengthy letter of sympathy, full of reflections on Steinhuber's remarks, to Ajace Antonio Alfieri, *Il Rinnovamento*'s editor-in-chief.[2] *The Tablet*'s Roman correspondent, who thought the letter was 'a most serious condemnation', commented: 'It is hardly necessary to say that this important letter has caused a great sensation in Italy, following so closely on the suspension *a divinis* of Don Romolo Murri. Your correspondent has reason to believe that it will shortly be supplemented by another act of the ecclesiastical authorities.'[3] Letters of sympathy began to pour in upon von Hügel from his friends both abroad and in England.[4] Perhaps the most moving tribute to the Baron, of all those rendered in reaction to Steinhuber's condemnation was the letter which Loisy wrote to Steinhuber himself.[5] Loisy told the

---

[1] These quotations from the letter are taken from its English translation as published in *The Tablet*, vol. 109, no. 3496, 11 May 1907, p. 733.

[2] *Diaries*, 7 and 9 May 1907.

[3] *The Tablet*, vol. 109, no. 3496, 11 May 1907, p. 734.

[4] *Diaries*, 11, 13, 14, and 22 May 1907. 'I have had *very* kind letters of sympathy from English and foreign Catholic scholars and clerics.' Von Hügel to Ward, 16 May 1907, WFP, vH MSS. 'I have had quite a number of notes and letters of kind sympathy, of so spontaneous and solid a kind as to cheer me greatly.' Von Hügel to Ward, 28 May 1907, WFP, vH MSS.

[5] This was eventually printed in Loisy's *Quelques Lettres sur des questions actuelles et sur des événements récents*, Ceffonds, 1908, pp. 81–2.

Cardinal that although the latter would probably consider his letter 'an act of extraordinary rashness if not of insufferable pride', it was, in fact, merely 'the straightforward and sad remark of a man who suffers because of the public insult, rendered in the name of the Church, to another man whom he loves and respects, and whom he knows not to have merited the harsh judgment passed on him'. Loisy told Steinhuber that he had respect for all of the men mentioned in the condemnation.

But the injustice done to M. von Hügel affects me most particularly, because he has been my intimate friend for so many years, and because I find it intolerable to see treated as a proud man, as a pseudo-Catholic who arrogates to himself the Church's authority and who dares to instruct even the Pope, this most humble of Christians, this most selfless individual, and the one most sincerely devoted to the Catholic cause, whom I have ever known in the whole of my life.

Loisy acknowledged that von Hügel united sincerity and courage to his scholarship and piety, that he did not hesitate to speak out when necessary, but always with modesty, reserve, and due deference toward church authorities. But is this a crime, Loisy asked! 'Are the successors of Peter unable to listen to anyone but flatterers, and is all independence of mind immediately suspect to them?' Loisy concluded by warning Steinhuber that an attempt to repress contemporary intellectual developments would work to the ultimate harm of the church, and told him that his attack on von Hügel was more to the Cardinal's discredit than to the Baron's.

Von Hügel himself referred to the condemnation as 'Cardinal Steinhuber's extraordinary vivacious censure', and he made up his mind 'to keep entirely silent' in the hope that in this way the incident would soon be dropped.[1] He was convinced that he had been condemned not for the content of the Briggs–von Hügel correspondence on the Pentateuch as such, but only because the correspondence had appeared in *Il Rinnovamento*.[2] 'But the Cardinal writes as tho' I had contributed

[1] Von Hügel to Ward, 16 May 1907, WFP, vH MSS. To Tyrrell von Hügel wrote: 'We have evidently, once more, a piece of administrative rhetoric – something intended not to define a reality but to affect a situation ... But I felt and feel that we should cultivate in our own interior and in our outward action, if not an infinite yet an indefinite amount of quiet and tough "sitting tight", of trust in the power of time and circumstances, as ultimately in the hands of God and as stronger than all the wit or wiliness of man.' Von Hügel to Tyrrell, 8 May 1907, BM, Add. MSS. 44930.27–8.
[2] Von Hügel to Ward, 16 May 1907, WFP, vH MSS. See also, von Hügel to Ward, 28 May 1907, WFP, vH MSS. One might presume that John J. Heaney, *The Modernist Crisis: von Hügel*, p. 124, was unaware of the publication of the Briggs–von Hügel correspondence in the first number of *Il Rinnovamento*. He writes, in reference to the condemnation: 'Ironically,

something *composed for* the Review,' the Baron told Wilfrid Ward,

whereas I did not write a line specially for them. And he speaks as tho' *previously* to my appearance there, I had already been a writer of ill fame; whereas I have never, so far, incurred any ecclesiastical reproof or check whatsoever, – indeed the very Letter specially aimed at here had been circulating for five months without any such reprimand.[1]

Il Rinnovamento was not even a year old, when Cardinal Steinhuber's condemnation fell on it. The Review's three lay editors, Alfieri, Casati, and Gallarati Scotti, were outstanding Milanese Catholics, notable both for their intelligence and piety, and for their courage and independence.[2] They accepted Steinhuber's letter with respect, but with honesty. In a deferential public letter they told him that they re-affirmed their submission to church authority, and that they were deeply pained by the attribution of motives to themselves which directly contradicted their true intentions. They also told him that, conscious as they were of their Review's defects and of their need to work harder, they could not in conscience simply abandon its publication.[3] Von Hügel was delighted with their tone and their determination. To Ward he wrote:

I think the young men have been most wise and courageous in deciding, – quite on their own initiative, – to declare their Catholic convictions and deference to Rome and their readiness to accept and apply any precise and detailed censure, – in scientific matters, from the scientific authorities; in

---

this is the only time that von Hügel was ever mentioned by name in a public Church document. The Baron had not yet written anything for *Rinnovamento*, though his name had cropped up in the review.' Actually, the only one of the four men mentioned in the condemnation who had not yet published in *Il Rinnovamento* at the time of the condemnation was Tyrrell. In the Review's first issue after the condemnation, and before the condemnation was known in England, Tyrrell had published his 'Da Dio o dagli Uomini' in *Il Rinnovamento*. This essay became chapter 13 of Tyrrell's *Through Scylla and Charybdis*, London, 1907, pp. 355–86. For von Hügel's criticism of what he considered Tyrrell's too great immanental tendency in this essay, see the letter of von Hügel to Tyrrell, 14 May 1907, in *Selected Letters*, pp. 138–9.

[1] Von Hügel to Ward, 16 May 1907, WFP, vH MSS.

[2] For an account of the origins of *Il Rinnovamento* and of its genuine independence of Fogazzaro's influence, despite ecclesiastical assertions to the contrary, see, Tommaso Gallarati Scotti, *The Life of Antonio Fogazzaro*, translated by Mary Prichard Agnetti, London, n.d., pp. 271–2. For a good account of the part played by *Il Rinnovamento* in the Italian modernist movement, see, Pietro Scoppola, *Crisi modernista e rinnovamento cattolico in Italia*, Bologna, 1961, especially pp. 185–220.

[3] This letter, written in Italian, and dated 13 May 1907, was published in *Il Rinnovamento*, vol. I, no. 5, 1907, pp. 611–12. It was preceded on pp. 610–11 by Steinhuber's letter. On 17 May von Hügel recorded in his diary: 'Long, important letter fr. Alfieri (w. their answer to Archb. of Milan's comm. of Card. Steinhuber's Letter). They are respectful & Catholic, do not abandon review.'

disciplinary ones, from the disciplinary authorities; and in theological and spiritual points, from theological and spiritual authorities. But that they could not, at the bidding of the Congregation of the Index, suppress at one sweep, an entire Review, which had been long planned and which had hardly yet been able to show its full bearings. That they had fully considered the possible grave consequences this their attitude might entail; but that they loved the Church too much, to do what they knew would at once constitute a weapon against it in the hands of her enemies, – since these enemies would at once find here a fresh proof that Catholics have, and can have, no liberty of research and speculation, however careful they may be to leave all official formulations, final decisions, or disciplinary matters to the ecclesiastical authorities alone. That they would pray and labour so as to make their tone and positions more and more profoundly Christian and Catholic, and would gratefully welcome every censure that would help them in this. We must now wait and see what Rome will do. I know that already, several leading Italian ecclesiastics, of markedly Conservative traditions, have been much struck and moved by such transparently sincere and dignified conduct. – We seniors must, clearly, stand aloof, so that our four names may not add to the young fellows' difficulties. – I doubt whether Rome is, really, moderately inclined just now; but we shall see. I shall be only too glad, to find that she is.[1]

The Baron's gloomy surmise was, of course, fully justified by events of the following months. The Roman authorities completely rejected the editors' plea, and *Il Rinnovamento*, like so many other publications, organizations, and individuals, was to fall victim to the aggressive anti-modernist campaign waged under the banner of papal authority.

Within a month of receiving the censure of Cardinal Steinhuber, von Hügel was actively engaged in yet another effort to demonstrate to church authorities that disagreement with their policies did not necessarily imply either a rejection of legitimate authority as such or a loss of the Catholic faith. On 3 June he received from his Roman friend Genocchi a copy of an anonymous brochure entitled 'What We Want: An Open Letter to Pius X'.[2] The letter was the work of a group of young Italian priests, and had been finally composed, apparently, by a twenty-four-year-old cleric named Piastrelli.[3] When Pius X had created some new cardinals in the previous April, he had addressed them with a

[1] Von Hügel to Ward, 28 May 1907, WFP, vH MSS.

[2] *Diaries*, 3 June 1907.

[3] Von Hügel met Piastrelli for the first time in late August 1907 in the Tyrol. He recorded in his diary: '... Piastrelli (Rome, – author of "Quello che vogliamo"), a young round-blue-eyed, strong-chinned, thin-lipped, cropp-haired [*sic*!], very clean, neat, alert & composed man of 24 in lay dress' (*Diaries*, 27 Aug. 1907). At the time of receiving the letter to Pius X, and while the translation was being prepared, the Baron was not aware of the document's authorship. See, von Hügel to Lilley, 11 June 1907, LFP, II, vH MSS.; and von Hügel to Lilley, 4 July 1907, LFP, II, vH MSS.

violent call to arms against the 'revolt' of progressive thinkers within the church.[1] A group of young Italian priests felt that they and their work had been the object of the Pope's denunciation, and they used the means of an open letter to deny the attitude and motives which the Pope attributed to them, and to try to show him what their real aims were. When the Baron read the letter, he was so impressed with 'the admirable thing' that he at once went to *The Times* editorial offices to ask for its publication.[2] He was promised an answer within two days, but was told that the letter could not possibly be published in its entirety and was asked for further information (not for publication) about the number of clerics the letter actually represented. On the following day von Hügel had a letter from *The Times*' editor, offering him half a column in the paper for summarizing the Italian letter. On that same evening he attended a meeting of the London Society for the Study of Religion where he discussed the letter and *The Times* offer with Lilley and Tyrrell.[3] They agreed that Lilley should write the article for *The Times*, as well as prepare a translation of the entire letter for publication in book form.[4] Lilley's article appeared in *The Times* on 15 June.[5] It was a full column and six lines in length. 'The thing is very well done', von Hügel told Lilley, 'and the "Times" has, for once, acted really handsomely, – promptitude, large type, position, – all is excellent. I am much pleased; and warm thanks to you.'[6]

Meanwhile, Lilley continued to work on the translation, and von Hügel advised him with points concerning both the translation and Lilley's introduction for it.[7] Lilley had first thought of asking Wells, the

---

[1] The entire Allocution, given in Italian, is found in *Acta Sanctae Sedis*, vol. XL, Rome, 1907, pp. 266–9. An English translation is appended to A. L. Lilley's translation of *What We Want: An Open Letter to Pius X*. London, 1907, pp. 67–71.

[2] *Diaries*, 3 June 1907.

[3] Lilley had been a member of the LSSR from its foundation. Tyrrell was never a member, but he attended the meeting on 4 June as a guest. See, *MSS. Minutes of the LSSR* (Dr Williams's Library, – WL80, OD.17); and *Diaries*, 4 June 1907.

[4] *Diaries*, 4 and 5 June 1907.

[5] 'An "Open Letter" to Pius X', *The Times*, no. 38,360, 15 June 1907, p. 8.

[6] Von Hügel to Lilley, 17 June 1907, LFP, II, vH MSS.

[7] *Diaries*, 19 June and 2 July 1907. Two points in the Italian Letter seemed to von Hügel to leave the way open for legitimate criticism. Consequently, the Baron asked Lilley to meet these criticisms in advance by saying 'a few words of the kind of softening interpretation, which you know so well how to put together', in his introduction to the translation. He described the two weak points for Lilley thus: '(1) The writer seems to assert that there is an *individual* obligation, now recognized by his group, and which will, in time, have to be recognized by all, to study, fearlessly and critically, the huge, indigest, mass of religious documents, – Brahman, Buddhist, Mahommedan etc. as well as Jewish and Christian, – *before* the final assent of faith to Xtianity and the C. Church, as englobing and exceeding them

publisher of Scott Holland's *Commonwealth,* to produce the full translation. When Lilley approached Scott Holland on the matter, the latter sent his letter on to John Murray's publishing firm instead. Murray had already read Lilley's 'article in the Times with the greatest interest without knowing its authorship', and he was definitely interested in the project of the book.[1] He wanted, however, some assurance from Lilley that he regarded the Italian letter not 'as a mere passing nibble on the sea of controversy, but as a Stirring of the Waters, and as such, likely to have permanent interest'. Lilley passed Murray's letter on to von Hügel, and it prompted from the Baron his own reflection on the probable significance of the open letter to Pius X from the Italian clerics. 'We are not God', he told Lilley,

and cannot possibly be absolutely sure as to what will come of it, and as to how far a sufficient number of Italian and other Cath. clerics (and laymen) will keep up this attitude, on and on, until an appreciable improvement of things has been permanently achieved. But I think we can say, most sincerely, that either this very document will form a crystallizing-point for efforts and effects which will leave their permanent mark upon religious history; or, at least, that it will remain one of the most remarkable of a series of manifestations which will end in such results. – In saying this, I am well aware that an element of faith determines this my prognostic. But is not every forecast, not of a physical or mathematical kind, informed by such a faith?[2]

all. It is surely plain that he can only mean and claim, that the *Church at large,* that certain sections and members of it, i.e. the Xtian and Cath. critics and philosophers, have such a duty, – and they indeed, a strict obligation, – thus to study, criticize and synthesize; and that they, *qua savants and critics,* may not assert that supremacy of Xtianity and the C. Church, prior to such painstaking research. The individual, life- and God-seeking soul, – whether not critical and philosophical (ever the large majority of souls) or also critical and philosophical (ever the minority), – must however have a much shorter and simpler means than those researches for reaching what at least implies that conclusion. Such means must exist, – for faith and love cannot wait, and death may come, at any moment. (2) The writer again, speaks as tho' Metaphysics, in any and every sense, were permanently played out. I take it that he can mean no more than that, *as a matter of fact and for the moment at all events,* they, understood as a method and a precise intellectualist system, are impotent in our hands, and that Xtianity must be able to express itself also in this new anti-metaphysical, or at least anti-metaphysical-seeming, philosophy. But it is, surely, plain, that the affirmations of faith are affirmations of a metaphysical world, of metaphysical reality, – in the very highest and deepest sense of the word. And again, even in philosophy proper, I cannot but be profoundly sceptical as to the permanence of this root-and-branch anti-metaphysical bent. On this point, I believe my studies to have been wider than those of the author of the "Lettera", or perhaps it is rather that I have not had to go through an early training in those rigid, and now largely childish metaphysics of the Neo-scholastics, from which the great, noble mind we are now considering is, I think, still suffering, in the sense of showing some (few) symptoms of an excessive reaction.' Von Hügel to Lilley, 11 June 1907, LFP, ii, vH MSS.

[1] John Murray to Lilley, 17 June 1907, LFP, ii, vH MSS.
[2] Von Hügel to Lilley, 20 June 1907, LFP, ii, vH MSS.

By the end of June Murray had accepted Lilley's translation, though Lilley and von Hügel had rejected Murray's suggestion that Paul Sabatier be asked 'to write a few words of preface'.[1] The little book was published in the course of the summer, but it was almost universally overlooked in the comment caused by the violent flood of Vatican reaction so soon to sweep away any such modest protests as the open letter to Pius X.

When the final condemnations actually came from Rome, no one was really surprised, least of all von Hügel. For nearly five years his scholar and clerical friends on the continent had been passing on to him Roman rumours about an impending syllabus of propositions, drawn from the writings of Loisy, Laberthonnière, Tyrrell, and others, which were to be condemned. Finally, on the morning of 18 July 1907 the Baron read in *The Standard* an announcement that the long awaited decree, containing sixty-five condemned propositions, was to have been published in Rome on the previous evening. On the 19th he received a telegram from the editors of the *Giornale d'Italia*, inviting his own and Tyrrell's opinions on the condemnations. On the 22nd he received a copy of the *Osservatore Romano* which had first published the decree, and at once he began a very careful study of this document known to history by its opening words, *Lamentabili sane exitu*. After reading the whole thing through very carefully alone, von Hügel went through it once again with Lilley, when the latter came for tea on the 24th. Again, on the following day he worked through the entire document with Dr van den Biesen, as the two sat in Kensington Gardens, referring from time to time to the notes which Tyrrell had drawn up on the decree and had forwarded to the Baron. A few days later he went through *Lamentabili* once more, proposition by proposition, with his old friend Mrs Adeline Chapman.[2]

In early August von Hügel gave Wilfrid Ward his considered opinions of the document. He first tried to determine what value and authority should be attributed to the decree on principles of current church law and practice.[3] Then he told Ward that he was certain the latter would

[1] *Diaries*, 21 June 1907; Murray to Lilley, 27 June 1907, LFP, II, vH MSS.
[2] *Diaries*, 18, 19, 22, 23, 24, 25, and 28 July 1907.
[3] 'Then you will have remarked that it is a Decree of a *feria quarta* session of the H.O. Already some twelve years ago, Duchesne and I were taught in Rome by a then member of the H.O. how that tribunal held two very distinct kinds of sittings, and issued two very different kinds of decrees, – sittings and decrees *Feriae quintae*, when the Pope either presides in person, or specially sends a representative to preside for him, – these are most solemn, and, in the eyes of the H.O. itself, quasi-irreformable etc.; and sittings and decrees *Feriae quartae*,

have noticed 'how prominent is the difference between two sets of propositions of which the "Lamentabili" document is mostly made up'. The first set of propositions were 'caricature-propositions', and 'burlesques of anything any of the writers even possibly aimed at has ever said or meant'. The Baron told Ward that he 'began by thinking that these must have been got in by some wily, hidden friend, for they would certainly be easily subscribable by us all (short of the humiliation of having to admit that men could think us capable of such stuff) and they give a fantastic look to the whole document'. Most of the burlesque propositions took some aspect of one or another critical scholar's conclusions and expressed it in such a way as to obscure and caricature his real meaning. The Baron gave Ward a number of examples of such propositions. Proposition ten was an instance: 'The inspiration of the books of the Old Testament consists in the fact that the Israelite writers have handed down religious doctrines under a peculiar aspect (*sub peculiari quodam aspectu*), either little or not at all known to the Gentiles.'[1] Von Hügel's observation on that proposition was that he had utterly failed to trace it 'to any one of the now all but countless Biblical scholars whose works I have consulted'. Again, proposition fifteen stated: 'The Gospels until the time the canon was defined and constituted were increased by additions and corrections; hence in them there remained of the doctrine of Christ only a faint and uncertain trace.' Of this the Baron remarked that the proposition 'in its protasis maintains a truth, or something near it, but which in its apodosis talks nonsense, and makes this nonsense the point of the whole sentence'. Proposition twenty-eight, another caricature, stated: 'Jesus, while He was exercising His ministry, did not speak with the object of teaching that He was the Messiah, nor did his miracles tend to prove this.' Von Hügel's

when the Pope neither presides nor sends, – these are quite secondary affairs, even in the eyes of the H.O. itself, and can readily be dropped or modified. (The day of the Pope's signature makes no kind of difference.) You will note then, that this is a *feria quarta* affair. The papers have already spoken of it as on a par with the condemnation of Galileo: they are wrong, – Galileo was condemned on a *feria quinta*; this is merely a *feria quarta* declaration.' Von Hügel to Ward, 8–9 Aug. 1907, WFP, vH MSS. All further quotations from von Hügel in this and the following two paragraphs are taken from this same lengthy letter. When von Hügel made his same Wednesday–Thursday distinction for Loisy, the latter observed with understandable cynicism: 'Touchant subterfuge, mais pratiquement illusoire, puisque Pie X exigera, sous peine d'excommunication, l'obéissance à *Lamentabili* comme à *Pascendi*. Rappelons-nous aussi que mes livres, en 1903, avaient été condamnés le mercredi, et que je n'en faillis pas moins être excommunié pour n'avoir pas souscrit sans réserve à la condamnation.' *Mém.* II, p. 547.

[1] The full Latin text of *Lamentabili* in its official publication is found in *Acta Sanctae Sedis*, vol. XL, Rome, 1907, pp. 470–8. An English translation is found appended to Paul Sabatier's *Modernism*, translated by C. A. Miles, London, 1908, pp. 217–30.

observation here was that the proposition 'declares the very contradictory of the teaching of Loisy and all the best N.T. critics, – for if J.C.
did not teach Himself to be Messiah, what on earth did He teach?' Of
proposition fifty-six, 'The Roman Church became the head of all the
Churches not through the ordinance of Divine Providence but through
merely political conditions', von Hügel asked: 'Whoever said this?
Holtzmann, Ranke, Sohm etc. would all admit that the Roman Church
acquired the head-ship of the other Chr. Churches by the will of Providence, and not thro' purely political conditions, – if such things exist.'
Of the final condemned proposition, 'Modern Catholicism cannot be
reconciled with true science unless it be transformed into a non-
dogmatic Christianity, that is into a broad and liberal Protestantism',
his comment was, simply, 'fantastic'. The Baron told Ward that a
friend of his had suggested 'that the Decree, in its original form, was
composed throughout of such-like props.; and that only later on were
many eliminated and was the other set of props., now to be found here,
introduced'.

The other set of propositions was very different from the burlesques
of the first set. These, in von Hügel's estimation, were drawn up by 'an
opponent of critical methods, intelligent enough to quote the propositions more or less exactly, ... only, he did not see how hopelessly in a
blind-alley and pinned against an un-scaleable wall, would be Church-
authority if it committed itself absolutely to such, finally suicidal,
positions'. Some examples of this second set of propositions were numbers sixteen to eighteen. These had to do with the fourth gospel, and
condemned any claims for its non-historicity and apostolic inauthen-
ticity.[1] But what was being condemned, as the Baron noted, was 'the
labours of some 70 years' of critical biblical scholarship. Propositions
forty-two to forty-four were statements about the evolution of the

[1] On 29 May 1907 the Pontifical Biblical Commission had published their responses to
three questions submitted to them concerning the historicity and authenticity of the Fourth
Gospel. The Commission affirmed without qualification that the Apostle John was the author
of the Fourth Gospel, and that it was genuinely historical in its narrative, even to the account
of the words attributed to Jesus. This document is found in *Acta Sanctae Sedis*, vol. XL, Rome,
1907, pp. 383–4. On 8 June von Hügel received a post-card from Tyrrell referring him to an
account of this Roman decision in *The Times* of the previous day. The Baron rushed out to the
Public Library where he read the account of the Biblical Commission's Decree, and noted
that the document had been signed by the Pope (*Diaries*, 8 June 1907). Three days later his
diary notes: 'Letter (important) to Dr. Briggs, abt. IVth Gospel & Rom. Bibl. Comm.
decision' (*Diaries*, 11 June 1907). On the same day he wrote to Lilley: 'You will have seen
that the Bible Comm. has now issued a purely conservative decision about the 4th G. Also am
writing to Briggs to prevent his more or less backing them, for on these N.T. points he is only
half satisfactory.' Von Hügel to Lilley, 11 June 1907, LFP, II, vH MSS.

doctrine and practice of baptism and confirmation, which condemned propositions von Hügel felt were 'questions for the historian, and hardly likely to be formulated very differently by the historian of the future'. However, it was not so much this or that anti-historical and anti-critical proposition which worried the Baron. Three of the condemned propositions, numbers one, twelve, and sixty-one, he felt to be the most important and far-reaching of all, not because of the detailed anti-historical bias implied in their condemnation, but because their condemnation rejected *in principle* the method of free historical and critical enquiry. He told Ward that

our science, like every other human science, is not infallible; and in one or other matter, or to a certain extent in all these matters, scholars may see more and differently in 50 or 100 years. Yet the question of *principle* will remain utterly unchanged: these matters and their solution will be then as now dependent upon historico-critical method and evidence. And to subtract them from the latter and put them directly under the jurisdiction of Church officials, or of Scholastic theologians, is not only to abandon the fundamental duty and condition of all sincere science, but also to ruin the logic and intrinsic necessities of the Catholic position itself, which ineradicably requires that its historical preambles and phenomenal facts shall be capable of and open to serious historical analysis and proof.

Since Ward was the editor of the ecclesiastically controlled *Dublin Review*, von Hügel took the liberty of suggesting three positions which he hoped that Ward would take up or imply toward *Lamentabili* if he found it necessary to write about the document. The first position was a careful limitation of *Lamentabili* 'to its real proportions and significance, – best attained by speaking but little, and only if and when unavoidable, of the Decree, and never with that insincere pomp and inflation now so painfully common'. The second position was to indicate the excess in the caricature propositions of the decree, and to show how easy of acceptance all these propositions were because of this excess. And the final position was 'a careful, clear, sober but unshrinking exposition of the danger *to the Church*, to its inherent logic and anti-fideist position, would be any pressing of the *principle* of the other set of props., even if they, each simply, expressed an historical "fact" which historical method and work would eventually disprove'. The Baron told Ward that he was convinced 'that we are still not at the apogee of the reaction, tho' it is certainly, by now, a bit difficult to see what more remains to be done in this sense'.[1]

[1] Certainly von Hügel would have disagreed with the protasis of a judgment by John J. |

On 1 August von Hügel left Victoria Station 'in a terrible holiday-crowd, at 11', to join his wife and eldest daughter in the Tyrol.[1] Gertrude had been at Levico since the end of 1906 because of her health, and Lady Mary had been with her there since the late spring. After four long and hard days of train travel the Baron reached Levico, and at once both his family and his Italian friends began to make great demands on his time and energy. He found Gertrude 'tho' better, yet delicate', and his wife 'very little well somehow'.[2] On the 6th Alfieri arrived at the Baron's hotel, and for two days kept von Hügel 'fully employed with talks on one's life-subjects', which included a full reading and discussion of *Lamentabili*.[3] He read through the same document with Gertrude later, and noted in his diary that he had talked with her 'on N[ew] T[estament] & Church authority questions, walking on high road to'rds Trent'.[4] He also began reading Schweitzer's *Von Reimarus zu Wrede* while at Levico.[5] But it was the problems faced by his young Italian friends of *Il Rinnovamento*, and their supporters, which primarily occupied von Hügel during those six weeks abroad.

On the 24th he received a letter from Fogazzaro asking him to meet with Scotti and himself at Caldonazzo Station, which the Baron did two days later. When the three men met, the two Italians persuaded von Hügel to go at once with them to Molveno where a meeting had been arranged with some other members of the Italian group.[6] After two train rides and five hours in a two-horse carriage up the mountain side, they

---

Heaney, *The Modernist Crisis: von Hügel*, p. 209: 'A careful analysis of the sixty-five propositions of *Lamentabili* shows that they were worded with great prudence; nevertheless a few were stated quite ambiguously.'

[1] *Diaries*, 1 Aug. 1907.
[2] Von Hügel to Ward, 8–9 Aug. 1907, WFP, vH MSS.
[3] *Ibid.* See also, *Diaries*, 6–7 Aug. 1907.
[4] *Diaries*, 12, 24, and 25 Aug. 1907.
[5] *Diaries*, 13 Aug. 1907.
[6] The Italian group had been planning a meeting among themselves since May. See, Scoppola, *Crisi modernista e rinnovamento cattolico in Italia*, pp. 237ff. John J. Heaney, *The Modernist Crisis: von Hügel*, p. 204, has suggested that von Hügel conceived of Modernism 'as a planned movement', and that the Molveno meeting was the single great moment of contact and agreement for the Italian modernists as a whole. Von Hügel did not consider modernism a 'planned movement'. Rather he considered it a spirit had in common by men engaged in various intellectual and social activities which inclined them to work toward a solution for the problems created for the Christian faith by their contemporary milieu. See, for example, his letters to G. E. Newsom, 7 Sept. 1909; Maude Petre, 13 March 1918; and Professor René Guiran, 11 July 1921, in *Selected Letters*, pp. 166–8, 247–9, 333–7. Moreover, the Molveno meeting was not a meeting of 'the Italian Modernists', but only of the *Rinnovamento* group and one or two of their closest sympathizers. Heaney's judgment seems overly influenced, perhaps, by Albert Houtin, *Histoire du Modernisme Catholique*, Paris, 1913, p. 177.

reached Molveno at 9.30 that night. The local hotel had no rooms available, so the Baron and Scotti had to share a room at 'a little albergo in the village'. Early the following morning von Hügel, Fogazzaro, and Scotti, went off to the village church to Mass, and then waited as the others began to arrive, – Don Brizio Casciola, Alessandro Casati, Ernesto Buonaiuti, Francesco Mari, Umberto Fracassini, and Luigi Piastrelli. The afternoon was spent in a nearby wood discussing the practical problem facing Fogazzaro because of a lecture series he had inaugurated and which was likely to cause trouble with the ecclesiastical authorities. In the evening von Hügel spoke to them about the efforts of their like-minded counterparts in England and the part which the Anglicans played in these efforts. Although he was up by 6.30 on the following morning, the Baron was too late for Mass in the local church, so he simply prayed there quietly for half an hour, before spending the morning discussing historico-critical problems with the group, again in the woods.

In the afternoon they discussed 'practical matters' which each of them would soon have to carry out in one way or another. They discussed what should be done if the Pope himself condemned *Il Rinnovamento*; what should be done if a submission were demanded of all priests to the Decree *Lamentabili*; and whether or not the group should undertake to write and circulate tracts among themselves and with interested fellow-thinkers on critical ecclesiastical questions. The tracts plan must have been carried, because von Hügel recorded his agreement to write a tract on critical methods, though he was never able to carry out his intention. On 29 August the group disbanded early in the morning, but not before the Baron had addressed them with a moving 'little parting speech'. He read them the last letter he had received from Loisy, and then he dwelt on the 'necessity of sincere, thorough critical work; of deep self-renouncing Xtian life; & of careful charity & magnanimity to'rds our opponents'.[1] Arriving back in Levico that same evening, the Baron remained there until he and Lady Mary left for home on 10 September. They broke their journey back to England twice, once to visit friends near Schwaz, and once at Baden-Baden so that the Baron could spend a day with his much-admired friend Professor H. J. Holtzmann.[2] This was the first and only meeting between

[1] *Diaries*, 26–9 Aug. 1907. See also, Ernesto Buonajuti, *Pellegrino di Roma*, Rome, 1945, p. 90.
[2] *Diaries*, 10–15 Sept. 1907. Holtzmann's death three years later, coming in the midst of all the Baron's other sorrows, was a great blow to him. 'On Sat. night I received the notice of the

the two men, though they had corresponded for years. By the evening of the 15th, after 'a good crossing' from Calais to Dover, the Baron and Lady Mary were once again in Kensington.

Within twenty-four hours of von Hügel's return to England, the papal encyclical *Pascendi dominici gregis* was published in Rome. This document, presented to the world in the Pope's name, and certainly composed under his personal authorization and supervision even if not entirely by his own hand,[1] was intended to represent for every Roman Catholic the authentic teaching of his church. The encyclical was presented as an act of supreme concern on the part of the shepherd for his sheep, as an attempt to protect good Catholics from evils and errors as widespread as they were insidious.[2] Unfortunately, the Pope was protecting his flock from something which neither he nor those who had collaborated with him in writing the encyclical really understood, and which, perhaps, they could not understand. The Roman Catholic clerical training of the period, and especially that of the Roman schools, with its limitation to scholastic philosophy and theology, and its general ignorance of nearly all modern modes of thought, especially the historical, was the background which produced *Pascendi*.[3] It was a back-

---

death of my most kind old friend, that fine N.T. scholar, Dr. Heinrich Holtzmann; and tho' he was 78 yrs. old – 20 years my senior, – he was still so fresh and active, so courageous, candid, and so full of faith in God and of generous ever watchful, love and sympathy for us, his friends, that his going is for me as the quenching of one of the few centres of ever-ready support and help.' Von Hügel to Juliet Mansel, 8 Aug. 1910, Juliet Mansel Papers, vH MSS. Miss Mansel kindly allowed the author to read through all of von Hügel's many letters to her.

[1] From the moment the encyclical was published, speculation on its authorship, and especially authorship of the doctrinal sections, was widespread. Louis Billot and Umberto Benigni were most commonly suggested as authors. See, Houtin, *Histoire du Modernisme Catholique*, p. 179; and Loisy, *Mém.* II, p. 566. The Reverend F. Nutcombe Oxenham, an Anglican chaplain in Italy, wrote back to England shortly after the encyclical was published that the authors of the document were said to be 'Father Billot (a Jesuit), Father Milzi d'Eril (a Barnabite), and Father Lorenzo Jansenns (a Benedictine)'. *The Tablet*, vol. 110, no. 3517, 5 Oct. 1907, p. 544. However, Jean Rivière, 'Qui rédigea l'encyclique "Pascendi"?', *Bulletin de littérature ecclésiastique* (Toulouse), vol. XLVII, no. 2–3, Avril–Septembre, 1946, pp. 143–61, seems to have demonstrated, on the basis of striking internal and external evidence, that the major role in drafting *Pascendi* was played by one Père Joseph Lemius, O.M.I., a Roman theologian who supposedly specialized in expounding refutations of Loisy's ideas.

[2] 'Pascendi dominici gregis mandatum Nobis divinitus officium id munus in primis a Christo assignatum habet, ut traditae sanctis fidei depositum vigilantissime custodiat, repudiatis profanis vocum novitatibus atque oppositionibus falsi nominis scientiae.' *Acta Sanctae Sedis*, vol. XL, Rome, 1907, p. 593. This is the official publication of the encyclical and the copy of that document used in these pages.

[3] The calibre of Roman education at this period can be judged by the memoirs of two Englishmen who experienced it, and who, while deeply loyal to Rome, are clear in their indictment of Roman education, – Wilfrid Ward and William Barry. See, Maisie Ward's *The Wilfrid Wards and the Transition*, pp. 66–7; and William Barry's *Memories and Opinions*, London,

ground which prepared its clerical products to view all principles, methodologies, and conclusions outside the scholastic system, as adversaries to be refuted. It was a background which had assumed, though never explicitly, that the scholastic theological system, in its general outline, was equatable with divine revelation. And it was a background which inevitably produced the self-righteous crusading mentality that could fight all adversaries of the scholastic system as though they were God's own enemies, or, even worse, heretics! Consequently, from its opening paragraphs to its conclusion, the encyclical presumed bad-faith and evil motives on the part of these adversaries of scholasticism whom it aimed to smite with God's own right hand of papal authority.[1] Unable to comprehend the minds of men who had broken out of the supposedly all-sufficient scholastic mould of thought, like Tyrrell or Loisy, or of men who had never been in that mould, like von Hügel and Fogazzaro, the authors of the encyclical created an imaginary system as an anti-system to scholasticism and termed it 'modernism', – 'the synthesis of all heresies'.[2] Having created a system, and given it a name, the encyclical then elaborated with considerable detail this so-called heresy: it was said to be composed of philosophical agnosticism, theories of vital immanence, deformation of religious history, evolution of dogma, experience as a religious criterion, scientific autonomy, and various symbolist theories. The encyclical concluded with a programme for exterminating modernism from all Catholic institutions, and from the Roman Catholic body as a whole. The chief remedy for wiping out this pestilential spirit and these destructive ideas, was to be through rigid enforcement of a carefully controlled study-programme of scholastic philosophy and theology, and by strict censorship of all reading material and personal contacts among Catholic clerics and seminarians.[3] 'Vigilance Committees' were to be set up in every Catholic diocese to carry out this pervasive control at the local level. Tyrrell remarked that the place of

---

1926, pp. 67–81 and 99–100. An indispensable *tour de force* on Roman Catholic clerical education of the period is P. Saintyves, *La Réforme intellectuelle du clergé et la liberté d'Enseignement*, Paris, 1904. Pages 161–91 and the whole of Part IV are especially important for anyone who would appreciate the mentality which produced *Pascendi*. On the author of this pseudonymous study, see the letter of von Hügel to C. C. J. Webb, 3 Oct. 1910, in *Selected Letters*, pp. 181–2.

[1] *Acta Sanctae Sedis*, vol. XL, 1907, pp. 594–6, 620, and especially 635.
[2] *Ibid.* p. 632: 'Jam systema universum uno quasi obtutu respicientes, nemo mirabitur si sic illud definimus, ut omnium haereseon conlectum esse affirmemus.' – See also, George Tyrrell, 'The Prospects of Modernism', *The Hibbert Journal*, vol. VI, no. 2, Jan. 1908, pp. 246–7.
[3] *Acta Sanctae Sedis*, vol. XL, 1907, pp. 640–7.

Pascendi in relation to modern life and thought was that of 'the dead in the midst of the living'.[1]

The encyclical seemed so totally and uncompromisingly reactionary in content, and so violent and uncharitable in tone, that only the most militant of ultramontanes and the most intransigent of anti-clericals remained unsaddened by its publication. It equated Catholicism with the narrowest of scholastic orthodoxies, and left no room in the Roman church for any efforts towards a theological synthesis which would take seriously the intellectual advances made since the thirteenth century. Moreover, the sweeping condemnations of the encyclical made it

possible to group together in one unholy fraternity, and under the same anathema, those who are sincere Catholics by conviction and those who, having lost all faith in the Church, continue Catholics in name and profession, whether through indifference, or self-interest, or consideration for the feelings of others. Men whose modernity is little more than an educated Ultramontanism are thus brought under suspicion of a secret sympathy with deists, atheists, and agnostics, and held up to the odium of the faithful at large.[2]

On 19 September von Hügel received a copy of the encyclical from his future son-in-law, Count Francesco Salimei. He had given it a careful first reading by the afternoon of the following day, when he went off with Tyrrell to Lilley's vicarage for tea and a discussion of the document. Tyrrell had been staying with the Baron since the 18th, and before he left on the 21st he showed his host the manuscript of the signed letter on the encyclical which he had prepared for the *Giornale d'Italia*.[3] Both the *Giornale d'Italia* and *The Times* had asked Tyrrell for his comments on *Pascendi*, and he complied with both requests.[4] After reading the published version of the Italian letter, von Hügel noted that he had 'read

[1] George Tyrrell, 'Mediaevalism and Modernism', *The Harvard Theological Review*, vol. 1, no. 3, July 1908, p. 310.
[2] *Ibid.* p. 304.
[3] *Diaries*, 18–21 Sept. 1907. The Roman correspondent for *The Tablet* told that journal's readers: 'The most painful commentary on the Encyclical is one which has appeared in the *Giornale d'Italia*. Readers of a recent Rome correspondence in *The Tablet* will remember something of the character of this Liberal organ. It took a leading part in the campaign recently organized by the Freemasons against the religious orders, and it never neglects an opportunity to provoke discord among Catholics, and disrespect for the authority of the Holy See. After the publication of the Encyclical it had the bright idea of securing the pen of the Rev. G. Tyrrell for a commentary. The commentary has been printed, and it is of a kind which unfortunately leaves no room for doubt as to the attitude of the writer. He not only refuses obedience to the teachings of the Holy Father, but uses language in regard to the Encyclical little short of insult against His Holiness. Incidentally the Tyrrell letter bears out with marvelous accuracy those points of the Encyclical which describe the "Modernists" and their tactics.' *The Tablet*, vol. 110, no. 3517, 5 Oct. 1907, p. 533.
[4] *Autobiography and Life*, II, p. 335.

Fr. Tyrrell's very strong, indeed vehement, but I expect, useful letter (Sept. 26) to "Giorn. d'It." on Encyclical'.[1] The vehemence of Tyrrell's tone and his seemingly personal attack on Pius X offended many of his Italian readers, including some of the *Rinnovamento* group and their friends. A considerable amont of persuasion from von Hügel was necessary before Alfieri and others could be convinced that they should stand by Tyrrell. 'Am busy rallying and steadying, for all I am worth', the Baron told Lilley, 'some (passing) dismay and alarm over T.'s "Gior. d'It." letter, among *some*, tho' by no means all, of his It. Catholic admirers.'[2]

Tyrrell's commentary for *The Times* appeared in the paper's issues for 30 September and 1 October.[3] The Baron had been visiting his mother in Cambridge while Tyrrell was preparing his *Times* articles, so he had no opportunity to see them before their publication. While in Cambridge, however, he had lengthy conversations with his friends James Ward, F. C. Burkitt, and Robert Hugh Benson, about the encyclical and the crisis it had precipitated.[4] Back in London by the evening of the 28th, von Hügel read Tyrrell's articles as they appeared on the mornings of the 30th and the 1st. In comparison with the Italian letter he found 'the "Times" articles are far more complete and could not be thus misunderstood. What grand things they contain and so little of the bitterness that shows in places excessively in the It. article'.[5] After reading over

---

[1] *Diaries*, 29 Sept. 1907.

[2] Von Hügel to Lilley, 3 Oct. 1907, LFP, 1, vH MSS. See also, *Diaries*, 30 Sept.; 1, 2, 4, and 5 Oct. 1907; von Hügel to Tyrrell, 1 Oct. 1907, in *Selected Letters*, pp. 141–2.

[3] *The Times*, no. 38,451, 30 Sept. 1907, p. 4; and no. 38,452, 1 Oct. 1907, p. 5. *The Times* commented on Tyrrell's articles with a leader, when it published the second article. On that very day the Anglican Church Congress opened at Great Yarmouth, and the leader concluded significantly: 'It is, perhaps, not too much to hope that Father Tyrrell's deliberate reflections will not be lost on the assembly which opens today at Great Yarmouth. There may be senses in which the English Church is "tied hand and foot", but even those who finger the trinkets of reunion may well take this Encyclical as an intimation that the trinkets would be very dear at the price' (p. 7).

[4] *Diaries*, 23–8 Sept. 1907.

[5] Von Hügel to Lilley, 3 Oct. 1907, LFP, 1, vH MSS. Canon James Moyes wrote a five-column article in *The Tablet*, vol. 110, no. 3518, 12 Oct. 1907, pp. 561–3, as a counter-blast to Tyrrell's *Times* articles ('The spectacle of a priest waging battle against the Holy See in the columns of *The Times* is one which even the few sympathizers whom he may have in this country will be very glad to forget. Such a contest is in itself far too absurdly uneven and too grotesquely preposterous not to bring discredit upon the misguided assailants whose ambition may tempt them to engage in it' [p. 561]). Merry del Val wrote to Moyes after reading *The Tablet* article: 'Mgr. Stanley, whom I saw last night, on his return from England, assures me that I am not mistaken in supposing that the recent article which appeared in "The Tablet", on the Holy Father's Encyclical & "Modernism" was written by you [the article was unsigned]. I feel I should like to tell you how very much everybody here has appreciated what you have written. I had the article translated & published in the "Osservatore" and it has

The Times articles twice, as well as the paper's own leader on them, von Hügel sent his impressions on to Tyrrell:

There can, I take it, be no serious doubt as to two things. One, that the substance of those two papers of yours, – the philosophical and theological analysis and positions, – are deep and true and great; and that there was and is a crying need for such expositions either now or soon ... The second thing is that although, perhaps, written less angrily than the *Giornale d'Italia* letter, this double paper is also, of course, very hot, vehement, and sarcastic. I hope very much that this heat, which, in some places, is so apt, and in all is so understandable, may not, in the long run at least, deflect otherwise likely and winnable minds from the substantial content and real, final aim of your papers.[1]

The Baron told Tyrrell that he was not criticizing his speaking out, nor questioning his mastery of the subject, but only suggesting a greater magnanimity in his personal tone when writing on this subject.

Several weeks after the encyclical was published the Baron had neither seen nor heard from Wilfrid Ward. 'Still no note from Wilf. Ward,' he told Lilley, 'who, poor fellow, will be unable to evade the fact that he and such as he fare at least as badly at Pius' hands as do Tyrrell or Loisy.'[2] Ward himself, always so cautiously moderate and ever scholastically oriented, felt this too. He wrote to Lord Halifax that he was 'properly dejected by the Encyclical. It shows the Pope to be out of touch with what is now a very large body of educated opinion among us. He has thrown himself (in his panic & anger) into the arms of Brandi and the *Civiltà*. Probably one of those *Civiltà* Jesuits wrote most of the argumentation part of the Encyclical.'[3] And he added that if only Loisy or LeRoy or 'even Tyrrell' had come in for censure in *Pascendi*, then Pius X might still 'have held the mass of opinion among us.' Finally, in mid-October von Hügel received a letter of commiseration from the dejected Ward, and at once he hastened to acknowledge Ward's thoughtfulness. 'Thank you much for your kind sympathy', he wrote,

especially welcome at a time such as this. With you I think that it will turn out a blessing in (a *very* thick) disguise, if all this astonishingly vehement reaction really brings out fully such elements and prejudices as have, by

---

been very highly eulogized by all who have read it, and the Holy Father desires me to send you a special blessing in His name.' Merry del Val to Moyes, 1 Nov. 1907, AAW, Unsorted Moyes Papers, no. 168.

[1] Von Hügel to Tyrrell, 1 Oct. 1907, in *Selected Letters*, p. 141.
[2] Von Hügel to Lilley, 3 Oct. 1907, LFP, I, vH MSS.
[3] Ward to Halifax, 1 Oct. 1907, HP, A4. 224.

diplomacy, been so largely hidden, but none the less mischievous for now three centuries, and especially since the last 100 odd years. I am especially not sorry that, – if once the thing was to be tried, – the attempt upon legitimate and necessary scientific liberty should have been mixed up with such a violently anti-mystical, utterly undevout frame of mind; with so reckless and shocking an imputation of motives; and with a complete lumping together of the extremest radicals with the most moderate of progressives. For thus three large classes of people will be made to feel uncertain, where these pronouncements are out of their depth: they will think: 'those dispositions, that temper which these documents show, are very painful and upsetting, – we will think of other things; there must, surely, be a screw loose somewhere, – possibly with those censured, but certainly, with the censurers. – One would, of course, so gladly have seen our authorities spared such reflections; yet if they *will* issue such unworkable orders, – or orders which, if carried out, would destroy all the Church's persuasiveness, – it is, surely, as well that these orders should make even ordinary hearers and readers pause and wonder ... I need not say how sincerely, in return, I sympathize with you, also. In some ways your position, – as Editor of a semi-official publication, – is more difficult and painful than my own. I feel, as tho' *I* must see to it, that nothing shall make me violent or bitter, or inert; and as tho' *you* should learn from this, how no taste or moderation in statement will make the militant scholastics tolerant of what you and I have got in common.[1]

The Baron's suggestion for the different ways in which he and Ward should react to the papal rejection of what they had in common was significant. At this stage of their relationship that common ground seemed relatively small, and the Baron's fear that Ward would try to explain away the obvious excesses of papal authoritanism, and thus make their common ground even smaller, was not misplaced.[2]

Shortly after the encyclical's publication the Roman Catholic hierarchy of England sent a joint letter to the Pope, affirming their complete acceptance of the document and re-affirming their loyalty and submission to the papacy. Apparently they had also indicated their desire to make this address public. Shortly after the letter was received in Rome Merry del Val wrote to Bourne that

the Holy Father fully appreciated the excellent address of the English Bishops and the sentiments expressed. He had of course no doubt whatever regarding

[1] Von Hügel to Ward, 15 Oct. 1907, WFP, vH MSS.

[2] Several years after these events, Ward discovered in his papers a copy of von Hügel's letter of submission to Vaughan at the time of the Anglican Orders decision, and he sent it on to Halifax with the comment: 'If you have not got the letter and would like to use it, I am sure I could get von Hügel's leave. I should not be sorry of the opportunity of communicating with him. He is a very old friend of mine, but he has been much more on the side of Tyrrell and Loisy than I have, and, though there has been no quarrel whatever between us, our intercourse has rather dropped, as disputing is too painful. This would be a matter on which I could write to him with complete agreement.' Ward to Halifax, 20 Jan. 1911, HP, A4. 224.

the orthodoxy and perfect loyalty of the English Bishops and of English Catholics at large. But there is one sentence which does not come very oppertunely just now, I mean where it is said that there is little or nothing of modernism amongst English Catholics. Just at present especially when Tyrrell is carrying on his scandalous rebellion and is proclaimed abroad as one of the leaders of the school, and perhaps the chief one, there is little doubt in my mind that if the address were published the remark would be made use of immediately in France, Germany and Italy and that we should be told that it was a slap in the face for the Holy Father. Obviously this would be a libel, but it would be propagated. Moreover, though there are not many English Modernists, there is quite a sufficient number of them, of *different grades*, in proportion to the comparatively limited number of English Catholics, clerical or _lay_, who are in a position to discuss such matters, half tinkered converts, etc. Hence, though the address is excellent in itself and in its true meaning, it would be better not to publish it.[1]

Pius X and his Secretary of State had, indeed, little to fear from the docile English hierarchy, but they were greatly concerned about Tyrrell and his sympathizers. Between the Roman authorities and the Roman Catholic Bishop of Southwark, Peter Amigo, it was decided that Tyrrell should be deprived of the sacraments and his case reserved to the Pope.[2] Although such deprivation and reservation were the canonical constituents of excommunication, Amigo insisted that Tyrrell had not been excommunicated.[3] Probably the technical term was avoided because technically Tyrrell had done nothing deserving such a censure. It was the two *Times* articles which had provoked the action by the authorities, and, as Tyrrell told Amigo, 'to write to *The Times* is not of itself a canonical offence meriting excommunication'.[4] And, for that matter, neither were bitterness nor personal insult, – the worst that could be said of Tyrrell's articles, – canonical offences meriting excommunication.

On 19 October Amigo received word from Merry del Val on the mode

[1] Merry del Val to Bourne, 17 Oct. 1907, AAW, MSS. Roman Letters, vol. 7, no. 111.
[2] *Diaries*, 24 Oct. 1907. See also, *The Tablet*, vol. 110, no. 3521, 2 Nov. 1907, p. 687.
[3] Tyrrell indignantly responded with a letter to *The Times*, no. 38,480, 2 Nov. 1907, p. 10: 'Sir, – The Roman Catholic Bishop of Southwark informs the public that I have not been excommunicated, but only deprived of the sacraments with a reservation of my case to the Holy See. According to the Catholic Dictionary (Ed. 1893, p. 359), excommunication "is an ecclesiastical censure by which a Christian is deprived of his right to participation in the sacraments". In acknowledging his Lordship's letter of Oct. 22, I spoke of my "excommunication". Why has he not written to me to correct me? Let the name pass; it is the thing that matters. What a thing is apart from all its qualities only a scholastic can tell. If I am not excommunicated, I am excluded from Communion – from the elementary rights of a Catholic – which is what plain folk mean by excommunication. What privilege is left? None that I shall heed or value.'
[4] Tyrrell to Amigo, 27 Oct. 1907, in *Autobiography and Life*, II, p. 341.

of proceeding with Tyrrell's censure. He communicated this information to the latter on the 22nd, and two days later von Hügel had a letter from Tyrrell containing the news.[1] Tyrrell was aware at the time of their composition that his *Times* articles were likely to provoke the near-hysterical authorities to excommunicate him; and von Hügel, while realizing that excommunication was possible, had hoped against hope that it might be avoided.[2] But after the censure had come, the Baron told Tyrrell that 'we have but to see to it, each one of us, that we may do, and advise, and influence, and be influenced, in the right, the best and deepest, the most fully Catholic direction'.[3] He also recommended a three-point programme for Tyrrell to follow over the next few weeks, and he even went over these points with Lilley, securing his agreement to them before posting them to Tyrrell. The Baron's three recommendations were that Tyrrell say nothing (except to several trusted friends) about the excommunication until the authorities publish the fact, that he write to Amigo apologizing for the tone and the personal attacks in *The Times* and *Giornale d'Italia* articles, and that he not publish anything further until at least the beginning of the new year.[4] Following von Hügel's advice, Tyrrell wrote a nobly apologetic letter to Amigo.[5] The prevailing mentality of the authorities, however, which accepted only total submissions and unqualified repudiations of one's whole life work and convictions, made Tyrrell's efforts a wasted expenditure. As to making known the fact of his excommunication, Tyrrell had not long to wait. Rome published the information on the 28th, and two days later *The Times* told its readers: 'We are informed that Father George Tyrrell has been excommunicated by the Pope on account of the two articles published by him in *The Times*, criticizing the recent Encyclical, and that the sentence of excommunication, passed at the petition of the Roman Catholic Bishop of Southwark, was communicated to him by that

[1] *Diaries*, 24 Oct. 1907.

[2] 'Had you read your Times of Mon. and to-day, as every good Christian does, you'd have seen that I am pre-occupied in pulling-down rather than in building up Churches; and that my days are spent in dodging the falling timbers and tiles. At a rough calculation I shall be excommunicated in ten days and for those ten days I am going to be a pillar of orthodoxy and intransigence.' Tyrrell to A. H. Mathew, 1 Oct. 1907, AEPSJ, Tyrrell MSS. CD/1 (copy). 'And I am deeply grateful and touched for and by that noble bit, in the second article, about your being and remaining a Catholic, whatever may happen ...' Von Hügel to Tyrrell, 1 Oct. 1907, in *Selected Letters*, p. 141.

[3] Von Hügel to Tyrrell, 24 Oct. 1907, in *Selected Letters*, p. 143.

[4] *Ibid.* pp. 143–4; *Diaries*, 24 Oct. 1907. In this diary entry, after summarizing his three points for Tyrrell, the Baron has later written: 'I fear this letter somehow changed his tone towards me for [a] time.'

[5] The entire letter is reproduced in *Autobiography and Life*, II, pp. 341–2.

prelate on Oct. 22.'[1] The controversies which raged in the press, both over his own position and over the other problems raised by *Pascendi*, made it practically impossible for Tyrrell to follow von Hügel's recommendation to refrain from publication during the last months of 1907.

Perhaps the chief problem raised by *Pascendi* was the question of just who was actually censured by the document. The so-called 'system' of modernism which the encyclical censured was so vague and so all-inclusive that almost everyone except the writers of scholastic text-books for Roman seminaries and colleges was rendered suspect. As soon as *Pascendi* was published Loisy wrote to the Baron that he would accept it as a definite censure of himself.[2] Tyrrell told Loisy that 'when I first read the document I, like others perhaps, found myself in every paragraph; but now I see that, in most cases, it is impossible to say whether I, or Laberthonnière, or Newman, or LeRoy, etc. be the culprit'.[3] And Wilfrid Ward was utterly shattered by the belief that Newman, the single greatest influence on his own life, and the subject of his major biographical undertaking, had been condemned by the encyclical.[4] But if Newman's condemnation was a shattering blow to Ward, it was also unsettling to a larger section of the English public than that represented by Wilfrid Ward. Newman was one of the very few figures at that time whose intelligence and integrity were admired by educated Anglicans and Roman Catholics alike, and for Rome to seem to condemn him was taken as a papal affront to Englishmen. The question of whether or not Newman had been condemned by the encyclical became a burning one which for weeks and months to come was discussed with heat in the English press.[5] Ward proposed to obtain from Rome some official statement discriminating the positions condemned by *Pascendi* in the moder-

---

[1] *The Times*, no. 38,477, 30 Oct. 1907, p. 10.

[2] *Diaries*, 20 Sept. 1907.

[3] Tyrrell to Loisy, 20 Oct. 1907, in *George Tyrrell's Letters*, p. 86.

[4] Ward to W. S. Lilly, 3 Nov. 1907, in *Insurrection versus Resurrection*, p. 268.

[5] Tyrrell really began the discussion with his mention of Newman in the second of his articles in *The Times*, no. 38,452, 1 Oct. 1907, p. 5. Some of the chief argumentation for and against the idea that Newman was condemned by *Pascendi* will be found by: Robert Dell in *The Times*, no. 38,459, 9 Oct. 1907, p. 13; Canon John Vaughan in *The Times*, no. 38,460, 10 Oct. 1907, p. 4; Eboracensis in *The Times*, no. 38,461, 11 Oct. 1907, p. 12; W. J. Williams in *The Times*, no. 38,480, 2 Nov. 1907, p. 9; John Norris in *The Times*, no. 38,481, 4 Nov. 1907, p. 10; F. A. Gasquet in *The Times*, no. 38,482, 5 Nov. 1907, p. 8; W. J. Williams in *The Times*, no. 38,483, 6 Nov. 1907, p. 13; F. A. Gasquet and John Norris in *The Times*, no. 38,484, 7 Nov. 1907, p. 4; A Catholic Layman in *The Times*, no. 38,485, 8 Nov. 1907, p. 10; R. Dell in *The Times*, no. 38,489, 13 Nov. 1907, p. 19; George Tyrrell in *The Guardian*, no. 3233, 20 Nov. 1907, pp. 1896–7; James Moyes in *The Nineteenth Century*, vol. LXII, no. 370, Dec. 1907, pp. 865–78; John Gerard, S.J., in *The Hibbert Journal*, vol. VI, no. 2, Jan. 1908, pp. 256–63; and Henry C. Corrance in *The Nineteenth Century*, vol. LXIII, no. 372, Feb. 1908, pp. 311–26.

nist 'system' from those positions of Newman which seemed to the intelligent lay reader to be very like, if not identical with, many of the condemned ideas. When Ward suggested this plan to von Hügel, the latter made some observations which clearly stated his own understanding of the situation created by *Pascendi*. 'Your plan is, I think, a good or bad one', he told Ward,

according as you would or would not make it turn upon, or work into it, two points.

(1) The real situation (the only thing to my mind worth all our efforts, – as distinct from the surface look of things, which has been all but exclusively looked to during 3 centuries or so, with the results now pressing so heavily upon us) would only be worsened, to my mind, if we (or any one) worked to get Rome, i.e. our present highest officials there, to make distinctions, and, say, whilst exempting St Thomas and Newman, or even Ward and Hügel, to concentrate their condemnations upon Loisy, Tyrrell and Fogazzaro. The latter three have done far too much for the Church's most difficult interests, the official spokesmen of the Church have, for the present, proved themselves far too little competent and just in these deep waters, for it to be right that we should do anything towards producing such a concentration, – should say or imply anything which could mean: 'do you restrict your condemnations as to persons, and we will back up those condemnations.' I speak without self-seeking, since I have as little doubt that they meant to strike me, as I have that they intended to strike you ...

(2) The thing would, to my mind, not be worth attempting, if it had to be restricted to Newman's case. Even at this moment they *may* shrink from publicly admitting that Newman was also aimed at ..., but I am certain that they as little like J.H.N. as they like you or me. It would only be a politic sense of such a condemnation producing too much commotion that wd. keep them back. No doubt N. is a cardinal; but so is Nicholas of Coes, and yet sympathy with N. of C. is solemnly declared (and has been now for years) to be a 'bad note' in any Catholic writer, by the S.J.s of Innsbruck. They will, no doubt, never now put J.H.N. on the Index nor do other such-like things; short of that, they will do everything to curtail and damage N.'s position and influence.

But what would at once back and strengthen the Newman case, would be if it were strengthened by the St Thomas case. And this latter case is easy to work. Not only St T.'s whole *analogy* doctrine, but also that (no doubt less frequently expressed but most important) teaching or admission as to man having a dim but real knowledge of what God is (the references are in my 'Exp. & Tr.' article), are most plainly angrily, contemptuously condemned. St. John of the † and St Theresa would have been horrified at such condemnations; indeed the Enc. leaves no standing ground for their central doctrines, their life's convictions. St Augustine is, of course, ruled out, by quite one half of his doctrine and habits of mind and soul, – by far the noblest, too.

If then you can draw up such a document without the implication or aim of a distinction which *now*, at the hands of the *present* executioners and of the *present* victims, would be even more unjust and intolerable than is the lumping together of all sorts of men which, as it now stands, of itself largely mitigates the document, – of course, through no intention of its authors; and if you can put in, in the forefront, not Newman but St Thomas with possibly St Augustine: I think your plan excellent. If these two conditions cannot or would not be worked, then I think it bad.[1]

Ward, apparently, would have been satisfied with a nominal declaration by some sufficiently important Roman official that Newman had not been condemned by *Pascendi*. For von Hügel the only thing that could make *Pascendi* tolerable would be a real, and not merely nominal, demonstration of how that document was in fact compatible with the best and the oldest aspects of Christian life and thought.

The Roman authorities, however, were in no disposition to care to justify their actions to anyone. Although for weeks following the publication of *Pascendi* the Roman correspondent for *The Tablet* kept informing his English readers of the numerous 'letters and telegrams of adhesion and gratitude' which poured into Rome from all parts of the world because of the encyclical,[2] the very serious rumblings of discontent could not be altogether drowned out by this triumphant chorus.[3] Within a month of the encyclical's publication a group of Italian priests had published *Il Programma dei Modernisti: Riposta dii Modernisti all' Encyclica Pascendi*, and a copy was in von Hügel's hands by the end of October. Almost at once he consulted the publishing firm of Williams and Norgate about an English edition, and Tyrrell eventually made the English translation.[4] The *Riposta* was a respectful but determined effort to demonstrate that the 'modernism' of *Pascendi* did not exist except in the minds of the encyclical's authors, and 'to expose the unfair attack which the Encyclical seems to make upon us, and to examine the teach-

---

[1] Von Hügel to Ward, 18 Oct. 1907, WFP, vH MSS.

[2] *The Tablet*, vol. 110, no. 3517, 5 Oct. 1907, p. 533; vol. 110, no. 3518, 12 Oct. 1907, p. 573; vol. 110, no. 3519, 19 Oct. 1907, p. 613.

[3] The protest was first most vocally expressed in Germany where Roman Catholics on the philosophical and theological faculties of the state universities seemed forced into a denial of academic freedom and intellectual honesty by *Pascendi*. See, 'Modernism in Germany', *The Times*, no. 38,481, 4 Nov. 1907, p. 4. Perhaps the most dramatic and impressive protest was the resignation from his bishopric of Tarentaise by Mgr Lucien Lacroix. The nominal explanation that the resignation was for 'reasons of health' misled no one, and the press made clear that it was because 'he was not in harmony with the reactionary policy of Pius X and his advisers'; and Mgr Lacroix did not deny it. See, *The Times*, no. 38,476, 29 Oct. 1907, p. 6; and no. 38,477, 30 Oct. 1907, p. 7; and *The Church Times*, no. 2336, vol. LVIII, 1 Nov. 1907, p. 560.

[4] *Diaries*, 31 Oct.; 2, 8, and 15 Nov. 1907. Williams and Norgate declined the offer, and the English edition was published by T. Fisher Unwin.

ings for which we are rebuked'. The authors stated that they would 'not offer excuses, still less are we going to beg pardon as offenders; we simply set forth our position and invite the judgment of our brethren upon it, and indeed the judgment of history'.[1] *The Tablet's* Roman correspondent told his readers that the *Riposta* had 'quite a mediaeval flavour', since 'it was nothing less than a counter-encyclical promulgated by a whole committee of anonymous little anti-Popes'.[2] The Roman authorities did not take kindly to this counter-encyclical, and on 29 October Cardinal Respighi, the Vicar of Rome, issued a decree of excommunication for the authors of the *Riposta* and for anyone else having anything to do with it. The book was said to have 'gravely scandalized the faithful', and anyone who dared to sell, read, or retain the book, was accused of committing serious sin (*culpa lethali*). The decree was only for the diocese of Rome, but Respighi made it clear that the Pope desired other bishops to promulgate the decree in their own dioceses.[3] As the year drew to a close, the very resistance manifested to *Pascendi* seemed to drive the Pope and curial Rome into ever more irresponsible statements and declarations. Under date of 18 November 1907 Pius X issued a *Motu Proprio* in which he declared all Roman Catholics to be bound 'in conscience' to accept all the decrees of the Biblical Commission, not only those already promulgated, but all the decrees to come in the future. And he added that anyone who dared to contradict in any way whatever the teaching of *Lamentabili* and *Pascendi* was automatically excommunicated.[4] When, a month later, the Pope held a secret consistory for the creation of four new cardinals, his exhortation to them consisted of a vehement attack on the modernists whom he accused of undermining the faith and papal authority.[5]

The last months of 1907 were especially painful for von Hügel, not only because of the general difficulties occasioned by the modernist crisis, but also because of the crisis of conscience which *Pascendi* occasioned for the *Rinnovamento* group. He learned in mid-November that the

[1] A. L. Lilley (editor), *The Programme of Modernism*, London, 1908, pp. 2–3.
[2] *The Tablet*, vol. 110, no. 3522, 9 Nov. 1907, p. 733.
[3] *Acta Sanctae Sedis*, vol. xL, Rome, 1907, p. 720.
[4] *Ibid.* pp. 723–6.
[5] *Acta Sanctae Sedis*, vol. xLI, Rome, 1908, pp. 21–4. 'Hi quidem, spreta tum Romani Pontificis tum Episcoporum auctoritate, methodicam invehunt dubitationem impiissimam circa ipsa fidei fundamenta; ac, praesertim si e clero sunt, catholicae theologiae studia aspernati, philosophiam, sociologiam, litteraturam e venenatis fontibus hauriunt; tum vero conscientiam quandam laicam catholicae oppositam pleno ore concrepant; sibique jus simul officiumque adrogant catholicorum conscientias corrigendi ac reformandi' (p. 22).

Archbishop of Milan had forbidden the sacraments in his diocese to all the writers and directors of *Il Rinnovamento*, and had declared sellers, buyers, and readers of it in his diocese to be guilty of mortal sin and, if they were priests, to have incurred a canonical irregularity. Dismayed, the Baron sent a telegram to Alfieri to encourage him not to abandon the conflict: *Profonde sympathie – vif desir ne pas changer dispositions – resolutions – Huegel*. He wrote to Scotti, too, expressing the same sentiments and quoting Walter Bagehot (whom he was currently reading and delighting in), telling him that he felt it wrong to give up *Il Rinnovamento* unless a financial crisis forced it, or unless 'their own consciences, sincerely interrogated, [made] them feel obliged to take that course'.[1] Scotti decided to leave *Il Rinnovamento* altogether, because he could not bear the prospect of excommunication. This decision greatly saddened the Baron, and he wrote to Scotti, encouraging him to persevere in his convictions and the engagements these entailed, even outside of the *Rinnovamento* group.[2] Some weeks earlier von Hügel had promised to write openly for *Il Rinnovamento*, if the group would agree to stand by Loisy and Tyrrell through the present crisis, and he honoured his promise by publishing four lengthy review articles on Loisy's *Les Évangiles synoptiques* in the course of 1908 and 1909.[3] In December the Baron went to Italy for his daughter's wedding at Genoa on the 8th.[4] Before returning to England on the 18th, he spent three days in Milan, trying to rally and encourage his friends of *Il Rinnovamento* for whom he had a special love because of the importance, in his estimation at least, of their work for the church.[5] Bremond undoubtedly expressed the thoughts of many

[1] *Diaries*, 16 and 18 Nov. 1907.

[2] *Diaries*, 18 and 26 Nov.; 2 Dec. 1907. See also, von Hügel to Bishop, 16 June 1908, in *Dublin Review*, vol. 227, no. 462, pp. 423–4.

[3] 'L'Abate Loisy e il problema dei Vangeli Sinottici' *Il Rinnovamento*, vol. III (Jan.–June 1908), pp. 209–34; vol. IV (July–Dec. 1908), pp. 1–44; vol. V (Jan.–June 1909), pp. 229–72 and 396–423. 'I venture to send you the off-print of a series of Papers by "H.", that appeared in the "Rinnovamento" on Loisy's "Évangiles Synoptiques". I believe that these Papers have not shirked any of the main questions raised by M. L.'s stout volumes, tho', of course, numberless other points remain untouched. Perhaps the pages on the religious meaning and worth of the *Parousia* expectation; on the probable nature and order of the events at the Last Supper; and the final pages on the Comparative Study of Religions and the Truth of Religion are the most important. The thing is semi-anonymous, and the writer prefers not to be publicly identified.' Von Hügel to Percy Gardner, 16 Dec. 1909, BL, MS. Eng. Lett. *c*. 55.220–1. See also, von Hügel to Bishop, 16 June 1908, in *Dublin Review*, vol. 227, no. 462, Oct. 1953, p. 424.

[4] *Diaries*, 3–5 Dec. 1907.

[5] *Diaries*, 10–13 Dec. 1907. The Baron promised to raise several hundred pounds a year to help support *Il Rinnovamento* through any financial crises occasioned by the condemnation, and his Anglican friends Lilley and Newsom undertook to raise a sizeable share of this for him as well as contributing themselves.

when, in sending his greetings to von Hügel for Christmas and the New Year, he told him that it was hard to see 'how 1908 could be worse that 1907'.[1]

[1] Bremond to von Hügel, 31 Dec. 1907, SAUL, MS. 2333. 'If there could possibly have been any doubt before the year 1907 as to which Church would exhibit the modernist crisis in its acutest form, there could be none after that date.' M. D. Petre, *Modernism: Its Failure and Its Fruits*, London, 1918, p. 113. 'The situation is really interesting here [Rome]. One does not hear much about the "Modernists". The Pope has adequately sat on them. But the tales which fly about are entertaining.' F. A. Gasquet to Moyes, 6 Jan. 1908, AAW, Unsorted Moyes Papers, no. 168.

CHAPTER II

TRIUMPH OF VATICAN POLICY

In *The Hibbert Journal* for January 1908 Tyrrell discussed the future prospects of modernism. Although he suggested that the immediate prospects were not very encouraging, he predicted that the distant future would vindicate the modernist rather than the scholastic mentality within Roman Catholicism.[1] But neither Tyrrell nor von Hügel would reach that distant horizon, and their immediate situation continued to grow darker. When Wilfrid Ward wrote an editorial in the *Dublin Review*,[2] tending to refute some of those who had been hostile to *Pascendi* and to make excuses for the excesses of the authorities, von Hügel told him that

it seemed and seems to me clear that, if you were determined to remain Editor of the 'Dublin Review', you could hardly say and do less about, or in apparent favour of, the document than you have done. But then the character of the arguments you are thus driven to use, and the (surely) certain fact that you still leave those you would satisfy, dissatisfied and pressing for more; make me very doubtful whether resignation of the post would not have been more simple and strong, more satisfactory to your own conscience and more useful to the cause, as not only I, but as I think you yourself understand it.[3]

Ward's situation was a difficult one and the Baron was not unsympathetic. Nevertheless, he felt Ward's position to be not wholly honest since Ward's own moderate liberalism was saved from 'instant repression by the now dominant authorities' only because of the more extreme liberalism of the men Ward would discriminate from himself. The Baron cancelled his subscription to the *Dublin Review*, suggesting that he would buy it issue by issue, depending on whether or not Ward returned to the encyclical question in future numbers. And he reiterated his hope that Ward would 'either not return to the encyclical, now, and to praise it; or that, if you cannot secure this condition, that you will resign'.[4]

---

[1] Tyrrell, 'The Prospects of Modernism', pp. 252–5.

[2] *Dublin Review*, vol. cxlii, no. 284, Jan. 1908, pp. 1–10.

[3] Von Hügel to Ward, 10 Feb. 1908, WFP, vH MSS.

[4] *Ibid.* After the April issue appeared, von Hügel wrote: 'I am much pleased at the new (April) "Dublin's" containing no explanation or modification of what was being pressed against in those previous articles of yours.' Von Hügel to Ward, 27 May 1908, WFP, vH MSS.

At the end of January the Archbishop of Paris, Cardinal Richard, died,[1] and was succeeded by Mgr Leo Amette who proved no less hostile to Loisy than his predecessor. At this time Loisy's two latest books, *Les Évangiles synoptiques* and *Simples réflexions sur le décret du Saint Office Lamentabili sane exitu et sur l'Encyclique Pascendi dominici gregis*, were published. Almost at once the new Archbishop condemned both books, threatening with an excommunication reserved to the Pope anyone who read, retained, printed or defended the books. Loisy wrote to von Hügel about this on 17 February, telling him that he had no desire to enter into controversy with Amette and his Vigilance Committee. His latest books were on the same lines as his earlier ones, and his primary aim, he told the Baron, was to establish the historical ground of the questions at issue, and only secondarily to suggest the necessity of more or less reforming the traditional theological concepts involved. He also mentioned to von Hügel that he presumed the latter had paid no attention to the rumours about himself expressed in some French journals. 'The genuine expression of my ideas is in my books', Loisy told him, 'and nowhere else.'[2] Loisy's expression of his 'views and intentions' pleased von Hügel.[3] However, within five days Loisy was writing again to tell the Baron that the Bishop of Langres, his canonical superior, had sent him a summons from Rome, demanding his complete submission to *Lamentabili* and *Pascendi*, without any reservation whatever, and under threat of major excommunication if he did not comply within ten days.[4]

The rumours in the French press about which Loisy had warned von Hügel chiefly concerned an interview with Loisy published in *Le Matin*. The interviewer had deliberately portrayed Loisy as a contemporary Voltaire, and had climaxed his account by announcing that Loisy had admitted that his distinction between the Jesus reached by historical method and the Jesus worshipped in faith was merely a rhetorical device

[1] 'Paris, 28 Jan. – Cardinal Richard died early this morning. His Eminence had nearly completed his 89th year, having been born at Nantes on March 1st 1819. He had been Archbishop of Paris for twenty-two years, and co-adjutor to Cardinal Guibert for thirteen years previously, so that his connection with the diocese had lasted for half an ordinary lifetime. The Cardinal was a man of sincere but narrow piety, who held in horror all "new ideas" and, in spite of his mildness of manner, showed himself anything but gentle to priests suspect of novelties. He was not popular with his clergy, but his sincerity, simplicity of life and unworldly disinterestedness won him general respect even from outsiders. He was extremely generous in his benefactions, and devoted to good works the greater part of the large revenues which came into his hands.' *The Church Times*, no. 2349, vol. LIX, 31 Jan. 1908, p. 127.
[2] Loisy to von Hügel, 17 Feb. 1908, in *Quelques Lettres*, p. 253.
[3] *Diaries*, 19 Feb. 1908.
[4] Loisy to von Hügel, 22 Feb. 1908, in *Quelques Lettres*, p. 253.

to silence theologians. An account of the interview was given in *The Tablet*.[1] The Baron had already read an Italian account of the same interview and had both interrogated Loisy and obtained a satisfactory answer from him about his intentions and authentic statements, when his attention was called to *The Tablet* account. Since *The Tablet* had used the *Matin* interview to justify Amette's condemnation of Loisy's books which it had published at the same time, von Hügel wrote to the editor to put the matter right. The Baron wrote his letter

in simple pursuance of the elementary duty of helping my fellow-Catholics in the sometimes difficult task of combining a sensitive Catholic faith and loyalty with perfect justice and fairness to their neighbour. In this case the neighbour happens to be a priest-scholar who, however large may be the element of error in his objective conclusions and hypotheses, has undoubtedly no intention of leaving the Church; and who, if he seems at times less direct and explicit in his answers than our zeal may require, is certainly thus determined not by any desire to deny or to evade the Catholic definitions of faith, but by the conscientious necessity of allowing for critical facts and of attempting such interpretations of the truths of the faith as will not collide with such facts or with what in all sincerity he feels compelled to think is thus real.[2]

The Baron's letter was published on 7 March, the same day on which the decree of Loisy's major excommunication was signed at Rome. In answer to his summons by the Bishop of Langres, Loisy had written that 'the total and complete submission of which Mgr Merry del Val speaks could only be a lie on my part; and, rather than a meritorious sacrifice, as Your Lordship calls it, this would be for me an act devoid of meaning and completely immoral'.[3] Excommunication was then inevitable. Von Hügel read of the fact in *The Daily Telegraph* for the 9th, and immediately sent a telegram to Loisy: 'Just read substance of new act – Seems relatively moderate – Accept expression continuous affection, respect, sympathy, and of conviction that we all will act with strength of chivalrous moderation – H – Kensington.'[4] Two days later he had letters from both Loisy and Archbishop Mignot, the former announcing his abandonment of clerical garb and his plans for future publications, and the latter expressing his sympathy and continued support for Loisy.[5] Although the Baron considered Loisy to be one of his really close friends to the end of his life, the growing divergence of their ideas, and Loisy's increased sen-

[1] *The Tablet*, vol. 111, no. 3537, 22 Feb. 1908, pp. 282–3.
[2] *The Tablet*, vol. 111, no. 3539, 7 March 1908, pp. 378–9.
[3] Loisy to Mgr Sébastien Herscher, 19 Jan. 1908, in *Quelques Lettres*, p. 250.
[4] *Diaries*, 9 March 1908.
[5] *Diaries*, 11 March 1908.

sitivity to any criticism, put much strain on the friendship.[1] ∤

At a special session of the London Society for the Study of Religion held on 17 March von Hügel gave an account of Loisy's *Évangiles synoptiques*. He began by acknowledging the need for ecclesiastical authority, and by insisting at the same time on its limitations. Then he discussed Loisy's critical principles and methodology, his main historical conclusions, his ideas on the relationship between science and religion, and, finally, the likelihood of the facts and convictions contained in *Les Évangiles synoptiques* ever being tolerated in the Roman Catholic church.[2] But regardless of von Hügel's own hopes and speculations on the matter, Loisy's relationship to the Roman church was permanently finished as far as he himself was concerned. Within a year Loisy would be appointed Professor at the Collège de France, and the construction of new relationships would be commenced.

After von Hügel's death, Loisy defended his own attitude and action at the time of his excommunication, by suggesting that his conduct then had been more in accord with truth than the Baron's had been.[3]

[1] Loisy has written at length of this estrangement in the third volume of his *Mémoires*, and especially pp. 14–25, and 142–70. His remarks are often bitter and ungenerous, and not infrequently self-justificatory. Undoubtedly von Hügel did become almost excessively anti-immanentist and anti-monist, but his tendency to extremes in one direction was largely occasioned by the excessive immanentism which was very really manifest in the evolution of the thought of some of the men he had worked with – and especially of Loisy himself. But even Loisy's sensitivity and sarcasm cannot totally obscure the old love and respect he retained for the Baron and which show through even in the final volume of the *Mémoires*. To his dying day von Hügel's loyalty to Loisy never flagged. Disagree with many of his ideas he did, indeed, but he also cherished his person to the end. – 'I was so glad too about what you told me concerning your attitude towards Loisy. We must not simply give him up. He is incomplete and contracting religiously; but a great scholar, a great, courageous soul.' Von Hügel to Newsom, 26 Oct. 1909, in A. H. Dakin, Jr., *Von Hügel and the Supernatural*, London, 1934, p. 259. – In 1911 von Hügel met Harnack at a luncheon given by Bishop E. S. Talbot. He conversed with Harnack after the meal, and they discussed Loisy. The Baron noted in his diary: 'I soon felt a prick at having not sufficiently spoken up for the great sides of L.' Some days later he wrote to Harnack 'completing and correcting my remarks on L.'; disagreeing with Harnack's own 'Lukan positions'; and expressing his 'scandalized feelings' at the review of Loisy's *Évangiles synoptiques* which had appeared in the *Theol. Lit. Zeitschrift* (*Diaries*, 5 and 11 Feb. 1911). See also, von Hügel to Kemp Smith, 30 Sept. 1920, SAUL, MS. 30420, in which von Hügel laments Loisy's negative and contracting attitude toward religion, but again defends Loisy's critico-historical work and the truly great dimensions of the man.

[2] *Diaries*, 17 March 1908; MS. *Minutes of the LSSR*, vol. I. (Dr. Williams's Library, WL80, OD. 17); *Mém*. III, pp. 12–13.

[3] *Mém*. III, pp. 13, and 24–5. With the publication of Jean Rivières *Le Modernisme dans l'Église: Étude d'histoire religieuse contemporaine*, Paris, 1929, the historiographical stance of ecclesiastically approved Roman Catholic writers towards Loisy became firmly established. This attitude towards Loisy was one which excused itself from the obligation in elementary justice to evaluate *all* the evidence about the man before passing historical judgments on his character and intentions, and which presumed that Loisy's extra-ecclesial position justified their attribution of the basest motives to the conduct of most of his life. J. T. Burtchaell,

According to Loisy, honesty demanded breaking with the church when he could no longer agree with the opinions of its highest rulers. Von Hügel also disagreed with Pius X and Merry del Val; yet he remained. Unlike Loisy, however, von Hügel did not equate the content of his Christian faith, as specified within the Roman Catholic church, with the opinions of the members of the Holy Office, of Pius X, and the Vatican Secretary of State. To stand against the governing body of the church was, obviously, not the ordinary stance for a Catholic, and no one recognized this more clearly than the Baron. But there could be times – as the whole history of the church from St Paul's day to the present indicated – when such resistance was not only allowable but a duty. In several letters written to Wilfrid Ward early in 1908, when the two men were discussing Ward's problems as editor of the *Dublin Review*, von Hügel made some comments which indicated his own understanding of his position in opposing the authorities. He criticized Ward's tendency to take acceptance and non-criticism of documents like *Pascendi* as an absolute obligation, and told him that even though

a Catholic will, or ought, to feel such acceptance, or non-criticism, to be *presumptively* due; it is impossible, I think, in view of history, to maintain that there cannot be, that there have not been exceptions. In these latter cases, the burden of the proof as to the necessity etc. ever lies with the infractor of the general rule; and such infraction can range, I take it, from the most frivolous or most un- or even anti-Catholic presumptuousness to an act of a most reluctant, costing, humble, devotedly Catholic character.[1]

Several weeks later he told Ward that his chief grievance against *Pascendi*

is that it *would* treat the movement as 'highly speculative', in the sense of 'occasioned or caused by *a priori* considerations'. Even the most speculative of its representatives, e.g. LeRoy, have, on the contrary, been set going by certain critico-historical brutal *facts*. And this the Enc. nowhere even implies. Let the authorities criticise or condemn the attempted solutions; let them not deny the tremendous pressure of most real facts. Abuse is no kind of remedy.[2]

This was also the real objection which von Hügel had to *Lamentabili*. Roman theologians, for the most part ignorant of contemporary scienti-

---

Catholic Theories of Biblical Inspiration Since 1810, p. 232, one of the most recent heirs of this uncritical tradition, dismisses Loisy as a 'petulant unbeliever'. Far more discriminating and genuinely historical is the recent estimate of Loisy made by Alec Vidler, *A Variety of Catholic Modernists*, Cambridge, 1970, pp. 20–62.

[1] Von Hügel to Ward, 10 Feb. 1908, WFP, vH MSS.
[2] Von Hügel to Ward, 26 Feb. 1908, WFP, vH MSS.

fic and historical method and developments, sat in judgment on historical and scientific questions, and made their pronouncements, when signed by the Pope or secretary of the Holy Office, binding on the obedience of Catholics. In order to make such authoritarian judgments more palatable, *Pascendi* had tried to encase the historical and scientific conclusions which it condemned in a would-be immanentist, subjectivist, evolutionist, pantheist philosophy which it attributed to men said to be possessed by the basest of motives, and which it called modernism. This refusal by authorities to acknowledge the legitimacy of the facts and working hypotheses brought forward by contemporary historical and scientific investigation, and the wholesale condemnation of those historical and scientific workers by a misrepresentation of their motives and their ideas, was what von Hügel was fighting in his struggle against the anti-modernist campaign. In June of 1908 he turned once again to the question of justified resistance to authorities. He told Ward that he

would only maintain that one cannot lay down a simply absolute rule, that, under no conceivable circumstances can what looks like 'disobedience' be licite as against the Church-authorities. For the Church itself is demonstrably based upon such a 'disobedience' on the part of Our Lord Himself. We can only maintain (and indeed are strictly bound to hold) that the *presumption* is ever on the side of the authorities and obedience to them; that only under pressure of obedience to even higher and still more costing claims and obedience to them can any 'disobedience' ever be licite; and that the 'disobedient' individual so acts ever at his own risk and peril to be justified or not in time and by God's own spirit working and expressing itself in and thro' the Church.[1]

For the Baron there was never any question of deliberately placing himself outside the church.[2] But to him the 'church' was much more than its ruling class. Moreover, he considered it his obligation to make every concession to the demands of legitimate authority, no matter how harsh or arbitrary or ignorant, short of compromising his own conscience. But to acknowledge as good or right or even justifiable the absolute positions of *Lamentabili* and *Pascendi* would have been thus to compromise his conscience.

In April of 1908 Houtin wrote to Loisy that 'modernism has been defeated, utterly crushed. The reign of terror holds sway in every diocese, and the young men have gone underground.'[3] All around him von Hügel

[1] Von Hügel to Ward, 5 June 1908, WFP, vH MSS.
[2] '... being myself very decided not to break with the Authorities, short of my most elementary conscience requiring it ...,' von Hügel to Petre, 3 July 1906, BM, Add. MSS. 45361.39.
[3] *Mém.* III, p. 29.

seemed to see evidence that the reign of terror had crossed the channel to England as well. When he sent a copy of Loisy's *Simples réflexions*, with a covering note, to his old friend Dr Christian van den Biesen, three days later the book was 'mysteriously returned, addressed by [a] hand unknown to me, with no answer to my note'.[1] For years van den Biesen had been professor of scripture at St Joseph's College, Mill Hill, and in the Baron's estimation was, perhaps, the most competent Old Testament scholar among Roman Catholics in England.[2] Some months after the mysterious return of the book, von Hügel met van den Biesen again and learned that the latter had, in fact, received the book and that the seminary authorities had been responsible for its return.[3] Later in the summer, while on holiday at Haslemere, von Hügel learned from van den Biesen that he was being sent away from Mill Hill, and the Baron noted in his diary that this was a case of another modernist purge.[4] The two men met again, and then van den Biesen left for Devon, where he was placed in charge of a Foreign Missionary Society sanatorium, never again to engage in his life's work of biblical scholarship.[5]

As the van den Biesen case was working toward its sad conclusion, von Hügel became involved in another instance of the systematic heresy-

[1] *Diaries*, 28 Feb. and 2 March 1908.
[2] See, von Hügel to Ward, 28 Aug. 1905, WFP, vH MSS.
[3] *Diaries*, 23 June 1908.
[4] *Diaries*, 5 Sept. 1908. Van den Biesen's only crime was competence as an Old Testament scholar, a critic familiar with contemporary historical method. However, such competence and methodology were interdicted by *Pascendi*. As the pursuit of 'crypto-modernists' became ever hotter, seminary professors became so strait-jacketed literally that they could do little more than enunciate propositions from approved textbooks. In 1910 the Sacred Consistorial Congregation gave a series of questions-and-answers on how to implement the decree of the same year *Sacrorum antistitum*. This latter decree aimed at 'purifying' Catholic teaching. One of the questions-and-answers was: 'An *quotannis* doctores in seminariis teneantur textum, quem sibi quisque in docendo propusuerit, vel tractandas quaestiones, sive theses, Episcopis exhibere, et ineunte anno jusjurandum dare? Affirmative.' *Acta Apostolicae Sedis*, II, no. 17, 1910, pp. 740–1.
[5] *Diaries*, 7 Sept. 1908. Van den Biesen died at the age of 87 on 17 November 1951 (information given the author in a letter of 20 September 1967 from the Reverend J. P. Thoonen, Archivist of the St Joseph's Missionary Society – to which van den Biesen belonged). Van den Biesen spent his last years in one of the Society's residences near Liverpool. The Rector of that house at the time of van den Biesen's residence there, the Reverend Michael Fox, wrote to the author on 29 September 1967: 'I was Rector here when Fr. van den Biesen came to retire. He was a very old man then ... I often had talks with him but he would never talk of the past i.e. of his days as a professor in Mill Hill. I never heard him once mention the name of Baron von Hügel. Brother Christopher here was a great friend of Father's. They went for walks together, on jaunts to Liverpool. He says that they talked about everything under the sun except of his days at Mill Hill; that was a closed book. He also says that he never mentioned any of the famous people he had met or corresponded with. I can only surmise that he had made a complete break with that period of his life and destroyed everything written dealing with those days.'

hunt for modernists. The Vigilance Committee in the Southwark diocese seemed the most active of those in English dioceses, and by August certain of the Southwark clergy, especially those with academic degrees like Dr Charles Dessoulavy of Greenwich and Dr Joseph Wilhelm of Battle (Sussex), were being required to sign the encyclical *Pascendi* as a token of acceptance of its teaching.[1] In August the Baron received a letter from the Reverend Raymond Hammersley, a young curate at the Catholic church in Chatham (Kent).[2] This priest, 'with a spotless moral and pastoral record, was delated by a senior *confrère*, for remarks made in friendly oral discussion with his brother priests alone, and who though prepared to sign all the Definitions of the Church, was suspended and dismissed'.[3] Encouraged, apparently, by Tyrrell and Dessoulavy, Hammersley sought legal advice on how to fight this injustice, and von Hügel paid the lawyer's fee.[4] However, Hammersley seems to have been able to do no more than print and distribute a Reply to his accuser, the Reverend James Warwick of Balham.[5] And the Baron sadly reflected that all this unhappy business was 'in the strictest conformity with the present ecclesiastical system'.[6]

Since Storrington was in the Southwark diocese, and since Tyrrell, often resident in Storrington at this time, was the most notorious of English and, perhaps, of all modernists, it was inevitable that he, and Maude Petre who sheltered him, should be harassed by ecclesiastical authorities and the Vigilance Committee's informers. In July of 1908 Tyrrell had published his *Medievalism*, a brilliantly written answer to Cardinal Mercier's Lenten Pastoral of that year which had attacked Tyrrell by name. In probably the most beautifully and certainly the most delightfully readable prose he ever wrote,[7] Tyrrell gave an account of his own

[1] *Diaries*, 25 Aug. 1908.
[2] *Diaries*, 26 Aug. 1908. There is some confusion over Hammersley's Christian name, though none at all over his identity. *The Catholic Directory*, London, 1907, pp. 308 and 405, lists his Christian name as Raymond. The Baron, in his diary refers to him as W. H. Hammersley (*Diaries*, 7 Sept. 1908). There was only one Roman Catholic priest in England named Hammersley at this time, and both *The Catholic Directory* and von Hügel's diary are agreed that he was curate at Chatham in Kent.
[3] Von Hügel, 'Father Tyrrell: Some Memorials ...,' p. 247.
[4] *Diaries*, 31 Aug.; 2, 3, 7, and 15 Sept.; and 2 and 30 Oct. 1908.
[5] *Diaries*, 10 Dec. 1908.
[6] Von Hügel, 'Father Tyrrell: Some Memorials ...', p. 247.
[7] Loisy's evaluation of Tyrrell's *Medievalism* seems just: 'Parmi les livres de Tyrrell, ce n'est probablement pas le plus profond, mais c'est peut-être le plus clair, le mieux ordonné, le plus facile à lire; bref c'est le plus beau manifeste moderniste qui, à ma connaissance, ait été écrit; c'est la critique la plus incisive et, à certains égards, la plus modérée, j'allais dire la plus miséricordieuse, qu'on puisse imaginer du système romain. Oeuvre éloquente, oeuvre

'modernism' and repudiated the 'medievalism' which Pius X was trying to identify with Catholicism and even revelation itself, and which
Mercier's Pastoral had endorsed. Von Hügel, who had read the book in
manuscript, was uncomfortable about it, mainly because he feared that
this type of writing would simply strengthen Tyrrell's habit of polemics
and create an occasion for a repetition of this class of literature from his
pen. He told Tyrrell 'that (brilliant as are your controversial, polemical
hits) God has made you for something deeper and greater, and that not
there, but in mystical intuition, love, *position*, do you give and get your
full, most real self'.[1] Almost as soon as Tyrrell had returned to Storrington after the publication of *Medievalism*, the Prior of the Premonstratensian monastery there, Père Xavier de la Fourvière, who also acted as
parish priest for the Roman Catholics of the village, asked Tyrrell, by
letter, to leave Storrington. This Tyrrell refused to do, though he wrote
a letter to *The Tablet* 'exonerating the Prior from all complicity with
modernism'.[2] The letter was never published. Since Tyrrell was already
excommunicated, there was little more that could be done to him, though
rumours of a major excommunication were bruited about from time to
time. Miss Petre, however, was still able to frequent the sacraments,
which she did with great regularity, and was thus open to intimidation
by the authorities. Bishop Amigo informed her through the Prior that her
frequent Communions in Storrington were a source of scandal. Not only
Tyrrell, but her three married sisters, all came to her defence by writing
to the Bishop, and Amigo eventually announced that he had no objection to her frequent Communions so long as they took place somewhere
other than at Storrington.[3] By the end of December the situation seemed
to have settled itself temporarily, and Tyrrell could inform the Baron that
the pressure at Storrington had been relaxed.[4]

The events of 1907 and 1908, and especially since the publication of
his *Medievalism*, had greatly oppressed Tyrrell. During this time he often
questioned his position in remaining within the church which had re-

---

sincère, oeuvre de foi. L'immanentisme de Tyrrell ne méritait pas l'anathème du Baron, et
l'auteur de *Medievalism* n'était pas le "pur sceptique" dont il paraît que Houtin a voulu
retracer le portrait pour la postérité.' *Mém.* III, p. 131.

[1] Von Hügel to Tyrrell, 27 June 1908, in *Selected Letters*, p. 153. The Baron's negative
judgments on *Medievalism* in his letter to Professor René Guiran, 11 July 1921, in *Selected
Letters*, p. 334, seem somewhat excessive.
[2] *Diaries*, 23 Oct. 1908.
[3] *Diaries*, 21 Nov. and 8 Dec. 1908.
[4] *Diaries*, 28 Dec. 1908.

jected him, and he looked with more than wistfulness at the peace that could be his by returning to the church of his childhood.[1] During these months, too, he was in especially friendly and sympathetic contact with the Old Catholics, through their English representative, Bishop A. H. Mathew, and through Dr Edward Herzog of Berne.[2] When G. C. Rawlinson asked von Hügel about a rumour regarding Tyrrell's intention to join Mathew's church, he confidently denied every substance to the rumour and wrote to Tyrrell about it. Tyrrell, who had kept most of his dealings with the Old Catholics from the Baron, answered with great heat because he felt that von Hügel himself believed the rumours. 'I did not, Friend, take those rumours seriously', the Baron responded,

in the sense that I believed you intended to join, or that anyhow you would join, any other body. I only thought, from the great definiteness of R.'s report, that you might, very understandably, have said or written things that had been interpreted in that way. And I wanted you, anyhow, to know what R. thought, since I could see that he was not speaking simply for himself.[3]

Tyrrell remained a Roman Catholic to his death. But his great sympathetic understanding for the Old Catholic movement and for the Church of England, especially, were not merely the result of the oppression and rejection which he experienced within the Church of Rome. 'If Modernism fails in the Church of England', he wrote,

(and by Modernism I always mean a synthesis of Catholicism and Science – not the supremacy of the latter) it may be abandoned as a noble dream. In the Roman Church it has not a fair chance because the other term of synthesis there is not Catholicism, but Ultramontanism, which is a species of Protestantism. My own work – which I regard as done – has been to raise a question which I have failed to answer. I am not so conceited as to conclude that it is therefore

---

[1] 'You can, again, most profitably insist upon his strong, *very* strong *attrait* back to Anglicanism, provided that, in pointing this out, as having possessed him during the *last six months or so of 1908*, you add that this almost irresistible fascination left him by the end of the year, and that conversations, letters, documents, his book about to appear now, are all there to show that the last six months of his life saw him fully re-established in his resolution to keep on within the R. C. Church.' Von Hügel to Newsom, 7 Sept. 1909, in *Selected Letters*, p. 167. See also, *Autobiography and Life*, II, pp. 366–78. 'I feel still that the reform of the Roman Church is *the* point for us whom Providence has made or allowed to be born, members of that Church, and that all the secessions, individual or corporate from it, have, whatever good they may (together, I think, with evil) have done to the seceders and to the bodies formed by or joined by them, but helped further to narrow the Church which they have left.' Von Hügel to Tyrrell, 7 Dec. 1908, BM, Add. MSS. 44931.68.

[2] *Autobiography and Life*, II, pp. 379–87. For Mathew's career see, C. B. Moss, *The Old Catholic Movement, Its Origins and History*, London, 1964, pp. 297–311.

[3] Von Hügel to Tyrrell, 7 Dec. 1908, in *Von Hügel and Tyrrell*, p. 181.

unanswerable. And I think it may be the destiny of the Church of England to answer it.[1]

In the depressing atmosphere created by so much violence and rejection on the part of ecclesiastical authorities, von Hügel seemed to respond with particular warmth to any intelligent sympathy for the cause and ideals he had so much at heart.[2] In January of 1908 Henry Barclay Swete, the Regius Professor of Divinity at Cambridge, had published a lengthy address on modernism, full of discriminating understanding of the values and dangers of the movement.[3] After reading the address von Hügel asked his friend F. C. Burkitt to arrange a meeting for him with Swete. On a visit to Cambridge in February the Baron met Swete, through Burkitt's arrangements, and spent part of an afternoon with him.[4] Burkitt also used this same Cambridge visit to introduce several young friends to the Baron, among whom was Edward Gordon Selwyn, the future Dean of Winchester and from that time a friend of von Hügel.[5] A week later, at a dinner party given by the Cecil Chapmans, von Hügel met for the first time Bishop Edward Stuart Talbot and, incidentally, Mrs Humphry Ward.[6] The Baron had been impressed with the primary Charge of the first Anglican Bishop of Southwark on 'The Church's Stress',[7] and two days after their meeting he wrote to Talbot: 'I do not

[1] Tyrrell to Arthur Boutwood, 13 Jan. 1909, in *George Tyrrell's Letters*, p. 119.

[2] 'Yet, even taking all the miseries and unsatisfactorinesses into account, I for one not only do not despair of necessary reform in and for the R. C. Church, but I actually see its process and *rationale*. And looking back in religious history, I see many, many illusions and delusions; yet one tops and entirely exceeds them all – hopelessness or non-labouring, non-fighting in the very thick of the conflict.' Von Hügel to Bishop, 16 June 1908, in *Dublin Review*, vol. 227, no. 462, Oct. 1953, p. 427.

[3] The Rev. H. B. Swete, '"Modernism" and the Church', *The Guardian*, no. 3243, 29 Jan. 1908, pp. 175–6. This paper had been read to a meeting of the London Society of Sacred Study at Sion College on 28 January 1908.

[4] *Diaries*, 7, 10, and 12 Feb. 1908.

[5] *Diaries*, 14 Feb. 1908.

[6] *Diaries*, 18 Feb. 1908. The Baron noted in his diary that he had 'some good talk' with Dr Talbot, and 'a little' with Mrs Humphry Ward.

[7] On the afternoon before the dinner party with Talbot, von Hügel read the section of Talbot's Charge entitled 'The Stress Upon the Church from the Condition of Modern Thought' (*Diaries*, 18 Feb. 1908). The Baron undoubtedly read there with approval these words: 'Some, on the other hand, stand rigidly by the identification of revealed truth with dogma, and are unable to read the lesson of Pharisee experience and to see how fatally truth may lose its vital character and become at once irresponsive and uninterpretative. We may go further and instead of judging others we may acknowledge that probably everyone of us errs, more or less, by holding too tightly what is of the form, or letting go too easily what is of the essence. But we can at least heartily rejoice in the effort of faithful and reverent men to work out in their several ways the problems of the relation of theology to revelation, of doctrine to that which it enshrines, of forms of speech or action to that which they express. Specially interesting is it to see this in the case of generous minds in the Roman Church which corpor-

know whether I am doing something tactful or the reverse in writing to ask you whether you would care to let me give you a copy of Loisy's *Les Évangiles Synoptiques* as a mark of sincere respect and of admiration for your declarations in your "Stress" Charge.'[1] Talbot must have answered sympathetically because the Baron sent him not only the two volumes on the synoptic Gospels but also Loisy's *Simples réflexions* and Maude Petre's *Catholicism and Independence*, and this exchange began a long and warm friendship between the two men.[2] Back in Cambridge in January 1909 to address the Cambridge Theological Society at Burkitt's request, von Hügel was surprised and disappointed to discover that all of his distinguished audience was 'more or less strongly conservative about the Fourth Gospel'.[3] But before leaving Cambridge he addressed, at Professor John Skinner's invitation, the 'young Presbyterian students' at Westminster College. 'I spoke to them on "Modernism"', the Baron noted in his diary, 'as R[oman] C[atholic]; as a "horizontal", not "vertical" difference; as not organized or unified; as composed of 2 main convictions; as opposed by the Protestantisers and Puritans; as going back to Erasmus, (Savonarola) & Synoptists, not Luther, Calvin, Augustine, St. Paul.'[4] In May von Hügel went to Oxford at the invitation of Albert Way, Librarian at Pusey House, to address a small group

---

ately bears so august a witness to the divine character and authority of Revelation, yet defaces and paralyses that witness by the position which it has given to its own traditions, and by such defiance as the late unhappy utterances under Papal sanction express to the good as well as the evil, the divinely-guided as well as the perverse in modern thought.' Edward Stuart Talbot, *The Church's Stress: Words on Some Present Questions of Thought and Action Spoken to the Clergy of the Diocese of Southwark at His Primary Visitation in the Cathedral Church of St Saviour,* London, 1907, p. 9.

[1] Von Hügel to Talbot, 20 Feb. 1908, in Gwendolen Stephenson's *Edward Stuart Talbot, 1844–1934*, London, 1936, p. 161.

[2] *Diaries*, 28 Feb. 1908.

[3] Among those in von Hügel's audience were H. G. Wood, T. R. Glover, J. K. Mozley (who, the Baron noted, had studied under W. Hermann, and had written on 'Ritschlianism'), J. F. Foakes-Jackson, S. A. Cooke, I. Abrahams, J. H. A. Hart, and others (*Diaries*, 28 Jan. 1909). As the publication date for his *Encyclopaedia Britannica* article on the Fourth Gospel approached, von Hügel became apprehensive about the sort of reception it would receive. Although it was not published until 1911, he had written it in 1906–7. Between the time of writing and publication his own church had condemned some of the ideas he expressed in the article, especially his ideas on the historicity and authenticity of the Fourth Gospel. Consequently, he was hoping for some sympathetic reception from his Anglican friends. The following diary entries are significant: '4.30. G. C. Rawlinson comes to coffee with me. Pleasant & bright, but did not stay long and did not seem to have much to say. Doubts whether Lacey or "Church Times" generally would support me, if I were attacked over my E. Br. article.' (*Diaries*, 15 Dec. 1910). 'Walter Frere came to tea,...Very satisfactory talk. I told him also about my E. B. article and the possible trouble that may come to me from it' (*Diaries*, 28 Dec. 1910).

[4] *Diaries*, 31 Jan. 1909.

there. He talked to them about W. R. Inge's recent article on modernism in *The Quarterly Review*, about modernism in Italy which he distinguished into four different varieties, about 'the two stages of the relations between the Church and the Bible', about the Fourth Gospel, and finally about the Eucharist and liberal views. The majority of his audience of seventeen seemed to him narrow and inclined to 'lumping together views', though he noted that 'several, Revd. Mr. Cartwright especially, appeared, from [the] first to be with me in the discriminations attempted by me'.[1] The publication of his *Mystical Element of Religion* at the end of 1908 was soon a source of new contacts and even friendships for the Baron too, though the anti-modernist campaign caused some of his Catholic friends and acquaintances to shy away from the friendly reception they might otherwise have given it.[2] Abbot Cuthbert Butler, for instance, called on the Baron to try to find out how the officials had received the book and to prepare the ground for a possible refusal to review it.[3] But the book's reception was largely positive, and often even enthusiastic.

About noon on 9 July 1909 von Hügel received from Maude Petre a telegram asking whether he could come to Storrington at a moment's notice to help with decisions concerning Tyrrell who was gravely ill. He answered 'Yes'. A second telegram arrived from Miss Petre at 4.00 p.m., and von Hügel was on the 5.10 train from Victoria. As soon as he reached Storrington he had a long consultation with Miss Petre on the problem of arranging for Tyrrell to receive the last sacraments of the church.[4] Tyrrell had never been charged with any specified heresy nor had he been nominally excommunicated. He had been deprived of the sacraments until such time as he made a formal retraction and submission to the Pope. But the submission and retraction demanded by Rome was total,

[1] *Diaries*, 29 May 1909.
[2] 'Genocchi writes me word that if any of the (in part intelligent and sympathetic) clerical book sellers in Rome were to accept sale-copies of my "M[ystical] E[lement]", he would receive an order for instant withdrawal of them from the Secretary of State, with the certainty of his business being crippled if he did not comply forthwith.' Von Hügel to Tyrrell, 7 Dec. 1908, BM, Add. MSS. 44931.68. 'I am very sincere when I say that I am unaware of having maintained any position, in any final way, throughout the book, which would be clearly incompatible with the soundest orthodoxy. And the main conclusions, certainly the great wish and aim, of the book, appears to be in substantial agreement with the great canonized mystics. Still I know how readily books just now have to face opposition for more or less personal, or external and accidental reasons; and so I shall be glad for whatever you can do, and not unduly vexed or surprised if you cannot do much.' Von Hügel to Ward, 3 Dec. 1908, WFP, vH MSS.
[3] *Diaries*, 5 Feb. 1909.
[4] *Diaries*, 9 July 1909.

including not only unqualified acceptance of *Lamentabili* and *Pascendi*, but also a complete repudiation of all his own writings. And this, obviously, Tyrrell could not do without seriously violating his own conscience. However, canonical practice allowed any priest to absolve a dying man, if the man showed signs of repentance or could be presumed to have a repentant disposition. The hitch, of course, was that by *signs of repentance* the authorities would insist in Tyrrell's case on nothing less than the fulfilment of their demand for an *unqualified* submission. Although this was more than any human authority had a right to demand, such a demand seemed inevitable under the circumstances, and its implications were what caused the dilemma for the Baron and Miss Petre. If Tyrrell received the sacraments and nothing was said about the circumstances in which he had done so, then the authorities could claim that Tyrrell had died 'piously' renouncing all his books and ideas and life's work and convictions – and implicitly endorsing *Lamentabili* and *Pascendi*. If he received the sacraments but evidently without making an unqualified submission, then the authorities might cause yet further trouble. After discussing the problem, von Hügel and Miss Petre decided that they knew of only four priests in good standing who could appreciate Tyrrell's situation and not press for more than was reasonably possible. These were Herbert Thurston, S.J., Basil Maturin, Henri Bremond, and Charles Dessoulavy. The last was the most accessible, and he was telegraphed to come on the following day as early as possible.[1] Less than forty-eight hours before Tyrrell died the Baron described the situation for Lilley:

I found, on arriving here, that he had had a violent *migraine* attack at supper on the Tuesday [6th]; and had been very weak and restless, more or less wandering in his head, with great pain in it, ever since then. On this Friday [9th] two trained Nurses had been installed. And the question of the Sacrs. was on. He had had a paralytic stroke on the left side (in arm and left side of mouth) which rendered his articulation most thick, and the mind was very wandering. No possibility of ascertaining *now* what he would wish. We decided according to the tenour of many a conversation, – recent ones, too, – that we had had with him; and decided to call in, next morning at once, a Southwark Diocese secular Priest, a friend of his, with full faculties, and to put to him what we were confident Fr. T. would wish done. This priest came at 1, midday; and, since the whole decision wd. have to be based upon interpretation and construction, – he made me take the responsibility for the following interpretation. Fr. T. would certainly wish to receive the Sacrs. and would certainly be willing and eager to confess, and to express penitence for, any and all excesses of speech or of writing, and unnecessary pain or scandal given to anyone, – and

[1] *Ibid.*

this also in specific instances that might occur to his memory. But he would, as decidedly, refuse any unlimited, absolute retraction, any unbounded submission; and would, sadly but firmly elect to die without the Sacr., if such a condition were insisted on. The Priest fully accepted these three positions, and saw T. twice, offered to hear his conf., and T. seemed very pleased to see him, – apparently recognizing him, and spoke much, – possibly his confession, – but it was impossible to make out what T. was saying, or whether even he realized the situation in general. The Priest gave him conditional Absolution, and asked to be sent for again, if he got still worse, for Extreme Unction; and, if he got better, for H. Com. Throughout Sunday T. lay restless, with the pain in his head, dozing a little now and then, – semi-aware, apparently of persons and things, but with still a curiously high degree of strength about him. The night to Monday was so alarmingly bad, that Miss Petre, on the Dr.'s advice, sent at 8 a.m., not for the distant secular Priest but for the Premonstratensian Prior here, who, as you know, used to be so friendly, and then became so hostile to him. The Prior, in the presence of 3 witnesses, Mr W. Tyrrell, Miss Petre, and her sister, Mrs Sweetman Powell, administered Extreme Unction to him, without attempting to extract even a merely interpretative recantation from him – a proceeding which would, it is true, have been physically blocked or impossible. We are all sorry he had to be called in, – not but that he was most kind and willing, or that we doubt his past good-hearted feelings towards T. . . . . Bremond arrives in an hour's time.[1]

Even at that stage of Tyrrell's illness the doctors were not agreed that it was really the final manifestations of Bright's disease and thought it might possibly be 'some bad nerve or brain break-down, with temporary kidney derangement'. If this latter were the true situation, then there would be a possibility that he might pull through. 'But the saddest feature of the case', von Hügel told Lilley, 'is that they are confident he can never again be the same man, – *some* diminishment of mind and will-power cannot fail to remain permanently. And if this were to be really considerable, we would all wish that he may *not* pull thro'.'

Tyrrell died at 9.15 a.m. on the 15th. Miss Petre was with him, but the Baron, who was staying at the White Horse Hotel, reached his bed-

[1] Von Hügel to Lilley, 13 July 1909, LFP, i, vH MSS. How careful the Baron was with the details which he records here is indicated by his conclusion: 'I know you will, kindly, be discreet in the dissemination of the news; especially would it be well, I think, to be very general and vague as to the ecclesiastical details, tho' it would be important to say that he was having every physical and spiritual help and attention. You will understand our motive: it is so very important that the higher official world should not begin to fusstle and to press, if not him, at least us. If he comes round fully, there may be difficult complications; but we must do nothing, by unnecessary communications of any sort, to bring these on. But you, his friend, much loved Friend, have a right to the above confidences; and I think it useful, too, that the facts of these days should thus stand, in black and white, upon paper, for future reference, if necessary.'

side too late.[1] At once the two, with Bremond's help, composed a statement for the press on the fact of Tyrrell's death and the circumstances of his reception of the last sacraments. Their purpose was to ensure that no rumours got abroad about the dead man's having made some sort of complete retractation.[2] Their statement appeared in *The Times* and in the *Daily Mail* for the following morning, and the matter of Tyrrell's dispositions regarding the sacraments was expressed in almost the same words that von Hügel had used in writing to Lilley earlier.[3] *The Times* letter angered and alarmed the Prior, and he insisted on consulting Amigo before proceeding with any funeral arrangements. Fearing trouble from Southwark, Miss Petre telegraphed to Archbishop Bourne: 'Difficulties have arisen about funeral here on account of *Times* letter – This letter compromises myself and Baron only – Will Your Grace to avoid scandal regard only plain fact that he received willingly and consciously though speechless full rites of Church and not raise difficulty about burial in your diocese.' By evening Miss Petre had received a telegram from Archbishop's House stating: 'Your telegram received. Archbishop abroad.' The Prior, too, had heard from Amigo, and the Bishop was firm in his insistence that unless Tyrrell had made a retractation there could not be a Catholic burial.[4] The Prior then tried to get Miss Petre and the Baron to publish a second letter, practically retracting the first one, as a means of bringing Amigo around to agreeing to the burial service. To this Miss Petre responded 'that our personal views had nothing to do with the case; that Dr. D[essoulavy] & he himself had administered the Sacrs. to the dying & speechless man, who was evidently most willing to receive them & in contrite dispositions, and that a man who has received the Last Sacrs. cannot be deprived of Cath. burial'.[5] On the 18th Mrs William Tyrrell showed von Hügel the copy of a telegram from her husband to Amigo 'pleading, as only living close blood-relation of Fr. T. for Bishop's allowing Rel. Fun., denial of wh. appeared to him unnecessarily harsh'.[6] Amigo replied that his decision was not a personal one,

[1] *Diaries*, 15 July 1909.

[2] *Ibid.* 'Miss P. and I were, of course, well aware of the unpopularity of what we were doing, – especially by this letter to the Papers. But we felt that the most elementary loyalty to our friend and to the great cause for which we have all laboured in common strictly *demanded* such a prompt declaration, so as to anticipate the upspringing of legend, which would have arisen in 24 hours, incapable of eradication any more.' Von Hügel to Bishop, 16 July 1909, in *Dublin Review*, vol. 227, no. 462, Oct. 1953, p. 429.

[3] *The Times* letter is printed in full in *Autobiography and Life*, II, pp. 434–5.

[4] *Diaries*, 16 July 1909.

[5] *Diaries*, 17 July 1909.

[6] *Diaries*, 18 July 1909.

that Tyrrell should have been made to make a retractation, and that without such a retractation there would be no Catholic burial.[1] Maude Petre and Henri Bremond spent much of the 18th and 19th in the London area, visiting various ecclesiastical officials, including Amigo himself, in a last effort to obtain some concession for the religious burial of their friend. Von Hügel remained in Storrington, where telegrams and letters of condolence from all over England and Europe arrived for him.[2] Only the communications from Mignot and Loisy depressed him. Loisy's note was 'distressingly cold and short', and Mignot's letter was 'disappointing, since as much official as sincere'.[3] With every possibility for Roman Catholic burial blocked, the hospitality of the Anglican Rector of Storrington was gratefully accepted and arrangements for burial in the parish cemetery on the 21st were completed.

Early on the morning of the funeral Bremond privately offered a *requiem* Mass for the repose of George Tyrrell's soul at the high altar of the priory church; Maude Petre, the Baron, and several other friends, communicated.[4] At 12.30 p.m. the small group of friends and relatives which had gathered in Storrington for the funeral assembled in the garden outside the room where Tyrrell's body lay. Bremond, wearing neither cassock nor surplice nor stole, addressed them briefly and without bitterness on the circumstances of the funeral and the entirely nonofficial character of it all. The procession then formed, Bremond leading, with William Tyrrell on his right and von Hügel on his left, and the coffin carried behind them. Everyone else followed behind the coffin. They walked through the village in silence to the churchyard. There Bremond read the traditional Catholic burial prayers, sprinkled blessed water over the grave in benediction, and read out a deeply moving and utterly unpolemic funeral oration. With those simple ceremonies Tyrrell's body was placed in the earth.[5]

[1] *Diaries*, 19 July 1909.
[2] *Diaries*, 18–20 July 1909.
[3] *Diaries*, 20 July 1909.
[4] *Diaries*, 21 July 1909.

[5] *Ibid.* Bremond wrote out his funeral oration (*Diaries*, 20 July 1909) and it was printed, among other places, in *The Guardian*, no. 3321, 28 July 1909, p. 1185. Loisy has accused the Baron ('Je tiens de bonne source...', *Mém.* III, p. 123) of hesitating to participate in Tyrrell's funeral because of the difficulties made about it by church authorities. This fits in well with Loisy's presuppositions and insinuations about the Baron expressed in the final volume of the *Mémoires*, but it ill accords with the evidence. Von Hügel went to Storrington on the very day when he first learned of Tyrrell's illness, and he remained there until the day after Tyrrell was buried. He took full responsibility for the decision regarding Tyrrell's presumed dispositions and his reception of the sacraments; he not only joined Miss Petre in publicly describing the situation in *The Times*; but he also composed a letter stating the same

The ecclesiastical controversy surrounding Tyrrell's death and burial was pursued by the authorities with dogged determination. Three days after the funeral Amigo suspended Bremond from all priestly functions within the Southwark diocese. Von Hügel, who had gone back to London after the funeral, returned at once to Storrington to help in the decision of what was to be done in this new crisis. Robert Dell wrote to Maude Petre proposing a document to be signed by all the Catholics present at Tyrrell's funeral protesting Amigo's act against Bremond. The Baron, Miss Petre, and Bremond discussed Dell's proposal and agreed against the plan because not all the Catholics at the funeral would be likely to sign the protest. But they also agreed that, if at any time it seemed desirable, Bremond should be free to publish the fact that the Catholics at the funeral had wanted to make such a protest and that he himself had asked them to desist.[1] However, before the Baron wrote to

thing even more definitely for publication in Italy in the Milanese *Corriere della Sera*. And then he had an English version of this Italian letter inserted in the English press: *Daily Graphic*, vol. LXXIX, no. 637, 31 July 1909, p. 12. He could hardly have nailed his colours more clearly to the mast, and if the authorities were to punish him it would be for his part in 'preventing' a dying and excommunicated priest from making a proper and ecclesiastically acceptable retractation, and *not* for joining other Catholics in attending an unofficial funeral which the authorities had tried to thwart. Moreover, von Hügel wrote to Edmund Gardner, a Roman Catholic who did not know Tyrrell really well, on 17 July 1909 (in *Selected Letters*, p. 166), saying: 'Come, please, to the Funeral if you possibly can.' It is inconceivable that von Hügel would have asked this man, under these circumstances, to do something which he himself 'hesitated' to do.

Maude Petre, whose own emotional entanglement with Tyrrell made her less than just to von Hügel, is certainly open to suspicion as Loisy's informant in this matter, since she has written: 'He [von Hügel] attended the death-bed of his friend; he attended his funeral, though he would, I think, have been glad not to do the latter...' (*Von Hügel and Tyrrell*, p. 199).

However, Bremond is more likely Loisy's 'bonne source', since the former wrote to the latter: 'Je ne suis rien du baron. Il est un peu déconcertant avec ses amis, surtout français et frivoles comme moi. Je ne sais comment il a pu vous pardonner d'être français. Ma soumission lors des funérailles Tyrrell ("regrette tout ce qu'il a fait de répréhensible") l'a irrité et cependent si nous l'avions écouté, les catholiques n'auraient pas accompagné le corps au cimetière, ce qui me paraissait plus odieux.' Bremond to Loisy, June 1913, in Henri Bernard-Maitre, 'Lettres d'Henri Bremond à Alfred Loisy', *Bulletin de littérature ecclésiastique (Toulouse)*, tome LXIX, no. 3, July 1968, pp. 176-7.

[1] *Diaries*, 26 July 1909. The list of those at the funeral, both Roman Catholic and Anglican, can be found in *Autobiography and Life*, pp. 441-2. The list which the Baron records in his diary agrees with this, except that he has also named T. Bailey Saunders as present. Apparently there was much discussion and criticism in certain English Roman Catholic circles of the Catholics who attended the funeral, and especially of Basil Maturin, the only Roman priest other than Bremond to attend. Wilfrid Ward wrote to Lord Halifax: '...Tyrrell's death has aroused a train of sad thoughts wh. will not consent to disperse themselves. Maturin was at the funeral, but I think wishes now that he had not gone. Whatever blame is due in high quarters I cannot doubt that Miss Petre in one way & Dell in another are taking a line wh. is quite indefensible' (Ward to Halifax, 27 July 1909, HP, A4, 224). And some days later he wrote again: 'I am still hearing more details about Tyrrell...It is all an ugly thing, & I am

Dell to tell him of the rejection of his proposal, Dell had already acted for himself. In a letter to *The Times* protesting the whole anti-modernist campaign as focussed on the sad affair of Tyrrell's burial, Dell wrote:

But the fact that the Roman Church had no place for George Tyrrell compels those of us who share his convictions and his hopes to ask ourselves whether that Church has any place for us. As I stood by his open grave in Storrington churchyard on Wednesday, I could not but feel that we too should be denied Roman Catholic sacraments, if we were as brave and as honest as he was. Have we the right to continue to avail ourselves of what was denied him without declaring as plainly and fearlessly as he did what we believe and to what we cannot submit? If, after such a declaration, we are allowed to remain in communion with the Pope, so much the better. If not, which of us would not choose to be in communion with George Tyrrell and with all that is best and noblest in humanity rather than with Pius X. and the spies, informers and professors of mendacity by whose agency he governs his 'docile flock of sheep'?[1]

As soon as the Baron read Dell's letter he wrote to him, admitting the 'truth and usefulness of many points in his "Times" letter', but also declaring his own 'deliberate impenitence at having done all, with Maude Petre, to get Tyrrell the last Sacraments and Ecclesiastical Burial'. He concluded by telling Dell that he was 'a Roman Catholic on and on (whatever may yet happen) please God!'[2]

Three days after the funeral *The Tablet* published a lengthy letter from the Prior of Storrington, excusing himself from any complicity in what had happened, giving an inaccurate account of the facts of Tyrrell's last days, and attributing defiant motives to Miss Petre and the Baron for the way they had handled the situation.[3] In the following issue of *The Tablet* both Miss Petre and von Hügel answered the Prior, the former supplying the background of the Prior's relationship with Tyrrell, and

---

sorry that Hügel should be mixed up with it' (Ward to Halifax, 8 Aug. 1909, HP, A4. 224). The following letter from Maturin to Bourne is also indicative of the atmosphere following the funeral: 'My Lord Archbishop, – I called on Your Grace a few days ago, but was told you were away. I have wanted to explain to Your Grace, in view of various rumours which I have heard, that my only reason for attending the funeral of Fr. Tyrrell was that he was an old friend of my family with which he has been associated ever since his boyhood. As a matter of fact I did not know that there was any difficulty about his burial till I got to Storrington. I do not know why any unworthy motive should have been attributed to me, nor do I care to explain my reasons to those who have spread this report, but I thought I ought to tell Your Grace & was sorry not to be able to see you.' (Maturin to Bourne, 7 Sept. 1909, AAW, Bourne Papers, 124/5).

[1] *The Times*, no. 39,022, 27 July 1909, p. 10.
[2] *Diaries*, 28 July 1909.
[3] *The Tablet*, vol. 114, no. 3611, 24 July 1909, pp. 130–1.

the Baron correcting the Prior's erroneous facts. 'As for his insinuations concerning the motives of Miss Petre and myself', von Hügel wrote, 'I would say but two words. Anybody who knows either her or myself knows also that we are utterly incapable of what the Prior has suggested; and those who do not know us, know, at least, that such grave accusations require proof.'[1]

When von Hügel first returned to London following Tyrrell's funeral, he found awaiting him 'a further great heap of letters', including an anonymous telegram concerning Bremond with rumours of some impending censure for Bremond's action at Tyrrell's funeral.[2] In forwarding the mysterious telegram to Bremond in Storrington, the Baron told him: 'Oh well, whatever may happen, and whatever may be the price you, or we all may have to pay, – the action, your action was nobly loyal, dignified and truly wise, I am very sure.'[3] Two days later followed Amigo's diocesan suspension of Bremond. By the end of July Bremond was back in France where he found the ultramontane press already in full attack.[4] For some reason he brought the local Southwark suspension to the attention of his ecclesiastical superiors in France and, at the express order of Cardinal Merry del Val, his local suspension was immediately made universal. When informing the Baron of this development, Bremond told him that he was preparing for Merry del Val 'a thoroughly *fenelonian* letter … with the puzzling readiness and humility more difficult to swallow than lutherian revolt'.[5] From the Malvern Hills, where von Hügel had gone with his family for a rest, he answered Bremond at once. '*Of course* I am very sorry', he wrote,

and (I suppose, equally of course) I think the line you have decided upon taking, wise and dignified …

On looking back now, over the whole course of events from July 9th downwards, I can only find two decisions which I feel uncertain about; which I would probably alter, were it possible to repeat it all, and were the decisions entirely in my own hands.

---

[1] *The Tablet*, vol. 114, no. 3612, 31 July 1909, pp. 181–2.

[2] 'My dear, brave, loyal Friend, – I have come back to find a further great heap of letters, – several of which may turn out interesting, tho' I am too tired to master them to-night. But this telegram I had better send on at once, though I not only trust but incline to think, that this is one of the "Correspondenza's" tricks, – and does not mean that they will really be so violent as to excommunicate you. I am clear that we must not budge, to the right or to the left.' Von Hügel to Bremond, 22 July 1909, SAUL, MS. 30284/37 (photocopy).

[3] *Ibid.*

[4] Von Hügel to Bremond, 10 Aug. 1909, SAUL, MS, 30284/38 (photocopy); *The Tablet*, vol. 114, no, 3613, 7 Aug. 1909, pp. 223–4, published a selection of the controversy from the *Universe*.

[5] Bremond to von Hügel, 8 Aug. 1909, SAUL, MS. 2336.

(1) I now feel as tho' it would have been better if, at the Funeral you had simply read the Prayers, and had invited all to follow your example, at the end, in the sprinkling of Holy Water on the coffin, thus differentiating the little service itself from a full Catholic funeral. And (2), – I have been puzzled as to why, on returning to France with that (no doubt unjust yet highly localized) suspension upon you, you did not simply resume your Masses, without any appeal against what, after all, had come to an end. I, of course, felt that *in ideal circumstances* that appeal of yours, away from the *profanum vulgus* to those two Princes of the Church, would be fine and dramatic. But, under our present *regime* and *personnel* it struck me as so obviously dangerous and in a sense, unnecessary, as to make me suspect that, on getting abroad, you had discovered conditions not known to, or at least not sufficiently realized by, myself. Perhaps it was practically impossible *not* to hold your tongue (to explain what had happened) and not to appeal thus to your immediate Chiefs. And we had all agreed that it was necessary that you should thus explain.

I suppose, from your P.C., that the Archb. of Aix did not move in the whole affair at all; but that Rome took the entire initiative, – at least for this stage, – and that it chose him as its most natural intermediary. I wonder, of course, how long this suspension will last, and what will bring it to an end. Certainly I shall wish much that (short of any really undignified or untruthful act on your part even suggested) this suspension may come to a speedy end. And I take it that precisely the course you have decided upon will give such a finale the best chance of coming to pass. Clearly, if the suspension is intended simply as a punishment, – 3 or 6 months of it may satisfy them. Let us hope they do not mean it chiefly as pressure put upon you to make some undignified, untruthful 'retraction' 'unconditional submission'.[1]

Apparently such pressure was indeed the chief intent of the suspension, and Bremond was required to sign a statement that he adhered without reservation to *Pascendi* and *Lamentabili* before it was lifted. On 5 November Bremond signed such a statement for the Vatican, at the same time 'regretting and condemning' everything reprehensible which he had said over Tyrrell's grave.[2]

[1] Von Hügel to Bremond, 10 Aug. 1909, SAUL, MS. 30284/38 (photocopy).

[2] 'Dans des sentiments de pleine et sincère soumission à l'Autorité Ecclesiastique et par l'entremise de Sa Grandeur Monseigneur l'Evêque de Southwark, l'Abbé Brémond déclares regretter et condamner tout ce qu'il a fait et dit de répréhensible au moment des funerailles du père Tyrrell. Il déclare en outre adhérer sans réserve à toutes les doctrines de l'Église et notamment aux enseignements contenus dans le décret "Lamentabili" et dans l'Encyclique "Pascendi". Fait à Aix en Provence, le 5 novembre, 1909. Henri Brémond.' *The Tablet*, vol. 114, no. 3628, 20 Nov. 1909, p. 807. 'One minds even the bit about the funeral and the discourse then. Still it is the last sentence (no doubt the one that Rome laid most stress on) that is *the* painfully trying part of the whole thing. Yet I know that Miss Petre, so brave and true herself considered that, if he felt in *his* conscience that he could do it, and if nothing wd. regain his eccl. status, he should do it, since he is so different from Fr. T. without any sense of a *mission*, and so little likely [not?] to suffer deep moral damage, if he let himself be made

How close the Baron himself came to some sort of ecclesiastical censure at this time he seems to have sensed,[1] but never factually to have known. On 30 July Merry del Val wrote to Amigo, asking for information as to whether steps should be taken against von Hügel and Miss Petre, and possibly some other Catholics who had attended Tyrrell's funeral. Amigo discussed the letter with Bourne, and the two decided to ask Bishop Hedley of Newport for his opinion before proceeding further. Hedley was not only one of the senior Roman Catholic bishops in England at this time, but he had been a personal acquaintance of the Baron for over thirty years, and during the earlier part of that relationship the two had been friends as well. Amigo interrogated Hedley, and received the following reply:

My information about what happened at poor Tyrrell's death is derived solely from the Tablet, and from your letter.

As far as I can see, no public sentence or canonical censure can be passed either on Baron von Hügel or on Miss M. D. Petre, in regard to what they are alleged to have said or done in connection with this matter. Even if the facts were not disputed, there is no expression (that I can find) of heresy, revolt, disobedience or favouring of heresy. The allegation I suppose would be that they prevented or suppressed a retractation, or prevented the access of a priest who would have made the dying man's duty clear to him. Whatever may be suspected, I do not think that either of these charges can possibly be proved. Moreover, I know F. von Hügel, and as he denies them, I believe him.

In any case, I think that before sentence is passed both the one and the other should be privately informed of the exact points on which they are to be censured, and given an opportunity of explanation.

I am not supposing that there is any intention, at present, of going back to anything that Baron von Hügel or Miss Petre has said previously. To do so at this juncture would seem to be very inadvisable.[2]

Amigo forwarded this letter to Bourne with the remark that 'perhaps the best time to act will be when poor Tyrrell's book [*Christianity at the*

---

into a déclassé. Yet, alas, alas, – no hope of true love for Rome by discerning minds, no spontaneous, proud admiration for the acts entailed, – as long as this system lasts; and when will it end?' (Von Hügel to Lilley, 20 Nov. 1909, LFP, I, vH MSS.).

[1] 'I feel too as though, at this crisis, we shall do so wisely, by, each time that hesitation is not excluded by dubious reasons, ever deciding rather for the few words than the many, for saying perhaps too little than perhaps too much. After all, it will be a *very great* point gained if you and I remain uncensured, or without their attempting to get us to subscribe to *Lamentabili* and *Pascendi*, with the alternative of suspension from the Sacraments. I know that we must not shrink from all that may be quite obvious to our consciences, whatever the risks, (but short of such cases, we shall, won't we, very largely mark time, and when we do act, act with an almost provocative reticence ...).' Von Hügel to Petre, 14 Sept. 1909, in *Selected Letters*, p. 169.

[2] Hedley to Amigo, 12 Aug. 1909, AAW, Bourne Papers, 124/5 (copy).

Crossroads] is published. So far though Miss Petre's conduct is strange, we have nothing positive to go by. I am glad that you will have the responsibility as the book will be published in Westminster.'[1] Bourne told Merry del Val of Amigo's consultation with him and sent him Hedley's opinion with the comment that 'this opinion seems to me wise and prudent'.[2] Bourne's letter to the papal Secretary of State stressed, as had the English Bishops' address to the Pope following *Pascendi*, that in England modernists were few and their influence negligible. He also pointed out that the circumstances of Tyrrell's 'death with the absolutely necessary consequence of the refusal of Catholic burial have shown people the horror of dying under the censure of the Church'. He added that

it is always dangerous to arouse in England the morbid unreasonable sympathy which people so readily give to every wrong-doer whatever the nature of his crime. It is most important that these persons should have no opportunity of posing as martyrs for a cause. Such Modernism as we have had here has been very largely sympathy with certain individuals rather than with their ideas. In dealing with the question I have had to keep this aspect always before my mind and carefully to avoid giving them any kind of advertisement. The result is that their books including Tyrrell's have practically no sale and they are not asked for in the lending libraries.

Judging from the reprints and translations of Tyrrell's books, one can discount Bourne's last remark as wishful thinking.[3] But the whole tone of his letter to Merry del Val was in keeping with his policy of not seeking trouble. He concluded by telling Merry del Val: 'Please let me know if there is any further information that you would wish to have or any action that you desire me to take.' The Archbishop of Westminster, at that time anyway, was not free to disregard the desires of the Vatican Secretary of State. But as far as modernist-hunting was concerned the initiative would have to come from Merry del Val, because Bourne's policy was and continued to be one of non-aggression.[4]

[1] Amigo to Bourne, 13 Aug. 1909, AAW, Bourne Papers, 124/5.
[2] Bourne to Merry del Val, 15 Aug. 1909, AAW, Bourne Papers, 124/5 (copy).
[3] 'Meanwhile, the brilliant volumes of the English (or rather Irish) Jesuit Father, George Tyrrell, were circulating widely among Anglo-Catholics early in the century. *Lex Orandi* was published in 1903. An Anglo-Catholic friend, now a Roman priest, presented me with several of Tyrrell's volumes in 1904.' H. D. A. Major, *English Modernism: Its Origins, Methods, Aims*, Cambridge, Massachusetts, 1927, p. 23.
[4] In 1911 the Jesuit Rector of Wimbledon College, the Reverend Daniel Considine, wrote to Bourne to inform him of two charges which were circulating against the Archbishop by certain Roman Catholics in England. These charges were that the Archbishop had misappropriated funds, and that he had 'leanings towards Modernism'. The proof of the latter charge was held to be that Bourne had not clamped down on professors and students at Wonersh Seminary and 'was considered to be in sympathy with a freer discussion and investiga-

During this same period following Tyrrell's funeral an indiscreet letter from Tyrrell to the Old Catholic Bishop Herzog was published. In this letter Tyrrell had violently challenged ultramontane extremism by denying ecumenicity to the Councils of Trent and the Vatican. *The Tablet*, delighted with such proof of Tyrrell's non-Roman ideas, reprinted the offending letter as justification for the way the ecclesiastical authorities had handled Tyrrell's funeral.[1] As Tyrrell's literary executor Maude Petre threatened *The Tablet* with legal action, if they should dare to publish further material by Tyrrell without her sanction.[2] The Baron, while regretting Tyrrell's remarks, asked *The Tablet*:

Would the sudden discovery of even a grave sin committed by one who had subsequently received the last rites of the Church, disqualify him for Catholic burial? One does not see how it could do so. Hence I cannot but regret that you should revive this distressing controversy once more, whatever you may have to say with regard to Father Tyrrell's orthodoxy.[3]

The Tablet, however, justified itself by insisting that its 'observations were addressed to those who have recklessly and unjustly accused the ecclesiastical authorities of narrowness and intolerance in refusing Catholic burial to Father Tyrrell'. And again it asserted that Tyrrell's letter to Herzog 'is plainly confirmatory of the justice of the action of the Catholic authorities, and it was only fair to them that we should have brought it to the notice of those by whom they have been attacked.'[4]

---

tion of Biblical subjects and Christian antiquities, and was supposed even to have joined in a petition of the Archbishop of Albi (?) to the Holy See that Loisy might not be condemned because his influence was on the whole stimulating to Catholic ecclesiastical studies and students'. Considine also told Bourne that people complained that he took no action against any of the clergy or others 'who were suspected of Modernist opinions, that the Vigilance Committee rarely meets, and does no business, and that no effort has been made to deal in any other way with what is (alleged to be) a present danger' (Considine to Bourne, 8 June 1911, AAW, Bourne Papers, 4/11.) Bourne has written across the top of this correspondence: 'This correspondence is kept to show my successors the wild and improbable accusations to which an Archbishop of Westminster may be exposed.' In late November 1924 von Hügel visited his Carmelite daughter for the last time before his death. She told him of a recent visit by Cardinal Bourne to the convent and of his words to her about and for the Baron: '"I have never got him into trouble & I never will", he had said only some days ago, upon sending me his blessing thro' T[hekla].' (*Diaries*, 28 Nov. 1924). Ironically, the official biography of Bourne does not even mention von Hügel and Tyrrell, nor is there in it any indication that there had ever been such a thing as the modernist crisis. One full chapter, however, is devoted to the Eucharistic Congress held in London in 1908. See, Ernest Oldmeadow, *Francis Cardinal Bourne*, 2 vols., London, 1940 and 1944.

[1] *The Tablet*, vol. 114, no. 3625, 30 Oct. 1909, pp. 690–1.
[2] *The Tablet*, vol. 114, no. 3627, 13 Nov. 1909, p. 776.
[3] *The Tablet*, vol. 114, no. 3626, 6 Nov. 1909, p. 738.
[4] *Ibid.*

Throughout this period of 'distressing controversy' Miss Petre, with some assistance from von Hügel, went on preparing for publication Tyrrell's last, almost completed, manuscript.[1] When she and the Baron examined Tyrrell's private papers, they also discovered that his letters from von Hügel were the only personal correspondence which he had not destroyed. The Baron, too, had saved all of Tyrrell's letters to himself, and he and Miss Petre agreed to publish the complete correspondence. They asked Edmund Bishop to act as editor for the proposed volume, and when Bishop refused the project was temporarily set aside and never resumed.[2] Bishop had suggested the idea of a full biography of Tyrrell, and this was the plan eventually chosen. Meanwhile the editor of *The Hibbert Journal* asked for three articles on Tyrrell for his January issue. The articles were to have covered Tyrrell's Anglican period and his earlier and later Roman Catholic periods. Tyrrell's childhood and lifelong friend, the Reverend Charles E. Osborne, who had travelled from his rectory at Wallsend-on-Tyne to Storrington for the funeral, was to write the Anglican article.[3] The Baron, of course, wrote the last in the series. But the article covering the early Roman Catholic period was never written, probably because of the difficulty in obtaining a writer who knew that period well and who would at the same time dare to write of it in a friendly manner. Throughout the months immediately following Tyrrell's death the Baron and Miss Petre not infrequently disagreed in their ideas about what did and what did not genuinely contribute to the true preservation of Tyrrell's name and memory.[4] Basically their difference was that between accepting and regretting Tyrrell's limitations while insisting on his true greatness and substantial right to devoted remembrance, and that of so idealizing the man that the limitations tended to disappear. The former approach was von Hügel's, and it was the approach he took in his *Hibbert* article. Before he published the article, however, he sent it off to Miss Petre for comment and criticism. 'I won't venture to say that I find the article as a whole quite

---

[1] *Diaries*, 23 and 31 Aug.; 8 and 11 Sept.; and 9 and 11 Oct. 1909.

[2] *Diaries*, 19 Aug. 1909; von Hügel to Bishop, 14 Aug. 1909, in *Dublin Review*, vol. 227, no. 462, p. 431.

[3] *Diaries*, 30 July 1909. Jacks, the editor, had originally suggested that Osborne, von Hügel and Maude Petre should write the three articles. Miss Petre declined the offer. 'His [Tyrrell's] mind & influence has been constantly with me for years past. I loved him beyond almost anyone else I knew, & what most attracted me in him was the union of profound & subtle intellect with a most generous & tender heart – Surely his message for the Universal Church cannot be in vain.' Osborne to von Hügel, 17 July 1909, SAUL, MS. 2902.

[4] *Diaries*, 28 July; 1, 12, and 29 Nov. 1909.

sympathetic', she told him after reading the manuscript.

I suppose it expresses what I have felt in my intercourse with you since his death, – viz. that you seemed more conscious of things to be excused than of things to be admired [Miss Petre has here crossed out the words: '& followed']. To me the full meaning and explanation of his life has come ever more fully with a fulness that has made me both proud and humble – indeed strangely so – since his death than it did before – to you it has perhaps been otherwise; and some things have come to you as a surprise which were familiar to me. I should not be honest if I omitted to say this. While liking so much a great deal that you have said. And I dare say you will think that I am not the best judge in the matter.[1]

Nevertheless, the Baron stood by Miss Petre sympathetically, and helped her with encouragement and suggestions through the next few difficult years especially. Once the World War came their paths crossed less often, and until the Baron's own death in 1925 Miss Petre seems never publicly to have criticized his relationship with and attitude toward Tyrrell. Only after both men were gone, and she alone was left with memories of broken hopes and battles lost did a touch of bitterness and something less than fairness sometimes come into what she wrote of von Hügel.[2]

The Baroness Elizabeth von Hügel, Friedrich's mother, and his brother Anatole, both living in Cambridge, were upset and worried about Friedrich's involvement in Tyrrell's now notorious case.[3] When the Baron visited Cambridge in September, on his return from Malvern, Anatole brought the matter forward for discussion. Friedrich defended his own and Miss Petre's actions, though he admitted much indefensibleness in the position which Dell had publicly taken. He found the conversation extremely provocative, though he managed to hold his temper and yet remain firm.[4] On the day after this conversation he

---

[1] Petre to von Hügel, 17 Nov. 1909, BM, Add. MSS. 45361.97.

[2] Petre, *My Way of Faith*, pp. 233, and 257–9; Petre, *Von Hügel and Tyrrell*, pp. 145–6, and 198–203. In reviewing this latter book Clement C. J. Webb has taken very discreet and subtle exception to some of the unfair conclusions implied in several remarks about the Baron. See, *The Journal of Theological Studies*, vol. XXXIX, no. 2, April 1938, pp. 214–15. Webb's own feelings about von Hügel are expressed in his journal for 27 January 1925, the day of the Baron's death. Hildegard von Hügel had telegraphed to Webb, telling him of her father's death, and Webb reflected: 'We have lost one whom we both [Webb and his wife] reverenced above all other living men: whose faith was a constant support and encouragement and whose sympathy one could seek always in perfect confidence. He was a religious genius: and withal a man of vast knowledge, of perfect intellectual freedom, of humour and of common sense; simple and candid, the surest of friends and a great gentleman. I count my friendship with him among the chief blessings of my life...' (BL, MS. Res. d. 181).

[3] *Diaries*, 6 Sept. 1909.

[4] *Diaries*, 15 Sept. 1909.

tried to show Anatole the 'touching side' of Dell's personality as well.[1] Even after Friedrich's return to London, Anatole pursued the question, writing a long letter criticizing his brother's theological attitudes and asking him to make a public repudiation of Dell.[2] To this letter Friedrich replied

that I have only him & my mother remaining as close, senior or contemporary, blood relatives, and feel that discussion of points on wh[ich] we differ by temperament, character or experience, w[oul]d only fix or increase our, fundamentally most legitimate and unchangeable, differences. That I so much love him and his Cambridge work, & hope that he may continue to [the] end loving & praying for me and my endeavours. That I c[oul]d publicly reprove & discriminate myself fr[om] D[ell] only if, at [the] same time, I published a whole series of recent Roman offic[ial] acts & proceedings which largely excuse, & in part even justify D[ell]'s vehemence. But that this would surprise and scandalise A[natole] amongst many others, & that truthfulness does not seem to demand of me more than silence on both points. That I must now drop all further talk or writing on this point.[3]

This letter seems to have ended the discussion, at least temporarily, but it did not end the sense of misunderstanding existing between von Hügel and some of his relatives as a result of the modernist crisis. Even at the end of 1912 he noted in his diary how 'fluctuating and uncertain' was his reception by Anatole's wife.[4] When he discussed the problems arising from Tyrrell's death and funeral with his own wife, she never tried to persuade him to one or another course of action, though she did greatly worry 'as to what the church authorities might do to me'.[5]

Von Hügel, however, was not pursued by the ecclesiastical authorities, though Maude Petre was. After spending the latter part of November 1909 in France, Miss Petre returned to Storrington and on the morning of 1 December went to the priory church there for Mass. Before Mass began the Prior 'rushed into church to forbid her going to H[oly] Comm[union]'.[6] When Miss Petre questioned him about his authorization for such a prohibition, he admitted that he had no orders from the Bishop. Miss Petre, consequently, appealed to Amigo. When

---

[1] *Diaries*, 16 Sept. 1909. On the afternoon of this same day the Baron went for a 'walk with Prof. James Ward to Grantchester. Excellent talk about Fr. T., *Rinn.*, the 2 kinds of Modernism, his 2nd Gifford Lectures course, Ladd's "Philos. of Rel.", sense of scent in ants, bees & dogs etc.'
[2] *Diaries*, 25 Sept. 1909.
[3] *Diaries*, 28 Sept. 1909.
[4] *Diaries*, 14 Dec. 1912.
[5] *Diaries*, 21 Nov. 1909.
[6] *Diaries*, 2 Dec. 1909.

von Hügel heard of these developments, he urged her to leave Storrington once and for all 'as soon as dignity will permit', and he warned her not to expect the Bishop to support her against the Prior. If the Bishop failed to support her, he begged her to consult 'some experienced person' as to her next move; but if the Bishop should allow her to receive Communion, he urged her 'not straight away to use her right'.[1] She in turn felt the Baron was pressing her, and to leave Storrington just then was psychologically impossible for her anyhow.[2] Amigo's answer was 'that she would help him in deciding the case between [the] Prior and herself, by declaring her sincere acceptance of *Lam.* and *Pascendi*'.[3] By return of post she answered

that she would have wished for a decision from the Bishop as to the point on which she had appealed and on which she had never contested the Bishop's authority; that nothing she could subscribe could add to such testimony to her faith as her life affords; and that the one reading, a long time ago, of those documents had (owing to their apparent discrediting of our greatest apologists, Newman & Tyrrell, rendering the acceptance of scientific and historical truth most difficult, and, in *Pascendi*, going contrary to simple Xtian charity), given her so much pain that, in any case, the Bishop would understand her shrinking from a reperusal of those acts.[4]

Amigo answered that he would not compel the Premonstratentian community at Storrington to admit her to the sacraments since they believed that she held 'modernist opinions', and she had not given him any assurance to the contrary. Miss Petre decided to drop any further correspondence with Amigo, and to go elsewhere for her Communions. The Baron congratulated her on this decision.[5]

Miss Petre, accordingly, began to make her confessions and to receive the eucharist at Greyshott in Surrey, which is in the Roman Catholic diocese of Portsmouth. She did this on the occasion of monthly or six-weekly visits to her sister who lived near there with her family. At the annual meeting of the Roman hierarchy of England and Wales, held during Low Week in 1910, Amigo asked the Bishop of Portsmouth, John Baptist Cahill, if he knew in what church in the Portsmouth diocese Miss Petre received Communion. Knowing nothing about her

[1] *Diaries*, 3 Dec. 1909.
[2] *Diaries*, 6 Dec. 1909.
[3] *Diaries*, 9 Dec. 1909.
[4] *Ibid.* The Baron wrote to Miss Petre about this letter, telling her that he entirely accepted her first two points, and, if the third 'was necessary, it could not have been better put' (*Diaries*, 10 Dec. 1909).
[5] *Diaries*, 11 Dec. 1909.

activities, Cahill answered that he 'thought Storrington was too far away from any church in the diocese to make it possible'.[1] Some weeks later, however, Cahill was visiting in Greyshott, and he discovered that Miss Petre was in fact receiving the sacraments there. The local priest, who had apparently been in a state of agitation for some time because of the situation, asked the Bishop what he should do. Should he tell her that he could not give her Holy Communion? 'This public refusal of the sacraments is a grave step', Cahill reflected, 'and I do not as yet see my way clear to order it.' Convinced now that Amigo had known all along where Miss Petre communicated and that he only desired to trap the Bishop of Portsmouth by his question, Cahill wrote to Bourne for advice. 'Do you think I ought to forbid her Comm. there on the ground that she is a known "fautor" of heresy? or do you think that before acting I ought to write to Rome and state the case?' Cahill asked. He concluded by telling the Archbishop that 'I incline to write to Card. Merry del Val, but perhaps you may say something which will put me off doing so.' Whether or not Cahill wrote to Merry del Val, Miss Petre was forbidden the sacraments at Greyshott. When she visited the Baron in September 1910 she told him of these latest developments.[2]

On 1 September 1910 a document was signed in Rome which 'layed down certain rules for getting rid of the danger of modernism', and which contained an oath against modernism to be required of various Roman Catholics, especially clerics, teachers, and certain officials.[3] The document seemed not to be designed for ordinary lay members of the church, but Amigo was to try to use it against Maude Petre nevertheless. On 8 October the Baron received a letter from Miss Petre enclosing a copy of a letter Amigo had sent her on the 5th. Amigo wrote: 'I hear that you still go to H. Com. in the neighbouring parishes. Until you are willing to submit in matters of faith to the authority of the H. Father, I must forbid you Communion in my diocese.'[4] To this Miss Petre replied

that it is now *for the first time* that you forbid me communion in your diocese ...

---

[1] Cahill to Bourne [no date], AAW, Bourne Papers, 124/5. The information contained in this paragraph is all taken from Cahill's lengthy letter to Bourne. Since the Low Week meeting could not have begun before the 4th of April 1910, and since Miss Petre told the Baron on 28 September 1910 that her refusal at Greyshott was a *fait accompli*, the letter had to be written between those two dates. Internal evidence suggests that it was written closer to the latter than to the former date.

[2] *Diaries*, 28 Sept. 1910.

[3] *Acta Apostolicae Sedis*, vol. II, no. 17, 1910, pp. 655–80.

[4] *Diaries*, 8 Oct. 1910.

But, my Lord, you have, I fear, given it to be understood on one or two occas. *before now* that I was going to communion in spite of your prohibition. This was not the case, since no such prohibition existed ... I must therefore ask Your Lordsh. to be so kind as to write me a letter, which I can show privately as often as may be necessary, exonerating me entirely from having gone to comm. in yr. diocese, in other churches than Storrington, contrary to yr. prohibition ... If you did not see your way to put me quite right on this point, then, with regret, I shd. have to make public a short history of the affair, to free myself in the eyes of those who might otherwise regard my conduct as lacking in honour and rightful regard for properly constituted authority. Yr. Lordship censures me as not submitting 'in matters of faith to the authority of the H. Father.' What have I said, done, or written to support this charge?[1]

Amigo responded by demanding that she subscribe to *Lamentabili* and *Pascendi* by taking the oath against modernism. To this demand Miss Petre protested that it was unjust to single out 'a lay person and a woman' to subscribe to such documents, 'and asking, since if she subscribed to all she wd. in conscience have to do so in Pope's sense and absolutely, whether each and all of the propositions and condemnations in those documents are *de fide*?'[2] Amigo, however, was adamant, and Miss Petre decided to write a public letter in protest. The Baron aided her with criticisms of details of her rough draft, and he helped her weigh up the pros and cons of publication.[3] On 2 November Miss Petre's 'Open Letter to My Fellow Catholics' appeared in *The Times*.[4] A leader in the same issue commented on Miss Petre's plight and concluded: 'When one thinks what a really progressive Pope might accomplish among the millions of people now longing for a faith in harmony with knowledge and life, the sight of this attitude of blind reaction is one that cannot be too deeply deplored.'[5] Clerical ultramontanes were not slow to respond, and Dom John Chapman announced that 'the Catholic Church is founded on absolute unanimity of doctrine, and her existence depends on her power of preserving doctrinal unity. It is always difficult to deal politely with people who outstay their welcome and will not take a hint. The method of asking them to sign a plain document is the traditional one.'[6] Even as late as 1913, on a visit to Liverpool, Maude

[1] *Ibid.*
[2] *Diaries*, 13 Oct. 1910.
[3] *Diaries*, 24 Oct. 1910.
[4] *The Times*, no. 39,419, 2 Nov. 1910, p. 6. 'What a fine Open Letter that is of Miss Petre! May her deep loyalty and high courage help us all and do her, interiorly, nothing but good! Thank you for your fine help and sympathy.' Von Hügel to Lilley, 29 Oct. 1910, LFP, I, vH MSS. See also, von Hügel to Petre, 3 Nov. 1910, in *Selected Letters*, pp. 182–3.
[5] *The Times*, no. 39,419, 2 Nov. 1910, p. 12.
[6] *The Times*, no. 39,421, 4 Nov. 1910, p. 15.

Petre was refused Communion when she presented herself in a church there.[1] In May 1914, on one of her increasingly rare visits to the Baron, he noted significantly that she 'looked very tired'.[2]

The publication in 1912 of Tyrrell's *Autobiography and Life* occasioned another outburst of reaction against those who had been responsible for it and those who sympathized with its subject. *The Tablet*'s editor, J. G. Snead-Cox, published a review of the book, written by himself but unsigned, which aimed at showing Tyrrell to have been so dishonest and shabby a person as to be unworthy of any sympathy or credit at all.[3] The review was in keeping with Snead-Cox's policy toward Tyrrell in the latter's last years and after his death, but its complete lack of taste, not to mention Christian charity, demanded an answer. Maude Petre asked von Hügel whether he would write a signed note to the editor of *The Tablet* protesting the review. The Baron let the plan 'simmer in [his] mind' for a day before attempting to compose a letter. His first attemps 'went badly somehow', and so much so that he wrote Miss Petre a note to say that he had begun the letter but did not know whether he could send it.[4] However, he did finish the letter and he sent it. It was published on 30 November, preceded by a lengthy letter from 'Sacerdos', which was so much a justification of the earlier review as to render the reviewer suspect as the author of the letter as well. After objecting to the review's injustice and misrepresentation, von Hügel concluded his remarks by suggesting that Snead-Cox and his readers would

be very clever if at last they can really find, deliberate and operative within one single soul – here the soul of Father Tyrrell – all the constituents of this elusive spirit 'modernism.' We who watched his life so closely can only find in it the operation, the travail of those supreme realities and needs – Theism, Christianity, Catholicism; the pressure of the intellectual and spiritual troubles and aspirations of our times, often so crude and ambiguous, from which none of us can entirely escape and which some of us would fain sincerely test and use; and the peculiar gifts, limitations, devotednesses, miseries, lights, errors, and sins of George Tyrrell, our friend.

Theism, Christianity, Catholicism – these are indeed our sole ultimate guides. Yet those very guides sternly forbid any injustice towards any man. Hence, in following them, we cannot accept unfairness towards one who

[1] *Diaries*, 6 and 17 Jan. 1913.
[2] *Diaries*, 24 May 1914.
[3] *The Tablet*, vol. 120, no. 3785, 23 Nov. 1912, pp. 806–7. Although the review was unsigned, Miss Petre later learned that Snead-Cox had written it and admitted doing so (*Diaries*, 6 Jan. 1913).
[4] *Diaries*, 25–6 Nov. 1912.

worked so hard for them, and who never, deliberately and finally, renounced these abiding realities and truths.[1]

The editor appended a retort to von Hügel's published letter. Probably expressing the thoughts of a number of English Catholics who were in no sense 'modernists', Basil Maturin privately thanked the Baron for his letter and told him how glad he was that 'some notice was taken of that most outrageous & mean Review of Tyrrell's life. I think there is only one man who could have written it. The effort to lessen the effects of the life by trying to impress the public with the idea that he was & confessed himself to be a liar, is contemptible beyond words.'[2] Maturin did not hesitate to add, though, that he regretted that the life had been written. 'I think it was a pity', he concluded, 'to rake up the past & it leaves the impression in the last few chapters of a man who had lost all balance of judgment & self control. One letter of yours to him towards the end moved me immensely.' The Congregation of the Index agreed with Snead-Cox, however, and the *Autobiography and Life of George Tyrrell* was placed on the Index of Forbidden Books on 17 June 1913.[3]

---

[1] *The Tablet*, vol. 120, no. 3786, 30 Nov. 1912, pp. 866–7. Nearly two months later Mrs Hubert Burke (née Florence Bishop), a Roman Catholic, lunched with Lady Mary and the Baron. After the meal von Hügel had an 'important talk' with her 'about the G. T. Autobiography and Life. She insisting she had found no one (not reviewers) who had not been shocked and perplexed. I defended M. D. P.'s motives for publishing and the fine self-knowledge and humility of Fr. T.'s self-revelation' (*Diaries*, 16 Jan. 1913).

[2] Maturin to von Hügel, 4 Dec. 1912, SAUL, MS. 2773.

[3] *Acta Apostolicae Sedis*, vol. v, no. 10, 1913, p. 276.

CHAPTER 12

CONSISTENT TO THE END

IN THE MONTHS immediately following Tyrrell's death the strain of the years from *Lamentabili* to the burial in Storrington churchyard began to take their toll of von Hügel's health. His nights became often more than ordinarily sleepless, he frequently complained of a 'buzzing' in his head, and the doctor diagnosed exhaustion.[1] With Tyrrell dead, and Loisy no longer concerned about the church and seeming to move ever further away from work and ideas which von Hügel could support, the personalities with whom his own chief work had been intimately connected for so long were removed from his life.

When the *Rinnovamento* group collapsed at the end of 1909, the last personal centre within Roman Catholicism around which his own efforts had revolved was withdrawn. During the years following these losses von Hügel sometimes seemed like a sad and lonely spectator at the grand collapse of everyone and everything for which he had striven and suffered. His friend Semeria was forced to submit to the modernist oath and then banished to Brussels.[2] Many books of old friends, and often books which had long before received the ecclesiastical *imprimatur*, were placed on the Index.[3] Even Duchesne's *Histoire ancienne de l'Église* did

[1] *Diaries*, 16 Sept. 1909. '...and my poor old head goes on buzzing badly, – it awakened and alarmed me last night, with its vehement noises.' Von Hügel to Lilley, 7 Oct. 1909, LFP, I, vH MSS.

[2] *Diaries*, 13 Sept.; 1 Nov.; and 10 Dec. 1910. Semeria was allowed by the Pope, personally, to take the oath with a mental reservation about the historico-critical positions expressed and implied in *Lamentabili* and *Pascendi*. 'Sad letter from Semeria – is banished by his General from Genoa and Italy to Brussels. Hopes to see me there and wants introductions' (*Diaries*, 17 Sept. 1912). See also, *Diaries*, 19 Sept.; 2, and 16–24 Oct. 1912.

[3] See von Hügel to Ward, 21 July 1913, WFP, vH MSS. – Even as late as 1920 this trend continued, and Scotti's utterly unpolemical life of Antonio Fogazzaro was condemned by the Holy Office, under Merry del Val's chairmanship. Scotti answered his summons to total submission 'by declaring that even tho' not understanding the reasons that have decided this official act, he will respect the authority of the Church by a complete silence and abstention from every defence or attack; but that he cannot go further, and formally accept a Decree with no reasons no details no limits, and which he could not thus accept without an insincerity which would dishonour not only himself but the Church. ... Meanwhile there was a fine, sober, strong article in the "Corriere della Sera", comparing what Dante had said about worldly Popes and worldly Curia, putting even contemporary office holders into his *Inferno*, and what Fogazzaro had written, even in his most daring moods – how mildly, in comparison! And then it described the official solemn participation of the Church authorities in the sixth centenary celebrations for Dante, and the condemnation of Fogazzaro. Why this difference asks

242

not escape, nor did Bremond's *Sainte Chantal* in 1913.[1] To the end of Pius X's reign the Baron watched the 'reign of terror' work itself out, and he suffered in the atmosphere of suspicion, fear, and narrowness, which it created and which would continue to make itself felt in the Roman church long after Pius X was gone.

But von Hügel only seemed to be a sad spectator. His temperament was not that of a mere spectator ever, and from the ruins about him he took a positive lesson and moved on into the future. He did not become embittered, nor did he give up working and struggling for what he always considered to be the goals of his life's endeavour. Moreover, both the violence of the authorities, and the falling away from genuine faith and viable philosophy by some of his friends, were instructive for von Hügel and determined both the tone and manner of his work for the last years of his life. When Maude Petre was preparing her little book on modernism in 1918, he wrote to her:

It seems to me that there are two, really (in substance) distinct, subject-matters which could be described under the term 'Modernism' – especially if we mean Catholic 'Modernism.' The one is a permanent, never quite finished, always sooner or later, more or less, rebeginning set of attempts to express the old Faith and its permanent truths and helps – to interpret it according to what appears the best and the most abiding elements in the philosophy and the scholarship and science of the later and latest times. Such work never ceases for long, and to it I still try to contribute my little share, with such improvements as the experiences of the Pontificate of Pius X have – in part only very slowly – come to show me to be desirable or even necessary. The other 'Modernism' is a strictly circumscribed affair, one that is really over and done – the series of groups of specific attempts, good, bad, indifferent, or variously mixed, that were made towards similar expressions or interpretations, during the Pontificate of Pius X – beginning, no doubt, during the later years of Leo XIII, but ending with the death of Fr. T. and with Loisy's alienation from the positive content that had been fought for, – also from the suppression of *Rinnovamento* onwards, and the resolution of so much of the very substance of the movement, not only, or even chiefly, under the stress of the official Church condemnations, but from within the ranks of scepticism dominating what remained of organs claiming to be 'Modernist.'[2]

---

the writer? "Because", he answers, "Dante is dead six centuries and Fogazzaro is dead a decade".' Von Hügel to Kemp Smith, 8–10 Jan. 1921. SAUL, MS. 30420.

[1] *Acta Apostolicae Sedis*, vol. IV, no. 2, 1912, p. 56; vol. V, no. 8, 1913, p. 216. The same decree of the Index which announced the condemnation of the *Autobiography and Life of George Tyrrell* also announced, with a cruel twist of irony, that Bremond *laudabiliter se subjecit* regarding the condemnation of his own *Sainte Chantal*.

[2] Von Hügel to Petre, 13 March 1918, in *Selected Letters*, pp. 247–9.

Miss Petre, of course, was writing about modernism in the second of the Baron's two senses. As she had asked for a list of his writings since 1914 to append to the volume, he told her that he could not 'see what my own, or indeed any one else's, writings, since that definitely closed period or crisis, have to do with your subject-matter'. He told her that the point was not merely an academic one, and that it did not spring from cowardice. It arises, he said,

from a strong desire not to appear (it would be contrary to the facts, and indeed contrary to my ideals and convictions) *as though all that action of the Church authorities had, in no way or degree, been interiorly accepted by me*. Certainly that action was, very largely, violent and unjust; equally certainly, if one had been required definitely to subscribe to this or that document without express reservations, one could not, with any self-respect left, have done so. Yet it is not cowardice or policy, it is in simplest sincerity, that I have come to see, more clearly than I used to do, how much of serious unsatisfactoriness and of danger there was especially in many of the philosophical (strongly subjectivist) theories really held which *Pascendi* lumped together. And Troeltsch has taught me vividly how profoundly important is Church appurtenance, yet how much appurtenance never, even at best, can be had without some sacrifices – even of (otherwise) fine or desirable liberties or unhamperednesses. These two things – the actual fact of a very real, though certainly not unlimited submission, and the duty of such submission – I care much should not be left uncertain on occasion, in my own case.[1]

The Baron's distinction between the two senses in which one can speak of Roman Catholic modernism is essential if one would understand the genuine and strong continuity between his thought and conduct before and during the modernist crisis and that of his last fifteen years of life. When von Hügel was still a young man, his much admired Huvelin had told him that truth, not orthodoxy, would be the real object of his life's search, and that it was orthodoxy's obligation to come to terms with truth.[2] This principle was operative throughout the Baron's adult life. Rather than being concerned with orthodoxy as

---

[1] Apparently John J. Heaney, *The Modernist Crisis: von Hügel*, p. 203, had never read that letter of von Hügel to Miss Petre, since he writes: 'From all that he said, from his love of the Church, it is impossible to come to any conclusion but this: if he had been faced with the choice of giving interior assent to some doctrine or leaving the Church, in utmost probability he would have assented.' The Baron himself has made it abundantly clear that he could not have made an *unlimited* submission, and unlimited submissions were all that Pius X and Merry del Val accepted. Since Heaney seems here, and elsewhere in his book, to use the term *Church* in an extrinsic sense, and also, chiefly, to equate it with ecclesiastical officialdom, his statement here seems even more indefensible.

[2] 'Oui, vous avez horreur de "bonne philosophie", "bien-pensant", parceque vous cherchez la vérité, point l'orthodoxie; il faut que l'orthodoxie s'arrange avec la vérité – c'est son affaire à elle.' Quoted in *Selected Letters*, p. 61.

such, he interested himself primarily in the pursuit of truth, trying to combine this with that purity of heart attained through the 'costingness' of church membership and the necessary (though never unlimited) submission to legitimate church authority. Von Hügel's life-long pursuit of truth consisted in attempting to understand and express the Christian mystery in the thought and experience of his own day.[1] It was a task that could never be adequately achieved, since the inexpressible cannot be expressed. Because Christianity is not only a religion of divine revelation, but of divine revelation *for men*, the attempt to grasp and express this reality, in some way and to some extent, remains the perennial privilege and obligation of each succeeding generation of Christians. St Paul understood this, as did Origen, and the Fathers of Nicea. But once the formulations of one age have been made, and have been accepted by ecclesial authority, the ever conservative tendency of later officials acts as a check on the search of new times and new men to re-express the always transcendent and infinite reality. For Catholic Christians at the end of the nineteenth century and the beginning of the twentieth to want to understand and express the object of their faith in terms of the thought and experience of their own time was not only normal, it was inevitable. From the first von Hügel was caught up in these desires and these efforts. Loisy's biblical criticism, Blondel's and Laberthonnière's philosophy, Tyrrell's apologetic, *Il Rinnovamento's* social comment, Murri's and *Le Sillon's* political thought and action, – all of this work and this insight could have been part of a new synthesis. But ecclesiastical authorities had neither sufficient acquaintance with contemporary thought, nor sufficient faith in the survival value of the church, to allow this ferment of ideas to work itself out, eliminating of itself the unworkable, and consolidating and expanding under the pressure of the various intellectual disciplines and practical applications involved in a new synthesis. The authorities destroyed a whole generation of thinkers within the Roman Catholic church, forcing those who would survive as members of that institution back into the thought patterns and formulae of another age.[2] The repression was not sheer

---

[1] Von Hügel switched his own philosophical emphasis from the epistemological problem to the metaphysical, from truth to reality, in the last years of his life. See his letter to Miss Petre, 2 Jan. 1914, in *Selected Letters*, p. 206. The manuscript which he left at his death, which would have been his Gifford Lectures at Edinburgh had his health allowed him to accept the invitation, and which was published posthumously as *The Reality of God, and Religion and Agnosticism*, (edited by Edmund Gardner), London, 1931, is a further manifestation of this altered emphasis.

[2] The judgment made by Carlo Falconi, *The Popes in the Twentieth Century: From Pius X*

reactionist hysteria, though it was certainly reactionary and it was at times hysterical. Some of the progressive thinkers did in fact become excessively immanentist in their philosophy; others became completely agnostic in their theology. But no human thought goes forward in a straight line, and intellectual extremes are righted not by repression but by the passage of time. Von Hügel acknowledged both the dangers and the mistakes. He accepted both the illegitimate rejection by the authorities of the entire contemporary movement to re-think the faith contemporarily, and their legitimate rejection of what was excessive or mistaken in that movement, – though he never approved of the former. He understood the right of the authorities to determine what did or did not pertain to Christian faith and acceptable Catholic practice, but he denied their practical claim to do so in a vacuum and without any reference to the thought and experience of the Christian body as a whole.[1] And especially did he deny their claim, made in the name of guarding the faith, to make arbitrary decisions which affected or even curtailed intellectual disciplines that also happened to have one or another aspect of religious history or philosophy as its subject-matter. Although he considered the specific development of ideas represented by Loisy, Tyrrell, and *Il Rinnovamento*, to be at an end with the close of the year 1909;[2] nevertheless, the last dozen and more years of his life were a sustained effort to continue, in whatever ways were left open to him, the never ending, nor endable, movement of thinking, expressing,

---

to John XXIII, (translated by Muriel Grindrod), London, 1967, p. 71, is not unjust: 'A temporary check in the field of ecclesiastical studies, as a prelude to further advance, might have done no harm. But the check ordained by Pius X was meant to be, and was, absolute, and it hit not only the scholars of his own time but future generations virtually right up to the pontificate of John XXIII. His anti-cultural measures produced a half-century of sterility that, taken in addition to the earlier slowing-down (it was not for nothing that Benedetto Croce described the Modernists themselves as "delaying factors"), was to weigh as a tragic inheritance upon the future of Catholicism.'

[1] At the very beginning of the period of condemnations which finally broke the men and destroyed the work which was the modernist movement, von Hügel wrote: 'I feel sure that we ought *never* to use the term "Church" pure and simple, for "Official Church", "Teaching Church". It is simply un-Catholic to restrict "Church" in such a manner. Though the "Eccl. Discens" is not, and should not aspire to be, the official tester, formularizer, and proclaimer of the collective Church's experience, tradition, analysis etc. that "Eccl. Discens" is an *integral* part of the material and means on which and by means of which the Eccl. Doc. thus acts. But let us frankly admit: we have a Pope who will have none of this. *Hinc illae lacrymae.* It is Tyrrell who, whatever may be his incidental faults of temper, is just now proclaiming this elementary, most dangerously forgotten truth, with splendid insight and courage. I should feel it a sorry return for so much help given, and at so great a cost, to dwell on faults or discriminate myself carefully from him.' Von Hügel to Ward, 4 June 1907, WFP, vH MSS.

[2] See von Hügel to Petre, 15 Oct. 1909, in *Selected Letters*, pp. 171–2.

and living Christianity intelligently and intelligibly in the contemporary milieu.

In the autumn of 1912 von Hügel accepted an invitation extended by W. Tudor Jones to address a Unitarian group at Essex Hall.[1] He decided to speak on 'The Present Battle and Problem of Religious Faith Amongst the Cultivated Younger Men of the Roman Catholic Church'. The address was given on 9 December before a group of about twenty-five men. The Baron 'insisted on 5 prominent dangers' to contemporary faith. These were 'pure immanentism', the 'elimination of all need of history', the 'denial of various *degrees* of truth and worth', the 'mantle of "magic" ', and, finally, the 'loss of deep asceticism in matters of sex and in matters of intellectual submission'.[2] This list was drawn from von Hügel's own experience in working with various Catholic clerics and laymen in Italy, France, and England, and contained the pitfalls intrinsic to the modernist movement as demonstrated by the lives of some of these men. In von Hügel's estimation the failure of the modernist movement was due as much to the partial triumph of these negative elements within the movement itself as it was to the negative reaction of church authorities.[3]

[1] *Diaries*, 21 Nov. 1912. Tudor Jones had been a student of Eucken in Jena; and, when he published his English translation of Eucken's *Wahrheitsgehalt*, von Hügel carefully revised the entire translation and himself translated the Index for him (*Diaries*, 8 and 27 Sept. 1911).
[2] *Diaries*, 9 Dec. 1912. On 7 July 1914 von Hügel addressed a group of scholars in Edinburgh as he passed through that city on his way to St Andrews to receive an honorary doctor's degree from the University. The Edinburgh address is published in *Essays and Addresses on the Philosophy of Religion*, 2nd series, pp. 91–131. When the Baron began to prepare this address, he 'hunted in vain for ms. of my Address at Essex Hall' (*Diaries*, 19 June 1914). Even though he had lost the text of the earlier address, the similarities and dissimilarities, in so far as these can be judged from the simple diary account of the first address, are instructive. The insistence on historical facts as necessary to Christianity and the warning against pure immanentism dominate both addresses.
[3] Michael de la Bedoyère, *The Life of Baron von Hügel*, p. 247. asserts that von Hügel's 'excessive historico-critical positions so hard to reconcile with his own great Catholic faith' were corrected by his 'increasing mistrust of the whole immanentist trend in Modernism – a mistrust which he never appears to have formally applied to his whole Catholic thought by revising point by point his earlier beliefs, but which worked within him, like a leaven, so that he gradually awoke to find himself a normally orthodox Catholic in all points for which he stood as public witness and teacher in the latter part of his life'. This assertion is based on several assumptions for which there seems to be insufficient, if any, evidence. Bedoyère *assumes* that von Hügel's historico-critical positions were excessive, apparently using the decrees of the Biblical Commission as his criterion, and ignoring the norm of historico-critical studies of the time and as they have developed, and the norm of truth. He also *assumes* that von Hügel became 'a normally orthodox Catholic', by which he would have to mean that von Hügel accepted the scholastic framework as expressed in *Lamentabili* and *Pascendi* as the sole legitimate framework for expressing the Christian faith. This von Hügel never to his dying day accepted in the absolute sense which would have made him 'a normally orthodox Catholic' of that era. If one assumes, as does Bedoyère, and as does John J. Heaney, *The Modernist Crisis: von Hügel,*

But if there were dangers intrinsic to the progressive movement within Roman Catholicism, there were equally serious, or perhaps more serious, dangers intrinsic to the extreme ultramontanism of Pius X and Merry del Val. These dangers, too, von Hügel was ever concerned to counteract as best he could. On 25 November 1912 he received from Semeria an article from *La Croix* reporting a recent address by Pius X to an Italian priests' organization on its fiftieth anniversary.[1] In the address the Pope went so far as to tell the priests that 'love of the Pope' was an important means to their own sanctification. He told them that this love should be shown in deeds rather than in words, and that this meant that they should obey him without setting any limits to their obedience, and not only him personally, but also the Vatican bureaucracy which acted in his name.[2] The Baron, who considered the address 'a monstrous effusion', could not directly attack it himself, so he mobilized his Anglican friends, Lilley, Rawlinson, and Alfred Caldecott.[3] Considerable effort was made to ascertain the accuracy of *La Croix's* report, and when they had satisfied themselves,[4] Rawlinson published in *The Church Times* two columns on the Pope's speech. 'We must say at once that we are convinced believers in the necessity of Church authority', Rawlinson wrote.

But it is not merely this that is implied in the Pope's latest utterance. He is not only claiming a general authority; he is not only claiming to have the last word when the faith of his children is threatened. He is asking for much more than that. In the first place, the obedience he claims is unlimited. It is not confined to purely religious or dogmatic questions, it is universal. It applies, for example, to politics. No good priest, and we suppose, no good Roman Catholic, has a right to a political opinion that it [sic!] opposed to the Pope's. If he insists on holding his own view, he is, *ipso facto*, proving himself to be one of those who insists on limiting the Pope's authority, and that is *une audace inouïe*. No disagreement of any kind with the Pope is allowed. Everyone is bound to agree with all that he says, that is, he must yield to his words a full

---

pp. 143, 192, 198, 201, etc. that the scholastic and Thomistic interpretation of Christianity is normative and absolute, then a just historical appraisal of the modernist crisis, and of von Hügel's thought and life, becomes impossible. If von Hügel is allowed to speak for himself, and if he is listened to in his own terms and accents, then one could never, as Heaney does (p. 143), hear him echoing St Thomas in the last phase of his life.

[1] *Diaries*, 25 Nov. 1912.
[2] Although *La Croix* stated that Pius X spoke spontaneously and without notes, this evidently was not so, as the whole Allocution is published in *Acta Apostolicae Sedis*, vol. IV, 1912, pp. 693–5.
[3] *Diaries*, 25 and 28 Nov. 1912.
[4] *Diaries*, 2, 13 and 20 Dec. 1912. See also, von Hügel to Lilley, 30 Nov. 1912, LFP, I, vH, MSS.

interior assent, while the Pope himself remains unbound. The utterances are not infallible. If they were claimed to be this it would be easy to understand. But they are not. Roman Catholics are asked to obey, and not to criticise, statements that may be retracted to-morrow ... Men are not even to wait till the Pope speaks. Even his desires are to be anticipated. In all seriousness we can't help saying that this will not work in favour of honesty, nor will it bring the best men to the fore. It will open the gates of promotion to the unprincipled, the time serving, and the corrupt.[1]

Von Hügel thought Rawlinson's remarks were 'very good', and he wrote at once to tell him so.[2]

The balance between libertarianism and authoritarianism, the balance which gives both freedom and authority their respective and co-ordinated due, was ever the stance which von Hügel attempted to attain.[3] In January 1914 he addressed the Hornsey Clerical Society at a luncheon held in the Kingsley Hotel in Bloomsbury. The Society's chairman, the Reverend H. B. Colchester, Vicar of Holy Innocents, had invited him, and several of those in attendance were his acquaintances. Von Hügel addressed them for thirty minutes on 'The Christian Conception of Liberty'. He talked about the elements which constituted this idea of Christian Liberty, and included among them the unique value which Christianity attributes to each individual, as well as a 'continuous sense of the prevenience of God, the givenness of religion, of our very freedom'. He traced the development of the concept of liberty through three stages of the New Testament, showing the relationship of the concept to the idea of the Kingdom of God, and insisting that the church is there manifested 'as partly preparing, and as partly identical with, the Kingdom of God'.[4] Ten days after giving this

---

[1] *The Church Times*, vol. LXIX, no. 2607, 10 Jan. 1913, p. 45.

[2] *Diaries*, 10 Jan. 1913.

[3] For a sympathetic comment which suggests, nevertheless, that the Baron never really attained this stance in a synthetic way, see Alfred Fawkes, 'Baron Friedrich von Hügel', *The Modern Churchman*, vol. XIV, no. 12, March 1925, pp. 662–6. For von Hügel's own observations on Fawkes's religious sense and judgment, see, von Hügel to Bishop, 16 June 1908, in *Dublin Review*, vol. 227, no. 462, Oct. 1953, p. 425.

[4] *Diaries*, 19 Jan. 1914. 'Among modernist religious writers Baron von Hügel holds a unique place. Much curiosity was therefore aroused when it was announced that he would address a mixed company of Anglican clergy and Free Church ministers on Christian liberty. A modernist who has not broken with traditional Christianity, a mystic who in his great book on Catherine of Sienna [*sic*!] has tried to give an intelligent account of the function of mysticism, a free-lance who yet believes in the institutions of Christianity, was sure to have something interesting to say, and the expectation was not disappointed. Making use of a new book by Professor Troeltzsch [*sic*!] as his text, Baron von Hügel pointed out that three prevalent types of Christian life find their sanction in the New Testament. Quakers and Independents are most naturally at home in the first three Gospels. The Epistles supply the foundation for all who lean on the traditional and institutional types of Christianity. The Johannine writings are

address he wrote to Wilfrid Ward on the practical troubles of Catholicism involved in the reconciliation of a true Christian liberty with church authority. He told Ward that

it is the men who have been cast out who brought into clearest relief certain principles and questions which have to be faced, and which acquire at most some kind of precarious toleration till the date, mostly some centuries away, when other living questions have taken the place of these. And meanwhile one feels keenly how, if these same authorities could have their full way, could get even what they claim, if not in documents considered by themselves to be absolutely final, yet still in pronouncements full of vehemence and disciplinary operativeness, none of the sciences and researches which trench upon religion could live, at least with a life of any sufficient autonomy and fruitfulness.[1]

To the end the Baron struggled to maintain the balance, not merely, nor even especially, in the world of pure thought, but in his practical Christian living within the church of his birth.

In 1919 von Hügel urged his friend Norman Kemp Smith to gain some 'definite Church membership, a clearly avowed and regularly practised traditional, institutional, religion'.[2] 'For myself', the Baron continued, 'such definite appurtenance has cost me much, all my life. Yet I am more than ever penetrated by the simply *immense* debt I owe (I mean, also, just *qua* philosopher of religion) to such appurtenance.' He told Kemp Smith that although he himself believed 'the Roman Catholic Church, to be the deepest, most comprehensive, and the most

the natural home of the mystics in all churches. The existence of these types in the New Testament is a guarantee that they will always have representatives in the Church as long as Christianity is a living movement. Religion differs from politics in its ability to recognize the uniqueness of different types of personal life. Equality as applied to human nature is a political dogma, and is often taken to mean merely that men are equal before the law, which is right, but also that one man is as good as another in the sense that they are inter-changeable, which is wrong. God is a God of particulars, and in religion every man is unique.

'Much of what Baron von Hügel said on this point would have satisfied the most Calvinistic of our fore-fathers. As against the modern habit of assuming that the Kingdom of God is something which we build up, the speaker insisted on the "givenness" of everything that belongs to vital religion. The Kingdom of God is something either already given or to be given, and, on our part, to be received rather than created. Perhaps the Baron does not realise quite sufficiently what Eucken has so well recognised – that modern religion has to satisfy a demand not made explicit until our time. If it is in any way to meet the needs of modern life it must find room for the living, believing, hoping, striving, suffering, sacrificing, achieving power which we know as the spirit of man. The modern task is to interpret the Christian religion in a way big enough to be in harmony with every worthy effort of the human spirit, and this is best done by quickening in the minds of men the ideals of the Kingdom of God and setting them to work towards their realisation.' *The Manchester Guardian*, no. 21,054, 29 Jan. 1914, p. 14.

[1] Von Hügel to Ward, 28 Jan. 1914, WFP, vH MSS.
[2] Von Hügel to Kemp Smith, 1 July 1919, SAUL, MS. 30420.

probing, of these great, irreplaceable training schools', he admitted that it was 'only one of such profound aids', and urged him to re-examine the Presbyterian and Anglican churches. More than two years later Kemp Smith asked von Hügel whether he really believed that the Roman church today could assimilate the best in the modern world as she had once assimilated the best in the Graeco-Roman world. The Baron answered that the question was

one that certainly, after suffering under Pius X, I ought fully to understand. My answer is threefold. (1) Single Roman Catholics – not only laymen, but priests, but religious – have, to my deepest mind and conscience, already achieved this assimilation: I am, of course, especially thinking of Huvelin. They have achieved an interpenetration, oh – how far more substantial and spiritually sane and solid than I can find even in Holtzmann and Troeltsch, in de Lagarde or Pringle Pattison! – I know, of course, that single men are one thing; an entire huge Institution is another thing. Still, in this poor world of trouble and inevitable, difficult choosings, it is not nothing to find such an assimilation a *fact*, and no mere hope. (2) Next, I do not feel that I can do more, with regard to the Church authorities, than to include such assimilative action of theirs, amongst the objects of my *faith*. I find I can believe such action possible, and even such belief I find to work well and ennoblingly in my life. After all, it is not as though my nine long stays in Rome had confirmed me in the fear, with which I first went to Rome, that the men in authority there were unanimously opposed to such assimilation; for very certainly it did *not*. At the very moment I know of several high authorities at the Vatican itself who are, as before Pius X, definitely friendly to, and believe in, such assimilation. – True, this enlightened part has not so far succeeded against the ultra-conservatives; and it is very certainly easier to think that this will continue on and on. Yet I do not, myself, find it impossible, even now, to believe in such a future triumph. (3) But, above all, and without any emphasis upon future possibilities, the essential the most indispensable of the dimensions of religion is, *not breadth, but depth*, and above all, *the insight into sanctity and the power to produce saints*. Rome continues – of this I am very sure – to possess this super-natural depth – possess it in far greater degree than Protestantism, and still more than the quite unattached Moderns.[1]

This profession of faith, – for such it really was, – represents a difference of emphasis, perhaps, than that which the Baron might have made in 1895, or in 1907, but it does not represent a different faith. Two years before his death von Hügel sent his New Year wishes to Lilley in words that set a seal upon this judgment. 'My best New Year wishes to you', he wrote,

friend of how many years; and what we have seen come and go, and how

[1] Von Hügel to Kemp Smith, 31 Dec. 1921, SAUL, MS. 30420.

much we hoped for has not come about! Yet it would be foolish and wrong not to hope and not work as though everything could, and will, come to fruition, all that is good in what we want. And for the rest, whether we see it to be poor or not, may it not come, even though its coming may rejoice our hearts.[1]

[1] Von Hügel to Lilley, 2 Jan. 1923, LFP, I, vH MSS.

BIBLIOGRAPHY

PART ONE: ARCHIVES AND MANUSCRIPT COLLECTIONS

Archives of the Archdiocese of Westminster. The Papers of Cardinals Herbert Vaughan and Francis Bourne, excepting certain restricted files. The Papers of Canon James Moyes. Various miscellaneous boxes of papers.

Archives of the English Province of the Society of Jesus. The later correspondence of George Tyrrell with the Jesuit Provincials. Copies of some of the letters from George Tyrrell to Bishop A. H. Mathew.

Archives de la Société des Bollandistes. Ten manuscript letters and five postcards from Baron F. von Hügel to Père H. Delehaye.

Balliol College Library. One manuscript letter from Baron F. von Hügel to Professor Edward Caird, and one manuscript copy of a letter from Caird to von Hügel.

Baron F. von Hügel's Manuscript Diaries. Forty-three volumes, for the years 1877–9, 1884–1900, and 1902–24.

Birmingham Oratory Archives. Four manuscript letters of Baron F. von Hügel to Cardinal Newman, VC 2, 22, 83, and 100a. Twelve letters from von Hügel to the Rev. H. I. D. Ryder, PC 205–6, and VC 20.

Bodleian Library. Two manuscript letters from Baron F. von Hügel to Professor William Sanday, MS. Eng. misc. d. 123 (2), fols, 609–13; one manuscript letter from von Hügel to Albert Dawson, MS. Eng. Lett. c. 196, fol. 62; twelve manuscript letters from von Hügel to Percy Gardner, MS. Eng. Lett. c. 55, fols. 195–229. The manuscript journals of Professor C. C. J. Webb, MS. Res. d. 181.

British Museum. Correspondence between Baron F. von Hügel and George Tyrrell, Add. MSS, 44926–44931 (five bound volumes of manuscript letters). Letters of von Hügel to Maude Petre, with one letter from Miss Petre to von Hügel, Add. MSS. 45361–45362 (two bound volumes of manuscript letters).

Downside Abbey Archives. The Edmund Bishop Library and Archives. The Cardinal Gasquet Papers. The Abbot Cuthbert Butler Papers, including five manuscript letters from Baron F. von Hügel to Abbot Butler, an outline of the history of Christian mysticism prepared for Abbot Butler's *Western Mysticism* by von Hügel, and one manuscript letter from Lady Mary von Hügel to Abbot Butler.

The Hickleton Papers. The Archives of the Wood Family of Hickleton and Garrowby, Co. York. The Church Papers of the second Viscount Halifax, MSS. A4, including six manuscript letters from Baron F. von Hügel to Lord Halifax, one manuscript letter from Cardinal Vaughan to Halifax, a large packet of letters from the abbé Portal to Halifax, a large packet of letters from Wilfrid Ward to Halifax, and numerous miscellaneous letters from Charles Gore, T. A. Lacey, and others to Halifax.

Juliet Mansel Papers. Twenty-five manuscript letters from Baron F. von Hügel to Juliet Mansel, and numerous miscellaneous notes and papers by von Hügel on the history and archaeology of Rome. Two manuscript letters from von Hügel to Mildred Mansel, three manuscript letters from von Hügel to Mrs Adeline Chapman, and various photographs of von Hügel and his family

Lilley Family Papers. These are in two collections: the first collection consists of sixty-three manuscript letters and cards from Baron F. von Hügel to the Reverend A. L. Lilley; the second collection consists of seven letters from von Hügel to Lilley, and two letters from John Murray (publisher) to Lilley.

St Andrews University Library. The complete personal library of Baron F. von Hügel, including numerous boxes of unbound pamphlets and article off-prints. Over a thousand letters addressed to von Hügel from a multitude of correspondents. Photocopies of twenty-three letters from von Hügel to Archbishop Mignot, and of sixty-four letters from von Hügel to Henri Bremond. Thirty-seven manuscript letters from von Hügel to Professor Norman Kemp Smith, MSS. 30420.1–37. Miscellaneous manuscripts written by von Hügel, including a lengthy biographical note on Padre Giovanni Semeria, three draft letters, two notebooks, and lengthy notes for remarks at the LSSR meeting for 1 May 1917.

Wilfrid Ward Family Papers. Two hundred and three manuscript letters and cards from Baron F. von Hügel to Wilfrid Ward. Five letters from von Hügel to Mrs Wilfrid Ward. Four letters from Wilfrid Ward to von Hügel. Manuscript notes (30 April 1896) by von Hügel on a paper delivered by R. H. Hutton before the Synthetic Society. One large trunk full of miscellaneous papers, including manuscript letters to Wilfrid Ward from the 15th Duke of Norfolk, Baroness Eliza M. Froude von Hügel, R. H. Hutton, Cardinal Vaughan, Father David Fleming, and others.

Dr Williams's Library. Volume one of the manuscript Minutes of the meetings of the London Society for the Study of Religion, 1904–25, MS. WL80, OD.17. Three manuscript letters from Baron F. von Hügel to J. M. Connell, MSS. 24. 103.6–8; one manuscript letter from J. M. Connell to von Hügel, MS. 24.103.9.

PART TWO: PRINTED WRITINGS OF BARON FRIEDRICH VON HÜGEL

Introduction, and translation: Carl von Hügel, 'The Story of the Escape of Prince Metternich', *The National Review*, vol. 1, no. 4, June 1883, pp. 588–605.

'Chronique', *Bulletin critique*, vol. vi, no. 2, 1 May 1885, pp. 175–8; vol. vii, no. 6, 15 March 1886, pp. 117–18; vol. vii, no. 7, 1 April 1886, p. 135; vol. vii, no. 24, 15 Dec. 1886, pp. 477–8; vol. xii, no. 6, 15 March 1891, pp. 119–20; vol. xii, no. 24, 15 Dec. 1891, pp. 478–9.

'The Spiritual Writings of Père Grou, S.J.', *The Tablet*, vol. 74, nos. 2589–90, 21 and 28 Dec. 1889, pp. 990–1, 1029–31.

Notes Addressed to the Very Reverend H.I.D.R. upon the Subject of Biblical Inspiration and Inerrancy, London: (privately printed), July 1891.

'The Papal Encyclical and Mr. Gore', *The Spectator*, no. 3438, 19 May 1894, pp. 684–5.

'The Roman Catholic View of Inspiration', *The Spectator*, no. 3440, 2 June 1894, p. 750.

'Fénelon's "Spiritual Letters"', *The Tablet*, vol. 83, no. 2821, 2 June 1894, pp. 587–8.

'The Church and the Bible: The Two Stages of Their Inter-Relation', *The Dublin Review*, vols. CXV–CXVII, nos. 231, 233 and 235, October 1894, April and October 1895, pp. 313–41, 306–37, 275–304.

'L'Abbé Duchesne and Anglican Orders', *The Tablet*, vol. 84, no. 2845, 17 Nov. 1894, p. 776.

'Communication to the Roman Society of Biblical Studies', *Revue Biblique Internationale*, vol. V, no. 3, 1 July 1896, pp. 470–2.

'Professor Eucken on the Struggle for Spiritual Life', *The Spectator*, no. 3568, 14 Nov. 1896, pp. 679–81.

'The Comma Johanneum', *The Tablet*, vol. 89, no. 2978, 5 June 1897, pp. 896–7.

'Impressions of Elizabeth Rundle Charles', *The Hampstead Annual*, London: Sydney C. Mayle, 1897, pp. 52–62.

'The Historical Method and the Documents of the Hexateuch', *The Catholic University Bulletin*, vol. IV, 1898, pp. 198–226, with seven separately-numbered pages of Appendices.

'Caterina Fiesca Adorna, the Saint of Genoa, 1447–1510', *The Hampstead Annual*, London: Sydney C. Mayle, 1898, pp. 70–85.

'A Proposito dell' Abate Loisy', *Studi Religiosi*, July–August 1901, pp. 348–50.

'The Case of the Abbé Loisy', *The Pilot*, no. 199, vol. IX, 9 Jan. 1904, pp. 30–1.

'The Case of M. Loisy', *The Pilot*, no. 201, vol. IX, 23 Jan. 1904, p. 94.

'The Abbé Loisy and the Holy Office', *The Times*, no. 37,331, 2 March 1904, p. 15.

Introduction to letters by Bailey Saunders and Loisy *The Times*, no. 37,382, 30 April 1904, p. 6.

'Du Christ éternel et de nos christologies successives', *La Quinzaine*, vol. LVIII, no. 231, 1 Juin 1904, pp. 285–312.

Letter (in reply to the Abbé Wehrlé) *La Quinzaine*, vol. LX, no. 238, 16 Sept. 1904, pp. 276–7.

'Discussions: M. Loisy's Type of Catholicism', *The Hibbert Journal*, vol. III, no. 3, April 1905, pp. 599–600.

'Experience and Transcendence', *The Dublin Review*, vol. CXXXVIII, no. 24, April 1906, pp. 357–79.

The Papal Commission and the Pentateuch, London: Longmans, Green and Co., 1906.

'The Relations Between God and Man in 'The New Theology' of the Rev. R. J. Campbell', *The Albany Review*, vol. I, no. 6, Sept. 1907, pp. 650–68.

'The Abbé Loisy', *The Tablet*, vol. 111, no. 3539, 7 March 1908, pp. 378–9.

Review of Loisy's *Les Évangiles Synoptiques*, *The Hibbert Journal*, vol. vi, no. 4, July 1908, pp. 926–30.

The Mystical Element of Religion As Studied in Saint Catherine of Genoa and Her Friends, 2 vols., London: J. M. Dent and Co., 1908.

'L'Abate Loisy e il problema dei Vangeli Sinottici', *Il Rinnovamento*, vol. iii, Jan.–June 1908, pp. 209–34; vol. iv, July–Dec. 1908, pp. 1–44; vol. v, Jan.–June 1909, pp. 229–72, 396–423.

Papers Read Before the Synthetic Society, 1896–1908, For Private Circulation. (Presented to the Members of the Synthetic Society by the Rt Hon. Arthur James Balfour, Aug. 1909.) London: Spottiswoode and Co. Ltd., 1909, pp. 235–9, 425–43. Von Hügel's first Paper was a response to a Paper entitled 'Authority a Reasonable Ground for Religious Belief' read by Wilfrid Ward in January 1899. Von Hügel's second Paper was an original one entitled 'Experience and Transcendence', and was read before the Society on 28 May 1903.

Obituary notice for George Tyrrell (written in conjunction with Maude Petre, but not signed by von Hügel), *The Times*, no. 39,013, 16 July 1909, p. 13. (This notice also appeared in the *Daily Mail* for the same day, on page 9.)

Letter on the circumstances of George Tyrell's death, originally published in the *Corriere della Sera* of Milan immediately after Tyrrell's death and retranslated into English by von Hügel and printed, *Daily Graphic*, no. 627, vol. lxxix, 31 July 1909, p. 12.

'The Death-Bed of Father Tyrrell', *The Tablet*, vol. 114, no. 3612, 31 July 1909, p. 182.

'The Late Father Tyrrell and the Faith', *The Tablet*, vol. 114, no. 3626, 6 Nov. 1909, p. 738.

'Father Tyrrell: Some Memorials of the Last Twelve Years of His Life', *The Hibbert Journal*, vol. viii, no. 2, Jan. 1910, pp. 233–52.

'Religione ed Illusione', *Coenobium*, anno v, no. 1–2, Jan.–Feb. 1911, pp. 5–59. Translated from von Hügel's English into Italian by Angelo Crespi.

'The Apostle John', *The Encyclopaedia Britannica*, 11th edition, vol. xv, Cambridge: The University Press, 1911, pp. 432–3.

'Gospel of St John', *The Encyclopaedia Britannica*, 11th edition, vol. xv, Cambridge: The University Press, 1911, pp. 452–8.

'Alfred Firmin Loisy', *The Encyclopaedia Britannica*, 11th edition, vol. xvi, Cambridge: The University Press, 1911, pp. 926–8.

Eternal Life: A Study of Its Implications and Applications, Edinburgh: T. & T. Clark, 1912.

'The Religious Philosophy of Rudolf Eucken', *The Hibbert Journal*, vol. x, no. 3, April 1912, pp. 660–77.

'Petite consultation sur les difficultés concernant Dieu', (written between 31 Oct.–20 Nov. 1912), printed as an Appendix in Pietro Scoppola's *Crisi modernista e rinnovamento cattolico in Italia*, Bologna: Il Mulino, 1961, pp. 368–92.

'Father Tyrell', *The Tablet*, vol. 120, no. 3786, 30 Nov. 1912, pp. 866–7.

'On the Specific Genius and Capacities of Christianity, Studied in Connection with the Works of Professor Ernst Troeltsch', *The Constructive Quarterly*, vol. II, nos. 5 and 8, March and Dec. 1914, pp. 68–98, 673–701.

'Christianity in Face of War: Its Strength and Difficulty', *The Church Quarterly Review*, vol. LXXIX, no. CLVIII, Jan. 1915, pp. 257–88.

'The German Soul and the Great War', *The Quest*, vol. VI, no. 3, April 1915, pp. 401–29; vol. VII, no. 2, Jan. 1916, pp. 201–35.

The German Soul in Its Attitude Towards Ethics and Christianity, the State and War, London: J. M. Dent and Co., 1916.

'What do we mean by Heaven? What do we mean by Hell? A Synthetic Attempt', *The Church Quarterly Review*, vol. LXXXIV, no. CLXVII, April 1917, pp. 50–82.

'Julius Wellhausen', *The Times Literary Supplement*, no. 842, 7 March 1918, p. 117.

'Religion and Illusion', *The Quest*, vol. IX, no. 3, April 1918, pp. 353–82.

'Eudoxe Irenée Mignot', *The Contemporary Review*, vol. CXIII, May 1918, pp. 519–26.

'Religion and Reality', *The Quest*, vol. IX, no. 4, July 1918, pp. 529–62.

'Christianity and the Supernatural', *The Modern Churchman*, vol. X, no. 3, June 1920, pp. 101–21.

'Cardinal Manning', *The Times Literary Supplement*, no. 1001, 24 March 1921, p. 195.

'A Great Book on Prayer', *International Review of the Missions*, vol. X, no. 38, April 1921, pp. 266–70.

'Morals and Religion: A Symposium', *The Hibbert Journal*, vol. XIX, no. 4, July 1921, pp. 605–10.

'Apologists of Religion', *The Times Literary Supplement*, no. 1040, 22 Dec. 1921, p. 860.

Essays and Addresses on the Philosophy of Religion, first series, London: J. M. Dent and Sons Ltd, 1921.

'Louis Duchesne', *The Times Literary Supplement*, no. 1062, 25 May 1922, p. 342.

Letter, *The Times Literary Supplement*, no. 1063, 1 June 1922, p. 364.

'The Rev. G. C. Rawlinson', *The Church Times*, no. 3133, vol. LXXXIX, 9 Feb. 1923, p. 158.

'Ernst Troeltsch', *The Times Literary Supplement*, no. 1106, 29 March 1923, p. 216.

Prefatory Note, and Introduction: *Christian Thought, Its History and Application*, by the late Ernst Troeltsch, London: University of London Press, 1923, pp. v–vii, xi–xxxi.

'Der Mystiker und die Kirche aus Anlass des Sâdhu', *Das Hochland*, Dec. 1924, pp. 320–30.

Some Letters of Baron von Hügel, F. R. Lillie (Editor), Chicago: (privately printed), 1925.

Essays and Addresses on the Philosophy of Religion, second series, edited by Edmund Gardner, London: J. M. Dent and Sons Ltd, 1926.

The Life of Prayer, London: J. M. Dent and Sons Ltd, 1927.

Letters from Baron Friedrich von Hügel to a Niece, edited with an Introduction by Gwendolen Greene, London: J. M. Dent and Sons Ltd, 1928.

Baron Friedrich von Hügel: Selected Letters, 1896–1924, edited with a Memoir by Bernard Holland, London: J. M. Dent and Sons Ltd, 1928.

Some Notes on the Petrine Claims, London: Sheed and Ward, 1930. (Von Hügel composed these *Notes* between 31 August and 7 September 1893. The Postscript was written on 17 and 18 September. They were composed for Madame Rhoda von Schubert who was on the verge of joining the Roman Catholic church, and were written in response to objections put by Walter Frere to Mme von Schubert in an effort to cause her to reconsider her proposed step.)

The Reality of God, and Religion and Agnosticism, edited by Edmund G. Gardner, London: J. M. Dent and Sons Ltd, 1931.

Juliet Mansel, 'A Letter from Baron von Hügel', *Dublin Review*, vol. ccxxv, no. 452, July 1951, pp. 1–11.

Nigel Abercrombie, 'Friedrich von Hügel's Letters to Edmund Bishop', *Dublin Review*, vol. ccxxvii, nos. 459–62, Jan.–Oct. 1953, pp. 68–78, 179–89, 285–98, 419–38.

Joseph P. Whelan, 'Friedrich von Hügel's Letters to Martin D'Arcy', *The Month*, new series, vol. 42, nos. 1–3, July–Aug. 1969, pp. 23–6.

Joseph P. Whelan, 'The Parent as Spiritual Director: A Newly Published Letter of Friedrich von Hügel', *The Month*, second new series, vol. 2, nos. 2–3, Aug.–Sept. 1970, pp. 52–7, 84–7.

Anthologies of von Hügel's Writings:

Algar Thorold, *Readings from Friedrich von Hügel*, London: J. M. Dent and Sons Ltd, 1928.

Franklin P. Chambers, *Baron von Hügel: Man of God*, London: Geoffrey Bles, 1945.

Douglas V. Steere, *Spiritual Counsels and Letters of Baron Friedrich von Hügel*, London: Darton, Longman and Todd, 1964.

PART THREE: GENERAL BIBLIOGRAPHY

Abercrombie, Nigel, *The Life and Work of Edmund Bishop*, with a Foreword by David Knowles, London: Longmans, Green and Co., Ltd, 1959.

Acta Apostolicae Sedis vols. i–vii, 1909–15, Romae: Typis Polyglottis Vaticanis.

Acta Sanctae Sedis, vols. i–xli, 1865–1908, Romae: Typis Polyglottae Officinae S.C. de Propaganda Fide.

Addis, W. E., 'The Pope's Encyclical and the Crisis in the Roman Church', *The Contemporary Review*, vol. xcii, Nov. 1907, pp. 585–96.

Altholz, Josef L., *The Liberal Catholic Movement in England: The 'Rambler' and Its Contributors, 1848–1864*, London: Burns and Oates, 1962.

Archambault, Paul, *George Fonsegrive*, Paris: Librairie Bloud et Gay, 1932.

Barbier, Emmanuel, *Le progrès du libéralisme catholique en France sous le Pape Léon XIII*, 2 vols., Paris: Lethielleux, 1907.

Barmann, Lawrence F., 'The Heresy of Orthodoxy', *Theology*, vol. LXXI, no. 580, Oct. 1968, pp. 456–62.

Barry, William, *Memories and Opinions*, London: G. P. Putnam's Sons, 1926.

Batiffol, Pierre, 'L'Évangile et L'Église', *Bulletin de littérature ecclésiastique (Toulouse)*, 3rd series, vol. V, 1903, pp. 3–15.

Baudrillart, Alfred, *Vie de Mgr. d'Hulst*, 2 vols., Paris: Ancienne Librairie Poussielgue, 1912–14.

Bécamel, M., 'Lettres de Loisy à Mgr. Mignot: A propos de la crise moderniste', *Bulletin de littérature ecclésiastique (Toulouse)*, tome LXVII, nos. 1–4, Jan.–Dec. 1966, pp. 3–44, 81–114, 170–94, 257–86.

'Autres lettres de Loisy à Mgr. Mignot', *Bulletin de littérature ecclésiastique (Toulouse)*, tome LXIX, no. 4, Oct.–Dec. 1968, pp. 241–68.

de la Bedoyère, Michael, *The Life of Baron von Hügel*, London, J. M. Dent and Sons Ltd, 1951.

Bernard-Maitre, Henri, 'Lettres d'Henri Bremond à Alfred Loisy', *Bulletin de littérature ecclésiastique (Toulouse)*, tome LXIX, nos. 1, 3, and 4, Jan., July, and Oct. 1968, and tome LXX, no. 1, Jan. 1969, pp. 3–24, 161–84, 269–89, and 44–56.

van den Biesen, Christian, 'The Authorship and Composition of the Hexateuch', *The Dublin Review*, vol. CXII, Jan. 1893, pp. 245–67.

Billot, Louis, *Tractatus de Ecclesia Christi*, 2 vols., 4th edition, Romae: Apud Aedes Universitatis Gregorianae, 1921–2.

Blondel, Maurice, *The Letter on Apologetics and History and Dogma*, translated by Alexander Dru and Illtyd Trethowan, London: Harvill Press, 1964.

Boys-Smith, J. S., 'The Intellectual Causes of the Modern Movement', *The Modern Churchman*, nos. 6–8, vol. XVII, Oct. 1927, pp. 302–17.

Bremond, Henri, *L'Inquiétude Religieuse*, Paris: Perrin et Cie., 1901.

The Mystery of Newman, translated by H. C. Corrance, with an Introduction by Rev. George Tyrrell, London: Williams and Norgate, 1907.

Browne, R. K., 'Newman and von Hügel: A Record of an Early Meeting', *The Month*, new series, vol. 26, no. 1, July 1961, pp. 24–33.

Brucker, Joseph, 'Le modernisme en Allemagne', *Études*, tome 115, 20 June 1908, pp. 738–51.

Buonaiuti, Ernesto, 'Religion and Culture in Italy', translated by P. H. Wicksteed, *The Hibbert Journal*, vol. XIX, no. 4, July 1921, pp. 636–44.

Pellegrino di Roma, Roma: G. Darsena, 1945.

Burnand, F. C. (Editor), *The Catholic Who's Who and Year Book*, London: Burns and Oates, 1909.

Burtchaell, James T., *Catholic Theories of Biblical Inspiration Since 1810*, Cambridge: The University Press, 1969.

Butterfield, Herbert, *Man on His Past: The Study of the History of Historical Scholarship*, Cambridge: The University Press, 1969.

Cardale, R. F., 'The Modernist Conception of Authority', *The Modern Churchman*, vol. IX, no. 9, Dec. 1919, pp. 408–18.

Carpenter, S. C., *Church and People, 1789–1889: A History of the Church of England from William Wilberforce to 'Lux Mundi'*, London: S.P.C.K., 1937.

Catholic Directory, The, London: Burns and Oates, 1887–1910.

Cenci, Pio, *Il Cardinale Raffaele Merry del Val,* Roma: Roberto Berruti e C., 1933.

Chadwick, W. Owen, *From Bossuet to Newman: The Idea of Doctrinal Development,* Cambridge: The University Press, 1957.

The Victorian Church, 2 vols., London: A. and C. Black Ltd, 1966 and 1970.

Chevalier, Jacques, 'The Biblical Commission', *The Expository Times,* vol. XVIII, no. 5, Feb. 1907, pp. 235–6.

Cheyne, T. K., 'Reform in the Teaching of the Old Testament', *The Contemporary Review,* vol. LVI, Aug. 1889, pp. 216–33.

The Hallowing of Criticism: Nine Sermons on Elijah Preached in Rochester Cathedral, London: Hodder and Stoughton, 1888.

Church Times, The, London, vols. XXXII–LXXII, 5 Jan. 1894–24 Dec. 1914.

Clark, Martin, 'The Theology of Catholic Modernism', *The Church Quarterly Review,* vol. CLXIV, no. 353, Oct.–Dec. 1963, pp. 458–70.

Clarke, Robert Francis, 'Mr. Gore's Criticism of the Papal Encyclical', *The Tablet,* vol. 83, nos. 2816–19, 28 April and 5, 12, and 19 May 1894, pp. 641–3, 681–3, 721–3, and 761–3.

'The Papal Encyclical on the Bible: A Reply', *The Contemporary Review,* vol. LXVI, July–Dec. 1894, pp. 280–304.

Clément, Maurice, *Vie du Cardinal Richard Archevêque de Paris,* Paris: De Gigord, 1924.

Cock, Albert, *A Critical Examination of von Hügel's Philosophy of Religion,* London: Hugh Rees, (no date).

'Friedrich von Hügel and His Work', *Speculum Religionis,* with an Introduction by F. C. Burkitt, Oxford: The Clarendon Press, 1929, pp. 195–213.

Conference of Bishops of the Anglican Communion. Holden at Lambeth Palace, in July 1897. Encyclical Letter from the Bishops, with the Resolutions and Reports, London: S.P.C.K., 1897.

Coore, George, 'Modernism and the Catholic Consciousness', *The Hibbert Journal,* vol. XI, no. 2, Jan. 1913, pp. 329–47.

Cornish, Francis Warre, *The English Church in the Nineteenth Century,* part II, London: Macmillan and Co., 1910.

Corrance, Henry C., 'A Vindication of Modernism', *The Nineteenth Century,* vol. LXIII, no. 372, Feb. 1908, pp. 311–26.

Coulson, John, 'Newman on the church – his final view, its origins and influence', *The Rediscovery of Newman: An Oxford Symposium,* edited by John Coulson and A. M. Allchin, London: Sheed and Ward, 1967, pp. 123–43.

Cox, Harvey, *The Secular City,* New York: Macmillan and Co., 1966.

Crespi, Angelo, *Contemporary Thought of Italy,* London: Williams and Norgate, 1926.

Dakin, A. Hazard, Jr, *Von Hügel and the Supernatural,* London: S.P.C.K., 1934.

Daly, Gabriel, 'Some Reflections on the Character of George Tyrrell'. *The Heythrop Journal,* vol. X, no. 3, July 1969, pp. 256–74.

'Tyrrell's "Medievalism"', *The Month*, new series, vol. 42, nos. 1–3, July–Aug. 1969, pp. 15–22.

Delaney, John J., and Tobin, James Edward, *Dictionary of Catholic Biography*, London: Robert Hale Ltd, 1962.

Dell, Robert, 'A Liberal Catholic View of the Case of Dr Mivart', *The Nineteenth Century*, vol. XLVII, no. 278, April 1900, pp. 669–84.

'The Crisis in the Catholic Church', *The Fortnightly Review*, no. CCCCLV, new series, 1 Nov. 1904, pp. 846–60.

'George Tyrrell', *The Cornhill Magazine*, new series, vol. XXVII, no. 161, Nov. 1909, pp. 665–75.

Denis, Charles, 'Pourquoi les dogmes ne meurent pas', *Annales de philosophie chrétienne*, 3rd series, tome III, no. 3, Dec. 1903, pp. 242–80.

Dictionary of National Biography (1931–1940), The, London: Oxford University Press, 1949.

Dictionary of National Biography, The: The Concise Dictionary, part II, 1901–50, London: Oxford University Press, 1961.

Dillon, E. J., 'The Papal Encyclical on the Bible', *The Contemporary Review*, vol. LXV, April 1894, pp. 576–608.

'Intellectual Liberty and Contemporary Catholicism', *The Contemporary Review*, vol. LXVI, Aug. 1894, pp. 280–304.

'Theological Book-Keeping by Double Entry', *The Contemporary Review*, vol. LXVI, Sept. 1894, pp. 351–73.

Dimnet, Ernest, *La Pensée Catholique dans l'Angleterre contemporaine*, Paris: Librairie Victor Lecoffre, 1906.

My New World, London: Jonathan Cape, 1938.

Documents of the Thirty-First General Congregation (of the Society of Jesus), Woodstock, Maryland: Woodstock College Press, 1967.

Draper, John William, *History of the Conflict Between Religion and Science*, 23rd edition, London: Kegan Paul, Trench, Trübner and Co., 1901.

Driver, S. R., 'The Cosmogony of Genesis', *The Expositor*, 3rd series, vol. III, 1886, pp. 23–45.

Dru, Alexander, 'Modernism and the Present Position of the Church', *The Downside Review*, vol. LXXXII, no. 267, April 1964, pp. 103–10.

Elliot-Binns, L. E., *English Thought, 1860–1900: The Theological Aspect*, London: Longmans, Green and Co, 1956.

Émonet, Benoît, 'Cas de conscience de M. Loisy', *Études*, tome 98, March 1904, pp. 737–58.

Essays and Reviews, 10th edition, London: Longman, Green, Longman, and Roberts, 1862.

Eucken, Rudolf, *The Truth of Religion*, translated by W. Tudor Jones, London: Williams and Norgate, 1911.

Collected Essays, edited and translated by Meyrick Booth, London: T. Fisher Unwin, 1914.

Rudolf Eucken, His Life, Work and Travels, translated by Joseph McCabe, London: T. Fisher Unwin, 1921.

The Spiritual Outlook of Europe To-Day, translated by W.R.V.B., London: The Faith Press, 1922.

Falconi, Carlo, *The Popes in the Twentieth Century: From Pius X to John XXIII*, translated by Muriel Grindrod, London: Weidenfeld and Nicolson, 1967.

Fawkes, Alfred, 'Modernism: A Retrospect and a Prospect', *The Hibbert Journal*, vol. VIII, no. 1, Oct. 1909, pp. 67–82.
    Studies in Modernism, London: Smith, Elder and Co., 1913.
    'Baron Friedrich von Hügel', *The Modern Churchman*, no. 12, vol. XIV, March 1925, pp. 662–6.

Ferrata, Dominique, *Mémoires*, 3 vols., Romae: Tipografia Cuggiani, 1920.

Fox, Adam, *Dean Inge*, London: John Murray, 1960.

Gardner, Percy, 'M. Alfred Loisy's Type of Catholicism', *The Hibbert Journal*, vol. III, no. 1, Oct. 1904, pp. 126–38.

Gerard, John, 'The Papal Encyclical: From a Catholic's Point of View', *The Hibbert Journal*, vol. VI, no. 2, Jan. 1908, pp. 256–63.

Girerd, F., 'Évolution et progrès en exégèse', *Annales de philosophie chrétienne*, 3rd series, tome III, no. 6, March 1904, pp. 621–33.

Gooch, G. P., *History and Historians in the Nineteenth Century*, Boston: Beacon Press, 1962.

Gore, Charles (Editor), *Lux Mundi: A Series of Studies in the Religion of the Incarnation*, 6th edition, London: John Murray, 1890.
    The Mission of the Church, London: John Murray, 1892.
    'The Problem of the Fourth Gospel, I and II', *The Pilot*, nos. 104–5, vol. V, 22 Feb. and 1 March 1902, pp. 203–4, and 229–31.

de Grandmaison, Léonce, 'L'Évangile et L'Église', *Études*, tome 94, Jan. 1903, pp. 145–74.

Green, Martin, *Yeats's Blessings on von Hügel*, London: Longmans, Green and Co., 1967.

Greene, Gwendolen, *Two Witnesses: A Personal Recollection of Hubert Parry and Friedrich von Hügel*, London: J. M. Dent and Sons Ltd, 1930.

Gruber, Jacob W., *A Conscience in Conflict. The Life of St. George Jackson Mivart*, New York: Columbia University Press, 1960.

Guardian, The, London, vols. XLV–LXIX, Jan. 1890–Dec. 1914.

Hales, E. E. Y., *The Catholic Church in the Modern World: A Survey from the French Revolution to the Present*, Garden City, New York: Image Books, 1960.

Halifax, Viscount, 'The Recent Anglo-Roman Pastoral', *The Nineteenth Century*, no. 291, May 1901, pp. 736–54.
    Leo XIII and Anglican Orders, London: Longmans, Green and Co., 1912.

Hanbury, Michael, 'Von Hügel and Tyrrell', *The Month*, new series, vol. 32, no. 6, Dec. 1964, pp. 323–6.

Hardwick, J. C., 'Modernism and Agnosticism', *The Modern Churchman*, nos. 6–8, vol. XVII, Oct. 1927, pp. 404–8.

von Harnack, Adolf, *What is Christianity?*, translated by Thomas Bailey Saunders, London: Ernest Benn, 1958.

Headlam, Arthur C., 'The Modernist Christology', *The Church Quarterly Review*, vol. XCIII, no. CLXXXVI, Jan. 1922, pp. 201–32.

Heaney, John J., 'The Enigma of the Later von Hügel', *The Heythrop Journal*, vol. VI, no. 2, April 1965, pp. 145–59.

The Modernist Crisis: von Hügel, Washington, D.C.: Corpus Books, 1968.

Hedley, John Cuthbert, 'Dr Mivart on Faith and Science', *The Dublin Review*, 3rd series, vol. XVIII, no. II, Oct. 1887, pp. 401–19.

'The Bishop of Newport's Rejoinder', *The Dublin Review*, 3rd series, vol. XIX, no. 1, Jan. 1888, pp. 188–9.

Heiler, Friedrich, *Alfred Loisy (1857–1940): Der Vater des Katholischen Modernismus*, München: Erasmus-Verlag, 1947.

Hemmer, H., *Fernand Portal (1855–1926): Apostle of Unity*, translated and edited by Arthur T. Macmillan, London: Macmillan and Co., 1961.

Hocedez, Edgar, *Histoire de la Théologie au XIXᵉ Siècle*, 3 vols., Brussels: L'Edition Universelle, 1947–8.

Hogan, J. B., *Clerical Studies*, Boston: Marlier and Co., 1898.

Hogarth, Henry, *Henri Bremond: The Life and Work of a Devout Humanist*, London: S.P.C.K., 1950.

Holmes, J. Derek, and Murray, Robert, *Newman – On the Inspiration of Scripture*, London: Geoffrey Chapman, 1967.

Houtin, Albert, *La Question biblique chez les catholiques de France au XIXᵉ siècle*, Paris: Alphonse Picard et Fils, 1902.

La question biblique au XXᵉ siècle, 2nd edition, Paris: Émile Nourry, 1906.

La Crise du Clergé, Paris: Émile Nourry, 1907.

Histoire du Modernisme Catholique, Paris: Chez l'Auteur, 1913.

Un prêtre symboliste, Marcel Hébert (1851–1916), Paris: F. Rieder et Cie., 1925.

The Life of a Priest: My Own Experience, 1867–1912, translated by Winifred Stephens Whale, London: Watts and Co., 1927.

von Hügel, Anatole, (Editor), *Charles von Hügel, April 25, 1795–June 2, 1870*, Cambridge: (privately printed), 1903.

Inge, W. R., 'The Meaning of Modernism', *The Quarterly Review*, vol. 210, no. 419, April 1909, pp. 571–603.

Jenkins, R. G. F., 'Tyrrell's Dublin Days', *The Month*, new series, vol. 42, nos. 1–3, July–Aug., 1969, pp. 8–15.

Knowles, David, *Great Historical Enterprises – and – Problems in Monastic History*, London: Thomas Nelson and Sons, 1963.

Kübel, Johannes, *Geschichte des Katholischen Modernismus*, Tübingen: Verlag von T. C. B. Mohr, 1909.

Laberthonnière, Lucien, 'La question de méthode en apologétique', *Annales de philosophie chrétienne*, 4th series, tome II, no. 5, Aug. 1906, pp. 500–15.

'L'Église et l'État', *Annales de philosophie chrétienne*, 4th series, tome III, no. 5, Feb. 1907, pp. 449–86, (incompleted).

'Dogme et Théologie', *Annales de philosophie chrétienne*, 4th series, tome IV, no. 6, Sept. 1907; tome V, nos. 1 and 5, Oct. 1907 and Feb. 1908; tome

VII, no. 1, Oct. 1908; tome IX, no. 3, Dec. 1909; pp. 561–601, 10–65, 479–521, 5–79, and 279–313, (incompleted).

Lacey, T. A., *Harnack and Loisy*, with an Introduction by Lord Halifax, London: Longmans, Green and Co., 1904.

Lagrange, M. J. *Au Service de la Bible: Souvenirs Personnels*, Paris: Editions du Cerf, 1967.

Lebreton, Jules, 'L'Encyclique et la théologie moderniste', *Études*, tome 113, 20 Nov. 1907, pp. 497–524.

Lecanuet, R. P., *La Vie de l'Église sous Léon XIII*, Paris: Librairie Félix Alcan, 1930.

LeRoy, Édouard, 'Essai sur la notion du Miracle', *Annales de philosophie chrétienne*, 4th series, tome III, nos. 1–3, Oct.–Dec. 1906, pp. 5–33, 166–91, and 225–59.

Dogme et Critique. Paris: Librairie Bloud et Cie., 1907.

Leslie, Shane (Editor), *Letters of Herbert Cardinal Vaughan to Lady Herbert of Lea, 1867–1903*, with an Introduction by J. Brodrick, S.J., London: Burns and Oates, 1942.

Lester-Garland, L. V., *The Religious Philosophy of Baron F. von Hügel*, London: J. M. Dent and Sons Ltd, 1933.

'Lettres Romaines', *Annales de philosophie chrétienne*, 3rd series, tome III, nos. 4–6, Jan.–March 1904, pp. 349–59, 473–88, and 601–20.

Lilley, A. L., 'Biblical Criticism in France, II', *The Guardian*, no. 2986, 25 Feb. 1903, pp. 267–8.

'L'Affaire Loisy', *The Commonwealth*, vol. VIII, no. 3, March 1903, pp. 73–6.

'A Roman Catholic Protest Against the Recent Vatican Policy', *The Commonwealth*, vol. XI, no. 7, July 1906, pp. 216–20.

(Translator), *What We Want: An Open Letter to Pius X*, London: John Murray, 1907.

Modernism: A Record and Review, London: Sir Isaac Pitman and Sons, Ltd, 1908.

(Editor), *The Programme of Modernism*, London: T. Fisher Unwin, 1908.

'The Religion of George Tyrrell', *The Commonwealth*, vol. XIV, no. 12, Dec. 1909, pp. 361–4.

'A Real Catholicism', *The Interpreter*, vol. VI, no. 3, April 1910, pp. 264–77.

'Modernism', *Encyclopaedia of Religion and Ethics*, edited by James Hastings, vol. VIII, Edinburgh: T. and T. Clark, 1916, pp. 763–8.

'Roman Catholic Modernism', *The Modern Churchman*, nos. 6–8, vol. XVII, Oct. 1927, pp. 333–44.

Lobstein, P., 'Modernism and the Protestant Consciousness', *The Hibbert Journal*, vol. XI, no. 1, Oct. 1912, pp. 63–84.

Lockhart, J. G., *Charles Lindley Viscount Halifax*, 2 vols., London: Geoffrey Bles, 1935–6.

Loisy, Alfred, *L'Évangile et l'Église*, Paris: Alphonse Picard et fils, 1902.

Autour d'un petit livre, Paris: Alphonse Picard et fils, 1903.

Quelques Lettres sur des questions actuelles et sur des événements récents, Ceffonds: Chez l'auteur, 1908.

Simples réflexions sur le décret du saint-office Lamentabili sane exitu et sur l'encyclique Pascendi dominici gregis, Ceffonds: Chez l'auteur, 1908.

The Religion of Israel, translated by Arthur Galton, London: T. Fisher Unwin, 1910.

Choses Passées, Paris: Émile Nourry, 1913.

L'Église et la France, Paris: Émile Nourry, 1925.

Mémoires pour servir a l'histoire religieuse de notre temps, 3 vols., Paris: Émile Nourry, 1930–1.

George Tyrrell et Henri Bremond, Paris: Émile Nourry, 1936.

The Birth of the Christian Religion, authorized translation from the French by L. P. Jacks, London: George Allen and Unwin, 1948.

Loome, T. M., 'A Bibliography of the Published Writings of George Tyrrell (1861–1909)', *The Heythrop Journal*, vol. x, no. 3, July 1969, pp. 280–314.

Louis-Lefebvre, M. T., *Abbé Huvelin, Apostle of Paris*, translated by the Earl of Wicklow, Dublin: Clonmore and Reynolds, 1967.

de Lubac, Henri (Editor), *Maurice Blondel et Auguste Valensin: Correspondance (1899–1947)*, 3 vols., Paris: Aubier, 1957–65.

Luzzi, Giovanni, 'The Roman Catholic Church in Italy at the Present Hour', *The Hibbert Journal*, vol. ix, no. 2, Jan. 1911, pp. 307–23.

McCormack, Arthur, *Cardinal Vaughan: The Life of the Third Archbishop of Westminster, Founder of St Joseph's Missionary Society, Mill Hill*, London: Burns and Oates, 1966.

MacDougall, Hugh A., *The Acton-Newman Relations: The Dilemma of Christian Liberalism*, New York: Fordham University Press, 1962.

McGiffert, Arthur C., 'Modernism and Catholicism', *The Harvard Theological Review*, vol. iii, no. 1, Jan. 1910, pp. 24–46.

Macpherson, Duncan, 'Baron von Hügel on Celibacy', *The Tablet*, vol. 223, no. 6741, 2 Aug. 1969, pp. 757–8.

Major, H. D. A., *English Modernism: Its Origin, Methods, Aims*, Cambridge, Massachusetts: Harvard University Press, 1927.

'Modernism and the Reunion of Christendom', *The Modern Churchman*, nos. 6–8, vol. xvii, Oct. 1927, pp. 409–18.

'Father Tyrrell', *Great Christians*, edited by R. S. Forman, London: Ivor Nicholson and Watson, 1934, pp. 553–74.

Mallebrancq, Paul, 'Y'a-t-il une crise du catholicisme?', *Études*, tome 113, 5 Oct. 1907, pp. 47–69.

Marlé, René, *Au coeur de la crise moderniste*, Paris: Aubier, 1960.

Martin, Luis, 'Epistola ad Patres et Fratres Societatis Jesu de Aliquibus Nostorum Temporum Periculis Cavendis', *Epistolae Praepositorum Generalium ad Patres et Fratres Societatis Jesu*, tome iv, Brussels: Sumptis Provinciae Belgicae S. J., 1908, pp. 268–332.

May, J. Lewis, *Father Tyrrell and the Modernist Movement*, London: Burns Oates and Washbourne, Ltd, 1938.

Merry del Val, Rafael, *Memories of Pope Pius X*, Forewords by Cardinal Hinsley and Cardinal Hayes, London: Burns Oates and Washbourne, Ltd, 1939.

Mignot, E. I., 'La méthode de la théologie', *Bulletin de littérature ecclésiastique*, (*Toulouse*), 3rd series, vol. III, 1901, pp. 253–74.

Mivart, St George, 'Modern Catholics and Scientific Freedom', *The Nineteenth Century*, vol. XVIII, no. 101, July 1885, pp. 30–47.

'The Catholic Church and Biblical Criticism', *The Nineteenth Century*, vol. XXII, July 1887, pp. 31–51.

'Letter from Dr Mivart on the Bishop of Newport's Article in Our Last Number', *The Dublin Review*, 3rd series, vol. XIX, no. 1, Jan. 1888, pp. 180–7.

'The Roman Catholic Church and the Dreyfus Case', *The Times*, no. 35,962, 17 Oct. 1899, pp. 13–14. See also, *The Times*, no. 35,993, 22 Nov. 1899, p. 14.

Moisant, Xavier, 'Qu'est-ce que le modernisme?', *Études*, tome 115, 5 and 20 May 1908, pp. 289–308 and 463–84.

Moss, C. B., *The Old Catholic Movement, Its Origins and History*, London: S.P.C.K., 1964

Moyes, James, 'Modernism and the Papal Encyclical', *The Nineteenth Century*, vol. LXII, no. 370, Dec. 1907, pp. 865–78.

Mozley, John Kenneth, *Some Tendencies in British Theology: From the Publication of Lux Mundi to the Present Day*, London: S.P.C.K., 1951.

Müller, Schmied, 'Un théologien moderne: Herman Schell', *Annales de philosophie chrétienne*, 4th series, tome II, no. 6, Sept. 1906, and tome III, no. 5, Feb. 1907, pp. 608–19 and 517–35.

Murphy, J., 'Dr Mivart on Faith and Science', *The Dublin Review*, 3rd series, vol. XIX, no. 2, April 1888, pp. 400–11.

Nédoncelle, Maurice, *La Philosophie religieuse en Grande-Bretagne de 1850 à nos jours*, Paris: Librairie Bloud et Gay, 1934.

La Pensée religieuse de Friedrich von Hügel, Paris: J. Vrin, 1935.

'Dr Angelo Crespi', *The Dublin Review*, vol. 224, no. 447, Jan, 1950, pp. 106–8.

'Un texte peu connu de F. von Hügel sur le problème de dieu', *Revue des Sciences Religieuses*, tome XXXVI, 1962, pp. 154–73.

Newsom, G. E. 'George Tyrrell', *The Church Quarterly Review*, vol. LXIX, no. CXXXVII, Oct. 1909, pp. 114–45.

'Baron von Hügel', *Theology*, vol. XI, no. 63, Sept. 1925, pp. 146–56.

Noether, Emiliana P., 'Vatican Council I: Its Political and Religious Setting', *The Journal of Modern History*, vol. 40, no. 2, June 1968, pp. 218–33.

Nouvelle, A., *L'Authenticité du Quatrième Évangile et la thèse de M. Loisy*, Paris: Librairie Bloud et Cie., 1907.

Oldmeadow, Ernest, *Francis Cardinal Bourne*, 2 vols., London: Burns Oates and Washbourne, Ltd, 1940–4.

Osborne, C. E., 'Father Tyrrell: Some Impressions by an Anglican Friend', *The Church Times*, no. 2426, vol. LXII, 23 July 1909, p. 121.

'George Tyrrell. A Friend's Impressions', *The Hibbert Journal*, vol. VIII, no. 2, Jan. 1910, pp. 253–63.

Palmer, William Scott, *The Diary of a Modernist*, London: Edward Arnold, 1910.

Partin, M. D., *Waldeck-Rousseau, Combes, and the Church: The Politics of anti-clericalism 1899–1905*, Durham, North Carolina: Duke University Press, 1969.

Petre, M. D., *The Soul's Orbit, or Man's Journey to God*, London: Longmans, Green and Co., 1904.

Catholicism and Independence: Being Studies in Spiritual Liberty, London: Longmans, Green and Co., 1907.

Autobiography and Life of George Tyrrell, 2 vols., London: Edward Arnold, 1912.

'The Advantages and Disadvantages of Authority in Religion', *The Hibbert Journal*, vol. XII, no. 2, Jan. 1914, pp. 295–305.

Modernism: Its Failure and Its Fruits, London: T. C. and E. C. Jack, Ltd., 1918.

George Tyrrell's Letters, London: T. Fisher Unwin, 1920.

'Still At It: The Impasse of Modern Christology', *The Hibbert Journal*, vol. XX, no. 3, April 1922, pp. 401–10.

'George Tyrrell and Friedrich von Hügel in Their Relation to Catholic Modernism', *The Modern Churchman*, no. 3, vol. XVII, June 1927, pp. 143–54.

My Way of Faith, London: J. M. Dent and Sons Ltd, 1937.

Von Hügel and Tyrrell: The Story of a Friendship, London: J. M. Dent and Sons Ltd, 1937.

Alfred Loisy: His Religious Significance, Cambridge: The University Press, 1944.

Pilot, The, London, vols, 1–9, 3 March 1900–21 May 1904.

Portalié, Eugène, ' "La Question Herzog-Dupin" et la critique catholique', *Études*, tome 116, 5 Aug. 1908, pp. 335–59.

' "La Question Herzog-Dupin" et la critique de M. Turmel', *Études*, tome 116, 20 Aug., and 5 and 20 Sept. 1908, pp. 506–38, 605–38, and 763–94.

Poulat, Émile (Editor), A. Houtin and F. Sartiaux, *Alfred Loisy: sa vie et son oeuvre*, Paris: Éditions du Centre National de la Researche Scientifique, 1960.

Histoire, dogme et critique dans la crise moderniste, Paris: Casterman, 1962.

Prestige, G. L., *The Life of Charles Gore, A Great Englishman*, London: William Heinemann, 1935.

Purcell, Edmund Sheridan, *The Life of Cardinal Manning, Archbishop of Westminster*, 2 vols., London: Macmillan and Co., 1895.

Quick, Oliver Chase, *Liberalism, Modernism and Tradition*, London: Longmans, Green and Co., 1922.

Raby, F. J. E., 'Baron von Hügel', *Great Christians*, edited by R. S. Forman, London: Ivor Nicholson and Watson, 1934, pp. 271–83.

Ramsey, Arthur Michael, *From Gore to Temple: The Development of Anglican Theology Between Lux Mundi and the Second World War, 1889–1939*, London: Longmans, Green and Co., 1960.

Ranchetti, Michele, *The Catholic Modernists: A Study of the Religious Reform Movement 1864–1907*, translated by Isabel Quigly, London: Oxford University Press, 1969.

Ratté, John, *Three Modernists: Alfred Loisy, George Tyrrell, William L. Sullivan*, London: Sheed and Ward, 1968.

Rawlinson, G. C., *Recent French Tendencies from Renan to Claudel: A Study in French Religion*, London: Robert Scott, 1917.

An Anglo-Catholic's Thoughts on Religion, edited with a Memoir by W. J. Sparrow Simpson, London: Longmans, Green and Co., 1924.

Reardon, B. M. G., 'Liberal Protestantism and Roman Catholic Modernism', *The Modern Churchman*, new series, vol. XIII, no. 1, Oct. 1969, pp. 72–86.

'The Modernist Movement in Retrospect', *The Ampleforth Journal*, vol. LXXV, part II, summer 1970, pp. 213–21.

Roman Catholic Modernism, London: Adam and Charles Black, 1970.

Reusch, Franz Heinrich, *Der Index der verbotenen Bücher. Ein Beitrag zur Kirchen- und Literaturgeschichte*, 2 vols., Bonn: Verlag von Max Cohen und Sohn, 1883–5.

Rinnovamento, Il, Milano, vols, I–VI, 1907–9.

Rivière, Jean, *Le Modernisme dans l'Église*, Paris: Librarie Letouzey et Ané, 1929.

'Modernisme', *Dictionnaire de théologie catholique*, tome 10, pt. 2, Paris: Librarie Letouzey et Ané, 1929, cols. 2009–47.

'Qui rédigea l'encyclique "Pascendi"?', *Bulletin de littérature ecclésiastique (Toulouse)*, vol. XLVII, nos. 2–3, Avril–Sept., 1946, pp. 146–61.

Roe, W. G., *Lamennais and England: The Reception of Lamennais's Religious Ideas in England in the Nineteenth Century*, London: Oxford University Press, 1966.

Roure, Lucien, 'Scolastiques et Modernistes', *Études*, tome 114, 5 Feb. and 20 March 1908, pp. 289–307 and 767–89.

de Ruggiero, Guido, *The History of European Liberalism*, translated by R. G. Collingwood, London: Oxford University Press, 1927.

Sabatier, Paul, *Modernism: The Jowett Lectures, 1908*, translated by C. A. Miles, London: T. Fisher Unwin, 1908.

'Modernism', *The Contemporary Review*, vol. XCIII, March 1908, pp. 300–7.

'De la situation religieuse de l'Église catholique romaine en France, à l'heure actuelle', *The Hibbert Journal*, vol. IX, no. 1, Oct. 1910, pp. 1–14.

Saint-Jean, R., *L'Apologétique Philosophique, Blondel 1893–1913*, Paris: Aubier, 1966.

Saintyves, P., *La Réforme intellectualle du clergé et la liberté d'enseignement*, Paris: Émile Nourry, 1904.

Sanday, William, *The Oracles of God: Nine Lectures on the Nature and Extent of Biblical Inspiration and on the Special Significance of the Old Testament Scriptures at the Present Time*, London: Longmans, Green and Co., 1891.

'The Work of Abbé Loisy', *The Guardian*, no. 2647, 26 Aug. 1896, p. 1317.

'An Anglican View of M. Loisy', *The Pilot*, no. 201, vol. IX, 23 Jan. 1904, pp. 84–5.

Scoppola, Pietro, *Crisi modernista e rinnovamento cattolico in Italia*, Bologna: Il Mulino, 1961.

Scotti, Tommaso Galarati, *The Life of Antonio Fogazzaro*, translated by Mary Prichard Agnetti, London: Hodder and Stoughton, (no date).

de Smedt, Charles, *Principes de la Critique Historique*, Liége: Librairie de la Société Bibliographique Belge, 1883.

Smith, Sydney F., 'What Is "Modernism"?', *The Month*, vol. CXI, no, 525, March 1908, pp. 284–301.

'Newman's Relation to Modernism', *The Month*, vol. CXX, no. 577, July 1912, pp. 1–15.

Smyth, Newman, 'Modernism', *Scribner's Magazine*, vol. XLV, no. 2, Feb. 1909, pp. 152–9.

Spectator, The, London, vols. 64–113, Jan. 1890–Dec. 1914.

Steinmann, Jean, *Friedrich von Hügel: Sa vie, son oeuvre et ses amités*, Paris: Aubier, 1962.

Stephenson, A. M. G., 'Liberal Anglicanism in the Nineteenth Century', *The Modern Churchman*, new series, vol. XIII, no. 1, Oct. 1969, pp. 87–102.

Stephenson, Gwendolen, *Edward Stuart Talbot, 1844–1934*, London: S.P.C.K., 1936.

Stewart, Herbert Leslie, *Modernism, Past and Present*, London: John Murray, 1932.

Sullivan, William Laurence, *Under Orders*, Boston: Beacon Press, 1966.

Swete, H. B., '"Modernism" and the Church', *The Guardian*, no. 3243, 29 Jan. 1908, pp. 175–6.

Tablet, The, London, vols. LXVII–XCII, Jan. 1902–Dec. 1914.

Talbot, Edward Stuart, *The Church's Stress: Words on Some Present Questions of Thought and Action Spoken to the Clergy of the Diocese of Southwark at His Primary Visitation in the Cathedral Church of St Saviour*, London: Macmillan and Co., 1907.

Testament of Ignatius Loyola, The, translated by E. M. Rix, with a Preface by George Tyrrell, S. J., London: Sands and Co., 1900.

Times, The, London, nos. 32,897–41,051, 1 Jan 1890–31 Dec. 1914.

Trevor, Meriol, *Prophets and Guardians: Renewal and Tradition in the Church*, London: Hollis and Carter, 1969.

Tyrrell, George, *Hard Sayings. A Selection of Meditations and Studies*, London: Longmans, Green and Co., 1899.

The Faith of the Millions, 1st series, London: Longmans, Green and Co., 1901.

Nova et Vetera: Informal Meditations, London: Longmans, Green and Co., 1902.

The Faith of the Millions, 2nd series, Longmans, Green and Co., 1904.

'The Abbé Loisy: Criticism and Catholicism', *The Church Quarterly Review*, vol. LVIII, April 1904, pp. 180–95.

External Religion: Its Use and Abuse, London: Longmans, Green and Co., 1906.

Lex Credendi, A sequel to Lex Orandi, London: Longmans, Green and Co., 1906.

A Much-Abused Letter, London: Longmans, Green and Co., 1906.

Lex Orandi, or Prayer and Creed, London: Longmans, Green and Co., 1907.

Through Scylla and Charybdis, or the Old Theology and the New, London: Longmans, Green and Co., 1907.

'The Pope and Modernism', *The Times*, nos. 38,451–38,452, 30 Sept. and 1 Oct. 1907, pp. 4 and 5 respectively.

'The Condemnation of Newman', *The Guardian*, no. 3233, 20 Nov. 1907, pp. 1896–7.

Medievalism, A Reply to Cardinal Mercier, London: Longmans, Green and Co., 1908.

'The Prospects of Modernism', *The Hibbert Journal*, vol. VI, no. 2, Jan. 1908, pp. 241–55.

'Modernism As a Gnosis', *The Church Times*, no. 2347, vol. LIX, 17 Jan. 1908, p. 68.

'Mediaevalism and Modernism', *The Harvard Theological Review*, vol. I, no. 3, July 1908, pp. 304–24.

'The Eucharist and the Papacy', *The Guardian*, no. 3289, 16 Dec. 1908, p. 2105.

'The Mystical Element of Religion', *The Quarterly Review*, vol. 211, no. 420, July 1909, pp. 101–26.

'The Point At Issue', *Jesus or Christ?*, being the Hibbert Journal Supplement for 1909, London: Williams and Norgate, pp. 5–16.

Christianity at the Cross-roads, London: Longmans, Green and Co., 1910.

The Church and the Future, London: The Priory Press, 1910.

Oil and Wine, London: Longmans, Green and Co., 1911.

Essays on Faith and Immortality, arranged by M. D. Petre, London: Edward Arnold, 1914.

Vaughan, Herbert Cardinal, and the Bishops of the Province of Westminster, *A Joint Pastoral Letter on the Church and Liberal Catholicism*, London: Burns and Oates, 1900.

Venn, J. A., *Alumni Cantabrigiensis: A biographical list of all known students, graduates and holders of office at the University of Cambridge, from the earliest times to 1900*, part II, from 1752 to 1900, vols. I–VI, Cambridge: The University Press, 1940–54.

Vidler, Alec R., *The Modernist Movement in the Roman Church, Its Origin and Outcome*, Cambridge: The University Press, 1934.

The Church in an Age of Revolution, 1789 to the Present Day, Baltimore: Penguin Books, 1961.

A Century of Social Catholicism, 1820–1920, London: S.P.C.K., 1964.

A Variety of Catholic Modernists, Cambridge: The University Press, 1970.

Viollet, Paul, *L'Infaillibilité du Pape et le Syllabus*, Paris: P. Lethielleux Librairie, 1904.

Virgoulay, René, 'Note d'exégèse blondélienne de l'Action à la Lettre de 1896', *Recherches de Science Religieuse*, tome 57, no. 2, Avril–Juin 1969, pp. 205–19.

'La Méthode d'Immanence et l'Encyclique Pascendi', *Recherches de Science Religieuse*, tome 58, no. 3, Juillet–Sept., 1970, pp. 429–54.

Ward, Maisie, *The Wilfrid Wards and the Transition*, London: Sheed and Ward, 1934.

Insurrection versus Resurrection, London: Sheed and Ward, 1937.

Ward, Wilfrid, *The Wish to Believe: A Discussion Concerning the Temper of Mind in which a Reasonable Man Should Undertake Religious Inquiry*, London: Kegan Paul, Trench and Co., 1885.

The Clothes of Religion: A Reply to Popular Positivism, London: Burns and Oates, 1886.

'The Scholastic Movement and Catholic Philosophy', *The Dublin Review*, 3rd series, no. L, April 1891, pp. 255–71.

William George Ward and the Catholic Revival, London: Macmillan and Co., 1893.

'Leo XIII', *The Fortnightly Review*, new series, no. CCCCXL, 1 Aug. 1903, pp. 249–67.

'The Pope and France', *The Nineteenth Century*, vol. LXI, no. CCCLIX, Jan. 1907, pp. 27–41.

'The Encyclical "Pascendi"', *The Dublin Review*, vol. CXLII, no. 284, Jan. 1908, pp. 1–10.

Last Lectures, with an Introductory Study by Mrs Wilfrid Ward, London: Longmans, Green and Co., 1918.

Watson, E. W., *Life of Bishop John Wordsworth*, London: Longmans, Green and Co., 1915.

Webb, C. C. J., 'Baron Friedrich von Hügel and His Contribution to Religious Philosophy', *The Harvard Theological Review*, vol. XLII, no. 1, Jan. 1949, pp. 1–18.

Weill, Georges, *Histoire du Catholicisme Libéral en France*, 1828–1908, Paris: Félix Alcan, 1909.

West, Austin, 'The Abbé Loisy and the Roman Biblical Commission', *The Contemporary Review*, vol. LXXXI, no. 436, April 1902, pp. 497–507.

Woodlock, Francis, *Modernism and the Christian Church*, with a Preface by G. K. Chesterton, London: Longmans, Green and Co., 1925.

W. S. T., 'The Abbé Loisy's Farewell', *The Nation*, vol. II, no. 20, 15 Feb. 1908, pp. 703–4.

INDEX

Abercrombie, Nigel, 1n
Abrahams, Israel, 12, 221n
The Academy, 11n, 81
Acton, *see* Dalberg-Acton
Aeterni Patris, 140
The Albany Review, 137n
Alfieri, Ajace Antonio, 184, 186, 194, 199, 208
Alfonso XII (Spain), 60n
Allard, Paul, 69n
Amette, Archbishop Leo, 211, 212
Amiaud, Arthur, 26
Amigo, Bishop Peter Emmanuel, 202, 203, 218, 225, 227, 229, 230n, 231, 232, 236–9
Anglican orders, 54, 55, 57–62, 70, 201n
Annales de philosophie chrétienne, 107, 111, 145
Aquinas, St Thomas, 40, 140, 205, 206, 248n
Ashmolean Museum, 9
Athanasius, St, 114
Augustine of Hippo, St, 40, 97, 205, 206, 221

Bagehot, Walter, 208
Bagshawe, Bishop Edward G., 128
Balfour, Arthur James, 1st Earl of Balfour, 4n
Balliol College, Oxford, 98, 124n, 176n
Barrie, Sir James Matthew, 69
Barry, William, 97, 98, 135, 196n
Batiffol, Mgr Pierre, 65, 87–8
Baylis House (Slough), 60n
Beardsley, Aubrey, 74
Beaumont College, 97n
de la Bedoyère, Michael, 3n, 129n, 133n, 247n
Benigni, Mgr Umberto, 196n
Benson, Archbishop Edward White, 56n
Benson, Robert Hugh, 199
Bentley, Richard, 14
Bergson, Henri, 130n, 137
biblical inspiration, 6–7, 17, 18–23, 27, 28, 33, 38, 43, 46–8, 51, 75, 76, 86
Bibliothèque Nationale (Paris), 26
Biblioteca Vittorio Emmanuele, 57
Bickell, Gustav, 11–14, 26, 31, 42
van den Biesen, Christian, 24, 25, 32, 33n, 35, 50n, 71, 104, 124n, 190, 216
Billot, Cardinal Louis, 156n, 196n
Birmingham Oratory, 18, 20n
Bishop, Edmund, 1n, 2, 61, 129, 130, 157, 234
Bland, Hubert, 129n

Blennerhasset, Sir Rowland, 129n
Blondel, Maurice, 62n, 69, 73, 96n, 120–3, 135n, 153, 168n, 245
Boer war, 72–3
Bollandists, Society of, 9, 147
Bonaventure, St, 140n
Bonomelli, Bishop Geremia, 126, 128, 183
Bossuet, Bishop Jacques Bénigne, 50
Bourne, Cardinal Francis, 104, 105, 123n, 129, 157, 172, 201, 225, 228n, 231–2, 233n, 238
Brandi, Salvatore, 55, 57, 200
Bremond, Henri, 73, 121, 146, 161–2, 166n, 168, 169, 175, 177, 208, 223, 225–7, 229, 230, 243
Briggs, Charles Augustus, 29, 133–6, 181, 185, 192n
British Museum, 8, 10, 11
de Broglie, Paul, 69n
Browning, Robert, 168
Bulletin critique, 8n, 9, 13n, 80
Buonaiuti, Ernesto, 195
Burke, Mrs Hubert, 241n
Burkitt, Francis Crawford, 124n, 134, 199, 220, 221
Burtchaell, James Tunstead, 213–14n
Butler, Abbot Cuthbert, 103, 124n, 175, 222

Cahill, Bishop John Baptist, 237–8
Caird, Edward, 98, 124n
Caird, John, 74
Caldecott, Alfred, 248
Calvin, John, 221
Cambridge Theological Society, 221
Cambridge University, 13n, 35, 57, 58, 88, 124n
Campbell, Reginald John, 137n
Casa Editrice Docca, 134
Casati, Alessandro, 186, 195
Casciola, Don Brizio, 62, 195
Catherine of Genoa, St, 92n, 123, 143
Catholic Truth Society, 163
Catholic University of America, 68n
Catholic World, 24
Cecil, Lord Hugh Richard Heathcote Gascoyne, 1st Baron Quickswood, 124n
Chapman, Adeline (Mrs Cecil), 109, 190
Chapman, John, 239
Charing Cross Station, 123n
Charles Borromeo, St, 10

273